The Post-Colonial State in the Era of Capitalist Globalization

Routledge Studies in Social and Political Thought

For a full list of titles in this series, please visit www.routledge.com

35 **Marx and Wittgenstein**
Knowledge, Morality, Politics
Edited by Gavin Kitching and Nigel Pleasants

36 **The Genesis of Modernity**
Arpad Szakolczai

37 **Ignorance and Liberty**
Lorenzo Infantino

38 **Deleuze, Marx and Politics**
Nicholas Thoburn

39 **The Structure of Social Theory**
Anthony King

40 **Adorno, Habermas and the Search for a Rational Society**
Deborah Cook

41 **Tocqueville's Moral and Political Thought**
New Liberalism
M.R.R. Ossewaarde

42 **Adam Smith's Political Philosophy**
The Invisible Hand and Spontaneous Order
Craig Smith

43 **Social and Political Ideas of Mahatma Gandi**
Bidyut Chakrabarty

44 **Counter-Enlightenments**
From the Eighteenth Century to the Present
Graeme Garrard

45 **The Social and Political Thought of George Orwell**
A Reassessment
Stephen Ingle

46 **Habermas**
Rescuing the Public Sphere
Pauline Johnson

47 **The Politics and Philosophy of Michael Oakeshott**
Stuart Isaacs

48 **Pareto and Political Theory**
Joseph Femia

49 **German Political Philosophy**
The Metaphysics of Law
Chris Thornhill

50 **The Sociology of Elites**
Michael Hartmann

51 **Deconstructing Habermas**
Lasse Thomassen

52 **Young Citizens and New Media**
Learning for Democractic Participation
Edited by Peter Dahlgren

53 **Gambling, Freedom and Democracy**
Peter J. Adams

54 **The Quest for Jewish Assimilation in Modern Social Science**
Amos Morris-Reich

55 **Frankfurt School Perspectives on Globalization, Democracy, and the Law**
William E. Scheuerman

56 **Hegemony**
Studies in Consensus and Coercion
Edited by Richard Howson and Kylie Smith

57 **Governmentality, Biopower, and Everyday Life**
Majia Holmer Nadesan

58 **Sustainability and Security within Liberal Societies**
Learning to Live with the Future
Edited by Stephen Gough and Andrew Stables

59 **The Mythological State and its Empire**
David Grant

60 **Globalizing Dissent**
Essays on Arundhat Roy
Edited by Ranjan Ghos and Antonia Navarro-Tejero

61 **The Political Philosophy of Michel Foucault**
Mark G.E. Kelly

62 **Democratic Legitimacy**
Fabienne Peter

63 **Edward Said and the Literary, Social, and Political World**
Edited by Ranjan Ghosh

64 **Perspectives on Gramsci**
Politics, Culture and Social Theory
Edited by Joseph Francese

65 **Enlightenment Political Thought and Non–Western Societies**
Sultans and Savages
Frederick G. Whelan

66 **Liberalism, Neoliberalism, Social Democracy**
Thin Communitarian Perspectives on Political Philosophy and Education
Mark Olssen

67 **Oppositional Discourses and Democracies**
Edited by Michael Huspek

68 **The Contemporary Goffman**
Edited by Michael Hviid Jacobsen

69 **Hemingway on Politics and Rebellion**
Edited by Lauretta Conklin Frederking

70 **Social Theory in Contemporary Asia**
Ann Brooks

71 **Governmentality**
Current Issues and Future Challenges
Edited by Ulrich Bröckling, Susanne Krasmann and Thomas Lemke

72 **Gender, Emotions and Labour Markets**
Asian and Western Perspectives
Ann Brooks and Theresa Devasahayam

73 **Alienation and the Carnivalization of Society**
Edited by Jerome Braun and Lauren Langman

74 **The Post-Colonial State in the Era of Capitalist Globalization**
Historical, Political and Theoretical Approaches to State Formation
Tariq Amin-Khan

The Post-Colonial State in the Era of Capitalist Globalization

Historical, Political and Theoretical Approaches to State Formation

Tariq Amin-Khan

Routledge
Taylor & Francis Group
NEW YORK LONDON

First published 2012
by Routledge
711 Third Avenue, New York, NY 10017

Simultaneously published in the UK
by Routledge
2 Park Square, Milton Park, Abingdon, Oxon OX14 4RN

Routledge is an imprint of the Taylor & Francis Group, an informa business

Typeset in Sabon by IBT Global.

First issued in paperback 2013

Library of Congress Cataloging-in-Publication Data

Amin-Khan, Tariq.
The post-colonial state in the era of capitalist globalization : historical, political and theoretical approaches to state formation / by Tariq Amin-Khan.
p. cm. — (Routledge studies in social and political thought ; 74)
Includes bibliographical references and index.
1. Postcolonialism. 2. Nation-state. 3. Capitalism—Political aspects. 4. Nation-state and globalization. I. Title.
JV51.A45 2012
325'.3—dc23
2011034708

ISBN 13: 978-0-415-71976-6 (pbk)
ISBN13: 978-0-415-89159-2 (hbk)
ISBN13: 978-0-203-12730-8 (ebk)

For Amin Hazien, Munira, Salman and Sameen

Contents

Acknowledgments

This book is the culmination of a long and complex process of reflection and articulation about the post-colonial state, which I began as a doctoral student. I refined and reworked my understanding of the post-colonial state over the years and was very fortunate throughout this process to have been associated with a number of wonderful people who, by their support, friendship, and knowledge, have helped me shape this study. My good friend and colleague, Mike Burke, provided invaluable insights during the completion of this work, while the friendly jabs of Joanne Dolhanty, Scott Milne, Thomas Ponniah, Abbas Syed, and Sanjay Talreja have allowed me to retain a sense of hope when dealing with the troublesome issues of imperialist subordination, racialization, and the grotesque divide between North and South based on the 'colour line'. Along the way, I have gained from the clear perspectives of fellow travelers, friends, and colleagues at our common place of work and struggle, Ryerson University in Toronto: Sedef Arat-Koç, Joanne DiNova, Grace-Edward Galabuzi, Doreen Fumia, Mustafa Koç, Lynn Lavallee, Colin Mooers, Lila Pine, Alan Sears, and Aparna Sundar. I was very fortunate to have met Hamza Alavi before his death—he was magnanimous with his comments about my critical appraisal of his work on peripheral capitalism. My thanks also to David McNally, my former doctoral supervisor in the Program of Social and Political Thought at York University, Toronto as well as to former committee members, Malcolm Blincow and Anaya Mukherjee-Reed—all of whom were very supportive of this work's first iteration.

Earlier versions of arguments and issues presented in this volume have been published in various journals, and some passages have been reprinted with the permission of the publishers mentioned here. My earlier critical assessment of Benedict Anderson's tendency to universalize the European experience in Chapter 1 was first published in Amin Khan, "Colonialism and the Common Origins of Discrete Post-Colonial Identities in India and Pakistan," *Canadian Review of Studies in Nationalism*, Vol. XXIX.1–2 (2002): 39–52 (published by the late Tom Spira and Henry Srebrnik, at the Department of Political Studies, University of Prince Edward Island, Charlottetown, Canada). Some of the material on political and militant Islam and the rise of the security state in Chapter 5, first appeared as Amin-Khan, "The Rise of Militant Islam and the Security State in the Era of the 'Long War'," *Third World Quarterly*, Vol. 30.4 (2009): 813–828 (published by Taylor and Francis Ltd, http://tandf.co.uk/journals). In Chapter 5, I also address the relationship between modernity and militant Islam, which was developed in an earlier article, Amin-Khan, "Issues of Power and Modernity in Understanding Political and Militant Islam," *Comparative Studies of South Asia, Africa and the Middle East*, Vol. 29.3 (2009): 544–555 (published by Duke University Press). The discussion on the state and society of early post-colonial Pakistan in Chapter 5 first appeared as Amin Khan, "Economy, Society and the State in Pakistan," *Contemporary South Asia*, Vol. 9.2 (2000):181–195 (published by Taylor and Francis Ltd, http://tandf.co.uk/journals). Finally, I have reproduced the table on page 179 of Hamza Alavi, "The Structure of Peripheral Capitalism," *Introduction to the Sociology of "Developing Societies."* New York: Monthly Review Press, 1982; the table is reprinted in this volume's Chapter 3.

I thank the Faculty of Arts, Ryerson University, for financial support during the final stages of manuscript preparation. I am also grateful to my research assistants, Reefa Mahboob and Shabnam Sarwary, for their help with some aspects of the research. The editing support of Linn Clark has been invaluable, and Routledge Research's Commissioning Editor, Max Novick, has been most helpful, encouraging, and accommodating. Further, I wish to acknowledge the valuable cooperation and support of Eleanor Chan of IBT Global in the production of this book. Thanks are also due to three anonymous reviewers for their helpful comments on parts of my manuscript. It goes without saying that I alone bear the responsibility for any errors in, and omissions from, this work.

The fruit of this work is due in equal measure to the loving support and encouragement of my partner, Munira, and to the love and youthful inspiration of Salman and Sameen.

Introduction

Renewed interest in state theory beginning in the 1970s sparked scholars and activists to question the nature of the capitalist state and led to the famous Miliband-Poulantzas debates in the pages of the *New Left Review*. It was in the context of these debates that Hamza Alavi penned his strident critique of state theorists' failure to account for the divergent histories of state formation in post-colonial societies, which he said should be differentiated from the Western state.[1] Alavi's critique fell on deaf ears, however, because the idea of the 'normal' European nation-state form was already considered the model for emerging post-colonial societies to emulate. Thus, theoretical advances in understanding the state since this time have really been about the Western capitalist state. Only recently, scholars with a post-structuralist orientation—postcolonial theorists, critical ethnographers, and some social geographers—have started to more intently examine the post-colonial state. Among these, many have theorized the post-colonial state based on empirical ethnographical studies, but the nature of the post-colonial state, its foundational character, remains elusive and is confounded by its characterization in either largely ambivalent cultural terms as a "cultural artifact"[2] (Gupta and Sharma) and as a "series of cultural acts and material production" (Joseph and Nugent) or in terms of "technologies of spatial power" (Radcliffe).[3] Before I discuss these confounding problematics in state theorization, I will clarify my use of the hyphenated form of the term 'post-colonial' in contradistinction with the non-hyphenated form widely used by poststructuralist/postcolonial studies scholars.

The term 'post-colonial' is used here to periodize from the colonial era the decolonization of the former colonies into supposedly sovereign states. However, the term's use also underlines the prevailing status of *inter*-national relations: colonialism may have formally ended only to be reinscribed by dependency, subordination, and underdevelopment in post-colonial societies. The term is thus used to represent both continuity with and a distinction from the colonial state form in the period since decolonization. 'Post-colonial' is therefore not deployed in a poststructuralist sense signalling the linguistic turn as it tends to in literary theory, postcolonial studies, or ethnographical studies of poststructuralist scholars.[4] On the contrary, the hyphenated form is used here to signal the start of another era of quasi-sovereignty, dependence, and subordination introduced (and now intensified) since decolonization and is based in a nuanced reading of the diverse set of states comprising the post-colonial world. In the context of the reinscription of dependency, I have avoided the term 'neocolonial' as it has been historically surrounded by controversy and its usage can be distracting.[5]

The term 'post-colonial' also helps to distinguish African and Asian states that emerged after the formal demise of colonial rule at the end of the Second World War from the 'normal' (European) nation-states. With respect to Latin American states, however, this distinction creates a dilemma: should Latin American states be considered post-colonial? If the broad description of post-colonial states mentioned previously—in the sense of the reinscription of subordination and dependency on the US and Western states, Western transnational corporations, and international financial institutions—then Latin American states share a similar reality. At the same time, these states have a different colonial and contemporary history than states of Africa and Asia (especially in relation to the emergence of nationalism and the presence of the Aboriginal population that still largely lives at the margins). Indeed, Latin American states were decolonized between 50 and 100 years before the African and Asian states. Moreover, the Iberian powers that colonized Latin America were marked by a very different, non-capitalist history (one typified by the rise of latifundia, minifundia, and other social differences based on Indigeneity/race and class rather than ethnicity/nationalism) as compared with much of Africa and Asia. As such, the application of the term post-colonial in the case of Latin American states is questionable. In distinguishing Latin American states from post-colonial states, my position is not very different from scholars involved in ethnographical studies of the state, although our reasons for doing so are divergent.[6] Nonetheless, this raises further questions about the relevance of using 'post-colonial' for states in the Americas. Thus, I confine the term here to the states within Africa and Asia that emerged during the post-1945 era of decolonization.

I should also clarify that the terms the 'Third World' and the (global) 'South' are used here interchangeably to signal and refer to states of Africa, Asia, and Latin America. In saying this, I recognize that the idea of the 'Third World' should be critically assessed as its usage could result in an easy slippage into generalizations that do not reflect the enormous differences between the various regions of the South, let alone the differences among states within the same region. Indeed, the idea of *tiers monde* was originally constructed to "define the structures of disadvantage" which echoed those of the peasantry (part of the 'Third Estate') within the social order of pre-revolutionary France;[7] therefore, the term Third World has been a descriptor deemed to identify 'inferiorized' parts of the world. But this description has not gone unchallenged. The leaders of the Non-Aligned Movement, not very long after decolonization, appropriated the idea of the Third World (not without complications) to invert its demeaning representation and to symbolize the notion of resistance against imperialist domination—as reflected in the idea of Third Worldism.[8] Thus, inherent in the use of the term here is the underlying concept of Third Worldism. However, by characterizing African, Asian, and Latin American states as the global South and as the Third World, I do not mean to gloss over the vast differences between them. Therefore, these two terms are used interchangeably, albeit sparingly.

Similarly, in using the term 'the West', or the 'Western world', my intention is not to reduce to a unitary entity the differences in language, culture, and/or history of the different states of Europe, North America, and Australasia. Rather, the terms' usage signifies for the different Western states a common broad commitment to capitalist culture ('Western values') and a determination to pursue common imperialist interests around the world. The 'West' as a construct also posits itself as the superior identity to its racialized and gendered 'other', the 'non-West' or the Third World.

WRITING THE POST-COLONIAL

The linguistic turn in the social sciences and humanities has undoubtedly challenged the more essentialist and reductionist understanding of racialized, gendered, and classed-based (among other) identities, although class (and even race[9]) has been blurred through interpretations of colonialism as more than a one-sided act of sheer dominance over the colonized—without dealing with the issue of class exploitation as such and the link between racism and capitalist accumulation/domination. Many postcolonial theorists instead view colonization as an *'encounter'* between an oppressive and a resistant force, thus signifying resistance and 'empowerment' of the colonized as well. This understanding is articulated by a host of postcolonial and subaltern studies writers, most notably Ranajit Guha, and Edward Said in trying to address the criticism against his *magnum opus*, *Orientalism.*[10] This is not the place to enter into a polemic with postcolonial or post-structuralist scholars on whether the resistance of the colonized was coeval with the power and domination of the colonizers or whether these scholars' understanding of colonialism introduces into the debate a degree of ambivalence and contingency that has, in the process, effectively disabled a more complete conception of power and domination. Even a cursory glance at the colonial 'encounter' uncovers the sad reality of resistance: of all the slave revolts, which were very violently put down, only Haiti's was successful. This 'success' only made hope turn into sorrow, however, because the imperialist powers ensured that Haiti's aspiration to *freeness* would be made into a terrible example that would never be repeated (France and the US not only placed a naval blockade around Haiti, they forced the liberated colony to pay reparations to France for freeing itself. Then the US decided to briefly occupy Haiti at the turn of the last century to ensure its subservience, which has continued into the present era making Haiti into a veritable neoimperial prison[11]). In raising this issue, I *do not* contend that resistance is futile; some national liberation struggles were initially quite successful, such as in Algeria, Indonesia, and Vietnam. On the contrary, Haiti's example highlights that the discussion of resistance—without an understanding of the structural composition of the colonial state and a political economy understanding of power—is incomplete and unable to explain how a handful of colonizers or settlers could effectively occupy and control (albeit imperfectly) vast numbers of colonized people. Incidentally, this structural legacy of the colonial state is deeply imbricated with the post-colonial state (see the discussion on the book's main argument next and Chapter 3). In other words, the Foucauldian perspective on power that informs critical ethnographical ideas of the state overlooks a structuralist understanding of power and resistance. This outlook can therefore celebrate resistance without a considered analysis of why examples of successful resistance to colonial or imperial power and even post-colonial state power are merely a few etchings on an enormous canvas.

In contrast to the contributions of critical ethnographers studying the post-colonial state, I attempt its more nuanced structuralist comprehension, which is rooted in social history and involves a political economy of the post-colonial state and critical understanding of power and resistance. The latter entails a recognition of how imperialist imperatives in the Third World and the clientalist role of most post-colonial states continue to underwrite the social and cultural fragmentation and economic dependency of post-colonial societies. That being said, I am sympathetic to Akhil Gupta and Aradhana Sharma's critique of an instrumentalist reading of the state, which they note has been so focused on the state's "structuralist and functionalist aspects as an instrument in the hands of the capitalist class"[12] that it ignores the "cultural dynamics of the modern state."[13] In focusing on culture as an antidote to instrumentalism, the gaze of critical ethnographers is directed by a poststructuralist reading that derives from an almost exclusive emphasis on local specificities, such as corruption, 'everyday practices', the bureaucracy or governmentality, and culture at various local institutional sites. However, the attention to these specificities, as objects of knowledge, and these scholars' empirical, cultural, and transnational approaches become so pervasive and intense that they ignore the external impulse and the structural dynamics of power, and pay scant attention to the need for mobilizing broader societal resistance against the oppressive power of the dominant classes and imperialist states—in order to move beyond the individualized stories of resistance. In this way, critical ethnographers reaffirm the state *not* as a pivot embodying the social relations of power but rather as "a dispersed ensemble of institutional practices,"[14] reflecting the dispersal of power against which they claim that resistance remains fertile. Such a perspective enables critical ethnographers to claim in Foucauldian terms that the "modern state is not the source of power but the effect of a wider range of dispersed forms of disciplinary power that allow 'the state' to appear as a structure that stands apart from, and above, society."[15] Mitchell goes on to suggest, "[w]e must analyze the state . . . not as an actual structure, but as the powerful, apparently metaphysical effect of practices [of control]."[16] Ignoring the intrinsic role of structures foregrounds the notion that power is dispersed in institutions and events rather than in classes. This negation of structure assumes that power is socially (or even ideologically) neutral. As such, this outlook benefits the state-framed and state-propelled class projects by neither analyzing nor interrogating their structural framework or questioning who benefits and who loses out.

In contrast, Poulantzas too did not view the state as a repository of power or as a subject or thing (unlike Hegel's idea of the state); rather, in contradistinction with Foucault, Poulantzas regarded the capitalist state as a relationship of forces or, more precisely, as the "material condensation of such a relationship among classes and class fractions."[17] For Poulantzas, this specific materiality of the state (embodied in state structures) is critical; otherwise, the state can be viewed as an instrument that is simply reducible to state power—that is, the class that can manipulate this instrument can capture the capitalist state.[18] Preceding Poulantzas, Marx and Engels originally argued against this instrumentalist view of the state when analyzing the failure of the Paris Commune to capture state power.[19]

This critical appraisal helps distinguish my own work and issues that are important to my research as I discuss some elements of a poststructuralist theorization of the post-colonial state. However, my critique of critical ethnographers does not entail complete rejection of their ideas: some generalizations made by these ethnographers about the post-colonial state have merit. What their research lacks is an effort to address more substantive questions about the state including the following: what is the nature of the post-colonial state in relation to the capitalist Western state; is the state apparatus autonomous or relatively autonomous of competing class, bureaucratic, and other interests (in other words, who rules, what forces control the state, and what are their roles in post-colonial states with respect to setting economic, political, and social priorities vis-à-vis imperial imperatives); how does the external impact the internal apparatus of the post-colonial state; and how is underdevelopment reinscribed in the post-colonial era—simply put, how is neoliberal globalization different from the first three or four decades of post-World War II capitalist development/domination?

In focusing on the nature of the state, my goal is not to attribute singularity to form and function of the post-colonial state. Instead, the assumption underlying questions about the nature of the state is that the post-colonial state is *not* a 'material condensate' of a dominant class in a classic sense like the Western capitalist state. As a result, the post-colonial state cannot be fully understood unless the players who wield power and influence on the state are identified. This brings us to the question of who rules and what is the form of the state; that is, is the post-colonial state capitalist, proto-capitalist, non-capitalist, or a combination?

Mobilizing efforts to make the state more representative requires the identification, as foes or allies, of contemporary players who control or influence the direction of policy and development in post-colonial societies. For example, if feudal elites have an abiding influence in controlling the functions of the state (a situation that is prevalent in many post-colonial states and societies), how can resistance be mobilized and extended when these same elites pretend to champion progressive transformative agendas and pay lip service to issues of democratization, alleviation of poverty, and land redistribution? Critical ethnographers are less interested in the nature of the state than in post-colonial state formation, which they claim is more encompassing in examinations of culture, territorial sovereignty, and the "mappings of state and citizenship [that are seen] as moving out of the state's hands and increasingly into a transnational space informed by indigenous social movements and multilateral development agencies."[20] Critical ethnographers and some geographers also suggest that there is much current 'rethinking of the state'. This process involves questioning the perceived role of the state in regulating social life while state sovereignty and its 'cultural legitimacy' face potentially undermining challenges from a variety of forces: ethnic/national movements, neoliberal globalization, and movement of people as migrants and refugees.[21] As I will discuss later, this type of theory rests on an assumption that the state is 'weak' in an era of rising transnationalism, an assumption whose validity needs to be critically assessed in the first instance.[22]

Anthropologists involved in critical ethnographic explorations view the post-colonial state, therefore, as a 'cultural artifact' or work towards the adoption of a 'denaturalized' attitude towards the state. This attitude stems from an avoidance of attributing a certain 'natural' essence to the state, and yet these same scholars often end up lamenting that the "paradox of inadequacy and indispensability has robbed the state of its naturalness."[23] Hansen and Stepputat noted that contributors to their edited volume, *States of Imagination: Ethnographic Explorations of the Postcolonial State*, such as Akhil Gupta, David Nugent, Sarah A. Radcliffe, and others

> all share this denaturalizing approach to state and governance in the postcolonial world; they all study the state, politics, and notions of authority empirically from a variety of ethnographic sites; and they all position themselves in the space between a Gramscian and Foucauldian position on power, government and authority where much of the reconceptualization of the state has been taking place.[24]

Investigating the post-colonial state using this approach involves two problems. First, it assumes what needs to be explained: whether the post-colonial state is actually a 'natural' embodiment of sovereignty and a source of social order. In other words, what are the naturalizing processes that generate awe and make people see the post-colonial state as a bastion of power, authority, and sovereignty? Conversely, what would a 'denaturalizing' process entail, and what would be the consequences not just for the state but especially for society? Furthermore, given that critical ethnographers are ambivalent about the nature of the state (viewing the state as a paradox or a cultural artifact), it is odd that a 'denaturalizing approach' does not involve an exploration of *how* (and why) the "institutionalized sovereign government remains pivotal in our very imagination of what a society is."[25] In the context of the post-colonial state, the assumption about state sovereignty has more to do with its roots in the Western imagination—propelled by the ideas of Hobbes and fed by the writings of ethnographers—without much appreciation of the external imposition that has most post-colonial states in a vice-like grip. Ordinary residents/citizens in *most* post-colonial societies are aware that sovereignty is actually wielded outside their respective states—by imperial and corporate political and economic powers that influence internal and external outcomes with respect to their state and society.

Second, this approach of striving for that in-between space that is populated by Foucauldian and Gramscian ideas may be the source of much confusion about the poststructuralist perspective of the state and consequent ambivalence about the nature of the state. Foucault and Gramsci take antipodal positions in examining a phenomenon which, I would argue, cannot be easily reconciled. Foucault begins with a discussion of the microphysics of power and its immanence in all social relations; because he considers that power solicits resistance it is easy for him to overlook the structural dimension (and pervasiveness) of power and imagine the diffusion of power in institutional and cultural practices. Gramsci, in contrast, begins at the macro level of class power and outlines how the state is a class hegemonic project, which is materialized in relatively autonomous state structures. For Gramsci, if the working class is to successfully overthrow the bourgeois state, it will have to be successful in the counter-hegemonic 'war of movement' and 'war of position'. Gramsci did, however, recognize (based on his involvement in the council movement in the Risorgimento) that resistance may be ambiguous when carrying out these 'wars': the subaltern may be progressive on some issues and reactionary on others.[26] So, if critical ethnographers situate themselves between Foucauldian and Gramscian perspectives, their position will not just be immersed in contradiction (as noted by Hansen and Stepputat);[27] rather, the force of the opposing polarities is such that mediation will eclipse either the micro or macro registers of power. But, because we are dealing with a poststructuralist understanding of the state, and because Gramsci's radical materialist notions contradict Foucault's micro-level ideas of power and resistance, it is quite conceivable that the latter will prevail over the former.

Beyond the poststructuralists, it is also disconcerting that other writers from both Weberian and orthodox Marxist perspectives articulate the post-colonial state as an undifferentiated entity that is largely indistinguishable from the 'modern' Western nation-state. Specifically, these scholars, and even developmental state theorists, have failed to account for the divergent histories of state formation in post-colonial societies (poststructuralist ethnographers excepted), the peculiar make-up of the bureaucracy, and the function of the post-colonial state in asserting the internal control of society while facilitating the external domination by Western states and metropolitan capital.[28] In contrast, ethnographic explorations have addressed the issue of colonialism in their inimitable style of an 'encounter', and although they have not distinguished the post-colonial state from the Western nation-state, they have argued quite correctly that the idea of the 'normal' nation-state was embraced by post-colonial elites at the time of decolonization.[29] Little attention has been paid, however, to the acquiescence of political and bureaucratic Third World elites to the demands of imperialist powers and their expectations that the former would fall in line on international issues, within the so-called community of nations. I will address some of these issues, as well as the significant historical differences between post-colonial states and Western nation-states, in the next chapter to provide context for the subsequent discussion of post-colonial states and why they cannot be classified as nation-states.

WHY THEORIZE THE POST-COLONIAL STATE?

In post-colonial societies, the state remains the most powerful force of political order and is the basis of multilateral, regional, hemispheric, and now supranational organization of the world. The power of this force notwithstanding, various kinds of proclamations have been made about the 'weakness' or the 'demise' of the nation-state to include post-colonial states.[30] This language of 'weakness', which was in vogue until recently,[31] had to be disentangled from the notion of transnationalism and demystified from the project of globalization to clarify the imperial imperatives that underlie both these ideas. "[A]lthough contemporary globalization has complicated the nation-state form, it has not rendered it obsolete as a form of political organization."[32] However, clarification of the character of the post-colonial state is difficult because theories are greatly divergent and are becoming more complicated as new modes of analysis are developed to theorize about the post-colonial state. For instance, the idea of transnationalism has emerged along with the project of globalization, enabling scholars to focus on social processes such as migrancy and social movements that are rooted in, and transcend, nation-states. But increasingly, the term 'transnationalism' is also casually employed by many poststructuralists to link the local with the global, where global becomes synonymous with globalization as a transhistorical idea—largely undistinguished from the ideological, political, and imperial projects that underlie contemporary globalization.[33] Marxists have long recognized that local struggles have an international dimension in the era of imperialism (some have termed the current conjuncture a period of 'new imperialism').[34] However, imperialist powers also consistently attempt to short-circuit this international dimension in order to prevent and subvert efforts to widen the span of local struggles on the international plane. As Petras and Veltmeyer pointed out, support for local struggles in the era of globalization has been effectively thwarted by the process of *NGOization*.[35] It would be imprudent to paint all non-governmental organization (NGOs) with a broad brush, but if NGOs mostly rely on Western donors or Western development agencies and corporate philanthropy for their survival, then it is not inconceivable that they will be influenced by their benefactors. Also, the rise of NGOs accompanied the intensification in social dislocations caused initially by International Monetary Fund's (IMF) structural adjustment measures throughout the 1980s, and the process was accelerated by the rise of globalization since the early 1990s. As a result, although some NGOs do meaningful work, organizing resistance on a society-wide platform—which is really a political imperative—for most of the NGOs, their work gets reduced in the current conjuncture to a fragmented and extremely localized social work initiative. Therefore, the term 'transnational' needs to be problematized to prevent mechanistic and casual labeling of any program, policy, or struggle as 'transnational'. In other words, application of the notion of transnationalism should be context-specific. In this way, the idea may become an organizing principle that can inform, coordinate, and conceivably organize internationally the local grassroots resistance and the work of indigenous social movements against imperial impositions, the neoliberal globalization project, and other forms of racial and gender oppressions and class exploitation. Realization of this potential, as opposed to rendering the idea of transnationalism into a mere rhetorical device, requires vigilance in two key areas: (i) the historicism inherent in not distinguishing contemporary globalization from capitalism's historical international trajectory since its infancy and (ii) the tendency to read mechanically a transformative potential to a program, policy, movement, or action and thus read its global (international) links without also identifying the ultimate beneficiaries (ordinary people versus the imperialized and imperialist holders of privilege).

The title of this book suggests that it uses a post-colonial perspective to analyze critically the imperatives of capitalist globalism, that is, its propensity of external domination of the post-colonial state. Based on this understanding, as I have argued elsewhere,[36] the project of globalization could only be realized once nationalist and independent-minded leaders in many post-colonial societies were overthrown or eliminated through the Central Intelligence Agency's (CIA) 'dirty tricks' and military coups, the developmental project was shelved, and the 'new' international division of labour was adopted in the late 1970s.[37] These measures subsequently opened the doors of most Third World states to the transfer of labour-intensive operations from the North, the establishment of Free Trade Zones and sweatshop assembly lines, the acceptance of the export-orientation bind on the economy with the consequent loss of an internal market, and the dismantling of the public domain for privatization and market access through the IMF's structural adjustment programs and World Trade Organization policies. These changes have not been part of some transhistorical process as Gupta and Sharma have alluded;[38] rather, the globalization era marks a qualitative shift involving a power transfer from the national (the nation-state/post-colonial state) to the global (meaning capital and corporations), a move in which, paradoxically, the post-colonial state has been fully complicit. In accepting this shift and the new reality of capitalist globalism, states in both the North and the South have worked hand-in-glove, not as 'weak' entities; rather, the proto-capitalist post-colonial states (weak in the sense of their client status) have been relatively strong vis-à-vis their own populace in enforcing the neoliberal shift in state and society. Before capitalist globalism came to pass, the national was paramount: the US with the support of most Western nation-states started to elevate the nation-state to mythical heights, beginning at the Bretton Woods conference in 1944, and the narrative of the all-powerful state has since navigated both imagined and real paths. Therefore, the challenge for theorists of the state is to make sense of the external impulses of the hegemonic Western state and international financial institutions and to analyze why and how the post-colonial and Latin American states have acquiesced in delimiting their power in relation to capital. For the post-colonial state, however, this dramatic turn to self-imposed delimitation of power vis-á-vis capital has created the dilemma for indigenous elites to create 'normal' nation-states—an idea that was internalized with the appearance of the colonial state and the eulogizing of the Western nation-state as the most effective vehicle of territorial representation and internal management of the populace. However, this self-imposed delimiting of state power has been realized by the force of external domination, a fact that state theorists have ignored in favour of analyses of internal state imperatives. This separation of external and internal state dimensions is one of the important issues addressed in this book and one of the key arguments for a theory of the post-colonial state. Incidentally, the case for integration of internal and external dimensions is specifically made in Chapters 2 and 3.

A post-colonial state theory can also explicate the ongoing impact of the colonial legacy on the state in post-colonial societies. However, these links cannot be articulated in an ahistorical manner. If we merely focus on the current era of capitalist globalism when most post-colonial states are trying to outdo and outbid one another in offering a favourable corporate climate for privatization and investment capital from transnational corporations, then we will miss examining the historical developments of the 1960s and 1970s. During this period, it was Western capital that was clamouring to get into post-colonial states and having much difficulty because of the restriction imposed on foreign direct investments. In the past 60 years or so of decolonization, links have been forged between the adoption of the capitalist path of development and the evolution of the post-colonial states in their current form. Even on a longer time horizon, admittedly, forms of Euro-US domination have changed over the past two and a half centuries, but the maintenance of a subordinate and dependent South is still the paramount imperialist goal with respect to states in the Third World. The identification of dependency as the common disabling tendency among Third World states should not become the basis of homogenizing the situation to all states of Africa, Asia, and Latin America. For the purpose of theorization, this generalization of dependency needs to be made more specific based on categories of post-colonial states' social and economic formation: as capitalist or proto-capitalist. Alongside, capitalist exploitation and race construction/racialization need to be understood as complementary social processes. These social processes even had some White people becoming racialized at one point in history (Irish, Southern and Eastern Europeans, and Ashkenazi Jews) who were subsequently de-racialized as they became part of the dominant Northern European communities in Europe and North America, whereas the historically racialized peoples, the Aboriginal and non-White from Africa, Asia, Australasia, and Latin America, continue to be oppressed and exploited in complex and contradictory ways for capital's benefit. However, even between the two broad variants of capitalist and proto-capitalist formations offered in this volume, a range of differences can be analyzed, including the composition and role of class forces, the differences in the nature of the state's relative autonomy, the question of whether understanding the power of dominant class forces should focus on the economic or political, or on their dialectical interplay. There is also considerable difference between capitalist and proto-capitalist categories that symbolize the incredible difference between the treatment of South Korea and sub-Saharan African states. Further, variations exist *within* each of these two respective categories. For instance, in the case of capitalist formations there are differences between India and China on the one hand and South Korea and Brazil on the other. Ultimately, these complexities are integrated in a meaningful theorization of the post-colonial state in Chapter 3, this volume.

THEORIZING THE POST-COLONIAL STATE

My primary argument in this book is that the post-colonial state has been the key mechanism in the global South's subordination (internally, by undermining civil society, and externally, by facilitating its imperialist domination) such that its populace remains largely fragmented and powerless as it is forced to yield to a unified front of mobile metropolitan capital that has the support of Western and client post-colonial states. The explanatory framework for this argument, which I introduced in the last section, can be synthesized as part of three complementary conceptual categories: (i) the *capitalism–nation-state nexus* and how it unfolds for Western nation-states and becomes the *capitalism–imperialism nexus* in colonial and post-colonial contexts, (ii) the problems with separating internal and external moments in state theory, and (iii) the primacy that state theorists have placed on either the economic or the political dimension without distinguishing the capitalist state from the proto-capitalist state. Most post-colonial states fall into the proto-capitalist category, whereas a few are capitalist entities. Distinguishing proto-capitalist from capitalist post-colonial states makes it possible to theorize the two variants of post-colonial states. In Chapter 3, I will begin with a broad theorization of the post-colonial state and then, in the final two chapters, shift to a concrete examination of state formation in India and Pakistan to clarify the capitalist and proto-capitalist variants, respectively.

I was motivated to conduct this research partly because of a resurgent interest in the post-colonial state and partly by witnessing how existing theorization has proceeded without either problematizing the ideological nature of neoliberal rule or foregrounding the external impulse of contemporary imperialist interventions and domination of the South. I also wanted to address the following significant omissions in post-colonial state theory: the differing natures of post-colonial states and the incompleteness of nation-building (failure to address the 'national question'), the impact of the colonial state, and the structures of internal and external domination. These omissions appear not only in the work of ideologues of neoliberalism and liberal social scientists but also in scholarship by various types of state theorists, including those of critical ethnography and of the developmental state. Three main limitations can be identified in the current 'discourse' on the post-colonial state: (i) a 'flattening of history', especially the history of the colonial state, whose imprint is deeply etched on the post-colonial state; (ii) a lack of comprehension of the capitalism–imperialism nexus and of the nature and role of the post-colonial state in facilitating the external imperialist domination of state and society; and (iii) an emphasis on culture, paradox, and ambiguity in identifying the state at the expense of a more nuanced structuralist understanding of the state.

Against this backdrop, my political economy and social history perspective is meant to critique the prevailing orthodoxy, which universalizes Western ideas and remains committed to a Eurocentric reading of the 'non-European' world. There is an apparent refusal to understand, or even notice, how colonial legacies shape the histories of post-colonial states; a characteristic current imperialist response is to demand post-colonial states to do more to support imperialist projects, while remaining silent about the North-South divide and the increasing dependency of the South on the

North. Currently, this involves a formal push for 'good governance' and democracy in the Third World within a privatized social framework that does not empower ordinary people and leaves the state relatively removed from issues related to the well-being of its populace including health, education, and gainful employment. Instead, Western states are eager to see a greater involvement of NGOs in local issues in Third World states and want an even bigger push towards privatization and the dismantling of the public domain in this age of neoliberalism. These observations underpin much of the work in the first two chapters.

I will begin Chapter 1 by foregrounding the conceptual framework of the *capitalism–nation-state nexus* and by addressing the larger historical context of capitalist development and the rise of the nation-state in Europe, which led to the extension of colonialism to Africa and Asia. This link demonstrates the very different context of the European nation-state formation compared with that of the post-colonial state. I will also contest the idea of the 'normal' nation-state and clarify how this notion was imagined by post-colonial ruling classes as they emulated the European experience of nationalism and nation-states formation. Similarly, I will critically assess theories of nationalism, most of which universalize the European nationalist experience to post-colonial state and society. I will address the problems inherent in Eurocentrism and distinguish my critique of universalization from Partha Chatterjee's so that I can analyze Benedict Anderson's celebrated work[39] and critically assess his ideas of nation and nationalism. My analysis of the colonial state's manipulative social policy will reveal that the nature of identity construction in the colony and its debilitating impact for the colonized have produced antagonistic conflicts, which continue in the post-colonial era. This chapter shows how the capitalism–nation-state nexus was central for the capitalist development of Europe and North America and how a new capitalism–imperialism link emerged as soon as capitalists (with full support of their respective nation-states' militaries) begin their search for new colonies from the mid-18th century. As the capitalism–imperialism nexus re-emerged in the post-colonial era, subordination was reinscribed on state and society through clientelism and US imperialist domination.

Chapter 2 provides the historical context to post-colonial state's re-subordination, and the analytical framework will assist in developing a theory of the post-colonial state in Chapter 3. Critical to this framework is the *capitalism–imperialism nexus*, which emerged during colonialism and has become the key instrument of re-subordination of post-colonial states. Because modernization theorists have played a pivotal role in introducing developmentalism to the global South and in encouraging post-colonial and Latin American states to serve as clients for the post-World War II capitalist/imperialist superpower, I will examine the ideas of two key modernization theorists. I will also briefly examine how the Cold War between the US and the Soviet Union became a hot war for post-colonial and Latin

American states. This happened with the formation of the US security state and the CIA, which resulted in the elimination or removal of nationalist post-colonial and Latin American leadership. I will then show how the developmental state was an effort to resist the capitalism–imperialism nexus but that the indigenous bourgeoisie began to dismantle the inward-oriented developmental state because of the economic stagnation and corruption accompanying this statist model and embraced the market-oriented path of capitalist development. The US, its Western allies, and international financial institutions took the developmental state's failure as an opportunity to pressure Third World states to privatize the public domain and introduce economic liberalization. At the same time, because the peasantry was being displaced from rural areas as mechanization and Green Revolution technology was introduced, Western states lost no time in introducing the 'new' international division of labour—effectively transferring labour-intensive production to the global South to take advantage of this captive reserve army of displaced and unemployed workers. With the demise of the Soviet Union, the priority for Western states was to extend neoliberalism for the eventual re-subordination of proto-capitalist post-colonial states. The combined effect of these changes and the pauperization of the urban working class that followed led to the emergence of the urban informal sector as the most exploited form of self-employment—in effect, the work of a disguised proletariat. The idea that families who are involved in the informal sector are complicit in their own *self-exploitation* is a relatively unexplored concept in the context of capitalist globalism; therefore, I will examine how self-exploitation is realized within the current capitalist framework. Finally, I will analyze how the division between North and South has been cemented by the new international division of labour, whereas the capitalism–imperialism nexus has intensified the re-subordination of post-colonial state and society in the period of neoliberal globalization.

The historical and social analyses of colonialism, nationalism, and the capitalism–imperialism nexus that I present in Chapters 1 and 2 provide part of the foundation for my theorization on the post-colonial state. Chapter 3 builds on this background by first examining the nature of the economic system and social relations that were dominant in the colony, as these have a bearing in the post-colonial era; most post-colonial states adopted the structures of the colonial state, which were quasi-capitalist or proto-capitalist. My theorization about the post-colonial state, therefore, includes three inter-related issues: the impact of the colonial state structure, the role of internal class relations, and the force of external imperialist domination of post-colonial state and society. In addressing these three issues, I am able to integrate the external and internal dimensions of the post-colonial state, which I consider to be central to a more comprehensive analysis of the character of the post-colonial state. By critically engaging with Alavi's theorization of pheripheral capitalism, I will examine colonial India's social conditions in order to demonstrate that, although the colony may have been a periphery of the metropolitan capitalist colonial power, its social relations, contra Alavi, were not capitalist or even peripherally capitalist. I will argue that the 'overdeveloped' bureaucracies of most proto-capitalist states have so encumbered and shackled their societies that feudal relations did not significantly weaken. As a result, capitalists and the working class are weak in proto-capitalist societies and, barring a few exceptions, do not enable the release of productive forces for capitalist, socialist, or some other form of social transformation. Following this, I will examine the nature of the post-colonial state more broadly by analyzing the character and roles of the bureaucracy and the propertied classes and how they contributed to managing the affairs of post-colonial state and society. Throughout much of this analysis I address the external meddling of imperialist power, integrate the external and internal moments, and discuss the need for a dialectical interplay between the economic and the political dimensions.

In addressing the nature or character of the state, I offer two variations of the post-colonial state: the capitalist and the proto-capitalist variant—the latter typifying most states of Africa and Asia. In this context, my research contributes to a new understanding of the post-colonial state in the era of capitalist globalism. There are very different implications for the post-colonial state depending on whether the state is analyzed as capitalist or proto-capitalist; hence the two case studies on state formation in India and Pakistan (Chapters 4 and 5, respectively) are my attempt to ground theory in practice.

Much of what I offer in Chapter 4's social analysis of early post-colonial India and its transition to a capitalist state is omitted in current ethnographical studies of the post-colonial state: an examination of the land question, an analysis of social relations in India, an assessment of the benefits derived by the propertied classes from the early social and economic policies of the Nehruvian state, and an examination of the role of the Indian bureaucratic elite. As the external dimension is an essential part of my broad analysis of India's state formation, I integrate it within this chapter. Moving from this integrated analysis, I will then examine the post-Nehruvian era: Indira Gandhi's stint with populism, the rise of regionalism, and how Hindu fundamentalism/nationalism gained prominence and captured state power. Through a careful analysis of the Indian bourgeoisie's aggressive moves to adopt neoliberalism and attack on the inward-oriented state-led developmental model in favour of economic liberalization, I demonstrate how India shook off the 'failed' developmental state label, rebranding itself 'incredible India'. Despite tremendous economic expansion and consistent high growth rates in the past decade, however, India's social fissures have not decreased, poverty has not been reduced, and the rural-urban divide is glaring. As a result, there is broad internal resistance to neoliberalism in India. In the final section, I will examine this resistance, which has taken the form of armed action of radical groups and *adivasis* (Indigenous people) to oppose corporate mining interests, the Indian state, and its paramilitary thugs. The challenge to neoliberalism, along with the nationalist movement in Kashmir, Assam, and elsewhere, has also led to the rise of the security-obsessed Indian state.

My case study of Pakistan's state formation in Chapter 5 will reveal that, in contrast to what happened in India, once the civil and military bureaucrats had taken firm control of the state apparatus in the immediate aftermath of decolonization, they completely aligned the country with the US. This decision made Pakistan captive to US demands and eventually led the country to become a client state of its US patron. My critical assessment of Pakistan's formative years shows that its very basis of existence as a homogenous Muslim '*nation*' was challenged from the moment of its inception by the assertion of ethnic and national identity claims. The demands for subnational rights and provincial autonomy were made by Baluch, Bengali, Pashtun, and Sindhi nations against the dominance of the bureaucratic elite from the Punjab and their junior partners (migrants from North India, who later chose to also identify themselves as the *Mohajir* [migrant] nation). I undertake an extended socio-political analysis of Pakistan's first three decades since decolonization, integrating internal and external dimensions. External factors affecting Pakistan were much more complex than those for India. The first three decades marked two long periods of military dictatorship between which was the civilian rule of Z.A. Bhutto. General Ziaul Haq's military dictatorship was extremely damaging for Pakistani society; its reverberations are being felt to this day. Haq not only deepened Pakistan's clientelist relationship with the US, in the context of the Afghan War against the Soviet Union, he also unleashed the forces of militant Islam. In a separate section of the chapter I will address the Pakistani state's role in enabling a rightward ideological shift and the radicalization of militant Islamists. The further intensification of Pakistan's clientelist relationship with US and the consequent rise of the Taliban against the US and North Atlantic Treaty Organization forces in Afghanistan and Pakistan, has also resulted in the Taliban attacking Pakistani state and society, which has made public safety and security in the country a number one concern. The Haq regime was also pivotal to the military's expanded involvement in the economy and impeded private industrial capital investment, whereas the power of the feudal elite has remained unchallenged. Consequently, the capitalist class has become weaker, as the civil and military bureaucrats, and now the civilian political leadership, have wreaked havoc with the already fragile economy. The result is that Pakistan remains a very dependent proto-capitalist state.

In the final section of the chapter, I will analyze the social and economic constraints, and investigate why economic liberalization in Pakistan has not received the kind of enthusiasm that it has in India. The rudderless Pakistani economy and the *rentier* nature of its key players' activities mean that the country is essentially on life support. Because the US has largely provided this economic support, even if it has been through the IMF and the World Bank, clientelism has become deeply entrenched, and Pakistan now is even more beholden to the US. The result of this dependency and subordination has been more intensively reinscribed in the period of capitalist globalization.

The importance of identifying the character of a post-colonial state as capitalist or proto-capitalist provides valuable clues about the internal makeup of society and the effect of external imperialist forces on both state and society. As the case studies of India and Pakistan reveal, there are serious implications for state sovereignty for *proto-capitalist states* in relation to the *capitalist post-colonial state*. The latter may still be dependent on Western capital and to a degree on Western nation-states, but it has more room to manoeuvre. In contrast, the sovereignty of *proto-capitalist states* is seriously compromised because they are made up largely of client states and dependent on the imperialist power. This dependency also has significant consequences for economic independence and for autonomy in developing appropriate social and political policy frameworks. The concluding thought here is that by returning to the larger structural questions and the legacy of the colonial state, by re-establishing the relationship between imperialism and capitalism, and by reintegrating the separations, the expectation is for a fresh understanding of the post-colonial state in the age of capitalist globalization.

1 Context of State Formation

Differentiating European Nation-States from Colonial and Post-Colonial States

The rise of capitalism, the spread of colonialism, and the creation of the European nation-state stand in stark contrast to the formation of the post-colonial state. Latin American states, which are similar to, yet different from, post-colonial states, are not part of this study, although I refer to these states in this volume.[1] Nonetheless, from the colonial to the post-colonial era, Africa, Asia, and Latin America have taken diametrically dissimilar trajectories of national identity, state, and societal formation compared with Europe and North America. In this chapter, I analyze these differential contexts and related issues in four interrelated sections. First, I provide a historical context for state formation in Europe by foregrounding the capitalism–nation-state nexus—that is, the integral link between the rise of capitalism and the emergence of nationalism and the nation-state in Europe and its transformative drive for Europe's capitalist development. The capitalism–nation-state nexus was critical, once ethnic groups became politically conscious about nation and nationalism, in breaking up the dynastic realms of the Habsburg, the Romanov, and others and in redrawing the borders of European nation-states. This European developmental path contrasts with the establishment of the colonial state in Africa and Asia at the behest of European colonial rulers. In the second section of this chapter, I show how the link between the rise of industrial capitalism and the emergence of European nation-states changed to the *capitalism–imperialism nexus* during the period of colonialism beginning in the late 1700s. Since the 1750s, however, the expansion of imperialist Western nation-states, beyond the Americas to Asia and Africa, was in pursuit of captive sources of wealth and raw materials to fuel European capitalist development and expansionism. Pursuing this economic drive, the metropolitan nation-state laid the foundation for colonial expansion and domination through the establishment of the colonial state, which stifled resistance and divided the colonized by manipulating conflicts among them around issues of identity based on religion, language, culture, and/or region. As these mechanisms of control, conflict-creation, and domination became more entrenched, culture became the terrain for the colonized to settle claims of inequity, injustice, and subordination through the assertion of caste, class, ethnic, religious, and linguistic identities. The emergence of these antagonistic conflicts among the colonized replaced the pre-colonial system of shared distribution of the society's surplus (albeit among privileged levels of right-holders) with a pattern of feudal domination in which the colonial state had absolute control over tribute extraction. As a result of this economic change and in this environment of conflict, various groups of colonized peoples began to perceive their oppositional group as the 'other'. In turn, these changes and the colonial state's manipulative social strategy laid the basis for the colonized to develop the ideas of ethno-culturalism, nation, and nationalism and led to another series of identity conflicts. In the third section of this chapter, I will examine the concepts of nation and nationalism, assess critically the tendency among major theorists to universalize the European experience of nationalism and nation-state formation, and clarify how identity formation among the colonized has a very different specificity. To do this, I draw on Benedict Anderson's most celebrated publication, *Imagined Communities: Reflections on the Origin and the Spread of Nationalism*,[2] which is useful here both for its distinct status and because his work is critical of Eurocentrism, yet universalizes the European experience to the 'non-European world', a tendency common to theorists of nationalism. In contrast to Anderson's thesis, I briefly examine the period of colonial rule in India to show its impact on national identity assertion in post-colonial societies and how it differs greatly from the European experience. I also show how identities that emerged in conflict under colonial rule tend to have a long afterlife and shape the formation of state and society in the post-colonial era. Before I have analyzed national identity assertions in colonial India, I also distinguish my analysis from Partha Chatterjee's approach to nationalism. In the final section of this chapter, I analyze the influence of capitalism–imperialism nexus on the social construction of the colonized peoples' identity, which plays out as antagonistic conflicts in the post-colonial era. These contradictions, along with the role of clientelism, have enabled the re-invocation of the capitalism–imperialism nexus in the post-colonial era—an argument that is addressed in Chapter 2, this volume. What ties the analytical frame of these very different ideas and concepts together is the treatment of nationalism and identity formation by most theorists as largely an internally driven impulse leading to a common underlying separation of the internal from the external. Regrettably, this almost exclusive focus on the internal has shaped not only the analysis of nation and nationalism but also theorization about the state. This separation of the internal needs to be remedied by examining the dialectical interplay of internal and external moments.

By addressing this separation and the separation of the political from the economic in Chapter 3, this volume, I support my central claim that the post-colonial state has been the key mechanism of its society's subordination (a role also shared by Latin American states)—both internally by fracturing and undermining civil society and externally by enabling the imperialist domination of the US and its Western allies. Faced with subordination in the era of capitalist globalism, the populace in post-colonial societies has become fragmented and rendered largely powerless in the face of an impositional unified front of powerful Western states, multilateral institutions, and corporate interests of mobile metropolitan capital that is able to move freely across territorial borders. Throughout this book, I aim to connect internal and external moments and to bridge the political and the economic within state theory. This approach differs from the dominant narrative that promotes such separations in social sciences more generally, especially in relation to state theory. The absence of an integrated analysis in state theory has hindered our understanding of the post-colonial state because the broad contours of Western capitalist nation-state theory have served as sketchy outlines for a theory of the post-colonial state. It is therefore necessary to examine the post-colonial state in its own specificity, especially in relation to the enormous legacy of the *unitary colonial* state.

In developing a theory of the post-colonial state, it is important not to simply advocate for the integration of internal and external dimensions without also being aware of the huge effect that the external, in the form of the capitalism–imperialism nexus, has had in shaping the broad structure of the post-colonial state. The dialectical interplay of these two moments is rooted in colonial history, as well as in relevant aspects of the colonial interlude (e.g., the historical trajectory of enclave production, export orientation, the determinate path of conflict among the colonized, and the inferiorization of the non-European world). The latter are recurring backdrops within even the integrated internal and external realities of the present post-colonial state. These historical threads need to be woven into post-colonial state theory, which I do beginning with this chapter, to clarify the historical antecedents to its character and propensities.

I CAPITALISM—NATION-STATE NEXUS AND THE EUROPEAN CONTEXT

The capitalism–nation-state nexus has been central to the development of capitalism in Europe and to the emergence of the capitalist nation-state with its demarcated borders. However, some have claimed that capital, by its very nature, tolerates no geographical limits to its expansion.[3] This is not to suggest, however, that capitalists do not need nation-state borders in order to protect their own 'national' capital. National borders first appeared, in the contemporary sense, when nation-states started to emerge in Europe during the late 1700s. For example, Eric Hobsbawm periodized the emergence of nation-states as beginning around 1780, situating this process as a result of capitalism's historical rise, which superseded the old regional boundaries; the map of Europe only began to be redrawn on the basis of nationalism after 1918.[4] Under feudalism, regional boundaries had been fluid because the parcellized sovereignty of feudal lords was based on a network of local and personal social relations, which gave way to the impersonal state of Absolutism that was largely under the control of centralized monarchies.[5] As industrial capitalism emerged, clear outlines of the modern nation-state also became discernible. The composition and role of the nation-state has changed over the course of the last two centuries, given the very nature of capitalist development: its unevenness, innovative ability, tendency towards accumulation and monopoly control, and its stranglehold over weaker states by means of colonization and imperialist domination. However, throughout this process, the nation-state has been indispensable, especially for the support of hegemonic capitalist states such as Britain and France during colonialism and the US in the post-colonial imperialist phase. The imperialist domination of past and present is a direct outcome of capital's expansionist trajectory. This relationship between capitalist expansion and imperialist domination is better understood by examining the capitalism–imperialism nexus, but before this link was forged, the capitalism–nation-state nexus facilitated the early drive for capitalist expansion outside the nation-state's borders. This expansionist thrust and the drive for domination is the formative specificity of the nation-state which, as will be shown later, is radically different from the post-colonial state. However, the capitalism–nation-state nexus has varied from the time of slavery and colonialism to the current phase of 'new imperialism' or capitalist globalism; it has changed depending on the mode of subordination used by the imperialist metropolitan state in support of 'national' capital.

The categorical link that I have drawn here between the nation-state and the drive for capitalist accumulation on the basis of colonial expansion is not a link made by most theorists of nationalism or of the state. Many theorists see a link between the rise of capitalism and the emergence of nationalism but do not seem concerned that European capitalist development was not a wholly internal matter; rather, the nation-state facilitated the external impulse of capital to move outside the borders of its state. Similarly, these theorists have offered very little in the way of explanation or background about the formation of colonial and post-colonial states.[6] Instead, analyses tend to universalize the European experience of nation and nationalism, as well as the European idea of the nation-state.[7] For much of mainstream social theory, the idea of the nation-state is equated with modernity and universalized beyond Western nation-states to be equally applicable for post-colonial and Latin American states in the South. Embedded in this outlook is the universalization of methodological nationalism—the notion that nation, state or society is the "natural, social, political form of the modern world."[8] Even those who explicitly reject methodological nationalism and wish to also respond to "post-modern relativism," end up universalizing the idea of the nation-state as well as the European basis of modernity.[9]

The problem of universalizing the European experience of nation and nationalism is an issue that also plagues much of the theorization on this subject. I will return to address this problem later, but here I will discuss how many scholars of nationalism do see the link between the rise of capitalism and the emergence of nationalism/nation-state. Well-known theorists of nation and nationalism (such as Ernest Gellner, Eric Hobsbawm, Elie Kouderie, and Benedict Anderson) as well as lesser known but perceptive theorists (such as Cornelia Navari[10]) all link, in one way or another, the rise of nation-states in Europe to the disintegration of dynastic realms and empires, such as the Austro-Hungarian or the Romanov dynasties. Within these formerly territorially bound empires lived diverse ethnic, linguistic, and cultural groups who increasingly began to assert their identities on the political stage after the beginning of the Industrial Revolution, from 1760 onwards. The idea of nation began to emerge, in other words, as ethnic groups in Europe began to affirm themselves politically on the terrain of nationalism. This was done through (often violent) ideological expressions of a group's identity as a nation, imagined or real, which may have harkened back to primordial roots or to a more contemporary beginning, such as displacement or migration of that group from a territory or a state. When coupled with claims of rights to a territory or a state, nationalism began to construct a people as a nation. In other words, linking the expression of nationalism, the political and/or ideological assertion of a nation's identity, with a particular territory of the nation (the state) or claim to a territory, produced the idea of a nation.[11]

However, it is important to emphasize that the acquisition of consciousness as a nation (national identity), and indeed the very manifestation of nationalism, was played out in fundamentally different ways in Europe, North America, and some of the settler colonies of Europeans, as compared with the formerly colonized peoples who now constitute the so-called Third World. I am making this distinction at the outset, because I will argue here and in following chapters of this volume that the formation of national identity and state formation in post-colonial societies have very different political goals (not to mention the very different experience)—different from the economic drive of emerging industrial capitalism in Europe to nurture the ideology of nationalism and national identity formation. Therefore, Western capitalist states have tended, in varying degrees, to protect the interest of their respective 'national' capital and indigenous capitalists and have steadfastly promoted the general interest of capital and the world capitalist system (WCS) beyond their borders, especially in penetrating the territory of former colonies and post-colonial states. In contrast, states of Asia and Africa that were decolonized after the end of the Second World War (identified hereafter as *post-colonial states*) alongside Latin American states, which are together known as Third World states, overcame colonization only to be locked into varying degrees of subordination by, and dependency on, the US and metropolitan states of Europe.

In establishing the relationship between the rise of capitalism and emergence of nationalism in Europe, I have relied on a number of scholars who have either established or implied such a link. For example, Ernest Gellner's work, *Nations and Nationalism* usefully establishes this relationship. However, Gellner's theorization has some problematic aspects: aside from his attempt to universalize the European experience, Gellner includes glimpses of neo-Malthusianism on the issue of population growth, and his attempt to show that industrial development in Eastern Europe within the category of 'industrialism' minimizes the social basis for the rise of capitalism. Nonetheless, he is one of the few theorists of nationalism to devote considerable effort to link the rise of capitalism ('industrialism') with the emergence of nationalism. Gellner's antithetical position to Marxism, as well an aversion to post-World War II developments in Eastern Europe under the control of the former Soviet Union, may explain his use of the term 'industrialism' instead of 'capitalism'. Gellner attributes to 'industrialism' many of the features of capitalism without distinguishing between how the centralized bureaucracies of the former Eastern bloc states were transformed compared to Western Europe, the transformation of which was directly related to the rise of capitalism.[12] His otherwise complex analysis of nationalism is simplistic with regard to his notion of 'industrialism', which includes some of the elemental features of capitalism, such as the complex division of labour, an entrenched bureaucracy, and a new rationality based on means-ends efficiency.[13] Application of this idea raises more questions than answers, but it is beyond the scope of this volume to address these questions.

In contrast, Cornelia Navari sees the emergence of 'modern nation-states' in Europe not simply "a tale of the withering away of old institutions."[14] The social changes described previously were introduced by capitalism and resulted in the destruction of the Old Order. Navari describes the "new creations—new institutions and new types of social relations—that knit society together in new ways"[15] as follows:

> Rationalism created the idea of the 'citizen'—the individual who recognized the state as his legal home. It created the idea of legal equality, where all citizens have the same status before that system of law. It created the idea of the state that exists to serve those citizens [. . .] Capitalism created the 'mass'—the masterless men who are free to sell their labour—and hence the material conditions for modern citizenship. It created the conditions for mass communication among them. It created classes and [. . .] tied those classes together by an intricate division of labour. It cast that division over vast territories, bringing hitherto distant regions into immediate functional relationships [. . .] The state created common languages and common education systems, and enforced common legal systems existing within clearly defined state boundaries [. . .] It created national bureaucracies and national armies that socialized people from different regions and classes [. . .] These features are the characteristic features of the modern state; . . . they are also the characteristic features of the nation-state, *the nation-state was created by them.*[16]

Navari highlights capitalism as the catalyst for the creation of the nation-state. She also acknowledges the homogenizing tendencies of capitalism, arguing that the system has been inherently disruptive of traditional European society, while also creating among those who live under capitalism "a peculiar characteristic: it makes them more or less alike."[17] Although these statements lend considerable support to my arguments presented earlier, the theory behind these claims is sketchy. However, Gellner posits a relationship between the rise of 'industrialism' (capitalism) and the emergence of nationalism, as well as capitalism's propensity towards cultural homogenization, which led to the formation of nation-states. Benedict Anderson took the discussion about the relationship between capitalism and nationalism a step further, claiming that the catalyst for national identity and the consciousness of nation was the emergence of 'print capitalism'. Anderson claimed that the "first modern-style mass-produced industrial commodity" was the printed book.[18] Similarly, Navari emphasized the need for a common language and education and legal systems, which were created and managed by the new type of state in Europe; in contrast, Gellner emphasized 'industrialism's' need for cultural homogeneity, whereas Anderson (borrowing the concept from Walter Benjamin) focused on the idea of 'homogenous empty time', a feature of capitalism and the media in which events are constantly (and somewhat aimlessly) changing and become the subject of newspapers and novels.[19] With regard to the publication of these newspapers and novels, the shift from Latin to the vernacular opened up new ways for imagining the community,[20] as ethnic groups acquired the consciousness to imagine themselves as nations.

When the modern nation-states first emerged in Europe around the mid to late 1700s, their borders provided both an important identity and the means of protection that was sought by national capital. In other words, the boundaries of the nation-state were an indispensible protective cocoon for the emerging 'national' capital. This link between the rise of the nation-state and the expansion of capitalism is acknowledged by the scholars mentioned previously, among others, but their theorization on this linkage has, as noted, been sketchy.[21] Notwithstanding the sparseness of literature on this topic, it can be said that capital required the borders of the nation-state for sustenance and protection, and this need was most pressing during the embryonic stage of capitalism. As capitalism began to mature, the same nation-state was expected to promote the free movement of capital outside its borders so that capital's expansionist drive would not be stifled. A contradictory process is at work in the capitalism–nation-state nexus: capital, as social relation, needs the protective environment of the nation-state during its nascent development stage, including protective trade and tariff controls and security of the captive home market, but once capital has integrated 'national' production it no longer needs to be confined within the boundaries of its nation-state; at this point capitalists have a hegemonic hold on society and an indirect influence on the state to safeguard their political and economic interests. In other words, as soon as capitalism matures, capital wants to burst outside its borders, mainly to meet its own survival needs of consistent expansionism and profit maximization. The important point here is that once capital moves outside the borders of its nation-state to satisfy its expansionist urge, the nation-state does not just wither away. On the contrary, at this stage, capital's need for the nation-state becomes more acute in order to provide legitimacy and a framework for its colonial (now imperial) expansionist project. History has demonstrated that this legitimizing function for colonial/imperial projects has been provided by the overarching cover of the nation-state, appearing in the garb of rationalizing doctrines such as the 'civilizing mission' claimed by Britain and France or the Monroe Doctrine of 1823 that provided a cover for the US to maintain its Latin American satellites.[22]

As capitalist development intensified, the process of accumulation resulted in a concentration of capital. I will not go into detail about the formation of monopolies and the emerging power of banks and financial cartels during the late 19th century and at the turn of the 20th century,[23] but these monopolistic institutions played an important role in the imperialist domination of about two thirds of the planet and have since ensured the continuing global presence of US and Western European capital. Even before the Second World War, monopoly control was already quite strong, and the export of capital was far-reaching on the international plane.[24] In the present era, the export of capital from the developed capitalist world has been on a truly phenomenal scale, with financial and industrial capital circulating in the remote recesses of the globe.

The next section will examine the spread of colonialism beyond the Americas into Asia (and later Africa) to show how the nexus between the rise of capitalism and the emergence of the nation-state changed colonial subjugation and imperialist domination in post-colonial societies.

II UNFOLDING OF THE *CAPITALISM–IMPERIALISM NEXUS* IN COLONIAL AND POST-COLONIAL CONTEXTS

The colonial state and the post-colonial state, respectively, have had a different imperative, distinct from the European nation-state, which has been crucial to the establishment of the capitalism–imperialism nexus that has undermined indigenous social and economic development in colonial and post-colonial societies. To understand how the capitalism–imperialism nexus emerges to undermine wellbeing in the colony in the interest of forging the imperialist domination of the 'non-European' world, whereas the capitalism–nation-state nexus continues to strengthen capitalist development in Europe, it is helpful to first identify key historical events that provided the specific economic impetus in Europe through colonial expansionism outside the Americas.

As industrial capitalism was starting to develop in England, it was also running into conflict with the slave trade and commercial capitalism. The abolition of slavery in the English Caribbean islands had as much to do with slave revolts and anti-slavery sentiments in 18th and 19th century England as it did with the realization that slavery was unproductive and inflexible outside large Caribbean plantations. However, long before slavery was abolished in England, the colonization of Asia was underway in the mid-18th century—just as capitalism was becoming a dominant economic system and wanted to bring much of the world into its fold through colonization by expanding its drive for plunder and extraction in order to maximize production and profits. Franklin Knight noted that industrial capitalism in Europe developed "with interests, which were, if not antagonistic to, certainly competitive with, commercial capitalism."[25] Therefore, the conflict was between the objective of securing stable sources of raw material for industrial capitalist development through further colonization and the need to maintain the slave system to sustain commercial capitalism. Ironically, the profits from "triangular trade," undertaken by commercial capitalists, were to "provide one of the main streams of accumulation of capital in England," which went on to finance the Industrial Revolution.[26] However, when industrial capitalism emerged as an economic powerhouse, the antagonism highlighted by Knight started to erode the base of commercial capitalism. Industrial capitalism eventually went on to displace commercial capitalism, but its displacement was drawn out and had a temporal span similar to abolitionists' attempts to end slavery (although the seeds of anti-slavery were sown in the 1730s, it was not abolished until more than a century later). The slave trade was first banned in 1807, but it took another 27 years for slavery to be formally abolished in England and its colonies, on 1 August 1834.[27]

Even before slavery was abolished and long before the start of the Industrial Revolution, emerging English and Dutch capitalists felt the need for firm control over sources of precious raw materials. Charter trading companies, such as the English and Dutch East India companies, were therefore authorized to explore the non-European world. The Europeans, especially the English, focused on Asia, with India as the largest jewel in the empire's assets. India was colonized by Britain's East India Company in 1757, coinciding with the commencement of the Industrial Revolution (1760 onwards).

Colonial policies were implemented with the express purpose of extracting maximum surplus; in addition, differences between various colonized groups were exploited to allow the divided society to be controlled more effectively. Colonial administrators separated groups that had hitherto lived relatively peaceably together: in India, this included Hindus and Muslims. In Africa, peoples who had historically lived together were separated, and those who had lived apart were forcibly grouped together within a single colonial state as the continent was arbitrarily divided by various

European colonial powers as 'the scramble for Africa' intensified during the 1884 Berlin Conference.[28] Furthermore, differences between discrete religious, ethnic, or linguistic groups were forcibly sharpened so that dormant or non-antagonistic conflict changed over the course of colonial rule into antagonistic and exclusionary relationships, for example, Hindus and Muslims, who are still divided in India.[29] This suppression of the identity of the colonized by means of arbitrary separation or forced coexistence of heterogeneous ethnic, linguistic, and religious groups meant that colonized states did not exemplify the link between capitalism and the emergence of national consciousness, which was so clearly apparent in the European context. Instead, the colonizers were determined to ensure that the colony remained a ready source of tribute extraction and surplus appropriation to fuel capitalist development in the metropolis, which would be possible by establishing the capitalism–imperialism nexus. The colonial domination of India serves as a useful guide to show how this nexus was established. India's colonization was critical in two ways: it removed the threat of a major competitor of British machine-made textiles (the first sector to be industrialized in Europe), and the colony became a captive source of economic surplus and raw materials to fuel capitalist growth in Britain.

Although medieval Indian society had a "high level of urbanization" and a well-established manufacturing foundation, the objective of colonial rulers was also to revert India to an earlier social form. Alavi noted that from its "developed manufacturing skills [base] equal to the best that Europe had to offer" just before colonization, India was de-industrialized to become a mere primary commodity producer after colonization.[30] This degenerating and regressive impact of colonial rule has prompted a number of Indian scholars, including Irfan Habib and Bipan Chandra, to suggest that pre-colonial India was on the "threshold of capitalist development" on the eve of colonial occupation.[31] Habib also analyzed the question of surplus extraction and its enormous increase after colonization, arguing that primitive accumulation was a vital factor enabling metropolitan capital to take advantage of pre-capitalist forms of accumulation in the colony to benefit Europe's own movement towards industrial capitalist development.[32] For this reason, colonial powers made the collection of surplus more extractive by intensively exploiting the colonized peasantry.

The first 100 years of colonial rule in India from 1757 onwards were managed by the British East India Company. The Company Raj was about maximizing the appropriation of surplus from India and extending and consolidating its tight grip on the tribute extraction process, while the export of Indian staples filled the coffers of the British state and its industrialists.[33] A direct result of colonization was that the Indian rural elite became stronger, while the British imposed even more oppressive feudal relations than the social form prevailing under Mughal rule. This resulted in dramatic social changes that further pauperized the peasantry, displaced artisans, and eliminated textile weavers involved in cotton production; poverty in India reached new levels.[34] In his enlightening paper "Colonialism and the Rise of Capitalism," Alavi pointed out that the main interest of the East India Company was to maximize the export of Indian textiles to Britain and Europe and to extract tribute through primitive accumulation:

> [by] the direct extraction of surplus from the Indian countryside, [which was] in the form of land revenue and other taxes and impositions. Conquest and plunder joined hands with trade. In the collection of land revenue, the penetration of Indian feudalism was replaced with the unmitigated avarice and greed of the faceless officials of the Company . . . Land revenue was collected with [a] rapacity and ruthlessness that was unprecedented . . . In the final year of the last Indian ruler of Bengal in 1764–5, the land revenue realized was £817,000. In the first year of the Company's administration in 1765–6, the land revenue realized in Bengal was £1,818,000. When Lord Corwallis fixed the Permanent Settlement in 1793, he fixed it at £3,400,000.[35]

This almost doubling of tribute (rent) in two years, and the more than four-fold increase within three decades of colonization, shows the extent of the rapacious exploitation of India. In addition to economic control, the English colonial rulers also used social policies to serve their own ends. By systematically manipulating class, caste, regional, and religious identities, the imperial powers superimposed a colonial system of exchange. The British took over a pre-capitalist form of economy that was conceivably on its way towards an epochal transformation and reintroduced antiquated social forms. They revived the *zamindari* system of the Delhi Sultanate (the dynastic realm preceding the Mughals) and adapted it along the lines of the English system of feudal lords and fiefdoms—making the Mughal state's complex system of extracting surplus even more exploitative and oppressive for the peasantry. As the British re-introduced the *zamindari* system, they dismantled the complex hierarchical system of superior right holders among *jagirdar, mansabdar,* and others (just below the Mughal ruler), who all had superior rights over the *zamindar;* the latter operated and oversaw the lower rung of the hierarchal system at the village level, namely the *Jajmani* system of tribute collection from the peasantry.[36] In other words, the British took a feudal form that was showing signs of breaking down and re-introduced a much more oppressive form of feudalism similar to the English fief (a system that was so oppressive that societal convulsions tore apart English feudal relations, as some theorists have claimed, and actually gave birth to the capitalist social formation).[37] In forcing this change, the colonial state *directly* appropriated the agrarian surplus which, in the pre-colonial era, was mediated through various levels of superior right-holders. This negated the sharing of surplus among different right-holding elites and led to the concentration of feudal power within a single entity: the colonial state and its representative at the village level, the *zamindar* who became the feudal lord.[38]

Compliant *zamindars* and *ryotwars* (peasant-proprietors) served the colonial rulers well by giving them 75% to 90% of the revenue. As Habib noted, this level of tribute collection made up about 30% of the capital formation in Britain, fueling its industrial development.[39] Thus, the dominant relations of production within the colonial state under the British became oppressively feudal at one level, whereas at another level, a supra-tributary mode of extracting the society's surplus was set up through the subsidiary exploitation of the lower strata of rural society, far exceeding levels in precolonial Mughal India.[40] Another consequence of this extractive tribute collection process was the export orientation of colonial India's economy, which meant India's forcible integration into the emerging world capitalist market. But the benefits of entry into the world capitalist market did not accrue to colonial India despite the wealth of its society and the skill of Indian craftspeople who could compete effectively with British machine-made textiles.

It was not until the late 18th century (once the British government was able to strangle Indian cotton textile production) that the British colonizers were able to block the sale of Indian textiles in the metropole, enabling the English textile industry to emerge as a formidable force on the world market.[41] The new technological developments of that era such as the steam engine and discoveries such as the principle of latent heat, Manchester's textile industry became the trigger for the industrial transformation and the first step of the Industrial Revolution in England.[42] While English textile manufacturers were struggling in the late 17th and early 18th centuries, the Indian textile industry, albeit at the craft level of production, was blossoming. The British recognized they were facing a losing battle and countered the trend by imposing a levy of 10% import duty on Indian textiles in 1685—long before the East India Company was to get involved in textile exports. By 1690 the situation had changed significantly: British textile manufacturers, despite their ideological commitment to *laissez faire*, were able to pressure the British government to double the import levy on Indian textiles.[43] This was the period when the British textile industry had supposedly come of age, but despite its lower costs and mechanized production, it was unable to compete with the finer quality of Indian textiles. By the time the East India Company began its wider conquest of India from 1757, the import duty on Indian textiles had gone up by another 50% (an aggregate levy of 70%).[44] This Indian example shows that a supposedly 'pre-modern' system of textile production was able to compete effectively, and even win, against a modern, mechanized system of production; extra economic means were finally required to squeeze out the handloom weavers. Alavi clarified a common misconception, explaining that it was *not* the mechanization of the English textile industry that killed off the Indian handloom industry;

rather, Indian handloom production had to be smothered before the English manufacturers could prevail:

> It is little realized that the *prior destruction of the Indian cotton textile industry was a necessary precondition for progress of the British industry.* It is a myth that is universally believed by economic historians (including Marx) that it was the mechanization of English textile production that killed the Indian textile industry. *That was not so.* Active steps had to be taken by the British government to suppress the flourishing Indian textile industry.[45]

This was the inauguration of the capitalism–imperialism nexus. The system of economic exploitation was perfected through the various steps described previously, as well as through the systemic process of de-industrialization pushed through by the colonial state, which has been so well articulated by Bagchi[46] and is supported by the case of Indian textiles. However, the British colonizers also realized that domination and ideological control in the arena of culture was an essential precondition for the continuation of colonial rule.

The normative framework for this cultural domination was the Eurocentric/Orientalist perspective, which warped the histories of the colonized people, stigmatized them, and more importantly, manipulated *difference* on the basis of region, language, and religion, generating new conditions of conflict and identity assertion within the colony. Under colonial rule, disparate ethnic groups were forcibly grouped together within the territorial boundaries of the colonial state without any concern as to the issues of incompatibility between these differing groups or as to whether they could even co-exist within the same colonial state. Africa is a classic case; new European colonizers such as Belgium, Germany, and Italy (alongside the older colonial powers) arbitrarily divided entire chunks of territory, claiming these as their respective African colonies and areas of control. The process of colonization and the establishment of the colonial state within the framework of a manipulative colonial social policy provided the Europeans with the opportunity to create in the colony an environment of *separateness, apartness,* and *unfreeness*, allowing them to control the colonized.[47] This environment promoted one colonized group over another, parceled privilege, and provided access to resources for select groups of the colonized elite, namely those who were willing to cooperate and collaborate with colonial rulers. The actions of the colonial state ensured that the colonized would be tamed and that the colony would remain in control of the metropolitan bourgeoisie; however, colonial social policy also formed the basis for serious tensions and conflicts among various colonized ethnic and religious groups.

The objective of the colonial state was not to foster indigenous capitalist development but to heighten imperialist domination of the colonized for the benefit of metropolitan capitalist expansion. In the environment of colonial domination, the colonized did not have the option of promoting cultural accommodation or separating from a larger, oppressive nation, as was done in Europe when differing ethnic groups/nations broke free of dynastic realms and formed separate nation-states. Also, for the most part, the bourgeoisies in these new European nation-states were able to foster an environment that was relatively *free* as long as capitalist-imposed homogeneity could be promoted in society. In promoting the homogenous idea of the nation, capitalist development in Europe took a different trajectory, a radical break from its feudal past, and went on to produce the 'Great Transformation'. The situation within the colony, however, was very different. Colonized societies could not even remotely be considered capitalist, although they were enveloped within the WCS. Furthermore, in contrast to the European experience, any breaks with the past in the colony were not transformative in character; on the contrary, the rapacious exploitation of the colony contributed significantly to Western capitalist development while inducing a pauperized existence for the colonized. These outcomes and their contexts are crucial in highlighting the differing conceptualization of nation and nationalism by the Europeans as compared to others in the colonized world. As well, the different context in the formation of the colonial state meant that colonized peoples began to embrace the ideas of nationalism and embarked on a course of conflict in making their respective national claims within a space that became more confined as the colonial state pursued its policy of separateness. Not surprisingly, this conflict has continued into the post-colonial era, affecting various ethnic and sub-national groups. As a result, the formation of Europe and Northern European settler colonies (North America, Australia, and New Zealand) had a very different developmental path[48] from that in colonial and post-colonial states.

In the 'non-European' world, the stifling environment generated by the colonial state enabled the cementing of divisions between differing colonized groups; this was a precise objective of colonial rulers because a divided populace ensured that colonialism could continue indefinitely. One of the more enduring and debilitating consequences of colonization and the capitalism–imperialism nexus for the post-colonial societies of Africa and Asia has been the continuation of unresolved ethnic, religious, and sub-national conflicts that began with colonial rule. Given that the magnifying of divisions between differing ethnic groups were largely the work of a manipulative colonial social policy, carried out by the colonial state through its bureaucratic apparatus and other extremely oppressive and authoritarian state structures, the conflict has had an enduring psycho-social impact on formerly colonized peoples. More importantly, the resolution of these ethnic and national conflicts between differing colonized groups *could not even begin to be tackled until the end of colonial rule.*

Ironically, the end of colonial rule did not mean an end to the colonially generated conflicts based on religion, ethnicity, or region. In most post-colonial societies, the ruling elite (composed of landholders, indigenous capitalists, and civil and military bureaucrats) were successors-in-interest of colonial rulers. The post-colonial elite, especially feudal landholders and civil and military bureaucrats, were former collaborators with colonial rulers and as such were schooled in the traditions of colonial rule. This had afforded them privilege during their years of collaboration with the metropolitan bourgeoisie, so the post-colonial elite were unwilling to abandon the tried and tested colonial state structures for fear of losing their power. Consequently, as the case studies of India and Pakistan in the final chapters of this volume will show, the reincarnated post-colonial ruling elites were only too eager to re-introduce the colonial state's structures of control. These state structures gave the ruling post-colonial elite even more power because the metropolitan bourgeoisie, although still dominant on a world scale, was formally removed from the post-colonial state's calculus of power. However, by transplanting colonial structures into the new post-colonial state, it has entrenched the capitalism–imperialism nexus.

Given the structure of the post-colonial state, the ruling elite in these societies has been unwilling to create relevant alternative structures of rule to meet the new realities of decolonization, that is, to accommodate the multinational character of its polity or to challenge the imperialist stranglehold on state and society. As a result, there has been a distinct lack of mechanisms through which to deal with the conflicting demands of ethnic/sub-national groups. When disputes arise, the elites in most post-colonial states avoid addressing ethnic and sub-national conflicts.[49] As a consequence, the 'national question' in most post-colonial societies remains unresolved. The ruling post-colonial elites are obviously implicated in this lack of progress, but imperialist domination also played a critical role, particularly the US domination in driving the capitalism–imperialism nexus. A detailed investigation of this is beyond the scope of this historical analysis, but briefly, the lack of a comprehensive analysis of post-Second World War imperialist domination of post-colonial states means that the central role of the US as imperialist hegemon is articulated more anecdotally. Extensive analysis is also lacking of the US's covert and not-so-covert operations in the early period of decolonization and thereafter, which were geared towards stifling a sovereign and self-interested course of development. For example, during the early years of decolonization, the US and its Western European allies were able to eliminate or remove nationalist post-colonial leaders such as Lumumba, Cabral, Senghor, Nkrumah, Soekarno, and others who had led national liberation struggles against colonial rule and appeared to be committed to the genuine social and economic upliftment of their respective societies.[50] The removal of these leaders stopped in its tracks the pursuit of a truly independent and people-centered path of development, in favour of clientelist rulers and pro-imperialist policies that made these societies dependent participants within the WCS. This project of dependency was promoted by the new client rulers such as Mobutu, Marcos,

Suharto, Pinochet, and a host of others—all military or ex-military leaders who were propped up in the emerging post-colonial or Latin American states. As a result, peoples in the global South continue to be blamed exclusively for a host of problems within their societies, including undemocratic rule, the non-resolution of the 'national question', and the raging conflicts that have ensued on the basis of ethnicity, religion, language, and region. Certainly, a large part of the responsibility for resolving these conflicts lies with the post-colonial elites who are in power. However, the consequence of imperialist meddling and arm-twisting by means of the capitalism–imperialism nexus cannot be ignored. What also cannot be ignored is the perpetuation of conflict in the post-colonial period based on ethnic, national, and religious identities. The post-colonial predicament is one of imperialist domination with many post-colonial client states having been complicit in actualizing the subordination of their state and society, whereas the ruling classes are also implicated in stoking the embers of internecine conflict by supporting the dominant ethnic, national, or religious group.

Moving from the post-Second World War US's meddling, the next section will demonstrate how theorists of nationalism have advocated for the emulation and the universalization of the European experience in post-colonial societies. This counsel is given by the likes of Benedict Anderson, whose arguments implicitly recognize the capitalism–nation-state nexus but fail to articulate the emergence of the capitalism–imperialism nexus and the harm that it unleashes.

III EMERGING CONSCIOUSNESS OF NATION AND NATIONALISM IN THE COLONIAL ERA AND ITS POST-COLONIAL MANIFESTATIONS

Much of the current theorization on nation and nationalism does not distinguish the European experience from the way identity has emerged and been manipulated in the non-European world. Although theorists of nationalism have highlighted differences in periodization and description pertaining to the emergence of nationalism in the two domains, they tend to universalize the European experience or explain nationalism as a conceptual framework that is Europe-specific. When Benedict Anderson published his now well-known text, *Imagined Communities*, he appeared to be breaking this mould: he offered the novel idea of "imagining a nation," which seemed to highlight the double standard in European and North American understanding and treatment of the Third World. Unfortunately, Anderson did not go deep enough to pierce the mould as he also relied on what I term 'the emulation hypothesis': claiming that the European experience of imagining the nation assumed a modular form that could easily be emulated by and "transplanted" to the rest of the world.[51] Anderson differed from other theorists in claiming less uncritically that the idea of nation and the concept of nationalism were introduced to colonies by colonial rulers and that these ideas were readily embraced by the colonized, especially their intelligentsia—offering an element of agency to the Indonesian or the Filipino writer whose imagined nation had a specific indigenous context. Still, this 'gift' of the colonizers, which Anderson's writing also evokes, has far more serious consequences for colonized people than has been hitherto acknowledged by Anderson or other scholars of nationalism. Consequently, the colonized have been saddled with identities that emerged under colonial rule, which have inherent disfigurements. Even after 50 years of decolonization, the toll continues to be extracted in the form of religious, ethnic, and sub-national identity assertions and conflicts in most post-colonial states. These ideas are briefly discussed later to show that despite his celebratory status, Anderson's theorization has not changed the Eurocentric thrust of theories of nation and nationalism. Before offering my critique of the emulation hypothesis, it is helpful to examine Partha Chatterjee's poststructuralist position on how nationalism emerged in the colony and shaped national identity formation, a position different from mine that he develops in the course of also offering his criticism of Benedict Anderson's work.

(i) Problematics of Partha Chatterjee's Critique of Benedict Anderson

As a self-professed 'Southeast Asianist', Benedict Anderson tried to introduce into his work various stories of the colonized peoples in Southeast Asia, especially those described in *Noli Me Tangere*, a novel by José Rizal.[52] He did this to show the development of colonized peoples' consciousness around the idea of nation but then catapulted to the conclusion that the phenomenon of nationalism was absorbed during colonial occupation. The examples of emulation offered by Anderson were really anecdotal—in some cases the stories and events were acknowledged as fictitious; as such, they cannot constitute a coherent basis by which to propound a theory. Yet Anderson could not forego the temptation of universalizing these examples to all colonized peoples.

Undeniably, resistance against European colonizers has had some influence on the development of national consciousness among the formerly colonized peoples. But this has to be understood largely in the context of how the identity of colonized groups was manipulated and interfered with in the interest of dividing the colonized communities, subverting resistance, and thereby consolidating colonial rule.

Because Partha Chatterjee linked the resistance of the colonized with the acquisition of national consciousness, and also criticized Anderson for his universalization of the European experience, it will be helpful to distinguish Chatterjee's view from mine on what is this different context of national identity formation in colonial and post-colonial societies—different from the European experience.[53] Chatterjee suggested that Anderson's "ethical universalism . . . does not deny the variability of human wants and values" from the crass universalism of Eurocentric universalists—correctly differentiating Anderson from these other Eurocentric theorists who have not bothered to question the "hard-headed developmentalist of the 'realist' school whose recipes for Third-World countries flow out of a cynical double standard that says 'ethics for us, economics for them'."[54] Chatterjee, although cautiously critical of Anderson's ethical universalism, was staking his claim for a different position about national imagining among the formerly colonized, identifying their assertion of national identity as "part of the ideological content of nationalism which takes as its adversary a contrary discourse, *viz.* the discourse of colonialism."[55] For Chatterjee, this contrary discourse reflected the nationalism of the colonized, and "[p]itted itself against the reality of colonial rule which appears before it as an existent, almost palpable, historical truth . . . [opening] entirely new political possibilities . . . that are propagated and defended in the battlefield of politics."[56] Chatterjee developed in the mid-1980s this view on nationalism of the colonized based on a Foucauldian understanding of resistance, making it coeval with power, which enabled him to view the colonized peoples' acquisition of national consciousness through a 'contrary discourse' as resistance. He published his more developed Foucauldian framework on nationalism in his well-known book *The Nation and Its Fragments*.[57]

In highlighting Chatterjee's perspective here, the purpose is to show that he considered nationalism in post-colonial societies to be rooted in the colonial *encounter*, in which the colonized resisted and, in the process, became conscious of the ideas of nation and nationalism. So far so good, but given his poststructuralist perspective, Chatterjee's discourse analysis is also very selectively textual, based on the novelist, essayist, and Hindu nationalist Bankimchandra Chattopadhyay (1838–1894) or on school textbooks of 19th century Bengal and *Puranic* texts that characterized Muslims in less than flattering terms: as 'foreign' conquerors and temple-destroyers, violators of Hindu women, and locating these moves in 'Muslim tyranny'.[58] Chatterjee's objective to identify this 'discourse' against Muslims as being pivotal to 'Hindu nationalist historiography of *hindutva*' is an attempt to locate the assertions of contemporary Hindu nationalism in India within 'contestations with the forms of colonial knowledge'—and so to place contemporary *hindutva* as part of the Indian imagination as a nation:

> My argument will be that such claims (historical claims to a *hindutva* identity) became possible only within the modern forms of historiography, a historiography which is necessarily constructed around the complex identity of a people-nation-state. To the extent that the genealogy of modern historiography in India is deeply implicated in the encounter with British colonialism, these historical claims of political Hinduism are also a product of the contestations with the forms of colonial knowledge . . . I will show that many of the themes that run

> through the contemporary rhetoric of Hindu extremist politics were in fact part and parcel of the historical imagining in the nineteenth century of "India" as a nation.[59]

This claim of Chatterjee's raises many concerns. At one level, one can be sympathetic with Chatterjee's project, which is to offer an explanation of the rise of Hindu nationalism in contemporary India and of the events that led the Bharatiya Janata Party, the political arm of *hindutva*, to capture state power. However, at a broader level—of comprehending the reasons for the rise of not only Hindu nationalism but also the trajectory of conflict between Hindus and Muslims in colonial and post-colonial India, the Partition and the creation of Pakistan, and how conflicts that developed into antagonisms between Hindus and Muslims in the colonial era have taken a life of their own in the post-colonial period—Chatterjee's 'discourse analysis' is not very illuminating. His textual analysis is bound by the limitations of the texts in question. More important, because this textual reading is devoid of a significant analysis of social history and political economy of the period in question, his work suffers from the same limited objective of these texts and their demonic characterization of the 'other'—which recreate a self-serving, one-sided, ahistorical reading of pre-colonial Indian history. In other words, even though he questioned Bankim's elitism, and also faithfully reported on the latter's anti-Muslim slants and utterances, Chatterjee made very little effort to question *how* the antagonistic conflicts emerged between Hindus and Muslims in the first place when there was largely symbiotic existence between them in the 900 years preceding colonial rule—symbolized for instance by the symbiosis of Sufi and Bhakti traditions. In the colonial Indian context, Muslims were made the 'other' in the process of constructing the edifice of Hindu nationalist imagining because the demonizing portrayal of the former would serve as the glue to bind the ideological project of *hindutva*—to eventually capture state power. Thus, Chatterjee, by focusing on Bankim, the Bengali-language school history books, and the *Puranic* texts, assumed what needed to be explained—that is, why was it necessary for Hindu nationalists to frame the demonization of Muslims when, as Chatterjee argues, the issue was about 'contestations with forms of colonial knowledge'? Even if one assumes that by 'forms of colonial knowledge', Chatterjee implies that it was the colonizers who demonized the Muslims, and the Hindu nationalists in turn internalized this outlook; then should not his focus be on the actions of the colonial state or a textual analysis of the colonial state's documents and policies and other relevant publications on the manipulative colonial social policy?

It is noteworthy, however, that although communalism in the form of Hindu-Muslim confrontation became common occurrences during the last decade of colonialism in India, and although there was a tragic loss of life on all sides during the genocide brought on by the Partition, Hindu nationalism was politically very weak, other than a brief spurt in the late 19th century and until its more contemporary manifestations emerged since the 1980s. The secular nationalists remained dominant in India during the last 50 years of colonial rule and for the first three to four decades of the post-colonial era. Thus, Chatterjee's claim that the Hindu nationalist historiography "is necessarily constructed around the complex identity of a people-nation-state"—a position not very different from the Eurocentric position of most theorists of nationalism—could only be made *after* witnessing the events during the decade of the 1980s when Hindu nationalists began to gain in strength and triggered the anti-Muslim carnage in India. Consequently, Chatterjee's outlook cannot frame the question that is key to my analysis: given the long period of symbiosis between Hindus and Muslims in pre-colonial India, what led to the emergence of conflict during the colonial era between these two colonized groups that shaped their respective national imaginary through the production of the 'other'? Chatterjee cannot or does not pose the question because his textual analysis points to a supposedly longer history of 'Muslim oppression' against the Hindus—as the authors of his interpretive texts suggest[60] and go all the way back to a time when Arab Muslim conquest happened around 711 AD that remained confined to the region of Sindh (when in fact it was Turkoman and Afghans who began founding loose principalities from 962 AD until Mughal rulers consolidated power from 1526 AD onwards). As a result, Chatterjee lets colonialism and the colonial state off the hook as he implies that the 'contestation' between the colonizer and the colonized was a match, an *encounter*, between almost equally matched parties—ignoring that the terms of the contest between the colonizer-colonized or between the dominant and subordinate colonized groups was mostly one-sided. The nature of the colonizer-colonized 'contestation' is central for Chatterjee which, in his view, produces the 'contrary discourse' and shapes national identity among the group imagining itself as a nation. However, the larger question is whether this contrary discourse had a chance to emerge during colonial rule or whether the mutual animosity and difference among the colonized were hardened. Of all the rebellions and revolts against colonial rulers, the one exception was Haiti: in 1804, Haiti had the only successful slave rebellion, against the French, but Haiti was later made into a terrible example to dissuade colonized and imperialized peoples from following.[61] Other exceptions might include the success of the few national liberation movements closer to the time of decolonization in Asia and Africa and the movement in settler colonies of North America: the 'Tea Party' thrown by the 13 colonies had its own specificity that cannot be generalized to the colonized peoples of Asia and Africa. Consequently, people in non-settler colonies of Africa and Asia and Aboriginal peoples in the Americas, Australia, and New Zealand not only had to deal with imperialist domination, they were also subjected to all kinds of social control experiments and assimilationist and manipulative actions of the colonizers. The gravity of these actions, as Frantz Fanon pointed out, was extremely debilitating for the colonized. Their culture became 'sclerosed' as its vibrancy was lost; their values were mocked, and their identities were inferiorized.[62] In this environment of subjugation, because privilege and entitlement were carefully parceled to suit the exigency of colonial occupation, differing colonized groups were pitted against each other, leading to the reformulation of their religious/ethnic/national identity. Under these conditions, the relative accommodation and accord that had existed historically between disparate groups gave way to a more generalized conflict and discord.

In contrast, I have argued that the colonial state's manipulative social policy intensified the antagonisms between different colonized groups, laying the trajectory for a peculiar kind of national identity formulation—one that is rooted in conflict—and having an afterlife in the post-colonial era. The crucial point is that when national identity formation takes place in a manipulative social environment of *unfreeness*, such as colonial subjugation—where group differences are exploited and intensely manipulated and where privilege or economic benefits are parcelled selectively—the conditions produce severe economic insecurities and social dislocations. The greater damage from manipulative colonial social policies—those that have created conflict among the colonized and made the opposed group as the 'other', posited superior and inferior identities respectively to the colonizer and the colonized, and normalized whiteness as positive and 'superior'—which were internalized, initially by the colonized and then by successive generations of people in post-colonial Africa and Asia. As one example, just look at the phenomenal market of skin whitening creams in India, other South Asian and post-colonial states. Another example in the South Asian context is how the British colonial state's conflict creation strategy, to perpetuate colonial rule, has resulted in serious harm to Muslims living in India, whereas the conflict between India and Pakistan, with its deep religious tinge, has continued well into the period of decolonization. This is the inevitable outcome of colonial social policy that purposely pits one group against another, as exemplified in the specific British moves in colonial India: among others, the 1905 partition of Bengal and the Separate Electorate Act which elevated Muslims and simultaneously demoted Hindus at one juncture and reversed this move at another point in colonial history.[63] In such an environment, the coordinated resistance of colonized groups was fragmented, and disparate groups that coexisted relatively peaceably for centuries inevitably began to question and distrust each other.

With that said, I should not end this subsection with a sense that all hope is lost. The former colonized people can recover their identity and dignity and their sense of belonging provided they are now willing to critically assess the period of colonial rule and its aftermath: challenge how the indigenous rulers of the post-colonial state have embraced colonial-era norms and legal codes and oppose the bureaucratic hold on society that has accompanied a clientelist drift of many post-colonial states. This involves not feeling helpless and blaming the colonizers alone for the social and political mess in most post-colonial societies; rather, it means becoming conscious of the social and economic harm of colonialism and then also becoming organized to address its internal and external consequences. Having distinguished my position from Chatterjee's, I can now conduct a broader investigation of Anderson's ideas and his theory of nationalism.

(ii) Anderson's Idea of 'Nation-ness' and Its Universalization

Benedict Anderson has introduced the notion of "print capitalism" and distinguished politicized ethnicity from nationalism; he also complicated the understanding of nationalism, but in doing all this he too largely excluded the role of women from national imagining.[64] Anderson propagates his theory of nationalism and tries to show that once the modern concept of nationalism surfaces, the consciousness around the idea of nation is so overwhelming and captivating that it can be transported through time and to significantly different terrains and cultures.[65] To this end, he ascribes a modular character to the idea of *nation*, which he claims has been embraced equally well by Europeans and by non-European colonized peoples. He stresses that modern nationalism actually emerged when the 'Creole pioneers' (White European settlers) in the Americas broke away from the metropole in Europe because they were not treated as equals and so began to assert their own imagined identity. Thus, he argues that, although linguistic nationalism emerged in Europe, it was actually the Creole pioneers in Latin America and North America who really acquired a national consciousness and developed the concept of *nation*, which was not based on language as it was not really the distinguishing marker of identity. So, although the Creole pioneers imagined their identity differently from mainland Europe and brought ideology into play, nevertheless, they influenced the development of 'national print languages'.[66] Consequently, it is this non-linguistic basis of nationalism, which he terms 'official nationalism', that really awoke Europe from its epochal slumber and paved the way for the emergence of the modern nation-state. For Anderson, official nationalism is "the willed merger of dynastic empire and nation, [and] it developed *after* and *in reaction to,* the popular national movements proliferating in Europe since the 1820s"—a phenomenon "emanating from the state and serving the interests of the state first and foremost."[67]

Anderson identifies official nationalism as imperialist and notices its equally easy emulation by the rulers of the British Empire, the Russian tsars, and the Meiji rulers of Japan.[68] In other words, official nationalism, once it configured the nation-states in Europe, took a modular form that enabled its easy transportation and transplantation to other domains with the eventual supplanting of the idea in the colonies.[69] Anderson acknowledges that, although official nationalism was conservative and reactionary (an outlook adapted from one aspect of popular nationalism), it was *universally* applied with equal force in India, producing Anglicized 'nationalists' such as Bipan Chandra Pal under British colonial rule, or in Korea under Japanese occupation, or in Malaya and French Indochina.[70] This kind of theorizing enables Anderson to make a leap from the popular and official imaginings in Europe to the rest of the world, particularly with regard to the adoption of the idea of the nation in the former colonies of Asia and Africa.

In applying the notion of official nationalism, Anderson tends to aggregate disparate groups and avoids the critical social analysis so necessary to unravel the analytical specificity of particular historical junctures: the powerful and powerless are similarly linked to the point where their identities get blurred. Thus, Anderson links imperialists and imperialized in a collaborative project that somehow engenders national consciousness within the colonial setting, with the result that he fails to differentiate between *three* important categories/groups of players in the colonial period: the colonial powers based in European metropoles; the colonial settlers in the Americas and elsewhere; and the colonized in Asia, Africa, and Latin America. Each of these three groups had significantly different bases for 'imagining the nation', which Anderson does not distinguish given that his category of analysis, official nationalism, is itself an amalgam. Surprisingly, Anderson treats the actions of colonial settlers in the Americas (Creoles) seeking independence from European *metropoles* as a movement for national liberation. This has Anderson confusing colonial pioneers with the colonized and their movements for national liberation, which were actual indigenous struggles of colonized peoples to free themselves of foreign domination and occupation. In blurring the distinctions between these two historically specific undertakings, Anderson confuses the two different realities.

Even when Anderson purports to engage in social analysis, this is largely anecdotal and the narrative traverses from Indonesia to the Horn of Africa in just a few short lines. His work appears to be rooted in cultural anthropology and cultural studies, rather than in a socio-historical or a political economy analysis that would identify distinctly different forms of social relations in Europe and in the rest of the world—especially the fundamentally different social reality in the colonies. This leads me to the second and the more serious problem with Anderson's approach: his uncritical application of the European experience of national identity formation to the very different spatial and temporal context of the colonized world. In particular, it is most unhelpful to see Anderson describe nationalism, nationality, or 'nation-ness' as "cultural artefacts of a particular kind"—but then universalize this "particular kind" of European experience to argue the following:

> the creation of these artefacts towards the end of the eighteenth century was the spontaneous distillation of a complex 'crossing' of discrete historical forces; but that, once created, they became 'modular,' capable of being transplanted, with varying degrees of self-consciousness, to a

> great variety of social terrains, to merge and be merged with a correspondingly wide variety of political and ideological constellations.[71]

Anderson's "spontaneous distillation" was the collection of a European condensate of nationalism that was meant to feed national movements *everywhere.* In fact, he expressly asserted that the European experience had the capability of "being transplanted . . . to a great variety of social terrains" and to be merged with an equally wide variety of political and ideological systems.[72] However, in identifying national imaginings as cultural artefacts, which are the spontaneous distillation of Europe's historical crossings, he betrays the very Eurocentrism that he is attempting to critique. In insisting that the "grammar of anti-colonial struggles" was conceived under colonialism, Anderson had in mind the introduction of such measures as census-taking and map-making by colonial rulers where "cartographers were putting space under the same surveillance which the census maker(s) were trying to impose on persons."[73] This argument is made more forcefully in his subsequent text, in which he claims that censuses, along with the newspaper, were responsible for the "impending collapse of colonialism."[74] Although Anderson is correct to point out that the census created divisions in colonial society, in terms of how it included and excluded peoples, how it described or mis-described people/groups, and how it recognized or ignored different groups under colonial rule, it does not necessarily follow that the census is responsible for the "impending collapse of colonialism."[75]

Historians of South Asia have pointed out that census protocols were used to parcel privilege and to define the religious minority in colonial India,[76] but Hindus and Muslims also utilized the process to advance their caste or social position.[77] Although the impetus for documenting religious and social identities was at the initiative of the colonial state, it also unleashed a torrent of caste and communal assertiveness in colonial India. The need for assertion and redefinition was felt not only by lower caste groups who projected themselves as belonging to higher caste categories but also by Muslims involved in less-valued work. People doing less-valued work such as weavers and butchers began to identify themselves with the respectable Momin and Qureshi lineages.[78] In the case of South Asia, at least, the census did not spell the 'impending collapse' of colonial rule. On the contrary, it contributed to the perpetuation of colonialism by contributing to the severance of historic ties of empathy and accommodation between Hindus and Muslims.

Anderson's theorization did not allow him to distinguish between the specificity of colonial rule in shaping national identity and the European experience of 'nation-ness'; the two were indeed conflated. The differences between them were not important to Anderson, who was trying to show how the European experience has been mimicked by the rest of the world and who neglected how this mimesis resulted in the gross disfigurement of colonized peoples' identity. His analysis neglected the motive force of the colonial era—the will of European colonial administrations—which was primed to consolidate colonial rule at any cost. This objective of colonial domination cannot be confused with the late 18th- and 19th-century nation-state formation in Europe,[79] where the environment was generally *free* for the emergence of national consciousness. Certainly, conquests and invasions occurred in Europe, such as the occupation of Germany by France, but there was also resistance against such occupation that was by and large successful.[80] In Europe, weak ethnic/national groups merged and were dominated, but during the process of nation-state formation, this was a 'willed-merger', as Anderson pointed out. Another option for these subordinate groups was migration to other parts of Europe to escape repression, as, for example, in the case of the migration of French Huguenots to other nation-states in Europe.

In contrast, under colonialism the only option available was for the colonized people to forcefully resist occupation, compelling the colonizers to flee and give up the colonial state. In the main, this did not happen; the colonizers did not flee in droves. Still, numerous efforts were made in many colonized areas to resist colonial oppression. With one exception, the case of Haiti discussed earlier, none of these attempts were successful until the mid-20th century, at which point imperialist rivalries had considerably weakened Western Europe. However, it is the specific social conditions in the context of British colonial rule in India to which I now turn to show how they have contributed largely to the disfigurement of colonized peoples' identities that have produced a troubled social development and have disembodied societal relations in the post-colonial era.

IV ROLE OF CAPITALISM–IMPERIALISM NEXUS IN IDENTITY CONSTRUCTION AND ENFORCING WESTERN HEGEMONY

One distinctive feature of South Asian history is how from the pre-modern period (and possibly earlier) India has been a multiethnic, multireligious, and multilingual society—much longer than present-day Western societies. During this long history, different groups and people from different regions fought each other, displaced a dominant group from power, made mutual accommodations, and, for significant periods, coexisted relatively peaceably.[81] This is not to say that caste, class, religious, and regional conflicts did not surface in India or that societal upheaval did not result as a consequence of successive invasions. The point is that when the dust settled, most invaders and their armies, with the major exception of the British colonial occupation of India (1757–1947), ended up adopting India as their new homeland. They integrated into Indian society and were influenced and affected in turn by its culture, languages, and social norms. In the process, difference had a way of being mediated and accepted in the subcontinent.

However, with the arrival of the British, the historical trajectory of occupation, mediation, and integration was radically altered because rapacious economic exploitation was at the root of the capitalist colonization project, which I have termed the capitalism–imperialism nexus. Given the Orientalist historiography and the economic objective of colonial occupation, the British did not desire to be part of Indian society, which they considered to be 'inferior and backward'. Instead, the colonizers were mainly interested in the continuation of their predatory urge—the maximum extraction of society's surplus. This objective acquired a greater urgency after the 1857 Rebellion[82] when the colonizers were shocked by almost being overthrown from power.

In the aftermath of the 1857 Rebellion in colonial India, the British elevated social engineering as a colonial state imperative with the expressed aim of maximizing differences between colonized groups based on religion. This was done to take advantage of the division between Hindus and Muslims, who, as indicated earlier, had co-existed relatively peaceably for centuries. However, once the British began to exploit religion and to sow seeds of distrust between the two communities, it was not long before the symbiotic existence began to turn into antagonistic conflict between Hindus and Muslims. In this realm of conflict, colonial social policy was designed to manipulate group differences and pit one group against another. These actions of colonial rulers worked to their advantage by turning historic non-antagonistic difference between the two groups into actual antagonisms. The colonized groups also internalized these antagonisms with devastating consequences: removing any possibility of future amity or accord between these groups.[83] Under colonial rule in India, Muslim and Hindu national elites were hostile to one another and treated each other with contempt. As this attitude against the 'other' was being translated at the political level as a consequence of nationalist assertions, Hindu and Muslim nationalists responded very differently. The Muslim League, a Muslim political party formed in colonial India, initially pushed for parity between Hindus and Muslims in terms of representation at the federal level, despite the latter's minority status. When that failed, it pursued the goal of a separate Muslim state.[84] This is not to deny that the Muslim League also took up narrow identity issues, but these remained largely the domain of smaller Muslim groups. In contrast, identity was the paramount drive for Hindu nationalists: beginning with Bankim as a mild version of a nationalist ideologue. By the mid-1920s, the Rashtrya Swamisavak Sangh had become a narrow nationalist ideological group with an expressly anti-Muslim outlook. Later, other groups such as the Vishwa Hindu Parishad and the Hindu Mahasabha (now known collectively as the *sangh parivar or hindutva*) became more vocal and expressive in their anti-Muslim actions. As these Hindu nationalists gained in strength during the post-colonial era, the Indian state, under Jawaharlal Nehru and subsequent leaders, as well as secular forces did not really challenge the steady growth of the *hindutva* outlook and narrow nationalist forces led by the *sangh parivar*, an issue discussed in Chapter 4, this volume. As a result, Hindu nationalism became ascendant—as can be seen from the attacks on Muslims with the destruction of the Babri Masjid (mosque) in Ayodhyia, the 2002 genocide carried out in Gujarat, and the ability of Hindu nationalists through their political party, the Bharatiya Janata Party, to capture state power until 2004. The Sangh forces have since been busy rewriting Indian history, have undertaken the Sanskritization of the Hindi language, and have adopted an intimidating and aggressively jingoist stance against other minorities as well.[85] In the context of the 2002 'pogram' against Muslims in Gujarat, Tanika Sarkar wrote the following:

> There is a dark sexual obsession about allegedly ultra-virile Muslim male bodies and overfertile Muslim female ones, that inspire and sustain the figures of paranoia and revenge. VHP [Vishwa Hindu Parishad] leaflets, openly circulating in Gujarat today, signed by the state general secretary, Chinubhai Patel, promise: "We will cut them and their blood will flow like rivers. We will kill Muslims the way we destroyed Babri mosque."[86]

The case of India exemplifies how the internalized perception of the other becomes indelibly etched on the national consciousness of formerly colonized peoples, whereby they end up in the post-colonial era by training their rifles on and blaming each other instead of directing their attacks against the imperialist power.

As mentioned earlier, Frantz Fanon discussed this tendency of internalization and made a compelling argument about its relationship to the process of inferiorization, which first comes about as colonized peoples' culture is demeaned and inferiorized whereas the culture of colonial rulers is elevated for its superiority.[87] Fanon argued that when the inferiorization process extends over a period of time under colonial rule, the culture of the colonized peoples is "lost" and, bearing a heavy imprint of colonization, cannot be reclaimed.[88] The inferiorization process is the most critical intervention of colonialism and leads to the disfigurement of religious, ethnic, and national identities.

Given that the manipulation and exploitation of group differences becomes the cornerstone of a colonial state's social policy, two issues remain to be examined. First, how does national identity formation under colonial rule differ from the European experience? Second, how can identity assertion among the colonized, expressed in terms of violent and vicious conflict, have a firm afterlife in the post-colonial era? There are overlapping responses offered to the two questions, but to begin by addressing the first question, colonialism imposes multiple layers of economic insecurity and deprivation, which makes it difficult to escape the stark social and economic realities that divide the exploiter and the exploited or the colonizer and the colonized. The manipulative social policy and sanctions as well as the economic subjugation imposed by colonial state is so thorough that it sets in motion a range of insecurities that affect the colonizers' well-being, their social cohesiveness, their culture, and their conduct with other religious/ethnic groups. Just as in the case of colonial India, most other colonized people in Asia and Africa were saddled with the *colonial mode of production.*[89] This mode of production imposed an enclave economy on the colony that limited the range of crop production in the interest of securing a large supply of reliable, continuous sources of raw materials to feed the capitalist demands of the metropolis. To enable this kind of exploitation, the subjugation of the colonized took a form by which dominant relations of production became oppressively feudal and allowed the colonial state to establish a supra-tributary mode of extracting the society's surplus.[90] Thus, the colonial division of labour imposed monocrop production and an export orientation, both in terms of tribute and raw materials' extraction, whereas the metropolis supplied the finished and processed goods to the colony. So, the colony was made part of the WCS, as a periphery, but given the nature of exploitation, especially the metropolis's reliance on tribute collection, the oppressive colonial fief made the peasantry captive and non-resisting or relatively docile—with the result that the relations of production in the colony remained mainly non-capitalist or merely inched towards proto-capitalist relations.[91] Additionally, the same peasantry and workers also had to service the interests of the indigenous elite, which meant that they had to suffer an added toll of oppression and exploitation. This resulted in multiple layers of subaltern exploitation of the colonial mode of production.

This super-exploitative impulse of European imperial capital can also be seen as establishing a relationship between capitalism and race. It is important to note that positing this relationship does not mean racism is an epiphenomenon of the economic or political for that matter; rather, this analysis will consistently show in later chapters of this volume that in the exploitation of the colonized has also meant the racialization of exploitation—capitalist exploitation of the colony through the colonial mode of production deeply embeds race. Although Satyananda Gabriel and Evgenia Todorova see a relationship between race and capitalism, they argue, contra Eric Williams and others, that "racism and capitalist exploitation must be understood as *distinct* social processes, shaping each other in complex and contradictory ways."[92] However, because Gabriel and Todorova are also at pains to not appear as economic determinists, they argue that "racialized subjectivity" is not an expression of economic or political projects, "but [is part of] a social process with its own effects on the social formation in question." [93] The concern of Gabriel and Todorova to examine how racism exists in (Western) society (outside of the formal economy) is a legitimate social exploration, but as the process of racialization has taken centuries to evolve, delinking its origins from capitalist exploitation is not helpful. Thus, my integrated social analysis, which links metropolitan capitalist exploitation with racialization (a process that introduces the notion of separate and inferiorized colonial subjects, a peculiar distortion in identity construction of the colonized, and the consequent emergence of conflict among the colonized) establishes an integral link between race and capitalism, embedding racialization with capitalist exploitation. The fact is inescapable that Western capitalism has gained tremendously from a racialized exploitation of the colony and now from the racialized underdevelopment of the global South and the creation of the North–South divide.

Another twist to the complex social relations in the colonies is the role of the indigenous elite. Although this group acted as intermediaries for the British and were the most privileged among the colonized, they too felt exploited and oppressed by the colonial state. Eventually, it was largely the economic and social insecurity of the elite forming part of different colonized groups that ultimately determined how the *other* would be perceived and how the colonized would respond to colonial domination. Fanon also discussed the role of the indigenous elite, once popularized as the 'national bourgeoisie', and cautioned that this class maintains the same relations of power and privilege as those held by former colonizers in the post-colonial period, to the extent of adopting the outlook of colonial rulers, in terms of the preoccupation with social control in the decolonized setting.[94] This keen observation is exemplified in many post-colonial societies that still continue to be governed by criminal, penal, and contract laws of the colonial state through a bureaucratic structure that is a holdover of the colonial period and whose emphasis is on manipulative social control rather than the protection of its populace and concerns for their well-being.

Given that capitalism–imperialism nexus has unleashed immense levels of exploitation, manipulation, and conflict as norms of colonial rule, it is not surprising that economic insecurity quickly led to social insecurity and identity conflicts. This happened as the colonized bourgeoisie jockeyed for favours with the colonial state, aware that the latter's intent was to use supportive indigenous overtures for the interest of colonial rule, the objective being to promote a supportive colonized group while simultaneously demoting the more recalcitrant 'other'. Ironically, despite this knowledge, the collaborationist elite continued to make their overtures to colonial rulers. So, does this mean that the colonized elite had no agency and were forced to undertake this collaborationist role? When viewed from the perspective of upper class interests—and if intra-colonized group conflicts and a manipulative colonial social policy are thrown into the mix—the choice becomes clear: resist in the first instance but when that fails or goes nowhere and class interests get threatened then collaboration appears a 'better' alternative for this opportunistic elite. In colonial India, the Hindu and Muslim elites both resisted at different historical junctures—the Revolt of 1857 when both groups were involved in challenging the colonial state, but with defeat and the formation of the colonial state under Westminster Raj, manipulation and conflict-creation became the social policy tools. As discussed earlier in the context of internalization, these tools were adopted by the two groups in their dealings with each other. As a result, Hindus and Muslims oscillated between resistance and collaboration, with the latter becoming dominant in the dying days of colonial rule. The colonial Indian bourgeoisie belonging to the Congress Party as well as the leaders of the Muslim League chose a largely collaborationist path mixed in with resistance, and their insecurities made them act less as free agents possibly because both Hindus and Muslims were not secure or confident either of their own subjective positions or about their respective standing vis-à-vis the colonial state—which itself was the instrument of perpetuating colonial subjugation and exploitation. This insecurity was overlaid by key policy instruments that the British had put in place in India, such as separate electorates, the partition of Bengal and its re-amalgamation, and the selective parceling of privilege and entitlement, which helped to create an environment of intense identity conflicts, Hindu-Muslim competition, and rivalry. The result of these complex manoeuvres was not so much the muzzling of agency; the social policy moves of the colonial state actually created the environment of conflicts and insecurity where collaboration became the more immediate and lucrative option, given the class positions of these respective elites.

Thus, social relations developed under the prerogatives of colonial rule were central in shaping identities and how Hindus and Muslims perceived each other—how they each chose to define their role in society and their actions towards one another and towards the colonial state. The colonial state had an enormous role in shaping the colonized people's perceptions of themselves as well as of the 'other', which formed the context for the 'imagining of the nation' that differed markedly from the European experience. The nature of the colonial state, given its structures of power that created a perception of powerlessness among the colonized, ultimately made the Hindu and Muslim elite become toadies to the powerful colonial state apparatus and to perceive the British colonial administrators as the final arbiter of settling inter-group differences. It could not have been otherwise, given the path chosen by the colonized elite. In the absence of necessary conditions that would promote free or revolutionary consciousness and because of the social fragmentation among the colonized, they were by and large unable to challenge the actions of colonial rulers or to largely question how power and privilege was dispensed. Moreover, given the rivalry and competition between the colonized groups, each group directed its anger at the other to settle perceived wrongs and inequities which, in reality, were engendered by the colonial state. This disfigurement of identity, which was neglected by Anderson, also led to adverse repercussions into the post-colonial period, fomenting the spiral of religious, ethnic, and/or sub-national conflicts.

Based on the discussion in the preceding pages, one of the (hypo)theses of this text is that the intervention of the colonial state has meant a qualitative break from the idea of nation and the nation-state model that emerged in the late 18th- and 19th-century Western Europe. The analysis thus far has elucidated the relationship between the rise of nation-states of Europe and the spread of capitalism. In contrast, the new relationship in the colonial era was based on the capitalism–imperialism nexus, which has been reintroduced into the post-colonial period. The colonial period did not leave the colonized areas and its peoples with the same opportunity as in Europe to evolve from the nascent stage of capitalist development, by way of an epochal shift from feudalism to capitalism, to make way for a nation(s) to form its own nation-state. The post-colonial state was the outcome of decolonization; it is deeply enmeshed with the colonial legacy. The external economic and imperial impositions on the post-colonial state have been enormous ever since its inception after decolonization, and this subordination of the state in the global South more generally has been presided over in large part by the ruling elite in most Third World societies, who have actively collaborated with the current imperial overlord.

To understand the post-colonial predicament, a good place to begin is by taking an inventory of what happened since decolonization to transform the idea of the Third World itself. This stock-taking reveals that the Third World, with some exceptions, has drastically changed: from one full of expectation and promise to its present predicament of dependency, misery, and gross neglect for the vast majority of its inhabitants. Thus, at the moment of decolonization a sense of buoyancy prevailed in many newly independent post-colonial states due to the successes of national liberation movements (such as in Algeria, the Congo, Ghana, and Indonesia) and even anti-colonial struggles. The ending of colonial rule kept alive the hope of a 'new tomorrow' brought about by independence. But this hope faded quickly. After the post-Second World War period, as soon as colonial rule started to come to an end, neo-imperial powers—with the US in the lead—became occupied with taming, opposing, or eliminating the new leadership in post-colonial societies. As a consequence of these imperial moves, the urgency that was needed to quicken the task of state-building and nation-building within a climate of supposedly *free* sovereign states simply did not materialize for most states. Instead, the Cold War-based rivalry of the two superpowers (the US and the former Soviet Union) introduced incentives to military and political elite in post-colonial and Latin American states to support the rival ideological power and its objectives—such as joining one of the defence pacts of the US or aligning the economy to favour either bureaucratic state control or allowing Western states and their corporations to influence policy. This process of alignment with post-colonial states actually helped the US. The reason was 'pragmatic' opportunism: because the departing colonial rulers handed power, wherever possible, to indigenous elite who had actively collaborated with the colonial state or had privileged positions within it, post-colonial elites were more than willing to support the US—more so because the former colonial powers also became part of the capitalist bloc led by the US. Consequently, it was no surprise that those in control of the post-colonial state went on to become clients of the US as the new leader of the capitalist world, whereas a few states became allied to the Soviet Union. To consolidate its gains, the US decided to stop recalcitrant nationalist leaders in their tracks and initiated or coordinated a number of military coups against them to install its client military or political group in power.[95] As a result, a self-reliant course of economic and social development in post-colonial societies was thwarted, whereas the larger questions of identity or subnational and ethnic grievances remained unresolved—leading to the re-invocation of the capitalism–imperialism nexus in the post-colonial era; this argument is further developed in the next chapter.

In general, the opportunity to address ethnic, sub-national, religious, linguistic, regional, and cultural claims after decolonization was actually squandered: some nationalist leaders tried to address this challenge, but most other post-colonial elites, who had been hoisted to power by departing colonial rulers or by the US, simply ignored it. With so many of these *client* post-colonial elites in power, the capitalism–imperialism nexus received a new lease on life. Because many states had retained the bureaucratic and governing structures of the colonial state, in some ways the colonial state appeared to be reinstated: just as colonial rulers had mastered the art of social exclusion, the new indigenous rulers of post-colonial states also managed to keep weaker or minority subnational groups out of the power equation. Thus, colonial-era tensions based on ethnicity, sub-nationalism, language, religion, and region began to ignite and finally to develop into open conflict, which has continued to this day, making a resolution appear more elusive under the clientelist leadership of most post-colonial societies.

2 The Post-Colonial State

Historical Antecedents and Contemporary Impositions

The specific nature, form, and function of the post-colonial state are inextricably linked to the capitalism–imperialism nexus. This nexus is not a transhistorical phenomenon: imperialist domination has been adapted from the colonial era to the moment of decolonization, which in turn has structured a more invidious re-subordination of formerly colonized regions in the current capitalist globalization period. As a result, state sovereignty for post-colonial states, with few exceptions, has been a token expression of self-rule. The integral link between contemporary imperialism and Western capitalist development has deepened and cemented the North-South divide and has promoted uneven development within and between post-colonial states. Regrettably, many scholars and state theorists have ignored the millstone this nexus has placed on post-colonial states, whereas their general disinterest in Asian, African, and Latin American states has largely eclipsed these states from the field of state theory.[1]

The tendency within the field of state theory is to focus mainly on the Western capitalist state without attempting to even understand the specificity of the post-colonial state. State theorists have also failed to distinguish between Latin American and post-colonial Asian and African states, which have had differing colonial histories and contemporary trajectories—a distinction that ethnographers working on the post-colonial state also emphasize.[2] Latin American and post-colonial societies must be understood differently within the context of post-World War II decolonization and the theory of developmentalism, from both Western/imperialist and Third World perspectives. As mentioned in my introduction, there may be a common thread of subordination running through post-colonial states of Africa and Asia as well as Latin American states, but there are significant differences between them. To add to what I have said earlier, Latin America is comprised of Southern European settler-colonial states that were decolonized 60 to 100 years prior to the decolonization of states in Africa and Asia, the latter being mainly non-settler colonies. The indigenous people within Latin America remain part of an internal colony, and they are still trying to decolonize their territory: indigenous successes, such as in Bolivia, are few and far between. As such, the character of Latin American states is different from post-colonial states. To guide the economic well-being of the Latin American dominant class and to resist the implications of imperialist dictates, the idea of the 'developmental state' emerged in Latin America in the 1960s and early1970s,[3] and the model was quickly embraced and applied to address post-colonial social and economic challenges. However, the developmental state concept does not help us understand the post-colonial state, especially its historical antecedents and contemporary manifestations that are helpful to comprehend not only its subordination but also its form and function. Nevertheless, some scholars still prefer to address the challenges of development in post-colonial societies within the framework of the developmental state.[4]

More recently, the notion of 'neoliberal' and 'post-neoliberal' states has also emerged, with the latter focusing on the widespread opposition and resistance against neoliberalism, particularly in many Latin American states.[5] In articulating the neoliberal or post-neoliberal state, scholars have failed to distinguish between the specificities of Latin American and post-colonial states and, therefore, have also not meaningfully analyzed how and why post-colonial states have stayed the course after taking the neoliberal turn or why many Latin American states have started to actively reject neoliberal policies. No post-colonial states appear to be following Latin America's lead (despite some popular anger, protest and opposition against economic liberalization), at least in the visible present. This is because, contrary to the Latin American situation, most post-colonial societies have not been widely critical of the neoliberal turn. Nor has there been substantive interest in examining how these states were persuaded to adopt neoliberal policies and bury the developmental state project through imperialist pressure and the coordinated actions of the International Monetary Fund (IMF), the World Bank (and now also the World Trade Organization [WTO]), and the US and its Western allies. Thus, if the re-subordination of post-colonial state and society is to be understood, it is more historically useful and analytically relevant to theorize about the post-colonial state instead of trying to articulate the 'neoliberal state' as a standalone theory.

In examining the historical antecedents that provide the foundation to build a theory of the post-colonial state from political economy and social history perspectives, this chapter analyzes their recent economic history and the contemporary impositions of Western capitalist states and their multilateral auxiliaries. These multilateral auxiliaries and manoeuvrings of Western states have paved the way for the emergence of the 'new' international division of labour (IDL), which has been pivotal in the re-subordination of post-colonial states. In this chapter, I also point out that, although the Cold War's professed objective was the defeat and elimination of the Soviet Union, its unacknowledged objective in the Third World was to trigger military coups leading to the removal or elimination of popular nationalist leadership and generally to keep the left in these countries on the defensive. The early period of Cold War alignments and the political environment surrounding the Non-Aligned Movement also had an impact on the post-colonial states' formation. Sustained imperialist pressure in the emerging Third World was enabled with the passage of the US National Security Act in 1947, which created the National Security Council and the Central Intelligence Agency (CIA) and led to the formation of the US security state.[6] This single step unleashed the Cold War. It was also central in determining whether post-colonial states under truly nationalist (in the most inclusive sense) leaders would be allowed to take a path of non-alignment and self-reliant development or whether such leaders would be removed or eliminated through the CIA's campaign of 'dirty tricks' in order to consolidate clientelism and dependency.[7] The gathering momentum of these developments have placed a stranglehold on post-colonial and Latin American states, enabling the US and its allied Western states to force Third World states to accept IMF's structural adjustment programs and adopt economic policies within privatized, marketized, and deregulated frameworks. The move towards economic liberalization is a good entry point to examine the push towards clientelism, explore the shifts from developmentalism to neoliberalism and from the colonial division of labour to the 'new' IDL, and assess histories since decolonization that bring us to contemporary developments affecting the post-colonial state. This approach, which I follow here, will provide the analytical and referential framework on which I will develop my theory of the post-colonial state in Chapter 3, this volume. This analytical framework will also help clarify the deep interconnections between the crisis of capitalism, changes in the capitalist mode of production, and the consequent imperialist drive of US militarism to block the self-reliant developmental path of the post-colonial state.

This chapter investigates how this developmental and autarkic path continues to be blocked, beginning with the role of modernization theorists from the 1950s whose theories encircled newly decolonized states with the object of placing most of them within the US's sphere of influence; the rationale was that these states had to be reoriented on the path of 'progress' of economic development and 'modernization'. I will show how the strategies of development outlined by modernization theorists, especially by treading a Eurocentric cultural terrain, served to further the imperialist ends of the US and other Western states.

After examining the motives of modernization theorists, I will then discuss the idea of the developmental state and the developmental project, which began in Latin America as a way to resist the imperialist stranglehold and to promote self-directed development. This idea was later also embraced by a number of post-colonial states. However, this developmental state project was short-lived. I will focus on the forces that propelled the shift from autarky and inward-oriented development to export and market orientation, which successively eroded the sovereignty and independence of post-colonial and Latin American states. Next, I will show how post-colonial states shelved the developmental state project by embracing economic liberalization and began restructuring their economy and society. The move to adopt neoliberalism cannot be blamed solely on imperialist measures: the acceptance of this ideology had the acquiescence of the indigenous bourgeoisie and other groups in administrative control of the post-colonial and Latin American states. As the path towards genuine national development in post-colonial and Latin American states was derailed, it was replaced by the 'globalization project'. This was not some naturalized progression of capitalist development based on technological imperatives and revolutionary changes in communication; rather, I will discuss the US and Organization for Economic Cooperation and Development's (OECD) strategy to pry open the markets and territories of post-colonial and Latin American states by reinvoking dependency, establishing the IDL, and transferring labour-intensive production to re-subordinate the Third World states.

I will show that the introduction of the IDL was carefully planned by the OECD. It was based on the understanding that the post-1945 era pact between the global North and South, and between capital and labour, would need to end in the wake of the capitalist economic crisis that had intensified since the 1970s. The timing of the peasantry's displacement in Third World societies, with the mechanization and introduction of Green Revolution technologies, could not have been more fortuitous for Western capitalists' intent on transferring labour-intensive manufacture from the North to the South.[8] The new IDL, alongside the US's unilateral abrogation of the Dollar-Gold Convertibility Accord[9] and the establishment of Free Trade Zones or *maquiladoras* in the Third World, set in motion the deindustrialization of the global North. The consequence of these changes, coupled with the continued displacement of the peasantry, opened the floodgates for the exploitation of the informal sector (IS). I will examine the notion of self-exploitation of self-employed families in the IS, which remains an unexplored concept. Finally, I will analyze how the division between North and South has been cemented by the new IDL, while the capitalism–imperialism nexus has ensured the re-subordination of post-colonial state and society in the period of neoliberal globalization.

As noted, state theory has not kept pace with these developments; the inward-oriented focus of theorists who simply examine the internal or domestic aspects of the Western capitalist state, has resulted in the occlusion of its militarist and imperialist dimension from their frame of reference. In the current anti-Marxist climate, it is precisely the insights of critical Marxists and their structuralist conception of the state that may need to be revisited and rearticulated to comprehend the reimposition of the capitalism–imperialism nexus.[10] To this end, I will argue that the shift towards globalization would not have been possible without the acquiescence of post-colonial and Latin American states. By historicizing the recent past, but also considering the colonial and post-colonial eras as separate epochs, post-colonial state scholars can grasp the intimate linkage between the past and the present.

I THE DECOLONIZATION CONTEXT

The Enlightenment era had two main trajectories: one path promoted a narrow idea of modernity in terms of 'progress' of technological and economic development; the other focused on the broader principles of rights, equality, and the embrace of democratic ideals, as enshrined in the slogan of the French Revolution: *liberté, egalité, and fraternité.*[11] The narrower ideal of economic development as 'progress' was embraced as colonial rulers began introducing themes of culture and identity during the colonial period and posited European culture as 'superior' to culture of the 'Orient'. Paradoxically, the narrow and linear conception of Western modernity as progress also implied an erasure of Europe's own history—a break with the past and with the traditions of the Old Order—that made its followers interpret the 'modern' conjuncture largely as a *tabula rasa.* I will return to this erasure of the past and its implications for both the colonized and decolonized worlds later.

As the economic transformation of Western societies unfolded, capitalism triggered the growth of 'instrumental reason' and a range of new social, cultural, and political tendencies. In this sense, contemporary ideas of modernity have become closely associated with the ideas of Euro-US liberalism and come together as a 'mode of consciousness' whereby modernity's historical significance lies in the manner in which "it self-consciously cut its links with all that had gone before."[12] As a result, modernity "unleashed forces which were able to vanquish the past and the horizontal present in the form of less technologically powerful cultures,"[13] which have been treated as patently inferior to the self-proclaimed 'superior' economic and cultural motif of Western modernity.

The Enlightenment project also cut links with its own historical past and with the 'non-European world'; Lawrence claimed this was done with "extreme violence."[14] This violence of modernity and the erasure of the high points of other cultures, which European colonial powers denied in the interest of treating colonized peoples as 'backward' or 'barbaric', also meant that the Eurocentric worldview would be privileged and universalized over the supposedly '*historyless* and *cultureless*' 'non-European' world. This erasure of the non-European gave the project of Enlightenment modernity a strong Eurocentric impulse that shaped empire-building projects and constructed the Occident and the Orient as 'superior' and 'inferior' domains. The colonized elite were inferiorized to the point that they internalized the ideas of modernity, especially the notion of the 'normal' nation-state[15]—an edifice that has enabled post-colonial elites, dominant Western states, and the present empire to place a stranglehold on post-colonial societies. This imperialist thrust of both past and present empires severely undermined and restructured the economic dimension of post-colonial societies, and its social and cultural legacies persist to this day. Specifically, I am referring to the colonial legacies of *separateness and apartness*, a trope that colonial rulers used to separate themselves and ensure that they lived completely apart from colonized subjects, whereas the insularity and control of the colonial state and the 'over-developed' colonial bureaucracy ensured absolute control over colonized society. In mimicking this colonial trope, the ruling classes in post-colonial societies have also remained insular and separate, whereas the bureaucracy has arguably become an auxiliary class that remains above the rest of society, subjugating and enforcing control.[16]

Chapter 1 of this volume discussed the *unitary* colonial state's legacy; in contrast, this chapter begins with modernization theorists and how they used cultural tropes and the colonial legacy-laced structures of the post-colonial state to realign these states with US's imperialist interests and to reintroduce more contemporary versions of Orientalism, Eurocentrism, and the narrow version of modernity. In the colonial context, the narrow notion of modernity was posited against the 'backward' traditions of the colonized and enabled the colonizers to ridicule and demean the culture of the colonized. In many cases, a Westernized elite was cultivated among the colonized by establishing school systems that mainly educated the children of this elite. The structure of the colonial state—which was crucial to the domination and control of the colonized, to the establishment of the capitalism–imperialism nexus, and to the extension of capital's imperialist thrust at the cost of derailing indigenous social and economic development during the colonial era—was retained by post-colonial elites with devastating results for most contemporary African and Asian societies. The retention of colonial state structures on the eve of decolonization into the new post-colonial state renewed this capitalism–imperialism nexus, reshaping it to suit the new post-colonial realities. This enabled the formation of a clientelist relationship between the US (as the new post-World War II capitalist role model) and many of the decolonized states of the global South. This decolonized reality can be understood as marking

> an era of formal horizontal symmetries of nations imagined as communities, dominated in fact by American power and its exigencies of 'self determination', 'open doors' and multilateral trade. Scholarship that projects the nation-state back to the Enlightenment has occluded imperial history, just as depictions of American power as 'neo-imperial' depict it too vaguely, and fail to capture the dilemmas. . .[of] decolonization as a beginning, not an end, exit from empires but also entry into a world newly ordered by American power.[17]

With the ascendency of US power during the post-1945 period, the national security state first emerged in the US to enable the exercise of its hegemony; I have previously analyzed this development with regard to the 'war on terror'.[18] However, the US security state, especially the creation of the CIA, was ostensibly structured to fight the Cold War with the Soviet Union, but another of its functions is largely ignored: the CIA's extensive resources were also devoted to eliminating or removing nationalist leaders in the Third World. The first such leader to be removed from power in 1953 was Mossadegh of Iran, who was committed to nationalizing the country's oil wealth, which was in control of British petroleum interests.[19] This process of taming and clientelizing the Third World has been a concomitant part of the US Cold War strategy, which has continued into the present and is now baldly called 'regime change'. However, the national security state strategy has been multipronged. At one level, violence and militaristic moves are used against recalcitrant post-colonial and Latin American states; at another, scholarship and cultural terrain are used to encourage Third World elites to embrace the US version of modernization, while the US organic intellectuals also promote US interests through their writings. This endeavour has involved a long list of modernization theorists, largely from the US, who have not only purveyed their ideas but have also begun advising holders of state power in the Third World about the policy of development and tokenistic commitment to democracy in an otherwise authoritarian framework of post-colonial states.

(i) Culturalism and Modernization Theorists: Paving the Way for a New Clientelism in the Post-Colonial Era

It was no coincidence that most modernization theorists, including Talcott Parsons, Samuel Huntington, and W.W. Rostow, were all very well connected with the US establishment. The argument of this section is that modernization theorists paved the way for a new clientelism to emerge in the post-colonial era in the interest of US imperialist expansionism, popularizing the perception of the Third World as 'backward' and needing to be rescued from itself by offering a theory of development—effectively involving the emulation of Western culture of modernity and capitalism—that essentialized culture and universalized the narrow notion of modernity as 'progress' in economic development.

Arguments for this Western cultural universalism within the ambit of this new US imperialism and clientelism has been provided by many professors in elite US academic institutions as well as US state functionaries. Academics with ideological agendas (such as Samuel Huntington and Talcott Parsons) have influenced US foreign policy and also provided a fertile environment for transnational corporations (TNCs) from OECD countries to operate in the Third World. These TNCs have been able to converge on historically captive sources of cheap raw materials, establish 'free-trade zones', continue the super-exploitation of Third World workers (especially women), and find markets (read 'dumping ground') for some of the Western world's excess production and speculative capital. When the US was building anti-Communist alliances with many Third World states during the Cold War, it relied primarily on two methods to achieve world hegemony. One method was reserved for its client states in the Third World, which joined the US and its Western allies in spewing the rhetoric of the 'free world' and anti-Communism as an ideological device to create the impression of a great divide between the capitalist world and the so-called socialist camp led by the former Soviet Union. In reality, the state-sponsored bureaucratic capitalism of the former Soviet Union, despite its socialist rhetoric, did not really operate outside the world capitalist system.[20] The other method was used against more noncompliant Third World 'nationalist' states; it involved a host of counter-insurgency measures or sheer physical violence to subdue or remove nationalist or anti-imperialist leaders. The CIA and other intelligence agencies were deployed to use their influence and resources in Africa, Asia, and Latin America to eliminate scores of other noncompliant Third World leaders who were removed from power between 1950 and 1980.[21]

As culture became the terrain of US power assertion, modernization theorists saw 'traditional' cultures of emerging decolonized states as *the* problem and began to counsel emerging Third World states to emulate the 'superior' European-North American culture. They portrayed the latter as worthy of emulation, especially if post-colonial and Latin American states wanted to leave the 'backwardness' of traditional society and move into the 'modern' age of developmentalism. This meant adopting 'Western values' (an amorphous concept that was never fully articulated) and embracing capitalism and capitalist values about individualism and the profit motive. Not surprisingly, as discussed in more detail later, democratic norms were not promoted; modernization theorists worked almost exclusively with compliant client military or authoritarian Third World regimes that eagerly adopted ideas about modernization. Modernization theory's lens of naturalism framed the so-called transition into modernity and industrialism as a supposed 'natural' rite of social passage for all 'traditional' societies. Accordingly, ideas about modernization were presented not only as harmless and innocuous but as helpful guideposts for 'traditional' societies that wanted to move towards economic development and industrialization. Some analysts with origins in the Third World who have internalized the ideas of modernization theorists argue that these theorists are not economic determinists but actually focused on 'culture' and 'internal causes' of 'backwardness' in the South.[22] The validity of such claims, because of their corrosive impact on the developmental path of post-colonial and Latin American states and societies, is briefly established next by examining the outlooks of two widely known modernization theorists: Talcott Parsons and Samuel Huntington.

Talcott Parsons was a founder of modernization theory; he may not have been an economic determinist, but his work was rooted in *cultural determinism,* and he followed the logic of Social Darwinism very closely. His earliest work, *The Theory of Social Action and the Evolution of Societies*, is infamous for essentializing the process of 'natural selection' to human societies. A decade later, during a 1963 seminar on evolution at Harvard

University, he tried to show that societies "evolve" from 'traditional' to 'modern' in a way similar to biological evolution through adaptation. He formulated this idea with reference to the concept of adaptation, which was fundamental to Darwin's theory of evolution.[23] Parsons claimed that adaptation "should mean not merely passive adjustment to environmental conditions, but rather the capacity of a living system to cope with its environment."[24] The really troubling aspect of Parsons's work is his theory of 'evolutionary universals':

> [it] is a complex of structures and associated processes the development of which so increases the long-run adaptive capacity of living systems in a given class that only systems that develop the complex can attain certain higher levels of general adaptive capacity.[25]

Evolutionary universals are related to "the capacity of a living system to [not only] cope with its environment; [rather, it] includes an active concern with mastery, or the ability to change the environment to meet the needs of the system."[26] Parsons argued that this cannot be attained by the "relatively disadvantaged system" which will have to "stand in a variety of different relations to the higher" system.[27] He insisted that the criterion of evolutionary universals, can still apply to 'primitive' and 'socially stratified' societies by helping them break out of a traditional "system of cultural legitimation."[28] Notwithstanding his hierarchy of evolutionary universals, Parsons claimed that a traditional society can be propelled into 'modernity' with the right mix of ingredients: a correct stimulus of social evolution via the complex division of labour would break down the intense social stratification of 'traditional society' and eventually lead to the rise of individualism and the development of the bureaucratic state.[29] In purveying this kind of crass universalism, Parsons made no reference to the 'overdeveloped' bureaucratic structure that is present in most post-colonial states. This was not the result of ignorance about history and social conditions in the colonies; rather, his objective was quite self-serving: to use a set ideological position to develop a modern-traditional binary that would serve the aims of US imperialism. Similarly, but in contrast to his notion of adaptation, Parsons also claimed that an alternative process of evolutionary transformation was possible by emulating the European experience: "the advantages of 'higher culture'" can be also universalized by "diffusion" in 'traditional' societies.[30] He completely disregarded the differences in social and economic situations between Europe/North America and the Third World.

Parsons's reasoning brings about a host of troubling conclusions. By embedding hierarchy in his concept of evolutionary universals, he explicitly states that only the most adaptive will advance to the higher social evolutionary stage. Even Parsons's idea of cultural system seems to have closed adaptive categories leaving it open for unfortunate conclusions. His vast generalizations about very diverse and heterogeneous societies throughout the non-European world came from a typically Eurocentric perspective, reminiscent of Weber, and a long line of European social scientists.

Modernization theory rests on problems such as essentialism, the Eurocentric impulse, and ignorance of social conditions in post-colonial and Latin American societies. These issues are still inherently problematic for contemporary adherents to modernization in 'multilateral' institutions such as the IMF and the World Bank, who keep insisting that the introduction of new technology and 'modern' culture in the 'developing' South—in the form of Western-style education, bureaucratic controls, Western languages, value systems, and so forth—will bring about the desired changes in the developing world's culture through diffusion. The most basic issue, the universalization of the European experience and the homogenization of incredibly diverse post-colonial and Latin American societies, hinges on the question of whether it is even possible to diffuse larger non-indigenous type social values. The short answer is no: changes in values cannot just happen without changing the underlying social conditions as a consequence of social and economic transformation. Parsons and other evolutionists have simply been unable to grasp this elementary materialist concept; or maybe the issue is less about the ability to grasp a concept and more about the exercise of power and ideological control—specifically, control of the Third World. The US and its allies have searched for compliant and subservient leaderships that can trade away the sovereignty of the Third World in the service of imperialist interests; in return, the ruling indigenous elite and corrupt regimes in the Third World receive their share of imperial spoils.

Huntington's theory was subtler than Parsons's troubling naturalism. Huntington did borrow from Parsons's diffusion hypothesis to explain his evolutionism, but for Huntington the fundamental problem was the concept of change. He was not interested in social or culturally relevant change; he was preoccupied with the evolutionary pre-determined change from 'traditional' to 'modern' society, which his predecessors have worked to elucidate since the late 1800s. Huntington argued that 'modern' humans have more control over their natural and social environment than 'traditional man', who remains passive and submissive and does not believe in either changing or controlling his surroundings.[31] As noted previously, this kind of large and troublesome generalization is characteristic of Eurocentric scholarship. Huntington was no different; he claimed that modern ideas have spread globally, but he made this claim without problematizing colonialism or imperialism. Although he admitted that the modernizing process is homogenizing, he claimed that the 'Grand Process of Modernization' was not only 'progressive' but also 'irreversable' and 'revolutionary' in character.[32] Huntington saw modernization's grand process as the pivot on which hinged the larger project of achieving American hegemony over the non-Euro-American world. Therefore, he was unable to question the relevance of the 'Grand Process' or even the desirability of emulating the European experience by people in the decolonized areas of the world. In fact, his determinist outlook on modernity—as a supposedly inevitable principle and outcome of human social evolution—did not even allow him to pose the question of relevance or context.

The manipulative aspect of Huntington's work was especially apparent in his 1968 text, *Political Order in Changing Societies*. He considered 'political instability' to be at the heart of non-implementation of the modernization project in the Third World. Although Huntington recognized the obvious role of the 'economic gap'—that is, how political stability and popular revolt are responses to economic inequality[33]—he chose to ignore economic inequalities in favour of urgently bridging 'the political gap'. He considered political order and stability to be of utmost importance, arguing that because the political gap signifies "a shortage of political community and of effective, authoritative, legitimate government . . . [in] modernizing countries of Asia, Africa and Latin America," it impedes social and economic 'progress'.[34] This seemingly innocuous statement has larger implications because Huntington's objective *was* to achieve political stability in the South at any cost to realize the larger imperialist project of the US: the maintenance of abysmally low commodity prices, the ready availability of a reserve army of compliant and extremely low-paid workers, and client regimes at the beck and call of the US. Huntington's text reveals (as has long been understood by people in the South) that democratic ideals are not upheld simply because there are enough ideological writers like Huntington who are concerned with a particular kind of political stability. In the Third World, 'political stability' has been largely achieved through authoritarian rulers, military dictators, or oppressive monarchs largely because they have the necessary instruments of control: oppressive bureaucracy and the military's coercive power to do incredible harm—and it is very difficult for popularly elected leaders to muster support from these groups if they have almost no allies within the state apparatus.

Huntington's real objective was to pursue political stability without any concern for economic, social, or juridical equality (let alone the attainment of substantive equality). His agenda must be understood within the larger framework of Cold War posturing between the US and the former Soviet Union; it was also intended to rein in independent leadership in post-colonial and Latin American societies. Huntington's interventions were in the interest of the US to expand its sphere of influence as far as possible over countries of the global South and in opposition to the former Soviet Union's similar expansionist plans; and given the US's imperialist designs, it was important to eliminate opposition to its imperialism by pushing for the notion of political stability. From the perspective of capitalist and Western interests, the pursuit of economic well-being in the South would have required shelving the entire project of imperialist control and domination of the Third World, which would have been the very antithesis of the developmentalism idea and the spread of capitalism. Thus, pushing for political stability in the South became the method and a coded language for installing subservient client regimes that were able to prevent their populace from resisting or interfering with the rapacious extraction of surplus by American, European, and Japanese corporations. Further, the alignment of the US with the Third World elite to achieve this objective had the added benefit of widening the anti-Communist alliance. However, given the horizontal and vertical polarization in most states in the South, political stability through stable democratic governance was a process that would need to evolve and would be long and drawn out, given the ravages of colonialism and the colonial legacy. This reality did not escape modernization theorists or the functionaries of the US government who were willing to exploit the vulnerability of the South and political conflict among different groups by relying on Third World militaries to bring about the required 'political stability' in their respective states.

The project of implementing political stability was thus really the American blueprint for imperial dominance, and people like Huntington provided intellectual support as well as the methodology to bring about the Third World's compliance. Modernization theory fulfilled US priorities, and academics such as Huntington counselled US state functionaries and military dictators in the Third World to enforce the principle of 'political stability' at any cost. Given this overriding objective, superficial political stability was made possible through authoritarian regimes or military dictatorships that had the blessing of the US and its allies for much of the five decades following World War II and even into the present. Ever since decolonization, the history of the South has been replete with innumerable such examples of dictatorial regimes that have captured power by overthrowing popularly elected leaders. The recipe for gaining political stability was followed in all regions of the Third World where the US had a foothold—Argentina, Brazil, Cambodia, Chile, the Congo, Thailand, Indonesia, Nigeria, Pakistan, Philippines, Iran, and many other states of Africa, Asia, and Latin America—and Huntington and his contemporaries were in the forefront, seeing their ideas put into practice. The modernization project has been a huge blow to the Third World's economic and social self-reliance, even by the criterion of 'development as progress'. As a result of this dismal failure, and also because of the massive social dislocations in post-colonial and Latin American societies, the impact of manipulating culture and identity are now coming to haunt key players in the modernization project, in terms of rising anti-Americanism and, in many cases, anti-Western resentment. This new turn of events is being increasingly identified as the phenomenon of 'blowback'.[35]

With the end of the Cold War, and the US empire not making much headway even after the demise of the Soviet Union, Huntington was again in the forefront, carving a new strategy in support of US and Western imperial interests. In the past, US expansionism had been couched in the language of modernization to fight the 'Soviet menace' of 'totalitarianism' and unbending nationalist leaders in the Third World. This meant getting as many Third World states as possible, especially those that were geographically strategic, onboard the anti-Communist platform and to have these states commit to an agenda of implementing modernization. Now, US expansionism is more concerned with threats to its world hegemony from Islamist forces and China. Increasingly, this 'threat' has been framed in American conservative and liberal circles in civilizational and cultural terms. Huntington has again figured centrally in purveying this slant to a mainstream Western audience, which sees its cultural values being 'overrun' by a wave of immigrants from the non-European world. So, he outlined and promoted a new expansionist project based on *The Clash of Civilizations and the Remaking of the World Order*: his more contemporary prognosis of a 'clash' with antithetical forces—specifically 'Muslims and Confucians' opposed to the universalization of Western values—has increasingly been portrayed as the new threat to Western 'civilization'.[36] This project, in contrast to his old focus on modernization, was couched in less obtuse, fictional, and imaginary terms, but not surprisingly the battlefield was still identified as 'culture'. This emphasis on culture is in the mould of the new Orientalism, which relies on the older version of Orientalism to create a new superior–inferior binary between the West and Islam/Muslims. The difference is that whereas in the past, the Muslims, Chinese, Asians more broadly, and Aboriginal and Black peoples—in a sense the 'non-European' world—was targeted by the older version of Orientalism, the new Orientalism is more specific. In as much as the Chinese people are still part of Huntington's thesis, the culture clash since 11 September 2001 in much of the Western world, especially in Europe—with the rise of extremist right-wing Muslim-hating racist groups such as the English Defence League and others—is with Islam and Muslims, with the latter becoming the main focus of the racist and xenophobic attacks and a peculiar Islamphobic interpretation of the present conjuncture to frame the new Orientalism. [37].

Scholars living in Latin America and post-colonial states understood development in a very different way than did modernization theorists. For them, the idea of development was not a homogenous concept; it could be understood using a conventional or radical perspective, or using a combination of the two outlooks. They deployed these perspectives differentially in formulating the notion of the developmental state. The next section discusses developmentalism and the idea of the developmental state.

II DEVELOPMENTALISM AND DIVERGENT TENDENCIES OF THE DEVELOPMENTAL STATE

Some scholars have traced the genealogy of the notion of development back to colonialism,[38] but the idea seems to emerge with the rise of industrial capitalism and the Enlightenment project itself. Its more contemporary version, identified as 'developmentalism' (i.e., 'progress' through economic growth) was a US initiative presented in 1949 when President Truman first enunciated his government's policy for the emerging decolonized states.[39] Modernization theorists adopted developmentalism as an ideological project with the aim of influencing newly decolonized Asian and African states, along a firmly committed path towards market capitalist, rather than socialist, development. In contrast, dependency theorists, initially in Latin American states, offered their own versions of state-led development models in the form of import substitution industrialization (ISI) as a way to challenge the ideas of modernization and resist US imperialism. The notion of ISI, as discussed next, is a concomitant part of capitalism, and the idea was adopted even before dependency theorists began to promote it. This developmental strategy began to emerge as Latin American states in the 1950s ostensibly as a way to overcome the capitalism–imperialism nexus.[40] Countries that followed an ISI strategy, as a state-led industrialization project, differed with regard to how they manipulated import tariff rates and whether they regulated currency exchange or opposed foreign direct investments (FDIs) while protecting the national market. Countries that regulated FDIs and used the capitalist market to export their manufactured goods, such as South Korea and Taiwan, had an affinity with modernization theorists but followed a state-centrist path of developmentalism. This kind of state capitalist orientation exemplified one form of the developmental state—the export-led outward-oriented developmental state. Another type of developmental state relied on a quasi-socialist or mixed economy model of inward-oriented development, as exemplified in Latin America, Tanzania, India, and other Asian states. In addition, some dependency theorists were firmly committed on a socialist development path. Dependency theorists, beginning with Raul Prebesch, started to explore the idea of the developmental state from a more radical perspective.[41] These three developmental state trajectories shared a commitment to following an ISI strategy. As an economic development strategy, ISI has been a key element in providing a protective enclosure around infant capitalist development—something Britain had done as the first capitalist state, more than 250 years previously. At this time, Britain was still trying to protect its infant machine-made textiles, the first sector to be industrialized under capitalism, from high-quality handloom imports from pre-colonial India. On the relationship between nascent capitalism and ISI, Werner Baer had this to say:

> that all countries which industrialized after Great Britain, went through a stage of ISI; that is, all passed through a stage where the larger part of investment in industries was undertaken to replace imports [. . .] The ISI wave in Europe and the United States occurred in the [19th century . . . and] in this early ISI process governments played an active role in encouraging and protecting the development of infant industries. Another characteristic of [19th century] ISI is its 'national' character.[42]

ISI strategy has played an important role in capitalist development, and this strategy was logically adapted for the developmental state. But the US and other Western states actively resisted this ISI strategy for the emerging Third World as it would work against the coordinated push of Western capital and imperialist states to subordinate post-colonial and Latin American states. Therefore, modernization theorists, imperial powers, and international financial institutions have all vociferously opposed ISI and the inward-oriented developmental state model. This opposition is more apparent in the current neoliberal era, and ideological critics of ISI have argued that adopting an industrial policy based on the developmental state model more generally is a poor strategy for post-colonial states in East Asia and other regions because this model is no longer applicable in the globalization era.[43]

The idea of the developmental state emerged as modernization theorists began to postulate economic and social/political theories about development. However, the ideas of developmentalism, as they initially emerged in the US, were also part of an imperialist imperative to incorporate as many resource-laden and strategically located post-colonial and Latin American states within the US's orbit to deny the Soviet Union the strategic advantage. This US state's imperial strategy was spearheaded by the State and Defense Departments to launch the Cold War against the former Soviet Union and a 'hot' war against nationalist leaders in post-colonial and Latin American states once the national security state was established after 1947.[44] It was no accident that the US's declaration of developmentalism and the formation of the US national security state originated at the same time, in 1947. Modernization theorists were also involved and began to work closely with US's imperial interests of replacing nationalist leaders with military and authoritarian regimes. After identifying emerging post-colonial states as 'flawed states', Huntington went on to (in)famously note that the 'problems' of the Third World could only be overcome by having praetorian regimes govern these states because (military) dictatorships, in comparison to democratic governments, were better able to build capacity, create order, erect stable institutions, and produce economic growth.[45]

As some developmental state theorists shared with modernizationists a commitment to the capitalist market, they were willing to accept a limited role for the state in the economic sphere. These theorists were even willing to embed the role of bureaucracy in an interventionist state to establish a layer of protection around infant industries, as exemplified in South Korea and Taiwan.[46] However, the acceptance of this role of the state is mediated by two assumptions: first, the actions of the state are expected to be heavily circumscribed within the capitalist mode of production, and second, a tripartite corporatist alliance between the state, bourgeoisie, and labour is usually cited as the way to achieve the objective of this particular form of developmental state. In the context of a corporatist alliance, the state and business interests have usually considered organized labour as a tenuous ally, although it is well known that labour has very little leverage in this arrangement. Capitalists and their bureaucratic allies in control of the state apparatus have mostly sought the acquiescence of the working class, but theorists of this market-oriented developmental state model rarely articulate this issue.

Market-oriented developmental state theorists have argued that unless state-centered economic activities are able to overcome two impediments or tendencies of *statecentricity*—the challenges of overcoming the state's drive as 'rent-seeker', and the tendency of state forces to subsume the market within the state-market binary—the post-colonial state risks falling short in terms of both sustained economic growth and social upliftment.[47] The inference is that if these two impediments are overcome, economic growth will translate into the people's well-being—albeit within an unequal wealth and income pattern but still supposedly better than the squalor in most Third World countries.

Scholars are still involved in resurrecting the developmental state model in the current age of capitalist globalism as an effective development strategy.[48] Be that as it may, by the second decade of post-World War II decolonization, Latin American states were re-examining their commitment to ISI; some states, including Brazil and Argentina, even discontinued the strategy around 1964. About the same time, many states in Asia and Africa began to embrace the inward-oriented version of ISI, which tended to give the state a dominant role in regulating foreign investments along with trade and industrial policy—a step seen by some scholars as part of the impetus of state autonomy in framing development policies.[49]

As an example of the Latin American case, Fernando Cardoso and Enzo Faletto, writing in 1971, saw their version of the developmental states first emerging in Mexico and Chile between 1910 and 1930 as a result of corporatist alliances between the bureaucracy, the emerging bourgeoisie, and the workers; in both cases, foreign investment in agriculture and industry was encouraged by the developmentalist state.[50] Despite the rhetoric of autonomy and self-reliance, Cardoso and Faletto were influenced by the economic successes of South Korea and Taiwan as well as the earlier experiences of Japan and Germany; they subsequently outlined, in their peculiarly Weberian tradition, the critical role of the bureaucracy in overseeing the success of the developmental objective.

Some of the more radical dependency theorists, including scholars such as Samir Amin, Giovanni Arrighi, Andre Gunder Frank, Raul Prebisch, Immanuel Wallerstein, and others who remained committed to the view that given the deeply imprinted legacy of colonial rule on post-colonial and Latin American states, it made more sense for these states to 'delink' or opt out of the world capitalist system and to develop their own economies along socialist lines. The ideas of dependency theorists about public ownership and state-centered development, first introduced during the 1960s and 1970s—although they may appear as an anathema in this phase of neoliberalism—were not viewed as controversial. This is because these ideas were first launched in the former colonies in the process of the anti-colonial struggles that were waged just as the influences of the 1917 Russian Revolution were being absorbed by progressive nationalists in the colonies.[51] Nationalist leaders in post-colonial states—or at least those who were able to capture power or influence others who wielded it—adopted a non-capitalist path of development (or, at the very least, a path somewhere between central planning and exclusive market dependency). As a result, many post-colonial states saw ISI strategies, formally promoted by dependency theorists, as the way out of poverty through the route of rapid industrialization. Unlike the discussion of modernization theory in the previous section, an in-depth analysis of dependency theory will not clarify how the Third World came to be re-subordinated; therefore, it lies beyond the scope of this chapter.

Once the state-led model had started to run its course, attention was focused on problems such as economic stagnation, resource limitations, bureaucratic ineptness, and corruption in post-colonial states. Coupled with these problems, the post-colonial state was facing tremendous pressure from the US and its imperialist Western allies to open its borders to Western TNCs and to orient their economies towards a greater role of the market. As a consequence of these parallel developments, the ISI model began to see its demise. Just as this dismantling of statist strategy was taking place, Western states faced the most significant post-World War II economic crisis in the mid-1970s. This crisis was compounded by the problem of stagflation, adding pressure on Western states to de-industrialize and move their costly labour-intensive operations to the Third World. This crisis also presented an opportunity for the US and its Western allies to 'tame' the Third World and pressure its leaders to accept the path of dependent capitalism. The shift was possible because most nationalist heads of these states were by this point either deposed or eliminated. This combination of circumstances led to the creation of the new IDL, which in turn led to the re-subordination of post-colonial and Latin American states. In the mad scramble to avert a catastrophic crisis of capitalism in the 1970s, Third World countries became the conduit for capitalism's resuscitation and the means for the free movement of TNCs, privatization of the public domain, open doors for FDIs, and increased mobility for metropolitan finance capital via a push for economic liberalization.

The mad scramble for economic liberalization coincided with the bourgeoisie's new-found strength and confidence in some post-colonial and Latin American states including Argentina, Brazil, Chile, India, South Korea, and Taiwan. In these states, the capitalists themselves were demanding that the statist development model be dismantled and that their governments introduce deregulation and privatization through economic liberalization. These different types of pressure, as well some of the technological and financial dependency of post-colonial societies on Western states, led to a push towards embracing the project of neoliberalism.

The shelving of the developmental state was not entirely the result of the internal contradictions of the post-colonial state. The overturning of the 'mixed economy' model or quasi-socialist tendencies of state-led development in favour of a market-oriented path of dependent capitalist development also had some very strong external compulsions. These included imperialist meddling in the affairs of post-colonial and Latin American states and societies as well as an atypical trajectory of dependent capitalist development in the periphery; the indigenous bourgeoisie, despite the protection of a dirigisme cover, looked Westward for sustenance without a serious commitment to national development goals. Chapter 1, this volume, used Fanon to exemplify how colonial and imperialist domination changed the character of the indigenous bourgeoisie, turning them into a class that was less committed to the objective of national development, and how the drive for self-interest turned them into compradors who became opportunistic self-promoters for short-term gain. This tendency underlies the specificity of a dependent and narrowly opportunistic bourgeoisie in the South. However, there is also a stronger and more resourceful indigenous bourgeoisie emerging in the current neoliberal conjuncture in China, Brazil, and India. It is too early to comment on whether this emerging bourgeoisie will follow a less-dependent path of capitalist development, but this group will have to be closely watched.

The external imperialist dimension underlying the capitalism–imperialism nexus since the 1970s, however, has played a critical role by shaping the new IDL and reinscribing dependency on the Third World. This external force has affected the post-colonial state and society, as evidenced by the impositions and interference of IMF, World Bank, and now the WTO in their domestic policies, the enormous economic influence of TNCs in the continuation of their export-based economy and the tearing down of protective tariff walls,[52] and by the enforcement of the new IDL. The combined effect of this external drag, along with the peculiar internal dimension of the post-colonial state and the subordinate character of its bourgeoisie and landed classes, meant that the paradigm of state-led development had to be dismantled and replaced by a stronger market orientation—a project that modernization theorists as well as the IMF and World Bank were meticulously cultivating since decolonization. This issue is ignored by many theorists of the state, who focus all their efforts on analyses of the developmental state itself—its internal dynamics—at the expense of analyzing the external dimension of imperialist domination that has promoted dependency and underdevelopment in post-colonial and Latin American states.

III FROM DEVELOPMENTALISM TO NEOLIBERALISM: TRACING THE PATH OF DEPENDENCY AND ECONOMIC RESTRUCTURING IN POST-COLONIAL STATES

The Business International Corporation was an influential business intelligence firm that was acquired by The Economist Group of publishers in the mid-1980s. Its 1977 report to the OECD included a warning to the world's poor as well as a very bleak economic forecast in the wake of capitalism's first major post-1945 economic crisis. This firm stressed not only that the crisis was going to challenge the very survival of Western corporations but that steps would have to be taken so that the poorest segments of the world's population would no longer have any expectations of improved living standards from future economic growth. This firm framed its concerns and objectives as follows:

> Two fundamental issues confront corporate management in the 1977, they are:
>
> > —the probability that the post-war era of unusual rapid economic expansion is over, and the probability that post-war era of unprecedented world economic and political cooperation is coming to an end.
>
> The world's departure from these patterns could force companies into the most radical and painful reassessments of their plans and strategies in living memory [. . .] Growth, translated into improved living conditions, has [. . .] become one of the basic expectations of all the world's citizens, including the poorest. These assumptions clearly must now be challenged.[53]

This excerpt highlights capitalism's serious post-World War II crisis, not unlike the more contemporary economic crisis sweeping Europe and the US, but Western capitalists and groups like the Business International Corporation were not about to become 'victims' of this economic slowdown. Instead, Western capital used a two-pronged strategy to deal with the crisis in the late 1970s. Part of the strategy involved laying the foundation for a 'new' (post-colonial) IDL, which would rapidly move unprofitable, labour-intensive operations in the West to the decolonized states of the South. The other involved attacking groups and constituencies such as labour and the poorest people worldwide to wrestle even more concessions from them, in the form of ever-lower wages through temporary or contingent work. Similarly, Western capital would rather have the very poor pay market prices for essential goods and services, thereby forcing on them the effects of price deregulation. During all these attacks, even the token relief that was once available in the form of food subsidies to the abjectly poor in post-colonial states ended. This began with IMF's conditionalities, which were entrenched in subsequent policies of structural adjustment programs (SAPs). At the same time, American and European TNCs stood to gain from the deregulated environment in post-colonial states as well as from the displacement of the rural poor to urban centres through mechanization and Green Revolution technologies. As mentioned earlier, this displacement, which swelled the ranks of the urban unemployed and underemployed masses, would result in pathetically low wages for sweatshop work in Free Trade Zones and the informal sector. Through these attacks on the poor, and other insidious changes that are discussed later, Western capitalists in Europe and North America, with the support of their respective nation-states, ensured that labour and the poor (both in their own countries and in the Third World) would no longer have any expectation of improved living standards from economic growth in the future.

In working to deny the poor any expected improvement in their living standards, the US and its Western allies decided to implement a series of drastic measures. One of the first steps was America's unilateral dismantling of the Bretton Woods-era Dollar-Gold Convertibility accord, which had enabled relatively stable currency exchange rates from 1945 to the accord's abrogation in 1971. This move wreaked havoc with stable currency values that most post-colonial and Latin American states had enjoyed ever since decolonization and resulted in currency devaluations ranging from 800% to 1,500% over a period of 10 to 25 years in African, Asian, and Latin American countries. This dramatically increased the debt of many Third World states over a very short period.[54] Further, by taking advantage of the money lender's leverage, the IMF and the World Bank implemented in the Third World the policy dictates of the US and other OECD countries through SAPs. This ranged from 'gentle' prodding to actual coercion of Third World states to remove protective tariffs, exchange control restrictions and food subsidies, among other measures, while the lending bodies pushed for market liberalization and for the privatization of the public sphere in the South. These pressures came at a time when the South was already under a huge burden of debt as a result of liberal loans granted by the World Bank in the mid-1970s under Robert McNamara, the former US Defense Secretary at the height of the Vietnam War. McNamara's move to provide loans at liberal terms to post-colonial and Latin American states was ostensibly to relieve the liquidity surplus of Euro Dollars (US dollars in European banks), which had accumulated from the windfall of the large oil price increase in 1973 by the Organization of Petroleum Exporting Countries. All this came at a time when many post-colonial states were still experimenting with state-led development through ISI. The ISI strategy, because of its state-led developmental impulse, was actively opposed by Western capitalist states that wanted to ensure privatization of the public domain and greater access to the global South for US and European TNCs. However, as discussed previously, there was also internal opposition against ISI. This stemmed from the fact that state-led development led to balance of payment difficulties due to the high cost of machinery imports and industrial raw material inputs; the state-led economy became top-heavy and mired in bureaucratic corruption and controls that largely benefitted state corporations and a small coterie of the big bourgeoisie. "It is clear that in most, if not all, Latin American countries, industrialization was carried out on too wide a spectrum, given limited capital and human resources and very narrow markets."[55] By the early 1960s, ISI strategies in Latin America had started to give way to economic liberalization, easing movement for foreign investments. Thus, Latin America preceded Asia and Africa by about two decades in dismantling ISI policies. The move towards economic liberalization also gained support as increasing numbers of pliant Third World leaders gained state power and became more willing to acquiesce to the demands of OECD states and IMF structural adjustment programs.

One reason for the Third World rulers' support for the US was an ideological commitment to the program of economic liberalization. Another was related to the new realities of an increasingly intrusive international economic order as the IMF and World Bank became 'lenders of last resort' and more post-colonial and Latin American states became dependent on these financial institutions, which were starting to acquire a supranational status. Whenever Third World states opposed imperialist interventions, a campaign of 'dirty tricks' was instituted against them.[56] At the same time, international lending institutions and a host of other bodies including the Trilateral Commission, the OECD, G-7,[57] and others played a crucial role in developing and instituting the ideologically based agenda of market reforms, deregulation, privatization, and a move towards greater use of free-trade zones. These zones became arenas where gross exploitation of Third World workers was and continues to be practiced with impunity as national laws and labour regulations remain suspended or are not enforced.

Ironically, a few years earlier in 1974, the Group of 77, which is made up of members from post-colonial and Latin American states, was able to get the United Nations to declare the need for a new economic regime for the global South. Before long, this new regime emerged under the name of the New International Economic Order (NIEO). Third World states made this move precisely to address the issues of economic injustice and the need for a fairer treatment of the South by the North. However, the rationale used by the United Nations (UN) to 'sell' the NIEO idea to the US and its allies was not primarily based on the notions of justice, equity, or fairness; rather, the UN formally acknowledged that "economic injustice was as much a threat to world security and peace as were military and political tensions and conflict."[58] Not surprisingly, the US and its allies were not buying the argument: they were unwilling to concede anything to the South and, therefore, the NIEO declaration became a non-starter.[59] One reason that Western states could take such a firm stand against the lobbying efforts of the Group of 77 was the internal dissension and internecine rivalries between Third World states. Their differences were rooted in historic inter-state/intra-regional animosities and were also in part due to conflicting allegiances to imperial powers.

By the 1980s, Western intransigence was increasingly buoyed by self-confidence among business leaders and right-wing groups and their think-tanks, who demanded immediate steps to cut deficit and trim 'big government'. The intensively orchestrated campaign of deficit cutting carried out in the North also influenced right-wing or military governments in the global South. Right-wing confidence in many Western states and the aggressive rhetoric of 'less government' and the search for 'market solutions' was having the desired effect on the electorate. Bolstered by the popularity of these ideas, the 1980s saw a dramatic ideological shift in key Western states, which led to the installation of three hard-right heads of states: Ronald Reagan in the US, Margaret Thatcher in the UK, and Helmut Kohl in West Germany. These right-wing leaders were determined to implement the neoliberal agenda in their respective countries and the rest of the world. The ideologically committed trio held power at a critical juncture of the super-power rivalry between the US and the Soviet Union, when the latter was becoming considerably weak economically. As a result of this rightward shift in Western societies, and indeed in much of the world, Western states successfully used the language of reducing 'big government' and 'waste' to eliminate or shrink social programs, whereas attacks on labour remained unabated; the implementation of tax cuts and support for corporations kept these neoliberal leaders in office. Furthermore, these ideologues held firm on the "unrepentant belief in market forces and [had] little sympathy for poorer countries to reach agreement on the need for concessions to the developing world."[60] By the time Thatcher, Reagan, and Kohl left office, right-wing ideas had been firmly planted in Western societies. With the demise of the Soviet Union in the late 1980s, the US had no rival for the title of the capitalist hegemon and the sole superpower. Therefore, it was not surprising that George Bush Sr. signalled the defeat of NIEO, by triumphantly declaring the establishment of the New Economic Order in 1991, soon after the US victory in the first Gulf War against Saddam Husain. This step marked the beginning of many Third World states' re-subordination and even the re-colonization of other weaker states.

(i) Neoliberal Economic Restructuring

The 1980s experienced a series of tumultuous developments: the collapse of the Soviet Union, the rise of the US as the sole superpower, the failure of NIEO, the elevation of the IMF and World Bank to supranational status, and the deindustrialization in the North. At the same time, the IDL changed dramatically. Client states in post-colonial and Latin American states also became more numerous, allowing the imposition of imperialist dictates that made broad and autonomous social, economic, and political upliftment more difficult in the Third World. Philip McMichael suggested that the rise of neoliberalism or the globalization project also simultaneously marked the end of the developmental project.[61] In the process, neoliberalism emerged as the new ideological outlook of triumphal capitalism. Another reading of neoliberalism sees it replacing the Keynesian-Fordist model in the first few years of the 1980s as a result of the capitalist crisis of the late 1970s.[62] In a bid to stop the declining fortunes of Western capitalists, Margaret Thatcher was the first head of a Western state to commence the implementation of neoliberalism in her country, beginning with a firm privatization and deregulation agenda. Her government simultaneously launched attacks against the working class in England, once the militant striking miners were overcome by her intransigence. The drive towards privatization and deregulation has since become a key policy of neoliberalism and has meant either the abandonment or a drastically reduced role of the public sphere. In such an environment, the freeing-up of public assets is done in the interest of private benefit, thereby creating the possibility of immense profit for capitalists and their private corporations. As a rule, "neoliberal economics does not concern itself with social policy . . . With privatization, health and education have become pieces of merchandise to be bought and sold in the marketplace."[63] User fees have been introduced for essential services such as health, education, and social welfare on the pretext that it reduces the burden on government and the public purse. However, very little is said about whether user fees may impede poorer segments of society from accessing services, and there is not any mention that user fees actually create a publicly funded welfare system for business.

When the current phenomenon was not even identified as neoliberalism, the G-77 and later the South Commission, as the Third World's representative for a more equitable economic order, was vociferously resisted by OECD states and failed to obtain a fairer economic arrangement between the North and the South. Since then, the capitalist world economy has been guided by neoliberalism with most Third World states facing more extensive subordination. Consequently, the Third World is forced to follow the dictates of the US and the G-8 states[64] through SAPs and cross conditionalities of the IMF and World Bank, which have become increasingly more onerous:

> The majority of Third World nations adopted structural adjustment programs to respond to their deepening economic problems. Policies of deregulation, desubsidization, devaluation, export drive, liberalization and tight fiscal control, in the context of poverty, political instability, corruption, declining foreign assistance and investments, appeared in the majority of cases, to have deepened the crisis of the developing countries. Beyond this, however, was the diversion of interest, aid and investments away from the developing world to Eastern Europe . . . Debt service [became] an avenue for draining the resources of the poorer countries to the developed countries especially by the IMF.[65]

Through these changes, the South has been made pliant and far more subservient than in the early years of decolonization. Following the defeat of Iraq in the first Gulf War, George Bush Sr. declared in 1991 the dawn of the New World Order, which was "the US's absolute [. . .] dominance of the world [capitalist] system."[66] It involved the ability of the US to get other states to follow its leadership, for example, in containing Iraq before the 2003 US attack, in eliminating opposition to the use (or even testing) of new hazardous depleted uranium weapons in the Gulf War,[67] in declaring which is a 'rogue' or 'terrorist' state, or even in dominating the UN. The US's declaration of the New World Order was really an assertion of its hegemony on a world scale and an affirmation of market triumphalism from the perspective of neoliberalism.[68] This domination of neoliberalism as an ideology that provides a market orientation to social and economic policy has resulted in somewhat different outcomes for the North and the South. In the North, there have been attacks on labour in the form of deskilling/casualization of work and in deep cuts to social spending, whereas financial liberalization and deregulation have created a bonanza for speculative investment and unprecedented windfall corporate profits that have accompanied concentration and monopolization within the corporate sector. However, as the more recent developments since 2008 have shown, financial deregulation has come at enormous costs to ordinary citizens in US and European states who are now facing the brunt of bailing out the big banks and insurance companies. In post-colonial and Latin American states, in contrast, the assault on the poor has proceeded full-throttle through the adoption of structural adjustment programs and a deep erosion in the living wage, which has intensified sweatshop work, especially involving women, and has led to monumental growth of the informal sector. The massive currency devaluations that have accompanied the fall in wages have skyrocketed inflation, and have resulted in severe pauperization among the poor and large sections of the middle class.

As noted, these attacks on labour and generally on the poor in the Third World were initially a response to the serious economic crisis of the 1970s, but in the ensuing restructuring of the world capitalist system they became an integral feature of neoliberal policy. Apologists of neoliberalism see these attacks quite differently; they claim the 'restructuring' was meant to 'integrate' the Third World into the capitalist world economy:

> During the 1970s, two-thirds of the world's population lived in countries that were largely outside the world economy, whether in socialist economies or in economies protected by trade barriers. At the turn of the century, this proportion is expected to drop to 10%. The opening up of China to foreign companies and capital and the collapse of the Soviet bloc have eliminated the most important obstacles to the expansion of capitalism.
>
> The integration of developing countries into the world economy has taken place as a result of political, economic and technical changes. The political decisions which allowed numerous countries to reduce their trade barriers have been accompanied by similar choices in the field of finance . . . The capacity to standardise core products while differentiating their appearance has played a decisive role in globalization. It has permitted companies to benefit from economies of scale in mass production while at the same time meeting specific market constraints

> ever more closely . . . Companies in the North have been able to *extend their profit sources by enlarging their production networks to countries of the South.* Companies in the South can enter these networks thanks to their *cost advantage* they have in terms of wages . . . Regional integration should not be confused with that of opening up. As Charles Oman points out, if globalisation is a centrifugal process, then regionalisation is in turn a centripetal one that involves the movement of two or more economies, that is, two or more societies towards greater integration with one another.[69]

These statements were made in 2000; a little more than a decade later they can be re-assessed to ascertain whether there has been meaningful integration and what has it meant for post-colonial and Latin American states. By 'regional integration', these authors mean the linking up of any G-7 (now G-8) state with another state or region of the global South. What is troubling, although not surprising, is the tone of Western 'benevolence' that underlies the necessity of integrating the South with the North. The global South is infantilized and portrayed as needing oversight and 'guidance' by developed Western capitalist states. This attitude is further exemplified by suggestions that "[d]ifferences in regional integration process . . . lie more in the role of the North as a development centre or regional leader, and the South's form of insertion; these differences also explain the context of *de jure* integration."[70] One material benefit of this integration for the North is the rise of supply chain capitalism or outsourcing as indicative of the 'continent-crossing' magnitude and inter-continental linkages between global capital and labour in the Third World, symbolizing the explosive growth of corporations such as Walmart and other box stores and the extensive reach and control of global brands such as Nike, Gap, and others.[71] Nike boasts on its website: "Nike's supply chain includes more than 660,000 contract manufacturing workers in more than 900 factories in more than 50 countries, including the United States."[72]

This 'integration' of 'two or more different economies or societies' is not between equals, and it is not self-willed by the South. Contributors to the myriad of OECD publications blatantly refer to Northern interests with an imperial arrogance concerned with how best to enlarge production interests and expand profitability for the North while ensuring that labour migration from the South remains very tightly regulated.[73] The OECD researchers cited previously, Bensidoun and Chevallier, did not appreciate the nature of dislocations and misery experienced by the people in the Third World since the commencement of the capitalist restructuring process; they simply saw North-South 'integration' as a win-win situation for both hemispheres. They were untroubled by the fact that the developed capitalist world takes advantage of the scandalously low production costs in most Third World states because these countries have been made pliant with an accompanying favourable political climate for Western capital—whereas working conditions in these countries, especially wages, almost simulate those of indentured labour.[74] One consequence of economic restructuring and the dismantling of the public sphere in post-colonial and Latin American states has been an unprecedented rise of the informal sector.[75] The International Labour Organization (ILO) estimates that the informal sector in states of Africa, Asia, and Latin America

> today [has] between half and three quarters of non-agricultural employment in the majority of these countries. The proportion of informal employment is even greater when agriculture is taken into account. Informal employment is generally a larger source of employment for women than for men. The majority of poor and extremely poor workers are found in the informal economy. Informal economy workers, and in particular women, often work in the most hazardous jobs, conditions and circumstances, and are especially vulnerable and unable to defend themselves against natural and man-made hazards and problems. The vast majority of these workers are not covered by social security schemes, occupational safety and health measures, working conditions regulations and have limited access to health services.[76]

The informal sector serves as an island of survival from dreadful poverty for extremely poor families who try to create work for themselves. In the process, these self-employed family members subject themselves in their own self-exploitation, which allows them to barely subsist in appalling living and working conditions. These conditions are at the heart of the human degradation brought about by imperialist subordination of post-colonial and Latin American states as well as from the callous disregard and utter neglect of poor and ordinary people by the ruling classes in these states. The self-exploitation of workers in these societies, because it involves exporting products of their own labour through intermediaries who serve the interests of TNCs and sources of FDIs, signifies the intensification since the late 1970s in the international valorization of labour in production processes of the Third World.

(ii) Self-Exploitation in the Informal Sector

The concept of self-exploitation was developed largely within the context of peasant economies.[77] It is relatively unexamined within a capitalist framework and much less so in relation to work in the informal sector.[78] The project of the South's subordination, as I have implied from the outset, relates to the very nature of capitalist development and the racial and gender subordination that the system has engendered. However, in the current era, for a host of reasons—including the deepening crisis of capitalist accumulation, the restructuring of the capitalist state, the falling rate of capital's valorization in the North, and the massive scale of dislocation from the phenomenal volume and mobility of both speculative and productive capital—it became necessary for the North to pressure the South even more to ensure that the expanded reproduction of capital and the rates of capital accumulation would not decline too drastically for Western capitalists. Given the various developments since decolonization in subduing post-colonial and Latin American states, it was possible for the US, as the new capitalist hegemon after World War II, to tighten its grip around the Third World state. The increased control of these states since the 1970s was intended to fulfill imperialist objectives of the American state and its European allies: to offset the internal crisis of capital accumulation by moving outwards into Africa, Asia, and Latin America and simultaneously ensuring access to cheap raw materials, fossil fuels, food, and value-added finished products. This has been possible with the privatization of the public domain, including a stranglehold on nature in the name of intellectual property/private property protection, to ensure complete mobility of capital and simultaneously to restrict the mobility of labour. At the same time, it has been made certain that Euro-American-Japanese TNCs would be free to roam the world, transfer production offshore, and export financial and industrial capital at will.

As client Third World states submitted to imperialist pressure in producing their own subordination, they also facilitated the super-exploitation of their own workers—a vast proportion of whom have now become part of the informal sector. Since the 1970s, there has been an explosive expansion in informal work, as people displaced from rural areas—because of landlessness, mechanization, and Green Revolution technologies—have had no option other than to move into urban areas and try to scrape an existence. It is the work of these urban poor, with no possibility to be absorbed in the formal economy, who are forced to become self-employed in the informal sector in which the production of surplus can be said to take the form of *self-exploitation*. This idea of self-exploitation appears to be relevant to both the capitalist and the proto-capitalist post-colonial states in which the informal sector has ballooned at an incredible pace.[79] The informal sector in much of the Third World began to emerge with the expansion of the new IDL, as labour-intensive industries in the North were dismantled and relocated in the South. Initially, American and European TNCs began to relocate only their branch plants in the South, but then they discovered the lucrative benefits of subcontracting and sweatshop work as a result of the IMF's neoliberal push that forced the South to open its borders to FDIs and to create export processing zones. This change also required the South to loosen or disregard the enforcement and/or development of labour and safety standards as well as laws to protect the environment. These factors led to the rapid expansion of casualized, flexible, and informal work in the Third World. The informal sector is made up of people who manage their own or their family's labour and organize production through home-based work, street vending, or small shops.[80] Much of this is in the form of subcontracted work that involves the poor and serves the poorest indigenous population; often the production is also for Western TNCs, but the producers have no direct relationship with these TNCs that actually realize the value of informal workers' labour. A significant portion of informal sector's production is composed of low-cost products or services for indigenous consumption, because the formal or organized sector is unable or unwilling to provide these goods and services. In effect, the informal sector serves to subsidize the formal economy.

The concept of self-exploitation in the way it has been used to understand peasant economies may help explain the nature of informal sector work under capitalism. However, the specific processes involved have not been fully articulated, nor has there been any substantive discussion about how the concept may apply in the context of sweatshop work and precarious work of the informal sector. A related issue, albeit a tangential one, has to do with how the concept may apply in the period of capitalist globalism. In the context of dislocation under capitalism, critical Marxist scholarship examines 'development' (the global South's 'underdevelopment') as a paradigm that produces dislocation.[81] Nonetheless, there is still no consensus about whether self-exploitation, as a mode of exploitation and displacement, is part of the present capitalist mode of production. Therefore, the concept needs careful scrutiny before any claims can definitively be made about its usefulness in explaining the nature of exploitation in the informal sector and its relationship to the world capitalist system.

Given these caveats, Chavanov, whose work Thorner has translated, argues in the context of the appropriation of the surplus from peasantry's labour, that self-exploitation occurs under the conditions of: (i) a substantive increase in the peasant family's labour input in terms of time (more hours of necessary labour time), (ii) an unusual rise in the intensity of work, and (iii) the simultaneous increase in number of hours of labour and its intensity.[82] Of these, the condition outlined in (iii)—the simultaneous increase in the necessary labour time and in the intensity of work—appears to fit the description of informal sector operations and the condition of work for the self-employed IS workers. As for the issue of self-exploitation, the extent or nature of exploitation is one part of the puzzle. The other is to ascertain who organizes production, appropriates the surplus from informal sector's work of the self-employed, and benefits from it. In relation to the informal sector, it is the household which, in managing its own labour, produces a surplus that is appropriated by some other level of organization without *directly* organizing this exploitation itself.[83] In other words, although the family in the IS organizes production to meet the sub-contractor's production requirement, the surplus created from producing the contracted goods is not substantively appropriated by the sub-contractor alone. Rather, it is either the formal sector company or the Western TNC, which awarded the contract, that ends up becoming the real appropriator of this surplus.

The people working in the informal sector, whether they are concerned with the home or the export market, often work for subcontractors. Contract work may be done in informal workshops or at home; people who manage their own labour and/or the labour of others in their operations produce goods whose value is realized substantively at another level of organization. This different level, where the value is realized, could be a local contractor who supplies the goods to the local market at reasonable gain. However, where TNCs are involved in working with subcontractors, the former attain substantial surplus from the product of subcontracted IS workers' labour, whereas the indigenous subcontractor who exports the goods from the IS also benefits. Consequently, the individually organized units in the informal sector see the appropriation of their potential surplus by different levels, both local and international, which are not involved in *directly* organizing surplus appropriation at the point of production. Thus, this mode of exploitation (increased intensity of work and longer hours of necessary labour time) when linked with how surplus appropriation is removed from the point of production in the informal sector, to another level(s), arguably constitutes the *self-exploitation* of people who manage their own labour, organize the labour of others, and produce a substantial surplus, but see it appropriated by others (such as TNCs) with whom the IS producers may not even have any contact.

Having offered preliminary thoughts about the notion of self-exploitation, I also recognize that the lengthening of the work day and the rise in the intensity of work also takes place under *formal* capitalist enterprises. However, the difference, as it relates to the IS, is that the extended/intensified work day is the everyday and sector-wise norm and pattern for self-employed work in the IS. It should be noted that informal sector units in the South largely involve women, many of whom even manage their unit's production, displacing their male family members in some instances.[84] This social change has had an impact in altering gender dynamics in the family, but it does not mean that women's oppression and social control through patriarchal domination is altered to any significant degree. On the contrary, "the forces of transnational capitalism simultaneously maintain and subvert the existing social structures; they uphold patriarchal constraints on women's mobility and change the gender dynamics in the family."[85] Thus, the beneficiaries of this *indirect* form of surplus appropriation, through a gendered exploitative system, are American/European/Japanese TNCs, their local agents in the Third World, and the indigenous capitalists. This extractive undertaking in the informal sector, facilitated largely by the current IDL, also implicates the post-colonial state, which either does not adopt appropriate laws or ignores existing laws that are intended to protect its workers.

A similar process of super-exploitation is underway in the South's agricultural sector; its impact, in effect, is also a form of re-colonization. Because informal work extends into the agricultural sector, the extremely low price of farm commodities helps facilitate the strangulating grip on the South. The high level of productivity in the North, along with large subsidies given by the US, Canadian, and European governments to their farmers, enable these farmers to sell their goods at very low prices in the international market. These low prices force Third World farmers to sell their produce at prices that really do not allow them to subsist even at the barest level of existence. This fact, coupled with the oligarchic control of the agricultural commodities market by a handful of US and European companies (including Cargill, Archer Daniels Midland, Dole and Chiquita, Nestle, and Monsanto, among others), places an imperialist chokehold on Third World farmers. Given the reality of rising Western agricultural productivity and the historically falling commodity prices, it is not difficult to surmise that if the prices of Third World agricultural produce do not reflect the quantum of labour required to produce them, farmers in the South will "never be able to accumulate enough capital to make their own agriculture more productive."[86]

IV CEMENTING THE DIVISION OF THE WORLD: CREATION OF THE 'NEW' IDL

The restructuring of the world capitalist system since the 1970s has resulted in two things: the establishment of the hegemony of imperial capital led by the US and the foundation of a 'new' (post-World War II/post-colonial) IDL that was laid as US-European TNCs began to move their low tech, labour intensive operations to the South. The latter is of particular importance, because the 'new' IDL really laid the groundwork for the movement of FDIs and later for the unfettered global mobility of financial capital. Henry Veltmeyer and Henk Overbeek have both provided cogent analyses of how capitalist restructuring affected the South and the rest of the world. They placed slightly different emphases on the consequences of the capitalist restructuring since the late1970s (which has been either understated or misidentified as 'globalization' by other theorists), but they agree that the emergence of the IDL in the late 1970s was a way to deflect the capitalist crisis from the developed North to the South. Veltmeyer maintained that since the 1980s, the restructuring of economies and societies across the world has been driven

> under conditions of deeply rooted systemic crisis—stagnant or slow growth of society's productive forces, high rate of structural employment and diverse forms of underemployment, low income and impoverishment. And while the OECD countries have successfully deflected the crisis to other world areas, such as the NICs [newly industrialized countries] and [other Third World states], the conditions of crisis remain evident. In fact, they represent 'transnational' social costs

> of adjustments on the backs (and in the families and households) of world's workers and direct producers. They also form the new global structure that reproduces these social costs [. . .] through the relocation of labour intensive and costly operations towards a major change in the international division of labour and the formation of the global industrial production system.[87]

In contrast, Overbeek's outlook resembled that of Fröbel et al., who in the 1970s were the first to offer an explanation of the then still-unfolding phenomenon of the 'new' IDL:

> The dramatic acceleration in the internationalization process followed the deep global recession of the mid-1970s. The response to the crisis on the part of Western capital was to intensify its outward orientation, which resulted in what was described as the New International Division of Labour: "a single world market for labour power, a true world-wide industrial reserve army, and a single world market for production sites" (Fröbel et al. 1980: 30).[88]

Both Veltmeyer and Overbeek argued that since the 1970s, the deflection of the crisis to the South and the ensuing restructuring of the world capitalist system have really shaped the IDL. This division of labour has been central to American and imperial capital's world dominance. The concept of IDL can be traced back to the period of colonialism; division of labour between the colonies and the metropole started to take shape when the colonies mainly extracted raw materials and the colonizers exported them to the metropole for processing and sold the value-added product to the world as well as the colonies. This relatively simple colonial division of labour persisted even after about two decades of decolonization. When the 'new' IDL was created in the late 1970s, this division of labour was correctly understood not as a clear division between the North and the South but as an ongoing process—one that would bring about "the increasing worldwide subdivision of the production process into separate partial processes."[89] The just-in-time production and supply chain capitalism of today really epitomizes the culmination of these separate partial processes, which have become far more numerous since the 1970s. Furthermore, today much of the worldwide subdivision of production has been perfected in the division between work done in the South (generally labour-intensive and of lower technological value) and work done in the North (generally high technology research/design, development, and some production). Another development related to the current IDL has to do with production in relatively more industrially developed Third World states such as China, Brazil, India, South Korea, Taiwan, and others that manufacture or assemble high technology products or take on many of the partial processes of high technology production that were once the exclusive domain of factories in the North.

Further, manufacturing of a finished product has been now increasingly subdivided into production fragments by most corporations, and these companies contract out much of this work to a string of contractors that are part of the supply chain.[90] In many cases, TNCs may contract out the entire manufacturing or assembly process and the contractor may be required to use its own manufacturing facilities or hire contract labour to produce the goods. Depending on what is being produced, contract production of fragments or parts could be given exclusively to the South, done in the North, or even be divided between the two hemispheres. By employing just-in-time manufacturing methods, the production facility becomes merely an assembly operation where parts are sourced and put together into a finished product. Just-in-time purchases now account for almost half of all purchases in textiles, "compared with one quarter in 1987; order cycles in the US electrical and electronics industry have been reduced from about five months in 1980, to seven weeks in 1990, and only about two weeks today."[91] This tight timing of inventories and availability of parts for same-day production has undoubtedly introduced some level of 'interdependence' between manufacturers in the South and buyers/manufacturers in the North. However, when globalization theorists discuss the idea of 'vanishing borders' and 'interdependence', they fail to acknowledge that this interdependence is on the most unequal terms. The disparity appears most obviously in terms of the wages paid to producers in the South and in the very low price for piece goods that is offered to Southern factory owners—not to mention the poor working conditions and a host of other social inequities.

When much of the dreary, labour-intensive manufacturing began shifting to the Third World in the 1970s, some researchers suggested that the IDL was shaping worldwide capitalist production. Fröbel et al. argued that the 'new' IDL was the imperialist states' response to the recurring crisis of capitalism that had followed the post-War II boom.[92] This kind of argument, although similar to Veltmeyer and Overbeek, is still very much a minority position in the extensive literature about globalization and transnationalization. However, it appears to provide the best analysis of the phenomenon of globalization, as well as the nature of the restructured world capitalist system and its impact on the South.

During the 1970s, TNCs expanded in an effort to ensure the survival of corporations and capitalism. At the time, FDIs (primarily from the US and Europe) had started to move South to set up textile, garment, footwear, and synthetic fibre plants. This began as these industries in the US and England were experiencing declining outputs, mass redundancies, and over-capacities because of increased competition from Japan and the so-called newly industrialized countries.[93] Investment from the North to selected areas of the South was not for the simple purpose of 'industrial relocation'; it was prompted by mounting challenges to the valorization and accumulation increasingly faced by Western capital.[94] In addition, the fear of social upheavals loomed large in the North: "if it became clear that the recession was not [just] a temporary crisis, but might mean the end of the whole epoch of the capitalist world economy."[95]

Thus, the relocation of plants to the Third World really spawned the new IDL since the late 1970s; this move produced two simultaneous developments. First, the movement of labour-intensive industries from the North to the South resulted in the de-industrialization of some sectors of the North: plants and manufacturing facilities were closed, particularly in the US and England. This selective de-industrialization in turn increased the pressure on the working class in the North and contributed to the phenomenon of deskilling of work.[96] These changes in the North came about as more and more workers lost not only their jobs but also their acquired profession.[97] To add insult to injury, these displaced but skilled workers had to sell their labour power as unskilled and semi-skilled workers at considerably lower wages, in tougher working conditions, and mostly without the protection of a unionized environment. In addition, because the US had to modernize its aging plants to compete with the newer and technologically advanced manufacturing facilities of Japan and Germany, newer American plants had a 'downsized' workforce.

It should be pointed out that the new IDL would not have become a reality had there not been an abundance of displaced rural migrants that began to move to urban areas of the South since the late 1960s. These rural migrants swelled the ranks of the reserve army of labour by the very fact of their displacement, which was the result of uneven technological and social changes in the agricultural sector during the so-called Green Revolution of the mid-1960s. The Green Revolution was a method employed by the US to push its International Rice Research Institute's seed development program in many states of Asia and Latin America (just as Monsanto now forces Western and non-Western farmers to use its terminator seeds). The Green Revolution forced peasants and small farmers to migrate to urban centres in search of a livelihood.[98] Compelled by proletarianization, these displaced people settled in the already choked cities of the South, eking out a living by creating slum dwellings that have become a permanent feature of the South's landscape.[99] These new urban slum dwellers (the new proletariat and in some cases semi-proletariat) became a critical element in the creation of the new IDL. Their displacement presented an 'opportunity' for self-exploitation, which was capitalized by Western and indigenous capitalists.

Even before the critical element of the new IDL (labour, and especially women's labour) was in place, the idea of the *maquila* factory or export processing zones were already taking advantage of displaced peasants from the rural areas. The export processing zones were the forerunners to the *maquiladoras* or the free trade zones as we know them today and were central to the establishment of the new IDL. The idea of an export-based economy was a prominent feature of colonialism;[100] in the post-colonial setting, Western capital has forced this self-serving objective with such determination on post-colonial and Latin American states that most Third

World states have abandoned the idea of developing an internal market for indigenous production. Instead, the bulk of production in most post-colonial states is destined for export. The IMF and the World Bank have consistently pressured Third World states with the goal of orienting their economies for export production. The TNCs with their *maquila* factories have only reinforced this pattern of export-oriented industrial production in the South.

Given the emphasis on production for export, it appears that imperial capital has perfected and expanded the idea of the *maquila* factory. The *maquiladora* has taken on new meaning in terms of the range and quality of products that are manufactured.[101] The sheer volume of production has exponentially increased since the 1970s, and because many of the *maquila* factories are just branch plants, their entire production is conveniently exported back to the principals in the core countries. However, the super-exploitative conditions of work in the South have worsened due to rampant poverty and the massive reserve army of labour. The wages of workers in *maquila* factories, whether they are in Mexico, Honduras, Indonesia, or the Philippines, are shockingly low. Many of the workers in these factories are women, stuck in extremely poor working conditions without the protection of a unionized environment. Even where unions exist, labour laws are often not enforced. ILO data point to an overwhelming presence of women workers in the informal sector.[102]

Parenthetically, it should be mentioned that the present division of labour has actually produced a 'duality' or segmentation of labour within the existing IDL: although the labour of so-called dynamic sectors of the information and communications economy is valued, the work of labour-intensive industries is downgraded.[103] This divide mimics the inferiorized position of Southern workers and the correspondingly superior status of labour in the Northern hemisphere. This segmentation also exists in Western countries, between new immigrant labour from the Third World and European immigrant labour or the local-born working class.[104] Ironically, the primary goal of the present IDL, as pointed out at the beginning of this section, was to alleviate the serious systemic crisis of the late 1970s (the simultaneous stagnation of growth and the inflation), but the 'benefits' of the IDL, through a deepened North-South divide and the re-subordination of the South, have been beyond the wildest dreams of Northern capitalists. The new IDL has created obscene wealth, mainly in the North, although wealthy capitalists in China, India, Brazil, and South Korea are trying to catch up with their rich Western counterparts. This enormous wealth creation has largely come about through speculative investments or by the increased valorization of Third World labour (primarily women), which has yielded super surpluses for the North.

However, by relocating labour-intensive production from the North to the South, and driving down wages by massively increasing sweat-shop production, North American and Western European states have also simultaneously introduced stringent measures to curb immigration of those who desperately want to escape the poverty and misery of the global South. Of those wishing to escape, a very limited number of highly skilled migrants from the South are very selectively allowed to enter the North as doctors, engineers and other professionals. However, the extractive impulse of North American and European states is to ensure that the wages of these migrants remain abysmally low. This is done by first strictly regulating the entry of highly skilled immigrants, and then not recognizing their professional skills and qualifications or, in some cases, regulating the entry of a small fraction of migrant professionals to practice their skills through a tightly controlled accreditation process. As a result vast numbers of migrant professionals are forced to work at very low wages, which has a dampening effect on native-born workers to restrict their demands for wage increases. Also, because temporary or contingent work has become the norm in most industries and the service sector (which again employs a high proportion of immigrants), this leverage of contingent work is used to restructure workplaces in various ways: by contracting out work, busting unions, or pressuring employees to accept employer's conditions of work at lower wages. Consequently, the presence of new immigrant labour in the North serves two particularly important functions for Western capital. First, it offsets the 'graying' of the Northern working class.[105] Second, the lower wage given to new immigrant labour (compared to their European or local-born counterparts) brings 'wage stability' for Western capitalists and even helps lower the threshold of real wages for all workers in the North.

With the primary element in the creation of the new IDL—cheap and unorganized labour—in place, the US and its allies were able to work on other changes to bring the new division of labour to fruition. One important change was the removal of 'protective walls' of high import tariffs around most Third World states. The TNCs involved in shaping the new IDL had to find ways to circumvent these protectionist measures, and they were able to do so with the determined support from their respective nation-states. In re-imposing the capitalism–imperialism nexus, the US State Department, the OECD, the IMF, the World Bank, and the General Agreement on Tariff and Trade (GATT) body (the forerunner to the WTO) provided the necessary arm-twisting and laid fertile ground for the new pliancy and subserviency of the South. When the South had built these protective walls in the 1960s, they were good ways to introduce tariff controls and exchange control restrictions, which were designed to nurture and protect the infant indigenous industries from foreign predators and cheap imports—to actually fend-off the impact of the capitalism–imperialism nexus. However, as a consequence of the 1970s economic crisis and the Third World's mounting debt burden, bureaucratic ineptitude, and corruption, the South eventually succumbed to pressure from Western states. These imperialist pressures, including prodding from GATT for tariff harmonization, the refusal of the US and its Western allies to implement the Group of 77's NIEO recommendation or to transfer technology, and instead impose the structural adjustment programs of IMF/World Bank in relation to loan disbursements were ultimately effective in bringing the South to its knees.

A critical point in the structural shift towards re-subordination and the reinscribed capitalism–imperialism nexus came at the end of GATT's 1995 Uruguay Round. Originally, GATT was concerned with liberalizing trade and harmonizing tariffs on commerce and industrial production. The Uruguay Round, however, added several 'new issues' to the liberalization/deregulation agenda: banking and insurance, investment measures, and agriculture.[106] These additions transformed GATT "from a contract among members to a full-fledged organ [of imperialist domination], giving birth to the WTO."[107] The Uruguay Round negotiations were complicated; most Third World countries did not know what they had signed, and were generally unaware of what was to come in the form of the WTO. The 'new issues' of the Uruguay Round were designed to strengthen the neoliberal changes that had originally been introduced by the IMF, the World Bank, or the OECD. They were meant to reduce, if not eliminate, the sovereignty of Third World states in social, economic, and political realms while simultaneously forcing open their borders and markets for transnational capital. "The WTO is a forum for trade rights of capital, on terms negotiated by the agencies of governments that represent the interests of capital. No other rights count."[108]

More than three decades ago, Fröbel et al. outlined three main conditions that enable the continued reproduction of monopoly capital on a world scale: (a) "[the] existence of a world-wide industrial reserve army, (b) the possibility of far-reaching subdivision of the production process into fragments, and (c) an efficient transport and communications technology."[109] These three conditions are not only applicable in the current neoliberal age; they have been perfected in the present IDL, and the reserve army worldwide is now at capital's beck and call. What began in the late 1970s as a new IDL has resulted in the perfection of a worldwide network of *maquila* production and a sophisticated system of production fragments in the so-called newly industrialized countries, and all the while more resources have been pumped into the production enclaves of Western Europe, North America, and Japan. In the process, the North-South divide has most oppressively undermined the South and has truly become a 'colour line', whereas the labour of women in the Third World has reached levels of super-exploitation and self-exploitation in the informal sector, as the capitalism–imperialism nexus has become deeply entrenched in North-South relations.

The historical and analytical themes discussed in this chapter and the preceding one meant to clarify the reimposed subordination of the Third World by imperialist states, metropolitan capital, and supranational financial institutions. The complicity of the ruling classes and the civil and military bureaucratic elite in post-colonial societies also must not be minimized:

their complicit actions shaped clientelism, dependency, and submission to imperialist demands, just as the post-colonial state, in control of these ruling classes, paved the way for its society's re-subordination. This reality is despite the promise of 'independence' made to the former colonies at the time of decolonization. This chapter has explored why and how this promise of Third World states' sovereignty has remained unfulfilled; the objective was to show that a rigorous analysis of the post-colonial state and society provides a more complete picture of how the current state of capitalist globalism has re-imposed the South's subordination—in contrast with the tendency to focus separately on the developmental state or the neoliberal state.

I have not addressed the consequences of neoliberalism for the US and other Western states—which are enormous given the severe current economic crisis, high unemployment, depressed wages and bank bailouts—as it is outside the purview of this study. These states, as is now apparent, have not been unscathed by the global South re-subordination. However, it should be said that the 'euphoric prospectus' of rising prosperity depicted by official propagandists of neoliberalism in the 1980s and 1990s showed a very different economic reality in the "transition from the twentieth to the twenty-first century," which Harry Shutt has outlined in his illuminating small book: the Western world now symbolizes the "grotesque disparities between rich and poor," the "[d]eepening economic stagnation," and the growing economic insecurity for 30% or more of the population of the richest countries, relegating them to a "seemingly permanent 'underclass'," whereas the rise of the 'bubble economy' has been unprecedented since the savings and loan scandal of the 1980s.[110]

In conclusion, it is worth noting that just as most, if not all, post-colonial states are firmly ensconced in implementing neoliberal policies, many Latin American states are starting to reject their earlier plunge into economic liberalization. Active opposition to neoliberalism is now appearing in Bolivia, Ecuador, and Venezuela, with somewhat less vocal opposition in Brazil and other Latin American states and Indigenous communities. Whether this movement to resist neoliberal globalization will be contagious and affect post-colonial states as well is yet to be determined—although recent rebellions in Egypt, Tunisia, and elsewhere may be signs of the change in the making.

3 Theoretical Understanding of the Post-Colonial State

A major theme in this book is the deep imprint left by the colonial state on post-colonial states and societies. The post-colonial state form includes both continuity with, and distinction from, the colonial state form, but the former can only be fully understood once the latter is analysed and distinguished. This approach can help clarify the post-colonial state's dependent relationship with Western states and show how indigenous ruling classes and the civil and military bureaucratic elite continue to rely on the colonial state's structure and its instruments of control—complete with colonial-era civil, criminal, and penal codes and property laws—to dominate and control post-colonial societies. The term 'post-colonial' and the period to which it refers also signals the beginning of another era of quasi-sovereignty, dependence, and subordination of the post-colonial state after decolonization. This subordination, as discussed in Chapter 2, this volume, is bound within the capitalism–imperialism nexus. Hamza Alavi first coined the term, post-colonial state, in 1972 when intervening in the Miliband-Poulantzas debate, with the goal of distinguishing between the post-colonial state and the Western capitalist state.[1] Alavi's analysis revealed that to fully examine the relative autonomy of the state requires a close investigation of the post-colonial state. The colonial era's 'overdeveloped' bureaucratic state structure has been re-incorporated by indigenous ruling classes in the post-colonial state, thereby allowing civil and military bureaucratic elites to dominate both state and society—enabling them to mediate the interests of propertied classes and to also privilege imperialist interests over the welfare of their people—in a word achieve *autonomy* over the competing class and group interests. Alavi's analysis has not received the recognition that it warrants: he offers insights not only about the state but also about colonial social formation in South Asia; the development of capitalism, nationalism, and ethnicity; and other topics. I have built on Alavi's work but move beyond it in my reconception of post-colonial states. However, inexplicably Alavi's work never really engaged the scholars of South Asia. Instead, it was African theorists, including Issa Shivji, and Africanists, such as John Saul, who worked to refute or refine his arguments.[2]

The work on the post-colonial state that began in the early 1970s was soon abandoned in favour of projects like the developmental state, dependency, and unequal exchange—coincidentally this was around the same time that strategies of import substitution industrialization and autarky were being discarded in Latin America (in favour of a greater market orientation and privatization of the public domain), whereas in a number of post-colonial societies the import substitution industrialization strategy was still followed. More recently (as discussed in this volume's introduction), the term 'postcolonial state' (without the hyphen) has been revived by some anthropologists who have undertaken ethnographical studies of this state form. Many of these ethnographers recognize the importance of clarifying the legacy of the colonial state and the problems associated with an uncritical embrace of the notions of modernity and the nation-state by the former colonized elites, but they have not delved deeper into issues, such as the nature of the state, the imprint of external domination, the balance of class forces and the state, or the ongoing impact of the colonial legacy and the contemporary imperialist stranglehold on the post-colonial state itself. As a result, ethnographical studies have tended to focus on issues that are symptomatic of poststructuralist concerns and the preoccupation with assertions of micro power and resistance. Thus, larger structural issues about the post-colonial state itself and its subordination to the demands of the Western state and/or imperialism remain under-theorized—a gap which I address in this and other chapters of this volume.

It is important to note that since Alavi's original contribution, his work has influenced scholars to identify a variety of other forms of post-colonial and Latin American states: developmental, patrimonial, prebendal (tributary state), overdeveloped, bureaucratic, rent-seeking, and so forth. These are largely different sub-forms of the proto-capitalist post-colonial state (discussed later)[3] and can distract researchers who are trying to comprehend the character of the state in post-colonial societies. I will avoid negotiating this maze or address the range of these different sub-forms. Rather, my focus broadly will be on the post-colonial state as such. I will begin at a point prior to this state form's emergence—the entry point being the period of colonial rule—and end up with a theoretical understanding of two broad forms of post-colonial states: the capitalist and proto-capitalist variants.

As it is important to assess how the colonial state shaped the structure of the post-colonial state, Alavi's polemical piece on peripheral capitalism[4] is a good beginning; his analysis of the Indian colonial periphery offers a good opening to offer a counter-analysis of concrete social relations within colonial India. I support some of Alavi's exegesis of colonialism in India but also disagree with his analysis of the nature of the colonial state and peripheral capitalism. A critical assessment of his claims, therefore, will enable me to compare Alavi's ideas about how peripheral capitalism affected colonial Indian society with my own position, which is supported by the findings of various social scientists who have examined the impact of British colonialism on India. My conclusions about the nature of society and state differ considerably from those of Alavi with regard to both the nature of colonial Indian society and, more generally, other post-colonial societies. When addressing the colonial state form and engaging with Alavi's work to assess the nature of social relations in the colony, I also examine the configuration of class forces and the role of external domination and its legacy on post-colonial state and society. Once I move beyond the colonial era, I begin to address the factors that have shaped the post-colonial state since decolonization: specifically its internal unitary state structure and its 'overdeveloped' character, as exemplified by civil and military bureaucratic domination. Classes and groups that hold state power also affect the internal structure of the post-colonial state and society, as does the powerful external political and economic pressure from imperialist states. The latter sections of this chapter, however, clarify the various complexities of the post-colonial state. I will also question Alavi's validity of assigning the specificity of the post-colonial state designation for most states in the Third World, without distinguishing post-colonial African and Asian states from Latin American states. I will then discuss some the critical aspects related to the character of the post-colonial state: the nature and role of bureaucracy, the analysis of propertied classes and their role in post-colonial state and society, and the impact of the colonial legacy of separateness and apartness, mentioned in previous chapters of this volume. A brief discussion will follow on the post-colonial state's relative autonomy and the auxiliary class character of the bureaucratic elite. The chapter's final section offers a theoretical understanding of two variants of the post-colonial state: proto-capitalist and capitalist versions. In postulating these two variants, the originality of my contribution is that, in the exercise of power in post-colonial societies, the primacy of proto-capitalist states is not on the economic; rather it is on the political and extra-economic means—whereas, for capitalist post-colonial states, the formal separation of the political and the economic does not constitute an actual separation.

I 'PERIPHERAL CAPITALISM' AND THE ENIGMA OF THE POST-COLONIAL STATE

Most post-colonial states are not developed capitalist entities. At best, most are *proto-capitalist states,* but there are exceptions: some countries in the global South may be considered capitalist states, such as Argentina, Brazil, China, India, Malaysia, South Africa, South Korea, Taiwan, Turkey, and possibly Chile and Thailand, based on the mode of production and the class that together are dominant in society. These capitalist post-colonial and Latin American states are not the classical periphery of the world capitalist system (WCS)—China is currently the second-largest economy worldwide and has hegemonic aspirations—but it would be premature to posit a post-imperialist era in relation to these states. However, given the dominant proto-capitalist character of most post-colonial states, analysts are faced with an apparent contradiction: proto-capitalist states are part of the WCS as the periphery, but they do not have a dominant capitalist class or feature internal social relations that are predominantly capitalist. Instead, feudal and capitalist relations often *coexist* in these states and *not just remnants of a bygone era*, which is the enigma of post-colonial state and society. In Europe, feudal and capitalist relationships never really coexisted because of their mutual antagonisms, although some remnants of feudal relationships continued during capitalism's nascent stage and dissolved as capitalism matured and capitalist culture became hegemonic—although many feudal cultural remnants still survive in Europe. In contrast, potentially antagonistic relations of production have coexisted in colonial, post-colonial, and Latin American states but have not generated serious antagonism or irresolvable contradictions between feudal and emerging capitalist elites. This enigma needs to be resolved and, in doing so, it is also my goal to move away from the universalizing of European experience to post-colonial societies because state theory is already rife with Eurocentrism. The enigmatic nature of post-colonial states will be addressed through the analysis of the nature of colonial and post-colonial states in this and the next section, but the following subsection begins with a discussion of Alavi's idea of peripheral capitalism and how he perceived the character of the colonial state.

(i) Alavi's Notion of Peripheral Capitalism

Alavi concisely presented his ideas about peripheral capitalism and his claim that post-colonial societies are capitalist in his article "The Structure of Peripheral Capitalism."[5] The article was first published almost three decades ago, but its implications are still relevant in the present era of 'free-market' capitalism or capitalist globalization. Alavi began with a critical appraisal of influential ideas in the late 1970s (many of which are still being debated): various theories about the nature of capitalist relations in the colonies and their relevance to 'modernization' and 'underdevelopment' as suitable diagnostic frameworks for post-colonial state and society. Alavi correctly dismissed the Orientalist views of his contemporaries (including Bill Warren) who championed the ill-informed ideas put forth in some of Marx's writings on India, in which Marx expressed his (in)famously cited notion of the 'double mission' of English colonial rulers, "one destructive and the other regenerating—the annihilation of the old Asiatic society, and the laying of the material foundations of Western society *in* Asia."[6] This justification of colonialism as the bearer of new social forces—"setting in motion the dynamics (and contradictions) of capital accumulation and development in the colony," as Alavi argued—had come to inform "the theory and practice of 'modernization' and 'developmentalism'."[7]

Alavi was also critical of Andre Gunder Frank and Immanuel Wallerstein, who presented similar and influential lines of inquiry with their respective theories of 'underdevelopment' and the 'world system'. According to Alavi, Frank and Wallerstein were not as concerned with social relations of production as their arguments addressed relations of exchange:

> Underdevelopment theory and Wallerstein's conception of the modern world system are grounded on a conception of capitalism in terms of trade and exchange rather than on social relations of production. The incorporation of society within the network of world trade is a sufficient condition for its designation as capitalist [. . .] besides, for Wallerstein, it is states, not classes, that are the essential units of his analysis, despite his disclaimers to the contrary. The argument tells us little about the origins and the *structural* and *class character* and consequences of capitalism and, specifically, peripheral capitalism.[8]

Alavi's argument focused on the 'structural specificity of colonial capitalism', which had a profound effect on pre-capitalist modes of production, moving them decisively towards peripheral capitalism and away from metropolitan capitalism. Alavi distinguished between peripheral and metropolitan capitalism by contrasting them with the feudal mode of production (see Table 1). The metropolitan bourgeoisie and imperial-capitalist domination have had a significant impact, leading to the dissolution of pre-capitalist modes, and relations, of production. Alavi argued that even where pre-capitalist social formations appear to have survived, the force of colonial capitalism not only produced indigenous capitalists but it also caused pre-capitalist modes to lose their character as they are subordinated by capitalism:[9]

> by an analysis of the modes of production and their contradictions we can understand the patterns of class formation and class alignment, and the class struggles that ensue as a consequence [. . . the focus needs to be] on the internal structures of pre-capitalist social formations in colonized societies that are incorporated within the domain of colonial capital, and the apparently *symbiotic* relationship between the two, as against the antagonistic contradiction between them, which has been advocated in classical Marxism.[10]

This symbiosis between pre-capitalist social formation and metropolitan capital was similar to some of the ideas suggested by Habib; he argued that 'primitive' (a historically poor translation of Marx's term, *ursprunglich*), previous, or primary accumulation actually aids the development of capitalism: "primitive accumulation continued to be an important means of transforming wealth gained from the non-capitalist world into capital simultaneously with the expansion of capitalist accumulation proper."[11] However, Habib's conclusions about the fate of the colony (colonial India, in this instance) differed from Alavi's conclusions about peripheral capitalism. Habib argued that in colonial India, capitalist production "essentially enlarged two pre-capitalist forms of accumulation, rent extraction and usury."[12] For classical Marxists, Alavi's observations are correct, but he did not point out the Eurocentrism in their views on colonial capitalism.

Classical Marxists correctly viewed the emergence of capitalist relations in Europe as an antagonistic process beginning in the conflict between the emerging European bourgeoisie and the feudal relations of production, eventually resulting in capitalists taking control of and overcoming the feudal hold on state and society. However, they were absolutely wrong in extending this view to the non-European world. Their classical perspective was rooted in examples provided by England and other European states, where feudalism, and later Absolutism, were violently and forcefully overthrown by an ascendant bourgeoisie. Classical Marxists generalized this trajectory of modern Euro-American state formation—an outcome of the struggle between the rising European bourgeoisie and the old feudal classes—as a universal feature of epochal transformation from feudalism to capitalism, even for the non-European world.

In contrast, Alavi, in his earlier, seminal piece on the post-colonial state,[13] accurately identified the social force responsible for the emergence of the post-colonial state. He showed that this state form's emergence was not the result of anything resembling a struggle between feudal and capitalist elites of Europe; rather, the post-colonial state was formed *by the colonial power*, and the two classes collaborate and coexist within the state's bureaucratic apparatus.[14] He also made an important observation about the *non-antagonistic* relationship between the feudal and indigenous capitalists within the colonial state, despite their differing economic interests, because the two classes did not need to struggle over the formation and control of the state as a ready-made colonial state structure was *made available* to both of them. To add to Alavi's earlier prescient analysis, it can be said that the potentially antagonistic interests of the two classes have since been mediated by the post-colonial bureaucratic elite within the colonial state structure, which has enabled the bureaucratic elite to share state power largely with feudal lords (and capitalists in a few cases)—in effect, actually making most post-colonial states as extensions of the colonial state.

This important distinction between state formation in Europe versus those in Africa/Asia and Latin America generates many questions about Alavi's subsequent hypothesis concerning peripheral capitalism. Some are related to the conception of the post-colonial state: do most post-colonial states have an ascendant indigenous capitalist class? Can indigenous capitalists assert their class interests within and through the post-colonial state independently of the metropolitan bourgeoisie? Are pre-capitalist social forces relatively too weak to compete with the indigenous capitalist bourgeoisie in social and economic life? Have capitalist relations sufficiently permeated post-colonial societies to qualify for the 'capitalist' designation, which Alavi has subsequently given to post-colonial states and societies?

These questions will be addressed in analyzing the nature of post-colonial states, but first it is important to clarify Alavi's position on *peripheral capitalism*. Alavi defined peripheral capitalism as a process whereby the colonial periphery is linked to the metropolis to complete the circuit of generalized commodity production. Consequently, "three classes [within colonial society] are located in a single structure of peripheral capitalism, which admits their competing interests without a structural contradiction between them."[15] Alavi identified these three classes as the indigenous bourgeoisie, the metropolitan bourgeoisie, and capitalist landowners.[16] He argued that these three classes would normally be considered fractions of a single class—"analogous to the division of the bourgeoisie in advanced capitalist countries"—but not in peripheral capitalist societies.[17] In a peripheral capitalist society, each of these groups constitutes a whole class because their roles are mutually exclusive rather than complementary. Therefore, they do not together form a single ruling capitalist class, as has been the case in Western capitalist societies; indeed, none of these classes can be unambiguously designated as the ruling class.[18] By stressing the importance of the three classes in the periphery, Alavi argued that, although pre-capitalist structures survive the colonization process, most indigenous ruling strata are transformed either into comprador or industrial/'national' bourgeoisie, or landowning capitalists in the agricultural sector. In essence, he claimed that this social transformation dissolves the extra-economic coercion of the dispossessed producer in the periphery; but this position is contentious and has not been supported by much evidence.

The pivotal point of Alavi's argument is that colonized societies become peripheral capitalist social formations as they undergo two major social changes that Marxists have usually considered to be synonymous to capitalist development: (i) the emergence of generalized commodity production and (ii) the emergence of extended reproduction of capital, which implies not only the replacement of capital used in a commodity's production from exchange (sale) but also the surplus value extracted from the worker in the process of commodity production, which contributes to capital accumulation and the enlargement of the producer's capacity. Alavi developed a chart (see Table 1) to clarify peripheral capitalism and distinguish it from the feudal mode of production (FMP) and the capitalist mode of production (CMP).

Table 3.1 Alavi's Characterization of Different Modes of Production

FMP	*CMP*	*Peripheral Capitalism*
Unfree labour: direct producer in possession of means of production (land etc.).	'Free' labour: (1) free of feudal obligations; (2) dispossessed—separation from means of production	As in CMP
Extra-economic compulsion for extraction of surplus	Economic 'coercion' of dispossessed producer	As in CMP
Localized structure of power: the fusion of economic and political power at the point of production—a necessary condition of coercive extraction of the surplus	Separation of economic (class) power from political (state) power: creation of bourgeois state and bourgeois law	Specific colonial structure
Self-sufficient localized economy supplemented by simple circulation of commodities	Generalized commodity production (production primarily for sale; labour power itself a commodity)	Specific colonial structure
Simple reproduction where surplus is largely consumed	Extended reproduction of capital and rise in organic composition of capital	Specific colonial structure

Reprinted from Hamza Alavi, "The Structure of Peripheral Capitalism," *Introduction to the Sociology of "Developing Societies,"* ed. Hamza Alavi and Teodor Shanin (New York: Monthly Review Press, 1982) 179.

Alavi's chart does not distinguish the two characteristic features of capitalism (the presence of 'free' labour and the prevalence of economic exploitation) between peripheral capitalism and the CMP—common characteristics have been outlined for the two modes. However, where generalized commodity production and the extended reproduction of capital are concerned, Alavi included a caveat about the 'specific colonial structure' of peripheral capitalism, arguing that the circuit of generalized commodity production is internally incomplete in peripheral societies:

> That circuit is completed only by virtue of their link with the metropolitan economy, by production for exports, and as markets for colonial imports. The structural condition of generalized commodity production in peripheral capitalism is satisfied only by virtue of the link with the metropolis. The same can be said about the process of "extended reproduction of capital" [. . .] The condition of capitalist development is thus satisfied but in a manner that is specific to peripheral capitalism.

> While both cases fulfill the conditions of CMP . . . the structure of peripheral capitalism and the dynamics of its development are, by virtue of these differences, quite distinct from those of metropolitan capitalism.[19]

(ii) Conceptual Relevance of 'Peripheral Capitalism' Idea to Post-Colonial State and Society

Alavi's claims raise a number of issues. First, a mere link with metropolitan capital cannot satisfy the conditions for generalized commodity production in a colony because the necessary capitalist relations were not present in the rural sector or even dominant in the colony's urban setting. Second, the fact that metropolitan capitalist production is linked to surplus (not surplus value) extraction in the periphery through tribute collection does not prove the existence of peripheral capitalism. It is even arguable whether surplus value is actually extracted from a colony or whether merely surplus (tribute payments) from primary or 'primitive' accumulation is realized.[20] Third, the role of 'primitive' accumulation in capitalist development goes unrecognized, although, as mentioned at the beginning of this subsection, Alavi alluded to this relationship. In this context, Habib's groundbreaking work and Luxemburg's modified[21] position on the value of non-capitalist markets in the sustenance of capitalism are instructive and will be discussed later in this chapter. Finally, Alavi obscured the role of the metropolitan bourgeoisie in propping up the feudal elite in the colony; the latter acted both as an intermediary in the extraction of surplus from the peasantry and as a buffer between the colonizers and the toiling exploited mass of colonized peoples. Ironically, this function of the feudal elite created an alliance between the *feudals*/rich peasants and the indigenous capitalists and enabled the simultaneous presence of capitalist and feudal relations of production in the colony without the overwhelming hegemony of any one class. In the post-colonial context, because of the dominant role of the bureaucratic elite and the relative weakness of the indigenous capitalists, the relationship between the two classes is still largely non-antagonistic. The important point here is that the supposedly antagonistic relationship between emerging capitalists and the feudal lords in the European context became non-antagonistic in the colony and continue to be so in the post-colonial era—at least for the proto-capitalist variant of the post-colonial state.

As much has been said previously in opposition to Alavi's claims about the existence of capitalist relations in the periphery, I will defend my position by examining some key historical developments in pre-colonial/colonial India and supporting the argument that social relations in colonial India were not predominantly capitalist. First, India was not a classically *feudal* society, and it had a relatively sophisticated tradition of craft manufacturing that was destroyed at the time of colonization. The British replaced the elaborate tribute collection system of the Mughals and the various hierarchal layers of superior right-holders[22] with the 'elemental fief'. Second, Habib noted that 'primitive' accumulation in colonial India drained its wealth and resources, whereas the extracted surplus helped fuel capitalist development in the metropolis. Furthermore, during the latter half of the 19th century (100 years into India's colonization), the dominant mode of production was still largely feudal, *despite the introduction of capitalist relations in the colony*. Finally, the survival of robust feudal relations and their coexistence with capitalism ('mixed modes of production') has since become a vital aspect of colonial and now post-colonial societies.

Alavi was correct about colonial India being Britain's periphery and being enveloped within the then-prevailing WCS. However, the question remains whether the colonial periphery was capitalist and whether the CMP was dominant within the colony. For Alavi, the answer was undoubtedly in the affirmative, because the "well-established landowning classes were no longer 'feudal'."[23] Alavi attributed the power of diffusion to the limited capitalist development in the colony, a power which was expected to have transformed pre-capitalist social relations. In drawing these conclusions, Alavi has confused the issue by generalizing and extrapolating from the *mode of exploitation*—that is, exploitation based on either feudal or capitalist relations in the periphery, which, for Alavi, was imposed along capitalist lines by the capitalist colonial power. Alavi tended to read this development as capitalist in a self-serving manner, locating it as having pervaded the entire periphery and thereby as having transformed the colony into a capitalist entity—albeit peripherally. In other words, pre-capitalist or primary accumulation subsists alongside spotty capitalist development in the colony, but the former actually aids capitalist development in the metropolis. Alavi alluded to this symbiotic relationship and actually referred to it more directly in an earlier article.[24] So, although the Indian colony was made part of the WCS as a result of colonization, *capitalist social relations within the colony were not dominant*. Rather, capitalist social relations existed alongside feudal relations, with the latter being dominant in rural Indian society during the colonial era.

The dependence on agriculture in regions like South Asia, as Alavi also acknowledged, actually increases under colonial rule as a result of the collapse of urban society, which during the pre-colonial era had a parasitic dependency on tribute; this source of revenue was lost when the colonial state began to appropriate the bulk of tribute collected from the peasants, and transferred it to the metropolis.[25] This loss, as Alavi acknowledges, caused a dramatic demographic decline in urban areas after colonization as those who were without work moved back to rural areas.[26] This reversal is in sharp contrast to the common assumptions of modernization theorists and classical Marxists, who contend that the force of modernization or development of capitalist relations moves 'backward' societies towards industrialization. In contrast, Dutt noted that the official census of colonial rulers since the late 1880s reveals a very different picture of Indian agriculture:

> The proportion of the population dependent on agriculture rose from 61.1 per cent in 1891 to 66.5 per cent in 1901, 72.2 per cent in 1911 and 73.0 per cent in 1921. The 1931 census showed the percentage as 65.6. This was not a real reduction, but only a formal one due to a change in classification. Since the 1931 census the percentage has again increased from 65.6 to 69.8—[this, after decolonization] in 1951.[27]

The overwhelming dependence on agriculture destroyed the balance between industry and agriculture that prevailed in pre-colonial India and worked to relegate India "to the role of an agricultural appendage of imperialism."[28] The dependence on agriculture "as the sole occupation for three-fourths of the people, is in its present scale a *modern* phenomenon and the direct consequence of imperialist rule."[29] Dutt's observations are supported by Habib's argument about how 'primitive' accumulation in the colony sustains the development of capitalism in the metropolis.

As discussed briefly in Chapter 1, this volume, an advanced pre-capitalist society like India can compete with an emerging capitalist power like Britain if its specialized industry—for pre-colonial India, textiles—is not shut down by extra-economic means or colonial subjugation. Industrialized Britain was only able to become an international machine-made textile presence *after* destroying the Indian textile industry. Thus, despite the 'midwifery' of British colonial rulers in fostering the emergence of indigenous capitalists in India, industrial capitalism was not encouraged in the colony. The reasons for this British attitude were well founded: industrial production in colonial India would only exacerbate competition and rivalry from Indian capitalists, which the British were eager to avoid. Consequently, the interests of the metropolitan bourgeoisie in Britain would not be served if capitalist development was dispersed throughout India.

The colonial state discouraged Indian industrial capitalism, but were capitalist relations even introduced into the vast Indian agricultural sector? Or were pre-capitalist feudal social forms still dominant in colonial India? Answering these questions will require a brief analysis of the impact of British colonial rule in India, especially its effects on the peasantry. By the turn of the 20th century, the super-exploitation of the Indian peasantry, undertaken by the British over 150 years to extract an ever-increasing surplus and to increase the dependence of "three-fourths" of all Indians on agriculture, took a heavy toll on the rural population. At this time, Indian agriculture was in severe crisis because of the "paralyzing burden of the existing [colonial] social system and barriers to technical improvement and large scale organization."[30] According to official reports of the Agricultural Area in British India (1939–1940):

of the cultivable area of 355 million acres, only 59 per cent was sown with crops, 13.2 per cent was fallow, and no less than 27.3 per cent was cultivable land left waste. The official return for the Indian Union for 1949–50 recorded that out of a total land area of 710 million acres, excluding forests, 283 million or 40 per cent were sown, 59 million or 8 per cent were fallow, and 233 million acres or 33 percent were uncultivated other than fallow.[31]

These figures clearly show two things. First, the peasantry was under immense pressure to pay tribute on *fixed* rates regardless of whether or not the land was fertile; this pauperized the peasantry and also meant that the land, whose use was also severely affected, was even more overworked. Second, the data do not indicate that the supposed wide-scale capitalist relations in colonial India's agricultural sector improved productivity or land use, as was claimed by Alavi. In contrast, as discussed in Chapter 1, this volume, Habib (supported by Fuller and Aziz) characterized the changes introduced by the British to the feudal structures of India's village communities as far more oppressive than pre-colonial social forms. In effect, British changes resurrected the elemental fief of feudal England in colonial India via the Permanent Land Settlement of 1793.[32] Colonial rulers did this by re-instituting and strengthening the *zamindari* system of the pre-Mughal rulers, the Delhi Sultans.

During the first 100 years of colonial rule in India, 'primitive' accumulation served the purpose of metropolitan capital accumulation, but this pattern of England's imperialist appropriation could not continue unabated. Two main developments brought change: the introduction of capitalist relations into the colony and the metropolitan bourgeoisie's need for more captive sources of raw materials and markets for goods produced in the metropolis. At the same time, tribute collection rates (rent) also became more extractive. However, the real catalyst for change was the aftermath of the 1857 Rebellion: English colonial rulers were almost toppled from power and began to understand the importance of having dedicated collaborators among the indigenous feudal elite. Consequently, although the feudal elite were strengthened (many were even knighted by the English monarch), the British also began to contemplate the introduction of a new economic regime in India. Work towards this new regime actually began with the Reform Act of 1832 when emphasis shifted from the levy of direct tribute through land revenue to the exploitation of India as a market for British goods and a source for its raw material needs.[33] These changes had the additional effect of increasing the concentration of land into ever fewer hands, eventually leading to the displacement of the peasantry. Some displaced peasants became wage labourers, but not in the sense of 'free' labourers as envisioned by Marx or by Alavi. Dutt noted:

> the majority of real cultivators if not already reduced to the position of landless labourers became unprotected tenants, mercilessly squeezed to maintain a horde of functionless intermediaries above them in addition

to the big parasites and the final claims of the Government. This process, carrying the whole system of landlordism to its final extreme of contradictions, has been one of the sharpest expressions of the developing agrarian crisis in India. Nor has the agrarian reform legislation of the Congress [in post-colonial India] availed to solve this deepening crisis.[34]

In a similar vein, Habib commented that although capitalist production in colonial India expanded a great deal:

> it essentially enlarged two pre-capitalist forms of accumulation, rent extraction and usury. The only partial exception was offered by tea plantations, where British capital was served by wage labour, often of a semi-servile kind. The near-total subjugation of the Indian market by British capitalism thus generated only a very weak impulse towards *true capital formation within India*. In other words, while it created a proletariat by destroying Indian crafts, it did not correspondingly generate capital that could either give it even partial employment.[35]

The impact of feudal and quasi-feudal or proto-capitalist servitude promoted by the metropolitan bourgeoisie in colonial India's rural sector was not confined to the colonial era. The impoverishment of the rural worker continued into the post-colonial period. Victor Rastyannikov, a Russian scholar who analyzed the semi-proletarian nature of the labour done by rural workers in post-colonial India, noted:

> The outside[36] labour enlisted in the agricultural socio-economic structures, which function on the basis of simple reproduction, obviously cannot be regarded as *hired labor* in the fully economic sense of this concept (i.e., as labor producing a surplus value for the sake of its further reproduction). The hired workers who put their labour effort into these structures constitute a type of agrarian *protoproletariat*. Under the conditions of the multiform structure of India's agrarian economy, this type of people is most widespread among those who sell labour power; the extent of their distribution by regions is in inverse proportion to the level of development of the capitalist structure, and in direct proportion to the level of development of the relative overpopulation. Not creating any surplus value (and in extensive sectors of the agrarian economy—simply exchange value), and not capable of achieving the necessary minimum for subsistence through their own labor, the hired worker of this type is a *pauper in the fullest, most complete sense of the word*. The scale of pauperization which reigns in the agrarian society of a certain region may be measured more accurately by the scale of spread and the size of personal consumption of the agrarian protoproletariat.[37]

Clearly, the system prevailing in colonial India cannot be classified as capitalist although nascent capitalism was possibly emerging in the early decolonization period. A capitalist periphery, such as colonial India, does not necessarily have capitalist internal structures, and the state does not automatically have a capitalist character. As Dutt and others demonstrated, India was at best a proto-capitalist state even at the time of decolonization, and its rural society was still in the grip of feudal landholders. The system of feudalism did not just disappear, and it was not considerably weakened, as Alavi implied. On the contrary, one of the first critical steps the new post-colonial Indian leadership took in the early 1950s was to implement land reforms and try to eliminate the *zamindars* who were the new feudal elite under British colonial rule.[38] Given this evidence, how should Indian society be understood? Capitalism as a social form is commonly understood to involve, among other things, the emergence of 'free' wage labour, commodity production, an instrumentalist rationality, the prevalence of capitalist social relations, and a dominant capitalist class that impacts culture and society. These markers were not dominant in India at the end of colonial rule, but India was also not completely a feudal state at the time of decolonization.

Divergent social and economic realities for the colonizer and the colonized produce very different results in the metropolis and the periphery: the colonizer gains at the expense of a racialized and gendered divide and a deeply exploited economic and social formation in the periphery. Those in the periphery do not merely lose economically; the social impact is much more devastating. As a result, whereas colonial subjugation is more apparent in the lives of the colonized, metropolitan capital accumulation has a more significant impact on rural displacement and exploitation more generally on the social plane. At the economic level, Habib demonstrated that primary accumulation in the colony contributes substantively to metropolitan capitalist development, as exemplified by colonial India. Through a slight modification of Luxemburg's somewhat essentialist notion of non-capitalist markets[39] (she considers these markets as existing in perpetuity for capitalist expansion), we can see that the role of primary or 'primitive' accumulation has benefitted British capitalist development. Thus, capitalist accumulation during the *early* development phase of metropolitan capitalism, which requires continuous extension of the market in non-capitalist sectors of the colony, changes during the mature or later phases of capitalism when capitalist development is no longer completely dependent on this sector. This modification of Luxemburg's theory is applicable to colonial India, and social changes leading to the Reform Act of 1832 reveal how primary accumulation in the colony contributed significantly to capitalist development in the metropolis.

My claim that social relations were not predominantly capitalist in colonial India implies that capitalist development in the colony is, at best, an aberration because metropolitan capitalist development, at least in its early stages (and in contemporary Western capitalism), relies on various forms of imperial impositions, contradictory actions, the realignment of social forces through the elevation or demotion of a particular religious community or social/ethnic group, and the manipulation of divisions among colonized/imperialized peoples on the basis of race, ethnicity, nationalism, and religion.

Taken together, these findings provide a framework within which I can return to dispute Alavi's characterization of peripheral capitalism in colonial India, outlined in Table 3.1. Alavi claimed that 'free labour' is an important characteristic of peripheral capitalism but did not differentiate between peripheral capitalism and the CMP. Further, he claimed that labour in the periphery is *free* of feudal obligations, because the dispossessed peasantry is proletarianized by being separated from the means of production. As the previously cited evidence shows, labour was not substantively 'free' in colonial India. At best, the dispossessed peasantry could be viewed as semi-proletarians, but even then they were 'tied' to the soil, a position from which it was extremely difficult for them to extricate themselves. In addition, the *unfreeness* of colonial subjugation was coupled with the super-exploitation of the feudal lord and the colonial state's demands of exorbitant tribute or rent payments from colonial subjects, adding another layer of *unfreeness* and super-exploitation.

Alavi argued that both the CMP and peripheral capitalism follow the pattern of generalized commodity production through extended reproduction and the associated rise in the organic composition of capital,[40] which, in the case of peripheral capitalism, is bound by its specificity. Although Alavi acknowledged that the colonial state appropriates much of the surplus from the colony to the metropolis, he viewed the circuit of extended reproduction as complete—even though the evidence calls into question this very claim, and whether there was even a rise in the organic composition of capital, given the prevalence of primary accumulation in the colony. Quite surprisingly, when considering the disappearance of extra-economic coercion of the dispossessed peasantry, Alavi argued that no fusion of economic and political power takes place at the point of production. This claim appears to disregard the immensely reconstituted power of the *zamindar* as an oppressively patriarchal feudal lord, a power manifested not only as extra-economic coercion but also as how the colonial state ended up enforcing his edicts. Still, Alavi argued, "the structural conditions of generalized commodity production in peripheral capitalism is satisfied *only by virtue of the link with the metropolis* . . . the same can be said about the process of extended reproduction of capital."[41] His position is tantamount to asserting, without really examining the existing social relations, that because the colony is part of a capitalist periphery, it must itself be capitalist. Given that the social relations in the colonial periphery differed greatly from those envisioned by Alavi, his claim about the existence of generalized commodity production in the colony appears to have weak foundations.

The social structure of colonial India appears to show an increasing prevalence of mixed modes of production—pre-capitalist/feudal relations alongside emerging capitalist relations. An emerging class of industrial capitalists was gaining some prominence, and because land was being concentrated in fewer hands due to the agrarian crisis, increasing numbers of peasants were displaced and became semi-proletarians or proto-proletarians. Land remained largely in the control of feudal lords who had a comfortable, collaborative relationship with the British colonial state. The surplus from 'primitive' accumulation in colonial India that had once served to aid metropolitan capitalists was also changing, as India was increasingly (after the mid-19th century) being seen as both a market for British goods and a source for Britain's raw material needs. This is the enigma of the colonial state to which I alluded to earlier, an enigma that continues into the post-colonial era in which pre-capitalist and capitalist social forms continue to co-exist.

All these developments (and more) took place within a periphery that was created by British colonial rulers and metropolitan capitalists, but the colony itself was not capitalist. In addition, capitalist relations within this colonial 'capitalist periphery' (India) were neither dominant nor widespread in society. To reiterate, colonial India was part of the WCS as a periphery with mixed modes of production: a feudal basis of production was organized in rural areas (with pockets of capitalist farmers) and an embryonic system of capitalism that was emerging in both industry and trade in urban areas. The colonial state was extremely interventionist and even determined how this peculiar form of dependent capitalist development and the intensification of primary accumulation in the colony would unfold. As mentioned previously, the elaborate tribute collection and distribution system of the Mughals through hierarchal levels superior right-holders, which provided some latitude to the peasantry (in case of fallow lands or bad harvest), was destroyed and replaced by a single intermediary, the *zamindar*, who as the representative of the colonial state was literally made into an extremely oppressive feudal lord. As well, the unique demographic reversal from urban to rural areas, and later (as land became concentrated in the hands of increasingly fewer indigenous landed elite) back to urban centres, took a toll on the handful of large Indian cites, which had limited infrastructure to absorb large influxes of people.

The colonial state did not simply set the rates of tribute; as outlined earlier and in Chapter 1, this volume, the state's manipulative social policies also shaped the relationships between different colonized groups, creating divisions among the colonized on the basis of religion, ethnicity, and region. This legacy of colonial state intervention in economic and social realms became an integral part of the character of the post-colonial state: shaping economic policy, controlling economic investment and public sector enterprises, creating rifts and divisions among various colonized groups in the way privileges were assigned, while completely blurring the lines between the political and the economic. Poulantzas and Alavi both stress that the separation of economic from political is an important component of capitalist production (and of the capitalist state),[42] but this separation is almost completely missing in the colonial and most post-colonial contexts—in the bulk of proto-capitalist post-colonial societies, feudal elites not only share state power but dominate rural society by having state functionaries becoming complicit in extra-economic coercion, whereas the capitalists are so weak that their economic activities and economic policy is dictated by the feudal–civil and military bureaucratic alliance.

Thus, Alavi's claim that peripheral capitalism entails a separation of economic and political moments, in that the ascendant economic class (the capitalist) is 'separated' from the political (state) power of the capitalist state, does not fully hold up to scrutiny. Admittedly, the class power of capitalists (economic) cannot be reduced to state power (political), and whereas economics may be central to capitalist social formation, the political dimension is not just informed by economics; rather, politics actually shapes state and non-state economic interventions. The separation, I would argue, is at best formal because the capitalist state ultimately serves to safeguard and promote the CMP, but under colonialism even this formal separation is just not visible. Another important development is that Western capitalist societies, including Japan, do not generally contain remnants of pre-capitalist economic/social forms (although some cultural practices, such as reverence for nobility and atavistic patriarchal practices, may still survive).[43] This is not to imply that these capitalist societies did not, in earlier stages of their development, involve other pre-capitalist relations within the CMP, such as slavery in the US or quasi-feudal relations. However, as will be discussed in Section III, separation of the economic and the political has little meaning in the case of the proto-capitalist post-colonial state. Most proto-capitalist post-colonial states must contend with an overdeveloped bureaucratic state structure—a remnant of the colonial state that enables the bureaucracy to act as an auxiliary class in the post-colonial state apparatus—to mediate the competing interests of propertied classes. Even in post-colonial *capitalist* states, bureaucracy still has some leverage over the bourgeoisie in terms of state policy, but the bourgeoisie is becoming increasingly powerful due to its growing hegemony in capitalist post-colonial society. Still, with regard to post-colonial states, it is important to focus on their nature: whether these states are predominantly proto-capitalist or whether some have acquired a capitalist character.

II SPECIFYING THE NATURE OF THE POST-COLONIAL STATE AND SOCIETY

Decolonization has produced different trajectories of capitalist development not only among South Asian states but also in other states in Africa, Asia, and even Latin America. Alavi's wholesale application of the term 'peripheral capitalism' to post-colonial societies tends to disregard these differences. For instance, post-colonial Indian state was able to keep predatory transnational capital more or less at bay until the late 1970s based on its statist policies and thus helped to strengthen its bourgeoisie and the industrial sector.[44] In contrast, since the late 1950s transnational corporations (TNCs) have found the doors of post-colonial Pakistan to be wide open, as the country became very dependent on the US and, therefore, on transnational capital.[45] Oddly, Pakistan was late in embracing the agenda of economic liberalization; when it finally did in the late 1980s, it was a feeble attempt.[46] Sri Lanka, in contrast, was one of the first few post-colonial states to implement economic liberalism; this was as early as 1977, likely only second to Pinochet's Chile and the junta-ruled Brazil.[47] However, the adoption of economic liberalization has only compounded the burden of imperialist subordination among people in South Asia and elsewhere in the global South, making them even more dependent on the North.

The impact of the capitalism–imperialism nexus is felt most keenly in the economic realm of post-colonial societies, but imperialist influence on culture and political control of many states in the global South has been largely conducted through extra-economic means, with the direction largely determined by the US. Economic liberalism has pressured Third World states to privatize the public domain and dismantle exchange control borders to ease the mobility of capital and Western TNCs, based specifically on the threat of Western capitalist states imposing tariff restrictions and export quotas on products from the Third World. These threats have been reinforced through the policies and dictates of Bretton Woods institutions through tariff harmonization attempts (General Agreement on Tariff and Trade) or the imposition of structural adjustment programs (International Monetary Fund [IMF]), which are ostensibly economic in form but actually have substantial social implications. The media and Western cultural production also play a role; people in the South are regularly exposed to global networks such as CNN, BBC, and MTV, which go hand in hand with American and European corporate cultural icons such as Marlboro, McDonald's, and Nike. This imperialist encirclement of the Third World has been strengthened and formalized since the establishment of the World Trade Organization (WTO) in the mid-1990s.

Since decolonization, the combined strength of Western imperialist states has had a tremendous influence on how capitalist development has unfolded. In some regions of post-colonial states, this has taken place alongside existing pre-capitalist social relations. In much of Southeast Asia, capitalist development was given priority by the US and its allies: South Korea and Taiwan emerged as capitalist states just a few decades after their formation. South Africa and possibly Egypt (Zimbabwe's status may have changed because of the current internal turmoil) are probably the only capitalist states on the African continent. In contrast, the history of Latin America differs from that of post-colonial Asia and Africa. Latin America has had a historically close relationship with Europe and gained independence almost a century before other post-colonial states. Argentina, Brazil, and Chile can be considered capitalist with either remnants or a significant presence of pre-capitalist social forms. In India, capitalists are a dominant social class, but other pre-capitalist social forms remain—and not just as isolated instances of rural life. It can therefore be said that although the US and other Western states may have influenced the course of capitalist development in states such as South Korea, Taiwan, Argentina, Chile (after Allende), Brazil, and South Africa, the situation in other capitalist post-colonial states is somewhat different. In regions such as India, and now China,[48] indigenous capitalists have been more assertive about guiding the state towards capitalist development and have minimally opposed the imperialist domination of their societies. Other states, which form the bulk of the Third World, are moving (or being moved) along a different development trajectory of capitalist relations and can be best identified as proto-capitalist.

The transformation of a society's pre-capitalist social relations into capitalism (or some other social form) is related to prevailing social conditions and social relations, the level of productive forces, the ideology and outlook of those demanding (or opposing) social changes, and the international balance of forces, including the role of imperialism. An analysis of the international dimension and how capitalist relations emerge in the colony and later in post-colonial societies is therefore central to clarify whether, and how, the introduction of capitalist relations transform pre-capitalist social relations. In the case of most former colonies (South Korea is one exception),[49] the colonial state was not really concerned with overhauling social relations that were historically tied to land. In other words, as discussed in the previous section, the breakup of feudal relations was not a serious concern for European colonizers. They were more focused on collecting huge tributes, transferring these funds to the metropolis, and quashing any resistance to colonial rule. Social transformation of the colony was really not a serious objective.

At the time of decolonization, many nationalist leaders worked to transform feudal relations of production, given the issue of landlessness and the prominence of the land reforms. However, as discussed in previous chapters of this volume, many of these leaders were either eliminated or removed from power through collaborative efforts of the Central Intelligence Agency and the indigenous military before meaningful land reforms could even be implemented. The client regimes that replaced these nationalists went through the motions of introducing a number of land reforms without really redistributing land or overcoming feudal relations of production—the prevailing system in many emerging post-colonial states at the time of decolonization. Thus, post-colonial state policy on land reforms or land redistribution was a key element in transforming colonial social relations, which were neither completely feudal nor fully capitalist. In colonial India, the logical course of action for capitalist colonial rulers would have been to implement land reforms and speed up the social process of capitalist transformation—as Marx had expected. But this was not to be. In fact, the opposite occurred in India; the British went on to re-construct the elemental fief that they had destroyed in their own homeland. This strengthened the fiefdom of Indian princely states and the role of the *zamindar*, contrary to Marx's expectations about imperialist England's 'double mission' in India. As discussed in the previous section, this strengthening of feudal relations in colonial India was necessary because the feudal elite were a main pillar of support for British rule, serving as a buffer to protect the colonial state from the wrath of the colonized. Consequently, colonial rulers could not address the question of land reforms unless they wished to undermine their own self-interest and antagonize their indigenous, largely feudal, collaborators.

To date, most post-colonial states have been reluctant to undertake meaningful land reforms.[50] In those states where reforms have been adopted, very few efforts have been made to deal with the resistance and bottlenecks to their successful adoption. For example, policymakers made inadequate efforts to deal with the historical Indian land tenure system.[51] In states where land re-distribution was successfully implemented, the feudal stranglehold on the peasantry and the rest of society has been greatly reduced; China, Japan, and some East Asian states are the few success stories of successful land reforms. It is not surprising that these countries emerged as the few capitalist states in the Third World. The one and only land reform program undertaken in India was implemented very soon after decolonization, but only an estimated 6% of its available farm land was redistributed, compared to land reforms "implemented after the Second World War in the People's Republic of China, Taiwan, South Korea and Japan; the extent of redistribution was 37 per cent in Taiwan, 32 per cent in South Korea and 33 per cent in Japan [of the total available land]."[52] In most other cases, land reforms were nominal insofar as actual land redistribution did not take place: most feudal landlords simply 'transferred' the land on paper to their relatives or trusted servants while maintaining full control over that land.[53] The US and its Western allies have been in a position to pressure most post-colonial states to undertake land reforms, but they have applied this influence selectively and sparingly, mainly because their interests in maintaining the global South's subordination are already being met by the historically prevailing social conditions in these societies. More recently, the World Bank has entered the fray; it now seems to be pushing for 'market-assisted' land reforms designed to counter the 'failed' state-led agrarian reforms. This move by the World Bank, which has not gained much traction, would actually have served to concentrate land into even fewer hands because the criteria was the market and the prevailing price of land, which would have furthered the corporatization of agriculture in those Third World states that had previously been insulated from the invasive presence of multinational agribusinesses.[54]

Thus, given the nature of the proto-capitalist state, if land is one factor that impedes the movement towards capitalism in much of the South, the post-colonial state itself can have significant influence in the dissolution of feudal and pre-capitalist relations. Therefore, attention is now turned to understanding the post-colonial state.

III COMPREHENDING THE POST-COLONIAL STATE

In the current period of globalization and imperialist impositions, when most states of Africa, Asia, and Latin America have less room to manoeuvre, and when many of these states' sovereignty is being violated or threatened, it is critical to grasp why and how post-colonial states have been re-subordinated in the 21st century. In the almost four decades since Alavi first developed his theorization on the post-colonial states of Pakistan and Bangladesh, a number of changes have occurred in the Third World state itself, in the global capitalist system, and in the drive for imperialist hegemony. Therefore, my analyses will focus on social relations in proto-capitalist and capitalist post-colonial states, their histories, and how they were affected by the forces of external imperialist domination. In this section I will rely on the concept of the capitalism–imperialism nexus to show how the increasingly invasive and expansionist role of imperialist states under US hegemony, particularly since the rise of globalization in 1990, has affected post-colonial states most adversely. This external dimension is of immense significance as it bears directly on the character and role of the post-colonial state.

In addition to my examination of imperialist domination over post-colonial states, I will analyze the enormous legacy of the colonial state, especially its centralized, unitary state structure. This is accompanied by another consequence of colonial rule related to the social and economic elite in post-colonial states: these privileged members are the successors-in-interest of the indigenous colonized elite, especially the landed classes, who originally began to collaborate with colonial rulers and have continued along that path in the post-colonial era. In the present period of capitalist globalism, this history of collaboration has meant that indigenous capitalist and even feudal interests have become mired in even deeper collaboration with Western capital and imperialist Western states. Together, these colonial legacies reveal that post-colonial states did not form as a result of the struggle between an emerging bourgeoisie and a decaying landed class, as was the case in the formation of European capitalist nation-states. Rather, most post-colonial states were actually set up by departing colonial rulers/metropolitan elites, with both indigenous capitalists and feudal landholders colluding with the indigenous civil bureaucracy to run the affairs of the newly decolonized states. In post-colonial states that achieved national liberation and removed colonial rulers through armed struggle, many of the committed nationalist leaders in these states were either eliminated (the Congo, Ghana, Indonesia) by imperialist powers not long after achieving decolonization, or the surviving nationalist leaders eventually chose to collaborate with the metropolitan bourgeoisie.

More important, both the nationalist and the collaborationist indigenous elites of the colonial era internalized the idea of the nation-state, especially the notion of the 'modern' nation-state.[55] As discussed in Chapter 1, this volume, European nation-states formed as a consequence of the rise of capitalism and the resolution of national conflict among different ethnic/national groups that were once part of European dynastic empires. Post-colonial states are not nation-states, and for their societies, the capitalism–nation-state nexus has been an alien concept: there was neither an initial indigenous route to capitalist development nor a resolution of the 'national question' that could result in the formation of nation-states in post-colonial societies. Benedict Anderson's 'imagined communities' were located mainly in Europe, and the 'horizontal comradeship' among different European groups and across different borders could only be realized *after* a number of simultaneous events occurred: the overthrow of dynastic realms, the emergence of a dominant capitalist bourgeoisie, a new conception of time in which 'cosmology and history' were indistinguishable, and capital's need of the nation-state's borders for capital's protection and expansion.[56] Moreover, these developments occurred in Europe within an environment of relative *freedom*. In contrast, the horizontal comradeships that existed in *pre*-colonial times were literally destroyed by colonial machinations, and replaced with conflict and discord between different ethnic, religious, and regional groups during colonization and in the post-colonial era. As a result, the colonized began to emulate the ideas of nation and nationalism introduced by colonial rulers in an aura enveloped by conflict and *unfreeness*. Further, given that the colonial state was the root of discord and division among the colonized, these conflicts could not be resolved within the borders of the colonial state, and the colonized had to wait until decolonization to begin addressing questions about identity and difference. The accommodation of difference has eluded most multinational post-colonial societies, so different national and ethnic groups have ended up in serious conflicts; violence and conflict based on ethnicity and nationalism now proliferate much of today's Africa and Asia.

Consequently, the promise of accord and harmony that was to accompany the demise of colonial rule was not delivered for three important reasons. First, the model of the European nation-state that was adopted (and internalized) by post-colonial states was ill-suited to handle the fallout from the forcible inclusion within the colony of a number of disparate ethnic groups that had historically lived separately in the pre-colonial era; the existing nation-state model is ill-equipped to meet the autonomy demands of disparate multinational/multiethnic post-colonial societies. Second, the structures of the colonial state were incorporated within the post-colonial state with adverse consequences. Finally, the indigenous ruling elites, who were schooled with a colonial mindset, became rulers of post-colonial states and the rest of society that was not part of this elite core has been facing social, economic and political exclusion. These factors, together with the pressure from the new post-1945 capitalist/imperialist power to bring post-colonial states within the US's sphere of influence, did little to placate the fears of weaker ethnic, sub-national, or religious groups among formerly colonized peoples. More significant, the non-resolution of the 'national question' during colonial rule meant that very few 'nations' at the time of decolonization would be able to constitute themselves into homogenous nation-states on the pattern of Western Europe. The result was that most post-colonial states became *multinational* states led by a dominant nation, whereas weaker nations and ethnic groups grew more resentful as a centralized and authoritarian unitary state structure was entrenched. These developments of the decolonization period have prompted some observers of state and national identity formation to claim that instead of a nation(s) forming a state (as was the case in Europe), the state was created before a nation was even 'imagined'—as in a *state-nation*.[57]

Post-colonial elites were so captivated by Western ideas, specifically the idea of the nation-state, that they were willing to see this as a 'superior' alternative to their own inferiorized perspectives. Thus, when the US (as the new post-World War II imperialist power and capitalist hegemon) began to promote the idea of multilateralism, the nation-state became the pivot on which the entire edifice of the United Nations, the international financial institutions (IFIs), and other multilateral institutions were to rest. As the concept of the nation-state was universalized, it paved the way for the 1944 Bretton Woods conference, which made the nation-state a paradigm and multilateralism the mainstay of emerging new institutions including the IMF, the World Bank, and later, the General Agreement on Tariff and Trade (now the WTO). At the same time, the internalization of the 'modern' nation-state idea produced its own dynamic among the indigenous elites in post-colonial societies, who embraced the concept with much enthusiasm to become a part of 'modern' industrialized society. As Thomas Hansen and Finn Stepputat noted:

> [it is] pertinent to remember that the Western imagination of the state, however traversed by myths and historical fiction, remains the globally most powerful idea of political order in the twentieth century, institutionalized in the international state system after 1945. The most central presupposition underlying this system is that all states in principle are, or will become, similar, or at least mutually intelligible, in their structures and in their rationalities governing their actions. Such an ahistorical understanding of the state was eagerly embraced by the nationalist political elites in the post-colonial world, anxious to transform their states into "normal" nation-states.

> [. . .] Other important interventions aiming at producing "normal" states were performed by development agencies, international donors, and the thrust of development theory that all supported the view of the state as an "agent of modernization," an island of modernity and rationality, a part of the so-called modern sector, and so on.[58]

Many post-colonial states sought a shortcut to their cherished objective of becoming a 'modern' nation-state. Just as the Russian Revolution was initially successful in transforming feudal Russia into a reasonably strong industrial society within a relatively short period, many Third World states looked for an alternative to the market to pursue social and economic development and break from the pattern of dependency on metropolitan capital. As discussed in Chapter 2, this volume, state-centred policies were put in place in post-colonial and Latin American states to further the objectives of more autarchic development. The *dirigiste* state enormously benefitted indigenous capitalists but actually became a burden on post-colonial society for various reasons: 'overdeveloped' state structure that led to bureaucratic corruption and ineptness; the nature of class forces, especially the demands made by capitalists and the powerful landed elite on the state; the absence of a strong internal market; and the perpetual resource crunch faced by the state. Thus, in most cases the dismantling of state-centered policies led to structural adjustments imposed by the IMF and Western states. These took the form of directives requiring those in control of the post-colonial state to re-structure and re-orient the economy and society towards the market, privatize the public sphere, and eventually, adopt the entire neoliberalism package.

This external dimension marked an inauspicious beginning for the post-colonial state and has since led to more serious social, economic, and political difficulties in most post-colonial and many Latin American states. Much of this chapter has been devoted to the internal contradictions of post-colonial state and society; but perhaps the greatest change since Alavi originally presented his thesis in the 1970s is the strong element of external domination. This has been exemplified by intensified imperialist subordination of the Third World, crafting of neoliberal agendas, and the declaration of a 'new economic order'. All of these were preceded by the introduction of the 'new' international division of labour and a more interventionist role on the part of the metropolitan bourgeoisie, which have been discussed in Chapter 2, this volume. The 'military-bureaucratic oligarchy' may have mediated the conflicting interests of Alavi's three capitalist classes during the first few decades after decolonization, but the proto-capitalist state also needed to oversee and manage the demands of feudal landed interests. Today, the situation in most post-colonial societies is quite different. The interests of the metropolitan bourgeoisie, promoted by the US, its Western allies, TNCs, and post-colonial and Latin American bourgeoisies are not just *mediated* by the civil bureaucracy. Instead, the actions taken by the US and its supporters determine the responses of privileged indigenous social classes and the functionaries of the state. Furthermore, the multinational finance and industrial capitalist interests articulated by TNCs, Western nation-states, the IFIs, multilateral bodies, and other Western institutions, under the hegemony of the US, *determine directly or indirectly how post-colonial states will deal with their own indigenous propertied classes.* This changed relationship between the post-colonial state and the interventionist metropolitan bourgeoisie is important in the present era of globalization, and exemplifies the disturbing reality of '*weak*' post-colonial states in comparison to the enormous strength of metropolitan capital and Western states. Examples include the 'no fly zone' instituted in Iraq in the 1990s and how the country was 'shocked and awed' in 2003; how Afghanistan was similarly targeted by US forces and forces led by the North Atlantic Treaty Organization (NATO); and more recently, the regime change that has been successfully exercised in Libya under the same cover of enforcing a 'no-fly zone' to 'protect civilians'; whereas in Northwest Pakistan, remotely controlled US aerial drone attacks are a regular feature and not a peep is heard about the violation of the country's sovereignty in the international media.

Paradoxically, the post-colonial state is also 'strong' compared to its largely disempowered populace. The authoritarian state can exercise significant control over society, so those in control of the post-colonial state apparatus can *ensure* the protection of their own class interests, whereas the interests of metropolitan capital and Western states have precedence over the well-being of people in post-colonial societies. This, in essence, is the explication of the central arguments outlined at the beginning of this chapter: the civil and military bureaucratic elites, by dominating both state and society, are able to mediate the interests of propertied classes and also privilege imperialist interests over the welfare of their people, whereas the post-colonial state signals the start of another era of quasi-sovereignty, dependence, and subordination (now intensified) since decolonization. Attributing this character to the post-colonial state implies that its bureaucracy acts as an auxiliary class in a manner that differs greatly from the 'bureaucratic rationality' suggested by Weber and latter-day Weberians.[59] As Alavi noted, the bureaucracy in most post-colonial societies has been historically *overdeveloped* compared to other state institutions such as the judiciary or media and other civil institutions. Scholars of South Asia have often referred to the colonial bureaucracy as the legacy of the legendary colonial 'steel frame'.[60] The now well-documented purpose of this 'steel frame', which was (over)developed during the colonial era, was to control colonized peoples and ensure their submission to colonial imperatives, specifically the extraction and transfer of surplus to the metropolis. This legacy has continued into the post-colonial era and has actually intensified in the present era of globalization.

From the formation of the post-colonial state, the bureaucracy has effectively controlled the reins of power with political parties or populist leaders, in most cases providing the cover for its legitimation. Even in those capitalist post-colonial states, such as India, where capitalists have become ascendant, they have relied on the bureaucracy's support. In a number of post-colonial societies, the military was still in a formative stage at the time of decolonization, so its alliances with civil bureaucracy took a few years to take shape before the two, under the leadership of the military generals, could begin to assert power. However, although a number of military and quasi-military regimes have held (or still hold) power in Asian, African, and Latin American states, my claim about the 'feudal-bureaucratic-military oligarchy' wielding power in post-colonial societies—because of the differences between proto-capitalist and capitalist states—cannot be generalized to *all* post-colonial states.

(i) The Character of the Bureaucracy

The class origins and other aspects of the civil and military bureaucratic elite differ from state to state in post-colonial societies. Although the upper echelons of the bureaucracy and the military leadership are largely urban-based from the middle class, they also have strong links with landed interests. On the other hand, the industrial and commercial bourgeoisie usually have fewer family members joining these two groups. In colonial India, indigenous bureaucrats were among the first 'Western-educated' Indians after the British replaced Persian (the pre-colonial official language of Northern India) with the "dual language policy of 'Anglo-Vernacular education'"[61] that made English the official language of the colonial state. At the same time, the colonial "state apparatus [became] the principal avenue for upward mobility and [. . .] the status of Indian higher civil servants or judges, which did not then extend beyond quite modest middle levels was, nevertheless, generally reckoned to be higher than that of other indigenous classes—the colonial bureaucracy was the new nobility."[62] The consequence of the colonial state's intervention in India was the emergence of a politically astute upper layer of civil bureaucracy, which was able to interact with both colonizers and colonized. Indigenous bureaucrats used their unique position to influence the nature of colonial Indian politics and the eventual Partition of India.[63] This attitude and privilege on the part of the bureaucracy was carried into the period of decolonization on both sides of divided India.

This peculiar makeup of the bureaucracy also appeared in most other post-colonial states, so the question is whether this group ought to be treated as a class in itself or whether it has an auxiliary class status. Alavi was somewhat ambivalent on this point: in some of his writings, he referred to the bureaucracy as a general 'class' in the Third World, but he also treated this group as an auxiliary class, even developing a new term, the *salariat*, to describe it.[64] I take the view that the bureaucracy in post-colonial societies acts as a self-interested group to further its own group interests, which are not always the same as those of the state. The members of the bureaucracy may have their origins from the landed class or the urban middle class, and in some cases even the working class, but when people from these differing class backgrounds became state functionaries, they have tended to form an insular group that generally acted as an auxiliary class in the post-colonial context—working largely to perpetuate their office and further their individual and group interests. This is exemplified by the rampant corruption among civil and military bureaucracies in most post-colonial and Latin American states; with the lack of even a semblance of accountability, ordinary people have little recourse against the offending functionaries. Another indicator is the power held by higher ranked functionaries such as a ranking police officer, a lower court judge, or a district official, which is often wielded to further the individual and his or her office, rather than justice or redress. Still another indicator is the sheer number of top-level functionaries in post-colonial societies who remain insular and unaccountable for their actions, especially with regard to benefits obtained by metropolitan capital and imperialist states and acquiescence to IFI impositions. The 'IMF riots' in the global South (street protests against removal of subsidies to the poor and against arbitrary increases in the cost of food, fuel, and electricity imposed by state functionaries to meet IMF conditionalities) symbolize this kind of insularity and unaccountability. These examples reveal the character of the bureaucracy's auxiliary class, but they also reveal how theorists such as Peter Evans and others who, by advocating the need to 'embed' rational bureaucratic traditions in Third World states as a capacity-building measure, have a poor understanding of the bureaucrats' role in post-colonial and Latin American states.[65] The attitude of these theorists belies a lack of understanding of the post-colonial state's character.

(ii) The Propertied Classes

Based on the discussion in this chapter, the composition of propertied and non-propertied classes in post-colonial societies can be broadly classified into the following categories: the emerging indigenous bourgeoisie (some of whom also represent the interests of metropolitan capital with a negligible presence of national or anti-imperial capitalists), feudal landowners, emerging capitalist landowners, the various layers of peasantry, and an emerging working class.[66] Civil and military bureaucrats also function as an auxiliary class. The power held by each of these classes are varied by the nature of the post-colonial state, that is, whether dominant relations are capitalist or proto-capitalist. In proto-capitalist states, as discussed earlier, feudal landowners have not survived simply as vestiges of a bygone era; they are able to co-exist quite well with emerging capitalist interests and the civil and military bureaucracies in many post-colonial societies. This is in stark contrast to the revolutionary transformation of Europe, where feudal landlords were overcome by the power of the rising bourgeoisie. The so-called bourgeois national revolution that took place in 18th- and 19th-century England, France, and Germany not only helped defeat feudal landlords and Absolutism but also helped propel the capitalist bourgeoisie to power. This ascendancy on the part of capitalists enabled them to form nation-states, a historically new entity that replaced the dynastic realms of Europe. The inauguration of the 'modern' European nation-state, therefore, was undertaken by the bourgeoisie, and the entity that emerged, as Marx pointed out, was a bourgeois state. Therefore, as discussed in Chapter 1, this volume, the formation of the first nation-states, from 1780 onwards, coincided with the start of the Industrial Revolution (1760).

In contrast, even though feudal and capitalist interests conflict in post-colonial states, they are not antagonistic in the same sense as they were in Europe. Feudal elites and capitalists in post-colonial states do compete, but they also coexist—both vying for state patronage. The indigenous bourgeoisie tend to be more accommodative of metropolitan capital's interests and the demands of imperialist states, but their interests converge with the *feudals* and the bureaucratic elite in the service of metropolitan demands in proto-capitalist societies. In capitalist post-colonial societies, the attitude of the big bourgeoisie is largely collaborative with TNCs, but there are instances when rivalry between them may introduce an oppositional element among the indigenous capitalists. However, even in capitalist post-colonial states, because the imposition of European (and now US) imperialism has a very long history, the path of bourgeois revolution was simply not open to post-colonial indigenous bourgeoisie: it was a relatively weak class compared to the indigenous feudal and bureaucratic elite at the time of decolonization. In post-colonial societies, where the bourgeoisie became stronger or ascendant, the supportive role of the post-colonial state has been critical. In most proto-capitalist states, though, the indigenous bourgeoisie was not only sidelined by feudal and bureaucratic interests; it was also undermined by the metropolitan bourgeoisie who largely 'bequeathed' the post-colonial state to indigenous feudal and bureaucratic interests. Alavi viewed post-colonial state formation completely differently, but his conclusions about the indigenous bourgeoisie's lack of input in state formation are nevertheless relevant:

> The bourgeois revolution in the colony insofar as that consists of the establishment of a bourgeois state and the attendant legal and institutional framework, is an event which takes place with the imposition of colonial rule by the metropolitan bourgeoisie [. . .] Additionally, it has to create [the] state apparatus through which it can exercise domination over *all* the indigenous social classes in the colony. It might be said that the 'superstructure' in the colony is therefore 'overdeveloped' in relation to the 'structure' in the colony, for its basis lies in the metropolitan structure itself, from which it is later separated at the time of independence

> [. . .] *The essential problem about the state in post-colonial societies stems from the fact that it is not established by an ascendant native bourgeoisie but instead by a foreign imperialist bourgeoisie.*[67]

Although the post-colonial state had an inauspicious beginning after the departure of colonial power, indigenous political leaders and the intelligentsia in post-colonial societies appeared to be unaware that the path of 'bourgeois revolution' was effectively blocked for indigenous capitalists. Because the indigenous bourgeoisie had a dependent character, it could not conduct itself as a 'national' bourgeoisie unless it was aided by the state. Chapter 4, this volume, will explore how during India's state formation, the Indian state actually helped strengthen its emerging bourgeoisie, but because the nationalist impulse was limited and due to the current embrace of neoliberalism the Indian bourgeoisie, as a class, has also had a strong collaborationist relationship with metropolitan capital. Still, the idea of the 'bourgeois revolution', as it was advanced by the Second and Third International, based on the strong influence of the European capitalist transformation, was internalized by many political leaders and those on the left in post-colonial societies. The emerging capitalists in a number of post-colonial states were, therefore, seen as the 'national bourgeoisie'—the assumption being that indigenous capitalists as a class would be not only ascendant but also anti-imperialist. However, the arguments in the preceding sections have shown that because the colony was neither capitalist nor peripheral capitalist—despite the fact that it was a periphery of the WCS—indigenous capitalists could not become the 'national bourgeoisie'. Frantz Fanon was one of the few Third World intellectuals to recognize the futility of trusting to indigenous capitalists; he tried to alert people in post-colonial societies about the inability of the so-called national bourgeoisie to build a cohesive national unit along anti-imperialist lines. Fanon expressed these views following his participation in the Algerian Revolution, having seen first-hand the character of the indigenous elite. He gave his prognosis at a time when the national bourgeoisie, as a class, was being increasingly viewed as having an intrinsic (and a 'progressive') role in the post-colonial state:

> The psychology of the national bourgeoisie is that of a businessman, not that of a captain of industry, and it is only true that the greed of the settlers and the system of embargoes set up by colonialism have hardly left them any other choice [. . .] The national bourgeoisie, since it is strung up to defend its immediate interests, and sees no further than the end of its nose, reveals itself incapable of simply bringing national unity into being, or of building up the nation on a stable and productive basis. The national front which has forced colonialism to withdraw cracks up, and wastes the victory it has gained.
>
> [. . .] The national bourgeoisie turns its back more and more on the interior and on the real facts of its undeveloped country, and tends to

> look towards the former mother country and the foreign capitalists who count on its obliging compliance.[68]

Fanon's awareness was an exception in the 1960s and 1970s when the idea of the national bourgeoisie was all the rage, and his prognosis seems to have withstood the test of time. Still, the establishment of the post-colonial state by a 'foreign imperialist bourgeoisie' is a historical reality that brings up important questions about how different class interests can generate antagonism in one case (Europe) and not others (post-colonial states). For example, it is clear how capitalists came to be ascendant in what was once feudal Europe but less clear in the case of post-colonial societies. Part of the confusion arises from overlooking the fact that historically antagonistic contradictions between feudal and capitalist interests (based on the European experience) can produce non-antagonistic mutual accommodation and coexistence (in colonial and post-colonial settings)—even advancing metropolitan capitalist development, as shown in Habib and Luxemburg's arguments.

The landed classes have played a complementary role to the indigenous bourgeoisie by collaborating with colonial rulers from the very beginning of colonial occupation. In the post-colonial period, the feudal elite has readily submitted to the demands of multinational agribusinesses and, where it has been part of the ruling troika, has been most willing to acquiesce to the dictates of imperialist states such as the US and the demands of IFIs. Under colonial rule, feudal landlords had received sustenance and support from the colonial state in return for their allegiance to colonial rulers and acquiescence to colonial domination. At the time of decolonization, this landed elite was able to exercise considerable influence in most post-colonial states in one of two ways. In largely capitalist post-colonial states (such as South Korea), the landed elite usually did not have joint control of the state (in contrast to proto-capitalist states). For example, the *cheabol* (powerful group of business families) in South Korea had collaborated with the military and civil bureaucracy to further their economic interests and did not need the support of landed classes which, as it were, in decline. However, in states where the landed elite was strong but not necessarily dominant at the time of decolonization (such as India), this landed class was able to pressure both the state and the ruling political party to temper the demands of land redistribution, such as the dilution of land reform measures. In some other states, where feudal landlords were dominant (such as Pakistan), the landed elite actually held state power in league with the civil and military bureaucracy. As a result of the feudal landlords' relative strength as well as the nature of post-colonial states and the balance of class forces, the conflict between the *feudals* and capitalists simply did not materialize in post-colonial societies.

Given the earlier discussion in this chapter, based on the absence of contradiction between the presence of feudal elite and primary accumulation and between extended reproduction and capital accumulation in the colonial periphery, the colonial state was not particularly eager to introduce land reforms or to deepen capitalist relations in agriculture. For the colonial state, it made no sense to antagonize feudal landholders by introducing land reforms when benefits, in the form of massive tribute collections, were accruing to the metropolis. More important, the emergence of capitalism has not been an indigenous process in the colonies because colonial rulers have largely decreed a dependent variant of the system in the periphery. The consequence of this type of dependent capitalist development in the post-colonial context is that the indigenous bourgeoisie remains dependent on metropolitan capital; in most cases, their nascent stage of development made it difficult for them to attain hegemony in society, especially against the landed classes. China is one exception, but it was never really colonized for any extended period of time, other than the brief Japanese occupation and British pressure during the colonial period. Further, because China was able to introduce land reforms and later socialize its economy and society, albeit in a statist and authoritarian manner, before it adopted the capitalist development path, it has not been saddled with many of the problems faced by other former colonies.

In the early 1960s, a handful of countries belonging to the Non-Aligned Movement attempted to protect their nascent capitalist system with mixed success. India successfully nurtured its bourgeoisie and even introduced a single land reform measure, but as will be discussed in Chapter 4, this volume, the Indian state was unwilling to move definitively against landed interests. In contrast, whatever statist measures Soekarno planned in Indonesia were nipped in the bud by the military coup (with the Central Intelligence Agency's support), which returned Indonesia to a more dependent form of capitalism. Even when some client states (such as Indonesia under General Suharto and Pakistan under General Ayub Khan) started to adopt a more inward-oriented economic policy, they relied on multinationals rather than indigenous capitalists. For example, when indigenous capitalists formed joint ventures with Western multinationals, they relied largely on their imperialist benefactors, especially economic 'aid'. For the most part, the post-colonial state left economic planning to American academics, "particularly to the large contingent from Harvard University."[69] Thus, whatever benefits might have been derived through a more inward-oriented economic development policy were negated by the enormous dependency on Western multinationals and tied aid. Pakistan and Indonesia are not the only examples; similar cases occurred in the Philippines, Thailand, and a number of African and Latin American states. This explains why so few post-colonial states are capitalist. This dependency has thwarted and seriously undermined the independent class interests of the indigenous bourgeoisie. Given the nature of unequal exchange between the metropolitan centre and the periphery[70] and its historically weak position in comparison to landed classes, the indigenous bourgeoisie has had very little choice in determining the outcome of its dependent relationship with the metropolitan bourgeoisie. Imperialist dependency represents a double assault on a nascent bourgeoisie that is unable or unwilling to fight for and demand its rightful place. Consequently, indigenous capitalists, even after decolonization, continue to look to their metropolitan patrons for sustenance. The term *comprador*, nebulous as it may be, is a signifier of this kind of dependant relationship.

Thus, formal domination of the colonial state may have ended in post-colonial societies, but formerly colonized societies have been re-subordinated by the succeeding imperialist power, the US, and its metropolitan allies. In furthering this imperialist domination, the US has also institutionalized a much larger and more powerful body of support, composed of IFIs; the Organization for Economic Cooperation and Development; the WTO; client states in Africa, Asia, and Latin America; various ideological right-wing think-tanks; and its own military muscle, to ensure that post-colonial and Latin American ruling classes continue to rely on the metropolitan bourgeoisie for sustenance. The claim that the capitalism–imperialism nexus has reasserted itself in the era of globalization does not mean that nothing has changed since decolonization: although the tentacles of US imperialism have spread wider, resistance against US meddling and occupation has also been on the rise, and American and NATO forces have not been successful in winning their wars and maintaining occupied territory. However, this resistance is extremely fragmented, which has allowed the US and other Western powers to violate the sovereignty of a non-compliant, 'rogue', or 'terrorist' state at will.

(iii) Bureaucracy and the Post-Colonial State's Relative Autonomy

I have already described the bureaucracy in post-colonial societies as an auxiliary class. This subsection explores the role of bureaucracy in post-colonial states and societies to articulate the notion of relative autonomy of these states. The analysis of the bureaucracy and the civil-military bureaucratic union in post-colonial states will demonstrate how, based on its auxiliary-class character and its entrenchment in state structure, upper level bureaucracy has become the arbiter of power and mediator of competing interests of propertied classes in proto-capitalist societies.

Many scholars have observed that the bureaucratic-military union originated with colonialism and that the colonial state facilitated the dominance of civil bureaucracy over the indigenous classes. This was the outcome of colonial occupation. The express intention of colonial rulers was to continue the domination of indigenous peoples in perpetuity, and colonizers made every effort to meet this objective by strengthening the colonial state. Thus, the propensity of the colonial bureaucracy was to dominate social classes and other state and non-state institutions, such as the judiciary and the media, which has continued into the post-colonial era:

> The colonial state is [. . .] equipped with a powerful bureaucratic-military apparatus and mechanisms of government which enable it through its routine operations to subordinate the native social classes. The post-colonial state inherits this overdeveloped apparatus of the state and its institutionalized practices through which the operations of the indigenous social classes are regulated and controlled.[71]

Alavi examined state formation in Pakistan and Bangladesh and used his observations of the 'overdeveloped' state apparatus in these countries to form conclusions about the institutionalized practices of the bureaucratic-military union, which he generalized for all post-colonial states. However, there should be a nuanced reading of Alavi's generalizations: he is correct that the bureaucratic-military union, given its powerful position in a number of post-colonial states, mediates the conflicting interests of the other indigenous propertied classes (the commercial and industrial bourgeoisie, the feudal landholders, and the weak working class), but his claim of the 'overdeveloped' bureaucratic apparatus may not be valid for all contemporary *capitalist* and *proto-capitalist* post-colonial states. India had an overdeveloped structure at the time of decolonization, but the situation has changed with regard to the bourgeoisie's strength. The Indian state still has relative autonomy over other classes and groups, but Indian society has also become capitalist, and the large Indian bourgeoisie is more powerful. The power of the bureaucratic-military union is also changing in other *capitalist* post-colonial and Latin American states. In Argentina, Brazil, China, India, South Africa, South Korea, Taiwan, Turkey, and even Chile, the ascendant capitalist class appears to be more interventionist and has successfully obtained protection for their class and material interests compared to other classes. However, despite the hegemony of capitalists over other competing classes, the bureaucracy in these capitalist states still mediates between the conflicting demands of different groups—often to the benefit of capitalists. Thus, the bureaucratic state apparatus has relative autonomy even in capitalist post-colonial societies, but the overdeveloped nature of this apparatus is no longer how Alavi had conceptualized it to be: other institutions and classes have caught up with the bureaucratic elite and with the power they once wielded. In *proto-capitalist* states like Bangladesh, Nigeria, Pakistan, and others, the state maintains a higher degree of relative autonomy due to the greater power and control wielded by the bureaucracy or the civil-military bureaucratic union, which is precisely the result of the overdeveloped state apparatus. Thus, the 'overdeveloped' nature of the state apparatus is not the key to the relative autonomy of the state, although this *overdevelopedness* or lack thereof may determine the extent of the state's relative autonomy. The state's relative autonomy is actually a result of the *relative strength* of the propertied classes, especially the bourgeoisie, compared to the power of the bureaucracy and the extent to which it is needed to mediate and reconcile the different demands of propertied classes.

In both capitalist and proto-capitalist states, the civil bureaucracy has acted on its own or in alliance with the military to utilize the state apparatus to protect their conjoined interests. In this way, the civil-military bureaucratic alliance conducts itself as an *auxiliary* class. When this military-bureaucratic union (or the civil bureaucracy when the military is not in power) governs at the behest of one or more political parties, it also acts to further its own group interests and that of the political group in power, as it mediates the competing interests of other classes. However, when the bureaucracy deals with imperialist powers or institutions like the IMF or the WTO, it generally acts as an auxiliary class within the state apparatus but balances its own interests with the interests of these powers and institutions and those of the propertied classes.

Because imperialist forces, IFIs, and other multilateral institutions usually work very closely with the bureaucratic state apparatus in the Third World, this relationship imposes another layer of complexity to the task of clarifying the nature of the post-colonial state. Some capitalist post-colonial and even Latin American states, based on their relative economic strength, are beginning to forge a different, less subordinated, relationship with the US and other Western powers. However, their bureaucracies are still not completely independent of the influence of the West. In the case of proto-capitalist states, because many of them have a dependent and clientelist relationship with the US and its Western allies, their bureaucracies continue to be beholden to the West. Compared to the Western nation-state, Western capital/TNCs, and the IFIs, the proto-capitalist state is *weak* and has very few options at its disposal to protect its people, whose interests are antithetical to imperialist demands. However, when rulers of the proto-capitalist state enforce their will over society and the people, the state is internally '*strong*' in the sense of enforcing bureaucratic authoritarianism. It is important to note, however, that bureaucratic authoritarianism can be enforced only in relation to the balance of class forces and the relative weakness of civil society. In states where civil society has achieved cohesion and strength compared to authoritarian political/civil governments—as witnessed recently in popular uprisings in Egypt, Tunisia, and other Middle Eastern states—the bureaucracy can quickly switch sides to protect its auxiliary class interests and act to channel the popular will of the people towards less transformative outcomes. In other words, most post-colonial states have a contradictory character—both strong and weak—in the dialectical interplay of internal and external dimensions. This feature and my position on the differential levels of relative autonomy of capitalist and proto-capitalist post-colonial states are new contributions to the theory of the post-colonial state. Moreover, the contradictory nature of the post-colonial state negates the claim of some globalization theorists who have argued that the era of neoliberal globalization has produced the 'weakness' of the nation-state.[72]

IV TWO VARIANTS OF THE POST-COLONIAL STATE

This final section demonstrates that most post-colonial states fall under one of two varieties: the proto-capitalist state or the capitalist post-colonial state. The previous sections have identified some of the distinctions between these two variants; here, the focus is the cause of the shift from feudalist to proto-capitalist and from proto-capitalist to capitalist state and society. Based on the analysis of the social and economic dimension of state and society offered in this chapter, and without being reductive, it can be said that it is largely correct to give causal primacy to the economic dimension when addressing the shift from feudalism to capitalism, but being careful to place economics in the mix with politics and ideology when analyzing state-society relations—which is to say that I am not invoking the orthodox Marxist understanding of base-superstructure. However, this assumption—the primacy of the economic—may not be a valid basis to understand proto-capitalist states. Furthermore, the assignment of this causality to either the economic or the political has a bearing on the conception of relative autonomy of the state. Clarifying how economic and political moments affect power in post-colonial state and society requires a brief examination of the colonial state.

First, it is not actually the economic power of metropolitan bourgeois interests in the colony that gave the colonial administrators political clout; on the contrary, political control of the state in the colony presented colonial rulers and the metropolitan bourgeoisie with all kinds of economic opportunities. This claim is counter to the popular causal explanation offered by many scholars, but colonial and post-colonial situations involve a different causal link of extra-economic force. This extra-economic force implicates the political power of the bureaucracy and other interests that made up the state apparatus in colonial and now post-colonial societies. These interests have given legitimacy and economic power to landed and emerging capitalist classes, and have sustained and further strengthened the state apparatus. The enormous political power that was contained in the unitary, centralized structures of the colonial state gave it a monopoly on coercive control of the colonized, principally to stop revolts, have the power to extract tribute and appropriate surplus in the colony, and to drain the wealth of the colonized peoples. This debilitated the colony and left it very resource-poor. The colony was drained not because the metropolitan elite had economic power; rather, the realization of economic power rested on the *political* control of the colonial state through extra-economic means to extract economic benefit (tribute extraction) and fuel metropolitan capitalist development. In establishing the colonial state, colonial administrators made alliances with indigenous landed classes to ensure social control of the indigenous population for the extraction of economic surplus and its transfer with relative ease to the colonial state and the metropolitan bourgeoisie.

This characterization of extra-economic force and political power does not imply that resistance from the colonized was invisible in, or entirely eliminated from, the colony. Rather, the close collaboration of external and internal forces through the colonial state produced a lethal combination of power that was difficult to overcome by a people who were fragmented, politically unconscious, and unorganized. Ever since the colonial occupiers found that force could be used to develop and nurture local alliances and to arm indigenous collaborators (with weapons and political authority), they have fine-tuned the trajectory of subordination and dependency of the colonized and now the imperialized: the peoples of Africa, Asia, and the Americas. Colonizers and occupiers have stuck to the tried and tested strategy, even in the 21st century, of enabling indigenous collaborators to scout, unearth, stifle, and eventually quash resistance. Before the imperialized and occupied can develop their fragmentary resistance into a cohesive force, they are overcome and overrun by the collaborative strength of indigenous and metropolitan powers. For now more than 500 years, the challenge for the colonized and oppressed (and now the imperialized) has been to convert fragmentary resistance quickly into a more cohesive force. This has been very difficult, and successes have been few and isolated. However, signs of change are also on the horizon. The quagmires of Iraq and Afghanistan for US and NATO forces, and popular revolts in the Middle East, are indications of the oppressed and imperialized becoming better organized and strategically dissolving divisions in their midst, utilizing new communications technology, and presenting a unitary and cohesive line of resistance.

However, the legacy of the colonial state and its unitary, centralized structure has been re-appropriated for the post-colonial state—complete with colonial-era bureaucratic structural supports. The alliance of propertied classes in post-colonial societies, with bureaucratic mediation, has been able to access economic power by taking control of political power (the state). Almost no post-colonial states were capitalist at the time of decolonization, so their proto-capitalist nature facilitated the adoption of the structure of the colonial state and allowed the new indigenous rulers the benefit of political power exercised by the bureaucratic elites and the propertied classes. However, some of these proto-capitalist states have now become capitalist states, which raises the issue of whether the claim of the political primacy of the colonial state would apply with equal force to the current proto-capitalist and capitalist states. The simple answer is 'no'; the explanation is more involved.

The previous discussion has shown that no one class is truly hegemonic in proto-capitalist states. State apparatus is dominated by civil and/or military bureaucracy, and the landed interest of feudal landholders and capitalist farmers is reasonably strong, although not hegemonic, just as the capitalist bourgeoisie, which also oversees the strong presence of metropolitan capital. The state uses extra-economic coercion to benefit the propertied classes, often by enforcing historically oppressive social codes (such as the degrading and dehumanizing treatment of peasantry, the non-enforcement of labour laws, and the existence of appalling working conditions) or using state functionaries (police, judiciary, and district administration) for political ends to benefit feudal elites and/or capitalists. This use of political power has a causal primacy in economically empowering the propertied classes as well as the bureaucrats. The military brass and upper level bureaucrats magically transform when they leave their lofty perch: from high-level state functionaries into successful industrialists, owners of large agribusinesses, or wealthy property owners. This transformation is a common occurrence in many post-colonial states: well-known examples include the Mobutos, the Marcos, the Suhartos, and others. With regard to the role of the proto-capitalist state in fostering and strengthening the propertied classes, J.F. Medard suggested that:

> [f]or all intents and purposes . . . [the propertied classes] have no *independent economic base* or class identity outside the state and its power. It is the control of the state which gives the [ruling coterie] access to power and wealth, especially where the role and stake of the state is substantial.[73]

Issa Shivji used the African context to outline how the military, the bureaucracy, and other propertied classes, through their control of the state, have reaped substantial benefit and broadened their base of economic power.[74] Military officers regularly gained from toppling civilian governments and taking state power, as do even weak propertied classes when they have been coalesced around those holding state power. As will be discussed in Chapter 5, this volume, the military in Pakistan has become a veritable *economic force* in society. These issues along with those introduced at the beginning of this section, are key to understanding the bureaucratic-military and/or bureaucratic-authoritarian states that form the bulk of proto-capitalist states.

Capitalist post-colonial states, in contrast, signify an ascendant bourgeoisie and its dominance in society. The bourgeoisie has economic hegemony, and although a few capitalists may become part of the state apparatus, the bourgeoisie effectively retains their dominance indirectly in society through bureaucratic and political state functionaries—a situation not dissimilar to Western capitalist nation-states. The bourgeoisie is *formally* outside the capitalist state, implying that it exercises significant political influence on the state apparatus through political and bureaucratic elites to further state policy in its interest. By exercising this influence from a position of economic strength, the bourgeoisie has economic primacy over the political realm (the state)—a causal relationship that resembles Poulantzas's views of the capitalist state. Accordingly, the primacy of an ascendant bourgeoisie (its economic power and hegemony in capitalist post-colonial society) enables the class to attain its political objectives without being formally part of the state apparatus. In this respect, capitalist post-colonial states may not appear to differ greatly from the Western capitalist state, but the two state forms actually operate very differently—in the sense that capitalists in post-colonial states may not have just an arms-length relationship with upper level bureaucrats and state functionaries; rather, their relationships are a lot closer, and part of it may be because of the material benefit that the bureaucrats obtain through bribes and graft.

The claim that the post-colonial bourgeoisie is not *formally* part of the political does not necessarily involve a separation between the economic and political dimensions, as suggested by Poulantzas, Alavi, and Jessop.[75] There is still no separation between the economic and political moments in the operation of the capitalist post-colonial state: the bourgeoisie relies on a range of strategies, including bribes and financial incentives, to influence the state apparatus and ensure the political elite in post-colonial societies guide state policy for its benefit. Because the bourgeoisie chooses to operate formally outside the state, although some actually become part of the state, this does not amount to a separation of the political (state) from the economic power of capitalists in post-colonial societies. Capitalists' moves to influence state functionaries are of a political nature and are made both inside and outside the state. Thus, the *formal* separation from the political dimension cannot constitute an actual separation of the political and the economic, especially when the bureaucracy, acting in the bourgeoisie's interest, placates and adjusts demands of other classes and groups in society. In other words, as the bureaucracy in post-colonial capitalist states upholds capitalist interests, it cannot also forego its role of mediating the demands of the landed elites, be they capitalist or feudal landholders. In this way, the role of the state differs from that of the Western capitalist state.

This chapter has identified two variants of the post-colonial state: proto-capitalist and capitalist states. Other variants of the state may exist in the Third World, but this issue lies beyond the scope of this volume. However, based on the theorization of these two state forms, most states in Africa and Asia can be characterized according to one of these two variants.

4 India
The Capitalist Variant

This chapter grounds theory into practice to assess through concrete social analysis the case of India's formation as a capitalist post-colonial state. Using the theoretical framework set out in Chapter 3, this volume, I examine empirical and historical evidence of India's state formation and demonstrate how India is a capitalist variant of the post-colonial state—Pakistan being the proto-capitalist example, which I address in Chapter 5, this volume. In Chapter 3, this volume, my theorization of the post-colonial state identified three important factors affecting state formation: the impact of retaining a colonial state structure on the post-colonial state, the role of internal class relations and the consequence of civil and military bureaucracy protecting its auxiliary class interests, and the dependency-induced external pressure that embeds imperialist domination as a recurrent reality of post-colonial (and Latin American) states. In identifying these key factors, I have integrated the external and internal dimensions of the post-colonial state—a synthesis that is vital to clarify the character of the post-colonial state (in relation to the Western capitalist state). However, beginning in Chapter 1, this volume, I have also consistently shown that theorists from various fields of study have ignored the impact of the external dimension or have separated the external from the internal structure of state and society. Most writers across disciplines have notably omitted the external or have not integrated the two moments, including theorists of nation and nationalism, the Western capitalist state, the developmental state, and 'new imperialism' and globalization. The integration of the internal and the external is vital for a complete analysis of the post-colonial state and society. This approach has underpinned my theorization of the post-colonial state and undergirds this case study of India's (and Pakistan's) processes of state formation and explains why India became a capitalist state (and Pakistan a proto-capitalist entity).

I will begin analyzing India's state formation by initially focusing on the course charted by India's first Prime Minister, Jawaharlal Nehru, and the Congress Party at the time of decolonization. Next, I will assess, among other issues, Nehru's vision of a secular India, which was accompanied by an ambivalence towards Hindu nationalism, which helped trigger the re-surfacing of communalism in post-colonial India. Within the context of the Cold War rivalry, I will touch on Nehru's role in the Non-Aligned Movement. Because the external dimension is an essential part of this study of the post-colonial state, it is woven into the analysis of India's state formation. As I assess the internal structure of the state and social conditions in post-colonial India, I will tackle issues related to developmentalism, the land question, and the beneficiaries of early economic and social policy of the Nehruvian state. The next section focuses on the post-Nehruvian era, which includes Indira Gandhi's brief flirtation with populism as well as the manipulative policies that she used to alter the structure of the Indian state. These steps, I argue, provided succor to previously less popular and less visible Hindu nationalist groups, such as the Rashtriya Swayamsevak Sangh (RSS), Vishwa Hindu Parishad (VHP), and the Bharatiya Janata Party (BJP);[1] these religious nationalist groups, after Nehru's death, gained prominence and became identified as the forces of *hindutva* or Hindu nationalism/fundamentalism.

I will examine Indira Gandhi's populist measures, which neither improved the performance of the Indian economy nor resolved many of the unsettled questions related to regionalism, sub-nationalism, and Hindu nationalism; the consequences of these unresolved questions have impacted the social and economic plane. Economic stagnancy took such a toll on the Indian economy that the capitalist class itself started to demand the dismantling of the old state-led model of development, which had helped it prosper in the first place. The next section examines the introduction of economic liberalization and how India moved from the claims of a 'failed' developmental state to 'India Shining', signifying an unfettered embrace of neoliberalism and the dismantling of the developmental state. This section shows how the Indian capitalists' demands for greater market-orientation actually coincided with the conditionalities imposed by the International Monetary Fund (IMF) for market reforms. Admittedly, market reforms were adopted as initiatives of the Indian state, but it should be noted that the state was not immune from IMF pressure at the time. The section focuses on how the adoption of economic liberalization affected Indian state and society, in particular how the bourgeoisie as a class grew more powerful in relation to the bureaucracy and how the latter's auxiliary class position was modulated after Nehru's death. This analysis will demonstrate that although the Indian bourgeoisie was an ascendant class at the time of decolonization, the landed elite was also a strong contender for power. State-led policies actually went on to strengthen the capitalist class, and with the shift towards economic liberalization, the capitalist class attained a level of hegemony in Indian society. Through these developments India was well on its way to becoming a capitalist state by the early 1980s. However, the assertions of the landed elite and other groups in society have been such that the Indian state still exercises relative autonomy over the competing interests of various class forces and groups in society. The final section examines resistance to neoliberalism and how the initiative has been taken on by more radical groups such as the Maoist or the Naxalite from non-governmental organizations (NGOs) and other social activists. The Naxalite are now actively involved in resisting the takeover of Indigenous people's lands, the privatization of forests, and corporate mining interests. Such a challenge to neoliberalism, along with the nationalist movement in Kashmir, Assam, and elsewhere, has also led to the rise of the security-obsessed Indian state. So, although the Indian state has defeated the Naxalite in the past, the popularity of the current movement and its reach across different Indian states (provinces) promises more serious challenges for the neoliberal Indian security state.

I INDIA'S STATE FORMATION: DIRECTIONS CHARTED BY NEHRU AND THE CONGRESS

Even now, more than 60 years after decolonization, India and Pakistan remain prime examples of the *continuing* political legacy of the colonial state. The formation of South Asian states has been intricately linked to, and shaped by, this colonial legacy. The colonized South Asian societies were cold-pressed for wealth extraction, initially by more than 100 years of Company *raj* and then by another 100 years of Westminster's British *raj*. These more than 200 years of colonial domination and empire-building have forged the social and cultural consciousness of South Asian peoples, especially the South Asian elite. However, the effect of colonialism on shaping the culture and social consciousness of the colonized is not specific to South Asia; it can indeed be generalized to most other former colonies of Africa and Asia. Post-colonial societies have felt the impact of colonial rule in the areas of politics, economics, and culture. In the sphere of politics, the 'overdeveloped' colonial state structure with the auxiliary class status of the bureaucracy has been retained in most post-colonial states, but the character of the ruling classes differs between states, even between the South Asian states of India and Pakistan. The bureaucratic-authoritarian state structure, as a legacy of the colonial state, also differs between India and Pakistan: India has developed strong traditions of political leadership, whereas Pakistan is still mired in quasi-military rule. In the realm of economics, dependent economic development is a strong continuing legacy of the capitalism–imperialism nexus, although India seems to be on a more independent development trajectory. Beyond the political and economic dimensions, the nature of the propertied classes and the role of the post-colonial state since decolonization have largely determined whether a given post-colonial state will emerge as proto-capitalist or capitalist in the ensuing period.

On the eve of decolonization, India was by and large a proto-capitalist state. The following analysis will show that although the Indian bourgeoisie was ascendant, the strength of the feudal elite, especially the intermediary interests of the *zamindars*, was palpable. This reality and the concerns expressed by big Indian industrialists triggered the push for the major Indian land reform implemented immediately after the Partition. The objective of the land reform was to eliminate the landed class. Although the "abolition of intermediary interests [was] implemented fairly well," the reform's impact was uneven in different regions, and the main objective of effective land redistribution met with very minimal success, with tenants and sharecroppers becoming victims of "large-scale ejectments."[2] In effect, only 6% of all cultivable land was re-distributed in India.[3] Although the impact of this early land reform measure will be addressed next, the immediate question this brief information about the measure raises is whether or not India's commitment was to a socialist path of development, given the impression people had of Nehru. The short answer is that Jawaharlal Nehru's plan to follow a state-led model of development was not at all about India taking a socialist developmental path, despite the rhetoric; rather, this model was a state-guided trajectory of capitalist development in which the bourgeoisie were actively involved.

Some scholars of India consider Nehru to have made an overwhelming contribution to the "reinventing of India." Corbridge and Harriss, for example, ascribe a leading role to Nehru and leaders of the Indian National Congress (the Congress) on the paths taken by the Constituent Assembly in 1946, roughly a year before India's independence. The Constituent Assembly eventually paved the way for the transition to decolonization, which according to Corbridge and Harriss (among others) really propelled Nehru to power. Corbridge and Harriss went on to argue that Nehru played a pivotal role in framing India's Constitution (adopted 26 November 1949):

> Nehru provided the template of the invention of modern India, *and* that what we shall call the mythologies of rule in Nehru's India (ideas of democracy, socialism, secularism and federalism) have consistently affected the political economic landscapes of India since 1947, even where they have been honoured more in the breach than in the observance. It is in this sense that we speak of the invention of India in the 1940s and 1950s. We are not claiming that Nehru invented India as a true *Light of Asia*, nor are we claiming that Nehru's prospectus for social change measured up to his own rhetorics of developmentalism, nation-building or democratization [. . .] What we do claim is that an idea of India was put into play during this period which contributed to a new understanding of India "abroad" (India as the world's largest democracy, India as a secular state, India as a developing country), and which contributed, slowly and imperfectly, to new understandings of what it meant to be an Indian within independent India. There was, to paraphrase Nehru, at least some of magic in the moment of transition from the old to the new.[4]

Obviously, individuals—especially powerful personalities—cannot be separated from the historical role they may have played in shaping society and outlining the direction of state policy. But by the same token, it is important not to forget or minimize the realities of a people's existence, the relations of the social sphere, the configuration of class forces, and the impact of external powers and economic forces. Memorable personalities tend to be those individuals who safely steer the 'ship of state' through such complex and difficult waters—and Nehru may have been just such an individual. However, as Corbridge and Harriss pointed out, much of what ails India today has Nehru's and the Congress party's inscription on it: "We shall argue [. . .] that many of the pathologies of misrule that became evident in the 1970s or 1980s emerged from decisions taken—or not taken—in the Nehru years."[5]

So how do the Nehru years measure up? The starting point was the turn of the last century when the Congress began to spearhead the mainstream nationalist movement. By the mid-1940s, the Congress, with Nehru firmly in charge along with Sardar Patel, and with Mohandas Gandhi in the background, began to negotiate the terms of British withdrawal, the question of Pakistan, and other issues. As decolonization began and colonial rulers began their hurried departure, Nehru eventually took power. At the time of Partition, Nehru and his coterie of Congress party members needed to consider the traumas and human suffering caused by the slaughter of Hindus, Muslims, and Sikhs on either side of the divide. On one hand, they needed to chart a course for the country's independent existence as a sovereign state amidst the ensuing hatred that this genocide had brought forward. On the other hand, they faced challenges related to the exceptionally fast-paced changes on the international plane—the commencement of the Cold War, the emphasis on industrialism and developmentalism, the pressures on newly decolonized states from the US and the former USSR to become part of their respective spheres of influence, the project of non-alignment and Third Worldism, and so on. These were coupled with the enormous task of governing India. Given his social-democratic leanings, Nehru had to balance his rhetoric of socialism and eradicating poverty with his own class commitments amidst the influence and power of the industrial/commercial bourgeoisie and the landed elite.

Faced with these challenges, the Nehruvian project was one of state-led economic development and promotion of secularism, Westminster-style democracy, nation-building, and non-alignment as a principle of building Third World unity. Outwardly, Nehru projected the image of an austere and egalitarian individual who was mindful of his Indian*ness* and wanted India to be a model of the 'modern', sovereign, and non-aligned state in the Third World. However, his project and policies betrayed, to some, a kind of Orientalism that the Nehruvian project had come to symbolize.[6] Nehru's internalization of the 'modern' nation-state model was not very different from the attitude of other Third World nationalist leaders. The notion of 'modern India' was not separated from the British or Orientalist ideas of modernity, which were seen as embracing the Westminster-style centralized democracy and an uncritical embrace of Enlightenment notions of modernity. The paradox of modernity and secularism unfolded in India amidst a strong commitment to upholding tradition and accompanying deep caste and class divisions, mirroring two diametrically opposed realities of urban and rural life. This paradox is steeped within a culture of authoritarianism alongside a most skewed distribution of wealth, gaping social divisions, untouchability, and dissemination of privilege on the basis of class and caste power:

> In one of the typical paradoxes of Indian society the very factors necessitating the politics of secular nationalism laid the basis for particularistic religious communalism. Despite the official creed of secularism, a succession of Congress leaders both before and after Gandhi had grasped the expediency of resorting to popular Hindu religious symbols. As assertion of cultural confidence against alien rule as well as a strategy for political mobilization, the use of the Hindu idiom did much to narrow the gap separating India's localized public arenas from the larger purposes of the nationalist leadership. Yet what was intended to paper over the innumerable cracks within the majority community had the unwitting effect of appearing to set Hindus apart from non-Hindus, Muslims in particular.[7]

The setting apart of Hindus and Muslims is one of the more enduring legacies of colonial rule, but the "manipulation of religious symbolism in a secular nationalist garb had deeper intellectual moorings"—extending all the way back to the late 1800s with the rise of Hindu nationalism, when the idea of the 'nation' was equated with the land of the mythological Vedic ruler, Bharat.[8] This historical basis probably informed Nehru and many Congress leaders, who in framing the Indian Constitution, introduced the notion of secularism and ideas about inclusiveness through at least 12 articles of the Indian Constitution, which P.K. Tripathi contends have outlawed "communal electorates," religious intolerance, untouchability, and religious education in public institutions, among other measures.[9] It should be noted that the "Indian Constitution did not contain the word *secular* as a signification of the state until it was done so by [the Indira Gandhi government through the] 1976 amendment"[10]—ironically, after she had monopolized power by declaring a state of emergency.

Soon after coming to power in 1947, the Congress was of the view that the real problem was caste and that communalism had much to do with casteism. Consequently, the Indian state would maintain a separation between politics and religion—a split between public political life and the private realm of religious practices. In making this separation, Nehru and the Congress were unmindful of the consequences of their action. In maintaining this division, they were backsliding on two fronts simultaneously: first, the imposition of a top-down edict of confidence-building measures between members of the Hindu and Muslim communities was made without providing the necessary social framework for dialogue and tolerance at the grassroots level—especially given the proximity of the horrors of Partition. Thus, in pursuing a formalistic top-heavy approach to bringing amity between the two communities, the Indian state opted to remain distant from any grassroots efforts at rapprochement. Second, although article 17 of the Constitution outlawed untouchability, the practice not only continued unchecked but gathered steam with the spread of religious nationalism. The Indian state's inaction in the private realm—its decision to do nothing to end oppressive religious practices—led to a public-private split, for which many writers have faulted Nehru, as he promoted a secularism that left the private sphere of religion in the control of Hindu communalist and exclusivist groups like the RSS—in essence providing them a fertile ground to recruit, build, and strengthen their intolerant religious cadre.[11]

Indian state formation differed qualitatively from the formation of European nation-states in that the Indian elite 'inherited' a ready-made state structure, if not the state itself. This state came complete with colonial-era penal, criminal, and civil procedure codes as well as with a sophisticated and 'overdeveloped' civil and military bureaucracy. Even after more than 60 years of decolonization, this structure remains largely intact, and the laws have only been very selectively modified. The retention of colonial state structures has a lot to do with the leadership in the anti-colonial movement and whether those who took the mantle of power from colonial rulers felt it was in their interest to continue with the prevailing colonial structures of governance or to make a radical break from them. The bourgeoisie in India opted for the former path, which has also been the case in most other former colonized states. Consequently, the Indian elite negotiated merely the relinquishing of power by colonial rulers and, in so doing, were forced to follow the colonial methods of administration and control. One insightful reading of the Indian state on the twilight of the "night-bitten dawn"[12] of 'independence' has captured the implications of the Indian state's burden of *inheritedness*:

> On the one hand, the Indian independence movement brought together large sections of society, with conflicting interests, against colonial rule. The movement was thus also the site of struggle between different classes for control over it; a struggle in which the growing indigenous bourgeoisie was able to establish its dominance well before independence. This class clearly perceived the Indian state as the vehicle through which it would transform the economy and strengthen its own position within it.
>
> On the other hand, the structure and apparatuses of the state *remained largely identical with those of the colonial state* which had

> been used to reshape the Indian social formation according to the needs of metropolitan capital. And the same alliance with the rural dominant classes which had enabled the bourgeoisie to dominate the independence movement now proved to be a major constraint upon capitalist transformation. The state thus became the focal point for a number of different contradictions whose strength varied over time: contradictions between different sections of the dominant classes, between the interests of imperialist and indigenous capital, as well as between the producing classes and those who appropriated their surplus.[13]

Therefore, as these contradictions began to unfold, the challenges to the Congress government grew to enormous proportions. On the economic plane, Nehru resisted the path of capitalist development advocated by modernization theorists, but ironically developmentalism was the key feature of his policy of state-led economic planning.

II SOCIAL CONDITIONS IN EARLY POST-COLONIAL INDIA

Despite being a predominantly agrarian society (70% of its labour force) on the eve of decolonization, India was the seventh-largest industrial country by volume of output.[14] At the time, India was not an industrial society. According to the widely accepted mainstream logic of capitalist development, a largely agricultural economy is constrained by the limits imposed by the demand of agricultural products as opposed to manufactured goods. Additionally, the high rates of tribute and interest during the colonial and post-colonial periods kept the peasants pauperized, leaving them with nothing to invest in land; consequently, no real structural transformation occurred from primary to secondary and tertiary sectors,[15] unlike in Europe. By citing the accepted and prevailing logic of economic growth or industrialization that presumes the 'onward' and inevitable goal of capitalist development as 'progress', my objective is to show that the history of policy and economic planning in India, and in the South more generally, has been strongly informed by such Eurocentric reasoning. The framework of colonialism has placed the former colonies in an economic straitjacket, compelling Third World leaders to follow this 'logic of development'—that is, capitalist development—at all costs (although there is, in some cases, also a willingness on the part of Third World leaders to pursue an alternative course of development).

(i) Re-Examining the Emulation Strategy of Early European Industrialization in the Context of Dependent Capitalist Development

The path taken immediately after decolonization by Nehru and his economic gurus, political pundits, and the bureaucratic elite suggested, at least on paper, a commitment to avoiding the blind pursuit of capitalist development.

At the time of Partition, there was much debate in India over whether to adopt capitalist, socialist, or a 'mixed' economic program. In this chapter I will briefly analyze these debates and the economic planning model adopted by the Nehru government, but first it is important to assess the validity of developmental state theorists' outlook and how they and others pressured post-colonial states to emulate the experience of Europe's industrialization. To this end, I will briefly examine some key issues related to European capitalist development and address whether modernization and the model of industrialization set out by market-oriented developmental state theorists—which pushed post-colonial states to emulate the European experience of market-oriented industrialization—bears any resemblance to the actual experience of capitalist development in Europe. In earlier chapters of this volume, I focused on the deeply embedded Eurocentrism in the emulation strategy and how the policies of international financial institutions (IFIs) and modernization theorists caused immense harm, devastating the lives of millions of people who survive at the very edges of society. In Chapter 2, this volume, I also discussed the ideas of the developmental state from different perspectives, but what I did not mention was that the ideas, be they of dependency theorists or inward-oriented or market-oriented developmental state theorists, the underlying commitment for all of them was to economic development (industrialization) as progress—whether it was achieved through the paths of socialist or capitalist development. Therefore, here, I will analyze some of the key issues underlying early capitalist development in Europe as yet another way of challenging this widely accepted 'logic of development'.

Analysis of the emulation hypothesis in the context of European capitalist development clearly reveals, even with a cursory glance at the experiences of various states in Europe, that England did not simply become the formulaic capitalist model for the rest of Europe to emulate *at will* by making the revolutionary transformation from feudalism to capitalism. Undoubtedly, revolutionary transformations took place in Europe, as people violently resisted their oppressors and exploiters at different conjunctures; however, the context and the mode of transformations varied widely. Even during Europe's economic and social transformation, capitalist development was not a simple evolutionary process, and it was not one by which Western Europe simply adopted England's experience of capitalist development. As a matter of fact, in England alone,

> it took a series of revolutions [. . .] from the sixteenth century down to the eighteenth for capitalist relations to be firmly established on the ground under the supervision of a group of triumphant profit-oriented landlords, merchants, and later on, industrialists. Adam Smith may have preached laissez-faire in 1776, but England pursued *nationalist* economic policies down to the 1840s when free trade was introduced in the interest of manufacturers and wage-earners, and that interest was firmly based on a global supremacy in manufacturing, trade and finance.[16]

Bagchi argued that a similar combination of 'economic nationalism' and political revolutions under a series of complex and specifically indigenous development also occurred in the rest of Europe and North America:

> The story of the spread of capitalism in the other countries of Western Europe and in North America cannot be told only as a kind of passive adaptation of capitalist institutions borrowed from England. In France, Germany, or the USA, or even the small Scandinavian countries, it was a story of political revolutions leading to the eventual victory of interests championing the cause of capitalism; revolutions which were often reversed in the short run only to break out afresh in the setting of a new national and international conjuncture.
>
> [. . .] The history of capitalism shows precisely that a country or a region that passively adapts to the dictates of the dominant fraction of international or transnational capital generally finds itself condemned to underdevelopment.[17]

Bagchi's connection between economic passivity/subservience and underdevelopment is valid for much of the South, but there are also exceptions (of which he is quite aware). For instance, South Korea, Taiwan, Singapore, Hong Kong, and others quietly accepted imperialist dictates, but their social developmental structures were not enhanced by substantial economic 'rewards' from the capitalist states of Britain and the US in the form of investments and economic aid. Rather, internal social relations and the cohesiveness of different groups in these countries (and elsewhere in the South) were seriously undermined. Nonetheless, this kind of 'development' and industrialization came at a high cost to these and other post-colonial states in terms of the loss of sovereignty, among a host of other deficits. Some developmental state theorists claim that these costs are the necessary consequence of becoming a 'modern', industrialized society—a claim that the former Soviet Union and China's early economic/industrial development does not support.

Beyond developmental state theory, comparisons are constantly made between South and North; the global South is expected to embrace the European experience, at least on the economic plane. But why is it that political revolution, which if Bagchi is correct swept Europe and its movement towards capitalism, is not on the agenda for the South? If the bourgeois transformation of society and the state in Europe was a revolutionary change that Europeans proudly adopted, then why cannot the same take place in the South? The simple answer is that most post-colonial states cannot even begin to have nationalist leaders who pursue a self-reliant path of economic and social development, which comes about in large part through social and political revolutions. The reason is the constant drumbeat of imperialist arm-twisting and interventions. The equally simple reason why self-reliant development will not be facilitated is that the capitalism–imperialism nexus cannot be easily severed. It took almost the last 60 years for the US and its imperialist allies to eliminate nationalist leadership in post-colonial and Latin American states and to break the mould of inward-oriented or state-led development—thereby facilitating the rise of neoliberal globalization and mobility of transnational capital. The US and its allies will not allow this process to be undone easily. Even in the recent 'Arab awakening' in the Middle East, the US and Western European states have been busy trying to tame the revolutions by intervening to determine favourable outcomes. As an example, the elimination of Muammar Gaddafi at the hands of North Atlantic Treaty Organization/ Libyan 'rebels' in contrast to the continued tacit support of oppressive leaders in Bahrain and Yemen (who have also killed scores of protestors) is part of creating or determining favourable outcomes for Western powers. The North has a lot to lose—in particular, the entire edifice of the world capitalist system (WCS) and its thoroughly exploitable periphery.

Post-colonial societies have a very different history than European societies. Revolutionary transformation did not come about in most post-colonial states, and although the colonial state and the collaborative indigenous colonized elite had everything to do with effectively blocking a wholesome and nationalist developmental path, it is now fruitless to blame colonial rule for these losses. It is important, however, to understand the nature and consequences of these losses for post-colonial states, especially in an era where dependency and subservience has become the norm, to be able to address them in the post-colonial context. Undoubtedly, indigenous rulers had a unique opportunity to resist imperialism and to turn the tide of dependency and domination when they took the reins of power at the end of colonial rule. Some in the Congo, Ghana, and Indonesia tried, others in Algeria and Vietnam were even successful for a while, but in the final analysis, the capitalism–imperialism nexus prevailed—helped along largely by the collaborative indigenous elite. That was a critical juncture at which the early post-colonial state had the possibility of changing course by dismantling and re-configuring the colonial state structure to suit post-colonial realities. At the risk of stating the obvious, dismantling of the colonial state structure would have been logical and necessary because the structures of the colonial state, as should be now quite clear, cannot just be adapted for use in the post-colonial setting because they were specifically designed to serve imperial interests. I have repeatedly implied in this book the fact that post-colonial states must break radically from the stranglehold of their colonialist past and imperialist present if they are to escape subordination by metropolitan capital. In this context, it matters little whether the indigenous elite inherited a ready-made colonial state (as in India) or whether a new state apparatus needed to be built (as in Pakistan); both societies required a radical break with the past to escape the cycle of dependency, domination, gross inequality, and poverty—the desired end to an ordinary person's misery. But it was not to be. Even those former colonized societies that had fought national liberation struggles against colonial rule, such as Algeria, Indonesia, and Vietnam, were unable to establish a post-colonial society that was a radical break from the colonial past.

If the former Soviet Union's early revolutionary developments were an inspiration for India's model of economic planning, Nehru did not adapt his policy to reflect the lessons learned from the 1917 revolution, and India also degenerated into an oppressive form of bureaucratic authoritarianism. Because revolutionary change was not a possibility in post-colonial India, the next best move would have been to replicate as much of its transformative potential as possible within a non-revolutionary framework: the state, in other words, could have become an enormous catalyst, if not the instigator, of significant social change. But even in this realm, the Indian state was a big disappointment for the downtrodden millions. Despite Nehru's socialist rhetoric, very little effort was made to institute land redistribution on a massive scale, which, as discussed next, could have eliminated *landlordism* and transformed social relations in agriculture. After the first land reform was implemented in India soon after Partition in 1947, the Congress government began to abandon the project due to pressure from large landholders.[18] As a consequence, the ideas of developmentalism remained, and after the brief period of a state-led model of social and economic upliftment, India has re-submitted, along with most post-colonial states, to the primacy of the market and the path of dependent capitalist development.

(ii) The Land Question

The project of land reform was abandoned very early after decolonization, but the Indian National Congress's Economic Programme Committee had done excellent work on the rural land question. The issue was addressed quite comprehensively in the *Report of the Congress Economic Programme Committee*, which was produced soon after decolonization in January 1948. The *Report* outlined, among other measures, the need to abolish the intermediary (*zamindari*) rights in land, to determine the size of maximum landholding, and to distribute surplus land to village cooperatives. However, when it came time to implement these proposals, the resulting legislation was skewed heavily in favour of big landlords: "the rural oligarchs, with the support of the legal machinery, forced the central Congress leadership to effectively shed most of the land reforms proposals except the abolition of intermediary rights."[19] Bagchi added that the

> constitutional provisions for concurrent State [i.e., provincial] rights to regulate agriculture underlined the nature of the consensus under which the central government could manage the visible commanding heights of the cities provided they left the rural mud fortresses of the rural oligarchs alone.[20]

The feudal elite were so powerful that the state actually opted to leave this group alone. However, some land in India was re-distributed because of constitutional provisions that placed ceilings on landholdings and abolished the intermediary interests of the *zamindars*.[21] However, radical land reform measures by which cultivable land in excess of 30% would be redistributed were not to be. Feudal oligarchs responded with relative calm to the abolition of *zamindari* rights because, even with somewhat smaller landholding, they still had considerable power in rural areas. Paradoxically, the Congress' blueprint for India's economic and social policy was trumped by the *Bombay Plan*, a document produced by Indian capitalists as a counter-proposal for India's economic and social development. The *Bombay Plan* took a stronger position on the idea of land reforms by insisting on the necessity of "institutional reform of a radical kind."[22]

The Indian capitalists' views on land reform in the *Bombay Plan* differed significantly from their approach to dealing with poverty, a quite conventional approach that was similar to that espoused by the Congress, which emphasized economic growth and industrialization of the Indian economy as *the* way out of poverty.[23] Despite the fact that the Congress eventually pursued a greatly watered-down plan for land reforms, alongside an economic policy that focused on public sector development, the role played by Indian capitalists in directing state policy cannot be minimized. It may be surprising to some that the Indian capitalists did not really want the state out of the industrialization process, despite maintaining their own vision of the public sector and a desire to shape the Indian economy. To clarify this uniquely Indian paradox and to identify the real beneficiaries of the Indian state's social and economic policy, it is necessary to sift through the actions of the state on one hand and Indian capitalists on the other.

(iii) The Beneficiaries of Early Economic and Social Policy of the State

All rhetoric aside, Nehru's views were not very different from those who developed the *Bombay Plan*[24] and the Indian elites more generally in terms of the centrality of industrialization as a strategy for 'modernizing' India and ending poverty:

> You seem to separate the three objectives—India's independence, the creation of a socialist state, and the solution of the problems of India's poverty and unemployment and you suggest that the last mentioned should be tackled first. I am afraid that this whole conception of our struggle is wrong. If all of us in India devoted ourselves to fighting poverty under the present system—political and economic—we shall not get rid of it. If we could get rid of it the problem is a simple one and the need for *swaraj* is not very apparent.[25]

To Nehru, *swaraj* (literally, self-rule) meant self-reliance, which could be achieved on the basis of self-directed industrialization that would supposedly take the place of foreign capital in India and allow 'free' growth of the country and its people via state-centered industrialization. This kind of thinking set in motion the direction of economic planning in India. However, as Bagchi pointed out, major Indian capitalists—G.D. Birla, Jamshed Tata, and others—were aware as early as 1936 that Nehru's talk of socialism was not accompanied by any real commitment when it came to practice or policy.[26] Big business was therefore quite willing to work with Nehru and support the Congress, and in turn, Nehru was equally willing to warm up to Indian capitalists, albeit within the framework of state-centered industrialization. Was there a contradiction between these two seemingly conflicting positions? Apparently not; in fact, Chaudhuri suggested that state-centered development actually benefitted Indian capitalists. As public sector-based industrialization pushed ahead through the adoption of five-year economic plans, the state effectively financed the costs of the necessary infrastructure: "the expansion of industries such as steel which required massive investments, and implicitly if not explicitly offered [Indian capitalists] protection [from] foreign capital."[27] In essence, the role of the Indian state was to weave a cocoon around emerging Indian private capital, allowing the Indian capitalist to grow with little disturbance from foreign competition. In carrying out this work, the state was effectively underwriting much of the costs of private capitalist development, "bearing a large proportion of costs and risks of development but taking much less of the surplus. For these reasons, Indian business was quite happy to finance the Indian Congress."[28]

As to the role of foreign capital in India, it can be said that investment policy was designed to discourage multinationals from setting up branch plants in the country during the 1950s and 1960s and that collaboration with foreign capital therefore took the form of joint ventures. This is an important point when considering the hype around limits placed on foreign capital. For instance, the "special statement" of the Congress government issued in 1949 assured that foreign capital's "existing bastions would not be assaulted by the new government and that it would be allowed to expand in most fields (with the exception of few sectors reserved for government)."[29]

The apparent symmetry in the visions of the Congress and Indian big business has been interpreted in various ways by different Indian and non-Indian economists. Some writers, including Bagchi, referred to an "elite consensus" at work. Others, including Chaudhuri, argued for the existence of a creative tension between the views of the two groups. However, state support for the development of capitalism as well as the nurturance of private capital appeared to be the paramount objective of both the state and the Indian bourgeoisie. Although the reduction of poverty would have been a preferred outcome, it could not be achieved without threatening to undermine the interests of capitalists or the bureaucracy in India. Poverty reduction thus came to be mired in one grandiose bureaucratic plan or another with very few concrete measures taken to actually alleviate the deplorable existence of the desperately poor in India. As a result, poverty continues to be an immensely troubling issue, despite India's extensive industrialization. The current (2009–2010) Indian Planning Commission (IPC) estimated that 32% of Indians live below the poverty line.[30] The IPC threshold of what constitutes the 'poverty line' (Rupees 20 [US 50 cents] per day per person in urban areas and Rupees 11 [US 28 cents] per day per person in rural areas) is so ridiculously low that even the Indian Supreme Court slammed the IPC for these arbitrary low poverty line cutoffs. One can well imagine the living nightmare of these 32% of India's citizens—and the living conditions of those who survive marginally above the poverty line are not much better.

However, it would be unfair to say that Nehru was insincere in his "rhetoric of socialism." His idea of socialism was articulated as part of the social democratic tradition that saw India's absorption within the WCS as a problematic situation. But his particular social democratic slant—which did not allow him to be very attentive to class/caste issues, other than seeing the emerging bourgeoisie as a 'progressive' social force or desiring an end to poverty without meaningful alleviation strategies that would alter class relations—meant that India would become part of the WCS.[31] In the mid-1930s, however, before the Partition, Nehru began to embrace economic planning policies in the belief that this was the path for "socialist" economies, and that it would weaken India's link with the WCS. His economic planning involved imbricating the state in resource allocation and creating an industrial production base. The objectives of economic planning within the Nehruvian framework, therefore, were (i) the alleviation/elimination of poverty through intensive industrialization, (ii) the adoption of a socialist pattern of development so as to weaken India's link with the WCS, and (iii) the determination to stay the course of self-reliant development.[32] At face value, these objectives appear to conflict with the aspirations of Indian big business, and therein lies the rub: in adopting these objectives, India was also effectively embracing the idea of developmentalism and a commitment not so much to socialism but rather to a state-led model of capitalist development.

To complicate matters, commentators who have analyzed early Indian economic policy have concluded that the record of planning was a failure because Nehruvian policy framework involved the ideas of developmentalism instead of the aforementioned three objectives.[33] India's industrial development chugged along at a pace that became known as the "Hindu rate of growth," but the concept of self-reliance had steered Indian industrial development towards reasonably sound footing. The declaration by some economic pundits during the 1980s and 1990s that the Indian economy was a "failure" has not only proved incorrect but also ill-founded.[34] Therefore, with the maturation of Indian industry, which has unquestionably come with immense social costs, the Nehruvian objective of industrialization cannot be regarded as a failure in terms of industrial policy. On the contrary, Nehru's policy anchored India's industrialization effort along a relatively less dependent path in relation to most other post-colonial and Latin American states. The failure, if it can be called a failure, was not so much a result of policy but more of Nehruvian vision: it was the choice to link poverty alleviation with industrialization. This decision did little for social upliftment, and it was not able to spread the wealth or to reduce significantly the ranks of the desperately poor. However, industrialization at any cost was the paramount objective of both Nehru and the Indian capitalists, and this has certainly been realized. Be that as it may, the Nehruvian legacy dealt some huge blows to the Indian polity. The support for secularism, as discussed previously, led to a public-private split and created the conditions for the re-emergence of Hindu fundamentalists within the private sphere—indeed, as a very strong political force—within a decade after Nehru's death.

In this analysis of India's early state formation, we can characterize the Indian state as having relative autonomy *albeit under the sway* of the indigenous bourgeoisie. This peculiar character resulted from a particularly Indian variety of capitalist development, but this does not mean that capitalists in India have in all cases prevailed over the other 'contradictions' mentioned in Wilson's passage cited previously.[35] For this reason, the Indian bureaucracy still maintains relative autonomy in relation to the competing interests of other classes and groups despite the hegemony of the bourgeoisie. Undoubtedly, the power of the Indian bureaucrats—with respect to the growing assertions of Indian capitalists—has been curtailed from the period of colonial rule and immediately following decolonization. Nonetheless, the Indian state is forced to mediate conflicting class, group, and regional interests, ensuring wherever possible that the dominant interests of the bourgeoisie are safeguarded. Another factor that consolidates the relative strength of the state apparatus is related to the involvement of the Indian state at the level of cultural and social issues, especially when it comes to addressing oppressive cultural practices. Whenever the state has entered the social and cultural arenas where the upper caste/class has strongly opposed popular demands, such as the inclusion and fairer representation of lower caste peoples, the state's role has remained formal and ritualistic. Beyond the banning of some horrendous religious practices, such as *Sati* (widow's immolation) and the introduction of laws for greater *Dalit* (lower caste groups) participation, there has not been a determined effort either to enforce these laws or to ensure they are socially accepted. As a result, the Nehruvian state's track record on social inclusion and equality rights has been very poor.

However, the state has been integrally involved in protecting the interests of the Indian bourgeoisie and landed elite. As discussed in the previous section about the relationship between Indian capitalists and the state shows, the *Bombay Plan* opted to implement a different role for the public sector, but the Indian capitalist elite eventually gave way once the state assured the protection of capitalist interests through a state-centered development strategy. On the other hand, although Indian big business had proposed radical land reforms, the state ensured that the interests of the landlords would be protected despite the abolition of *zamindari* rights and without otherwise significantly affecting the interests of Indian capitalists. This has been possible because, as discussed in Chapter 3, this volume, landed and capitalist interests can co-exist in colonial and post-colonial contexts, unlike in the European period of early capitalist development.

III THE POST-NEHRUVIAN ERA: POPULISM AND DERAILMENT OF THE SECULAR STATE IDEA

The derailment of secularism is the one significant development that challenges the ascription of relative autonomy to the Indian state. The notion of secularism was threatened as the state began to pander to the demands of Hindu nationalists and as the leadership of the Congress was passed from Nehru to his daughter, Indira Gandhi. The Indian state failed to address the excesses of the dominant Hindu fundamentalists against the minority interests of Christians, Muslims, Sikhs, and others, but it also failed to protect *Dalit* groups against upper caste oppression and excesses. Many Indians and others are still concerned with how the Nehruvian secular state has been eclipsed by the rising wave of Hindu fundamentalists, who until recently had literally taken control of the state when the BJP rose to power. The BJP's rise to power marked the post-Nehruvian shift that reshaped the Indian state and its commitment to secularism under Indira Gandhi and subsequent political leadership.

Under Nehru, the Congress was said to have a wide base of support among the poor and the people of the rural hinterland. However, this support was not the result of Nehru's policies actually making a difference in the lives of these resourceless and wretchedly poor people. Rather, it was the result of class/caste convergences among the elite, which came about primarily through methods of "vertical patterns of mobilization with rural big wigs who commanded the allegiances of [lower] castes and powerful local factions" and were able to enlist the poor's support for the Congress.[36] In other words, the enormous control of landlords in villages has historically forced the ordinary peasant or rural worker to fall in line and follow the dictates of large landholders. Because these village bosses have controlled the countryside, they have been delivering large vote banks to the Congress for decades as an act mainly of self-service. In return, Congress has safeguarded the interests of the landed elite, for example by refusing both the recommendations of the party's own parliamentary committee and the radical land reform measures suggested in the *Bombay Plan*. This tried and tested 'vertical form of mobilization' by the elite seems to have been well-suited to the merging of elite and state interests.

Indira Gandhi also relied on this method of elite/state control when she was chosen for the Congress leadership after the death of her father. In 1966, however, Gandhi was more vulnerable to the power of "the 'syndicate' bosses who had come to control the party organization after Nehru's death in 1964 [and] selected [her] as their prime ministerial candidate, certain of keeping her at their beck and call."[37] But the years of social neglect under Nehru, set against the backdrop of inflation, food shortages, and high unemployment, eroded people's loyalty to the Congress, forcing the party to take notice and deal with people's anger. The ensuing resentment among the people, however, was the trigger for many defections from the Congress and other challenges to its leadership; some regional 'big wigs' also began to withdraw support from the Congress. All these developments were enormously significant and worked to erode the party's support base, as reflected in the results of the 1967 general elections when the party lost control of eight states. In the aftermath of these developments, regional parties gained ascendancy and there was "a general heightening of social conflict along class and caste lines [that] had serious ramifications for political stability at the state level."[38]

Old party bosses, therefore, began to switch allegiances, regional parties began to gain prominence, and the base of support of the Congress consequently started to shrink. In these circumstances, Indira Gandhi was able to free herself from the stranglehold of 'syndicate' bosses. By 1969, the worldwide shift towards radical politics and the gross neglect of the poor in India had also triggered radicalization of Indian society. This process not only played out along class lines, but caste, gender, tribal, and linguistic identities also began to be asserted. As a result, the Congress had to take drastic actions for its own survival, and Gandhi took the lead by moving left. In so doing, "she opted for an explicitly populist socio-economic program."[39] However, the leftward shift was not ideologically motivated—it was purely a tactical turn on Indira Gandhi's part.

The radicalization of the late 1960s was not peculiar to India; it grew to regional, national, and global levels. On a regional basis, the parties in South India were demanding fairer representation and a stronger voice at the centre, whereas radical and class-based demands were also being made in Bengal and elsewhere. A rising tide of radicalism also appeared in other South Asian states: in Pakistan, general anti-American sentiment mobilized students and workers, in turn galvanizing successful mass protests against the dictatorship of General Ayub Khan and ending 11 long years of military rule. As a result, populist leader Z.A. Bhutto was propelled to power in Pakistan. Similarly, Mujibur Rahman had to move further left as students in the former East Pakistan (Bangladesh) started to demand the separation of the province from Pakistan. Globally, the American civil rights movement was changing the social landscape of a highly racialized society, and even Europe was witnessing challenges to state power by workers and students.

As Indira Gandhi moved left, she upset the mango cart of the old bosses of the Congress. In the ensuing split within the Congress, Gandhi decided to form a minority government with the support of Communists and the populist regional party from South India, deciding, in the process, to embrace a populist platform. Populism in the South Asian context can be described as an opportunistic response on the part of upper class/caste elites, who tolerate a charismatic leader with the aim of subverting the genuine socio-economic grievances made by the marginalized and the most vulnerable groups in society. This opportunism marks the making of promises, for instance, to eliminate poverty and social inequality, with the larger, underlying objective to protect upper class interests—and this is precisely how Indira Gandhi's actions can be characterized. In her bid to gain popularity in preparation for the 1971 elections, Gandhi began to woo the lower castes, especially in the critical states of Gujarat and Uttar Pradesh, and tried further to mobilize support among the Muslims. Gandhi's efforts to widen and deepen her support base were accompanied by her adoption of a more interventionist state policy: she nationalized banks, introduced a more restrictive import licensing policy, and abolished the privy purses to princely families.[40]

With her preparations complete, Indira Gandhi called an election for 1971, all the while raising the populist slogan of *gharibi hatao* (remove poverty). Incidentally, Indira Gandhi's popularity also derived, in no small measure, from India's victory in the 1971 War with Pakistan that helped to establish the new state of Bangladesh. These moves facilitated a comfortable victory by which Congress members won a strong majority in parliament. However, serious challenges lay ahead despite this electoral victory. These challenges came from the Hindu right, which had been nurtured literally within the framework of the secular state ever since Nehru had declared that religion was a subject of the private realm of home and *mandir*. This declaration allowed Hindu fundamentalist/ethno-nationalist groups, such as the reactionary RSS and the Jan Sangh, to continue mobilizing and building cadres of their respective organizations by invoking the Vedic texts and declaring that the idea of *hindutva*—literally Hindu-*ness*—required the creation of an avowedly Hindu state. The political party of the Hindu right, the BJP, and its ideological arm, the RSS, are not merely revivalist; rather, they considered *hindutva* to be synonymous with *Indianness*, implying that those who do not subscribe to the *hindutva* outlook have no inherent right to call themselves Indian.[41] This effacing and exclusionary outlook has re-surfaced mainly to target Indian Muslims but also Sikhs and Christians.

Looking beneath the anti-Muslim actions, such as the targeting of Muslims in Ahmadabad and Mumbai and the burning of the old Babri mosque (supposedly built on the grounds of an ancient Hindu temple), the rhetoric of *hindutva* activists and right-wing Hindu nationalism symbolizes an upper caste reaction to *Dalit* assertions for inclusiveness and equal treatment. Ironically, it is the very same *Dalit* members, the poor and lower caste Hindus, who have been enlisted to contain the 'common enemy', the Indian Muslims. This deftly manipulated strategy of Hindu nationalism exemplifies *hindutva's* anti-Muslim sentiment, but the Indian state, under Nehru's leadership, has either been powerless or, as under Rajiv Gandhi, has been complicit in allowing relatively free rein to *hindutva*. This rise of Hindu fundamentalism is at the heart of the decline of secularism in India. A more detailed investigation of this decline is beyond the scope of this book; my objective here is to examine the twists and turns in the formation of the Indian state and the ways and means of protection it has afforded to upper caste/class.[42]

With the rise of Hindu fundamentalism and the challenges from regional parties, Indira Gandhi reverted to the tried and tested authoritarian and social manipulation tactics used by old colonial rulers, including sowing political and religious divisions while strong-arming weaker segments of society. She strengthened these political moves after her return to power in 1980, following her defeat in the 1977 elections. Her defeat was related to her policies and the actions of her son, Sanjay Gandhi, who played a pivotal role in the Indian state's adoption of draconian measures including the declaration of an internal Emergency (October 1976—January 1977), effectively denying citizens' civil and democratic rights. It was during this period that the practice of forced sterilization was adopted, coinciding with neo-Malthusian ideas gaining currency among a segment of the Indian ruling elite[43] and the bureaucracy. This segment of the elite blamed the poor for India's population crisis: the enforcement of the sterilization program "took the form of brazen class oppression, the entire might of the oppressive machinery of the state, including the police force, [which was] used to sterilize millions against their will."[44] These and other excesses led to the fall of Indira Gandhi's government in 1977.

When Congress and Indira Gandhi re-emerged to win the 1980 elections, the populism of the charismatic leader was quickly replaced—in a bid to consolidate power—by a manipulative political policy to exploit India's regional and religious fault lines. Gandhi's calculating moves were played out in the state of Punjab where Akali Dal, a regional Sikh party, was challenging the Congress. In response, Gandhi tried to groom an opposition to Akali Dal from within the Sikh community. This backfired badly, resulting in the Indian military storming the Sikh community's holiest place, the Golden Temple. The aftermath of these ill-thought and ill-advised actions was tragic insofar as Indira Gandhi lost her own life, but at another level they set in motion developments that challenged the very idea of the secular state. First, as a result of Indira Gandhi's assassination and then the ensuing massacre of Sikhs in Delhi and elsewhere, the *hindutva* forces made enormous gains. Later, the storming of the Ayodhya (Babri) mosque by Hindu fundamentalists was made possible during Rajiv Gandhi's government as it became plain that his government would be unwilling to confront the ethno-nationalism of the Hindu right. As a result, the forces of *hindutva* gained in strength, and just as they began to challenge the holders of state power, their actions started to reveal the fragility of the secular state. As the RSS, VHP, Shiv Sena, and the political arm of right-wing Hindu fundamentalism, the BJP, began to flex their muscles, secular parties were unable to offer an alternative to the saffron surge. Progressive and left-wing forces were sidelined and watched helplessly as the *hindutva* forces gained strength from one massacre of Muslims to another.

Incidentally, this rise of the Hindu right was accompanied by a deep economic shift that gathered steam once the Indian bourgeoisie as well as the IFIs began to demand that state-centered economic policies change to a strong market orientation and adopt an economic liberalization strategy. Thus, on the economic front, Indira Gandhi abandoned the state interventionist policies that she had adopted with much celebration in the early 1970s, one decade later. After the IMF sanctioned a five billion dollar loan in 1981 to 1982, the Indian state moved decisively in favour of market reforms and began to deregulate steel and cement prices and to ensure the easy entry and expansion of industrial firms, especially multinationals.[45] After Indira Gandhi's assassination in 1984, her son, Rajiv Gandhi, made more decisive moves towards economic liberalization. The next subsection examines this shift, focusing on whether the replacement of the Indian state's carefully crafted policies of state-led economic development with the new strategy of neoliberalism or economic liberalization marked the maturation of capitalist development in India.

IV ASSESSING THE INDIAN STATE'S TURN TOWARDS ECONOMIC LIBERALIZATION

India is among the few Third World states that willingly adopted neoliberal market-led reforms. In India's case, this adoption was largely self-enacted by the big bourgeoisie as well as the state on its own terms. Most other post-colonial states were forced to accept the package of neoliberal reforms, which came in the form of lending conditions imposed by the IMF, first through the program of conditionalities and later through structural adjustments. In India, as in Argentina, Brazil, Chile, South Africa, and South Korea, whereas the IMF pressed for the dismantling of state-led development strategies, the bourgeoisie in each of these states demanded an increased market-oriented economy. India's pursuit of economic liberalization is nevertheless quite unique, as the following analysis will show. There are as many reasons for India's ready adoption of economic liberalization as there are analysts and economists writing on the subject of India's economic transition. Due to space constraints I cannot include all of the different views on the subject, but this section will focus on some of the more popular and cogent arguments and plausible reasons. First, it is important to clarify the events that led to the failing health of the Indian economy and the subsequent demands of the Indian bourgeoisie for liberalization.

The Indian economy did not grow during the first three decades after the Partition; as Table 4.1 shows, India experienced an overall contraction in industrial development. When Nehru died in 1964, the Indian economy was in a state of crisis and industrial growth continued to fall. The Indian economy was still contracting when Indira Gandhi called the 1971 elections and instituted populist measures that signalled greater state intervention.

Quite surprisingly, it was during the 1970 to 1977 period, when her populist programs were launched—meaning greater state intervention—that actual growth of the Indian industry was recorded in an otherwise long period of contraction. However, economic growth diminished in the late

Table 4.1 India's Annual Industrial Growth

Period	*Average Annual Growth Rate (%)*
1951–1962	–7.0
1965–1970	–3.3
1970–1977	+4.8
1979–1980	–1.4
1982–1989	+6.6
1990–1995	+6.0
1996–2000	+5.2
2001–2005	+7.4
2006–2009	+8.6

Note: For 1982 to 2009 figures, reliance is on World Bank Group, "India's Industry, Value Added (annual % growth), 1982–2009" [Data file], World Bank National Accounts Data, and OECD National Accounts Data files. 25 October 2011 <http://databank.worldbank.org>.

For 1951 to 1995 figures, reliance is on Sumit Roy, "Liberalization and the Indian Economy: Myth and Reality," *Industry and Agriculture in India Since Independence,* vol. 2 of *Social Change and Political Discourse in India: Structures of Power, Movements of Resistance*, ed. T.V. Sathyamurthy (Delhi: Oxford University Press, 1994) 136.

1970s, just before market reforms and price deregulations were instituted. On the surface, India appears to have undergone long periods of industrial decline since the 1950s during its implementation of statist policies. But is this the whole story?

Simple analyses of industrial or economic growth figures can be misleading, offering an incomplete and generally inaccurate account of an economy's health. This is the case for India: although the figures from the Nehru years show consistently negative industrial growth over almost two decades, they do not reveal the extent of support for private capital's infrastructural development, which was heavily subsidized by the public sector during these lean years. The industrial base in India was on firmer ground because of this nurturance, so when the time came, the Indian bourgeoisie was ready to take advantage of a more market-oriented drift. Big Indian capitalists, in other words, were strengthened for competition in the international market during the period of state-led development; when the protective cover of the state was removed, the Indian bourgeoisie was prepared to become an effective player on the world stage. This fact is exemplified by the wealth generation and the current buoyancy of the Indian economy: between 2006 and 2009, the Indian gross domestic product has grown by more than 9% annually, with the exception of 2008, when the growth rate was at almost 5% even during a period of worldwide recession.[46]

Without a check on imperialist interference and without the necessary mechanisms and resources for its effective implementation, state-centered development could not have served as a panacea for the social and economic upliftment of Third World societies. At the same time, the state-centered model of development had some rather serious problems, including corruption, bureaucratic ineptitude, and stagnant economic growth. The economic stagnation under the state-led development strategy in much of the Third World was a result of various factors, but two in particular stand out. First, the nature of the bureaucratic elite, especially its auxiliary class character, became a major impediment in the stalled 'national' development in most post-colonial societies. Second, the incorporation of the colonial state structure by the post-colonial state created a disincentive for participation and decision-making at the regional or sub-national levels. In other words, the federal centralized political structure in post-colonial India did not conform to the objectives of inclusion and democratic decision making in India's states and geographical regions. The increasingly politicized expansion of centralized decision making led to increasing social resentment as regions, and Indians more generally, continued to feel excluded and marginalized by the pace of socio-economic development. Instead of addressing these problems, the state adopted ever more confrontational postures in dealing with issues of caste, ethnicity, and region.[47]

The patronage of elite groups, along with bureaucratic ineptitude, self-interest, and corruption, seriously limited the ability of the state-led development model to achieve the goals of autarky and self-reliance laid down by Nehru and the Congress government. This fact, along with the peculiar nature of the propertied classes in India, needs to be incorporated in any analysis of the 'failure' of state-led development strategy. In the case of India (and South Korea), analysts tend to forget that the bourgeoisie was actually *nurtured* under state-led development. When economic liberalization was introduced, Indian capitalists were thus prepared to take advantage of joint-venture opportunities with and technology transfer from Western transnational corporations (TNCs). Furthermore, because India refused simply to succumb to the dictates of the IMF and the Western states (when embracing economic liberalization), the Indian bourgeoisie could exercise significant leverage over foreign capital, unlike most other Third World states, which were ill-prepared for market reforms.

However, it should be also acknowledged that the lack of competition and the protective environment resulted in a very lethargic industrial development in India until a decade ago. In the first three decades of India's post-colonial existence, the Indian public sector went on to absorb, in large part, the losses from industrial failures of the private sector. Some evidence also indicates that many 'sick' industries in the private sector—"exemplified by jute mills, mini steel plants, pharmaceutical and engineering units, and a large part of the textile industry"—were taken over by the state to prevent massive social fallout in terms of job losses from the closure of these plants.[48] At the same time, sick industries were also operating within the public sector and drained the treasury. To add to these problems, India's political and economic scene is known for its sophisticated network of patronage, subsidies, backdoor deals, and kickbacks by which those who are 'connected' can reap substantial dividends, whereas the neediest or best qualified are usually excluded. The tax base of the Indian state has remained small, but as the following discussion will show, considerable effort has been made to enlarge it by directly taxing the agricultural sector. The long-term effects of resource constraints were exacerbated by the state's extreme patronage, which created enclaves of privilege and wealth, whereas a sea of humanity remained on the margins of misery and neglect. In these circumstances, resource availability and capital formation became pressing matters.

Taken together, these problems placed the state in an extremely challenging situation: given the falling rate of average annual industrial growth, it became difficult to raise resources and to act in the interest of Indian industry, whereas the state had insufficient funds for even minimal social programs. This is a plausible explanation of why the Indian elite embraced economic liberalization, but it does not explain why Indian industry was not expanding and how the tide was reversed once economic liberalization was adopted. At first glance, it seems that all credit should go to the policies of economic liberalization, and indeed this is the argument made by the purveyors of the market ideology. However, surface appearances can be deceiving. The rest of this section will dissect what the three decades long shift towards economic liberalization has meant for the ordinary Indian, the bourgeoisie, and the landed elite—and whether the once-interventionist Indian state has been willing to take a backseat in the face of bourgeois demands for privatization and a larger role for the private sector. It will also focus on the oft-mentioned claim that liberalization was the 'natural' course to follow for the state and the Indian bourgeoisie given the economy's "Hindu rate of growth" during the first three decades after decolonization.

As touched on previously, Indian social scientists have long debated why India so readily adopted the policies of economic liberalization. In general, they agree that these policies began when the short-lived Janata government of the late 1970s began to adopt policies of de-control and liberalization, which were then seized upon by Indira Gandhi when she returned to power in the early 1980s. After her death, the trajectory of liberalization was furthered by Rajiv Gandhi and his successors. Other writers point to a definitive shift towards economic liberalization beginning in 1991.[49] Whether the neoliberal shift is identified as beginning in the early 1980s or as being definitely embraced by state and society since 1991, social scientists have tried to explain the dismantling of state-led development in India by offering various underlying causes for the shift towards market reform. Four major explanations can be culled from this debate: First, imperialist pressure has been combined with the desire of a dominant segment of the Indian capitalist class to collaborate with foreign capital. Second, the shift towards reform and deregulation in the economic sphere was related to the 'inefficiencies' of a *dirigiste* state. Third, the peculiar nature of Indian 'state capitalism' meant that it was imploding from within and needed to be reformed. Finally, the rivalry between various groups of capitalists ('nationalist' and comprador), as well as bureaucrats, state actors, and the bourgeoisie supporting economic liberalization, made the bureaucratic elite perceive these players as the dominant force, and together with bureaucratic support, this group has therefore been able to push for economic reforms.

The first explanation closely mirrors the classical Marxist view (see Patnaik[50] and others): briefly, it states that a "beleaguered bourgeoisie was unable to ensure [economic] growth within the old ways, therefore, they were willing to compromise with imperialism [allowing] a closer integration within the world capitalist system."[51] In other words, the Indian bourgeoisie as a class has inherent weaknesses and has been forced to make peace with imperialism as it is incapable of achieving sustained economic growth on the basis of an import-substitution strategy. As a result, Indian capitalists have been willing to examine the Brazilian and South Korean models of development (two states that followed the inward- and outward-oriented import substitution industrialization (ISI) policies, respectively, until they accepted neoliberal market reforms) as strategies worthy of emulation. In contrast, other well-known commentators, including S. Mundle, have taken a different view. Writing in the 1970s, Mundle suggested that 'capital reorganization' had been underway for some time in India and that its industrial structure would be altered most likely along the lines of Meiji Japan, such that large and small-scale private industries would form collaborative arrangements under the leadership of the big bourgeoisie who would provide sustenance to small capitalists.[52] The problem with this view is that the private sector in India during the period under discussion was supported by the state, so the case of Meiji Japan, in which the private sector was largely independent of the state, does not appear to be applicable to the Indian context. Variations on this 'capital re-organization' argument, discussed later in a little more detail, have been also espoused by Pedersen, Baru, and others, who suggest that a 'new breed' of Indian capitalists has emerged. The claim here is that a 'contractor class' has become prominent as a result of the state policies promoting higher education and infrastructure development (Baru). Other researchers argue that the rivalry between the so-called 'national bourgeoisie' and the comprador capitalists (who have historically sided with foreign capital in India) has resulted in the latter group's dominance and influence in the framing of market-based economic policies (Pedersen).

The second and third explanations are variations of a similar position, and more straightforward supporters of liberalization argue for a predictable conservative argument: India's economic transition was the result of a need for efficiency and a need to stimulate economic growth.[53] A more optimistic explanation is that Indian capitalism has come of age and that the Indian bourgeoisie has now gained the confidence necessary to face global competition and is now seeking the removal of state restrictions on the 'free' interaction of market forces.[54] Although this explanation appears somewhat simplistic, it has been popular with the Indian media, in turn influencing the views of the people.

It is important to recognize the fact that the Indian state has historically financed its policy of state-led industrialization largely through foreign assistance and deficit financing, which, given the challenges, is itself a huge feat. India's achievements in terms of industrial development must be considered in the context of how imperialist sponsors have used foreign aid everywhere else in the South—not only to open markets for Western TNCs but, more importantly, to stifle meaningful industrial development in post-colonial states. In India's case, 'aid' dollars began to dry up as the capitalist economic crisis of the 1970s started to seriously hurt the US and its Western allies. Once these 'aid' sources began to decline, the weight of budgetary constraints on Indian economic planning began to increase, resulting in a further increase in deficit financing. Deficits can only be financed to a certain point, beyond which their strain on the economy would be intolerable. Unlike the US, which can compel more vibrant capitalist economies, such as Germany and Japan, to finance its deficits—as Michael Hudson explains in the reprint of his 1970s text[55]—India could not remain on the path of deficit financing. Under these constrained circumstances, the Indian bureaucrats who were nurtured under the old system of economic planning, under the watchful Planning Commission, were at a loss to adjust to the new realities. Additionally, the bureaucracy's failure to address the endemic problem of economic stagnation weakened them as a fraction of the ruling elite in comparison to the Indian bourgeoisie and those who were ready to accept economic liberalization. These old-system-bred civil servants, moreover, were out of step with those bureaucrats who had forged links with indigenous and foreign capital and were promoting deregulation and economic liberalization as the only way out of economic stagnation.

In trying to clarify the altered character of the Indian bureaucracy, Pranab Bardhan and other statists have suggested that the push for economic liberalization came from this new group of neoliberal bureaucrats, but they also tend to concede that the Indian bourgeoisie in the age of neoliberalism has enabled the autonomy of state actors.[56] This statist viewpoint fails to recognize that the conversion of Indian civil servants to neoliberalism was a survival tactic of this auxiliary class and marks a structural shift of the Indian state: the abandonment of the Nehruvian interventionist developmental state in favour of the neoliberal structure. In other words, as the Indian bourgeoisie became hegemonic, the bureaucracy was made relatively weak. However, the newer generation of Indian bureaucrats, in a bid to stem the decline of their influence and to protect their auxiliary class interests, has also made the transition to support neoliberalism, consequently strengthening the capitalist character of the Indian state and making the bourgeoisie more hegemonic in Indian society.

These four different explanations of India's adoption of economic liberalization each contain elements of truth, but even taken together they cannot fully account for a major influencing factor in the adoption of market-driven reforms in India. This is because they largely ignore the role of agriculture and its support in India's drive towards industrialism, as will be discussed briefly later. Further, resource constraints in India's annual budget have in the past been made up by borrowings and foreign aid, but this kind of dependency did not overly concern political elites and state functionaries. However, declining foreign aid remittances magnified the problem of budgetary constraints. The Indian state could have taken steps to overcome the budgetary shortfall by relying on direct taxation on landed elites or increasing the effective rate of tax levy on those groups that have historically had the ability to pay their due share but evaded payment of their taxes. The Indian state chose to disregard this very viable source of revenue generation because the ruling party did not wish to displease the old 'syndicate' bosses among the landed elite upon whom it relied for political support.

With regard to revenue generation in the agricultural sector, it is remarkable that agricultural income is virtually free of direct taxation in India: only about 1% of all agricultural income is directly taxed, with the regressive flat tax, known as land revenue, making not even the smallest dent in the incomes of the landed elite.[57] Throughout the post-colonial era, agriculture has contributed to about one third of the national income, but in the period when productivity was increased as a result of public investment and the adoption of the so-called 'Green Revolution', increases in agricultural income did not translate into proportionally higher tax revenues for the state.[58] Even more disturbing is the fact that these productivity gains did not significantly reverse the pauperization of rural workers and peasants. This was the result of various factors but most notably the high rates of rural displacement due to mechanization and land concentration, which forced workers and peasants to accept extremely depressing rates of remuneration. This reality, coupled with how the process of uneven development unfolded, meant that productivity increases were limited to only a handful of Indian states including Punjab, Haryana, Tamil Nadu, and a few others. Likewise, the gains from productivity have not gone to the state; the landed elite or the rich peasantry has benefitted, whereas large numbers of poor workers and peasants continue to live in squalor or have been displaced and forced to migrate to India's already choked urban centres.

The impact of agriculture and the state of agrarian capitalist relations in Indian society has received scant attention in the debates on economic liberalization. Although landlordism still persists in many Indian states, capitalist relations have deepened in the countryside.[59] With regard to this issue of deepening agrarian capitalist relations, Baru argued that agrarian capitalism has provided a strong contribution to India's industrial development,[60] but this impact remains unrecognized in much of the literature about India's neoliberal shift and even in state-centered development literature:

> Public investment in agriculture and the development of agrarian capitalism has initiated the process of locally based industrialization in several regions of the country. This stands in direct contrast to the colonial pattern of industrial growth which was characterized by its enclave nature, delinked as it was from the immediate hinterland in which such industrialization (in terms of the accumulation process and the home market for industrial produce) was taking place. The best examples of such agriculture-led industrial growth are to be found in Punjab-Haryana, Western Maharashtra-South Gujarat, Andhra, Karnataka, and Tamil Nadu regions.[61]

By contrasting this kind of agrarian capitalism-linked industrialization with the 'colonial pattern' of industrial enclaves or fragmented industrialization, Baru seems to be saying—contra Alavi—that a more integrated development is possible in the periphery provided the state has a meaningful rural development/investment strategy. Baru did not really develop his views on rural development strategies beyond a few brief statements, so an alternative perspective is not really available to challenge Alavi's position on peripheral capitalism.

Rural development expenditures under neoliberal reforms actually diminished from 1985 to 1990, the beginning of economic liberalization in India, and remained very low throughout the 1990s. Utsa Patnaik used data from the Government of India's Annual Economic Survey to show that from 1985 to 1990, the average expenditure for rural development was 3.8% (of the net national product for rural development)—already a low figure given that rural employment in 2008 to 2009 was more than 58% of the total Indian workforce[62]—and that this level has consistently declined throughout the 1990s to a low of 1.9% in 2001.[63] In 2006, public investment in rural development increased to 2.8% of the gross domestic product and reached a high of 4.27% in 2009 to 2010. Despite bureaucratic constraints and turf wars, this increased rural development investment has helped the level of rural infrastructure. Although construction has proceeded quite slowly, unevenly, chaotically, and imperfectly, state investment has nevertheless greatly improved the network of roads, communication, and other facilities. A related consequence of this state investment has been the emergence of a new class of contractor/venture capitalists, a group that has sustained the swifter pace of construction since 2005, making it another source of capital formation in India.[64] Alongside this infrastructure development, public investment in higher education, "especially professional education, such as medicine, engineering and [business] management[,] has created a large pool of skilled individuals" who have emigrated to the West or the Middle East or have joined the traditional South Asian trading communities in Africa.[65] Many of these diaspora Indians have returned, and some have invested substantial capital in India under the state-sponsored program that offers these 'non-resident Indians' significant incentives and financial benefits to invest in the country. Together with the infrastructure built by the state-directed development policy and the state's current support for its big bourgeoisie, these developments have contributed to India's economic expansion ever since the change towards neoliberal market reforms was realized.

These developments have also provided the impetus for two kinds of changes: (i) the necessary conditions, imperfect as they may be, for capitalist development to proliferate in India and (ii) an environment for increased rivalry among capitalists. However, India's industrial capitalist development in the neoliberal era has proceeded in a dependent and most uneven manner. In this case, 'dependency' does not mean the classic reliance on, and submission to, metropolitan capital; at least it is not the kind of dependency at the root of dependency theory, especially its enabling concept of core and periphery. India certainly relied on foreign technology when its capitalism was in its infancy, and Indian capitalists sought joint-venture partnerships with Western transnational corporations. This happened very soon after decolonization when the country was the recipient of American, European, Japanese, and Russian 'aid'. However, India differs from the classic peripheries exemplified by most proto-capitalist states—even capitalist states, such as South Korea or Argentina. If TNCs showed interest in investing in India, the state was also able to set limits on foreign direct investments (FDIs) and on how these investments could be deployed. More important, India was able to exploit the Cold War rivalry between the US and the former Soviet Union by resisting the demands of metropolitan states in a way that was not possible for other post-colonial or Latin American states. In so doing, India was able to have a largely independent domestic and foreign policy and mostly to avoid submitting to imperialist dictates in the ways most Third World states were forced to submit.

India's experience as a post-colonial state, therefore, is quite unique. However, India's character as a capitalist state can be generalized to other post-colonial states—although its specific context of dependency and relative independence vis-á-vis the capitalism–imperialism nexus differs from other capitalist states such as Brazil or South Korea. India and China are among the few Third World states that were able to pursue state-directed development to the point of establishing a viable industrial base and its attendant infrastructure, whereas also pursuing a largely independent foreign policy. Most Third World states had to abandon the ISI strategy before significant gains could materialize, as their respective debt burdens and the absence of internal demand forced them to submit to imperialist-directed structural changes a la neoliberalism. In contrast, even India's adoption of economic liberalization was at the instigation of its indigenous bourgeoisie, and it is committed to pursue this policy even to this day. This is not to say that there has been little or no opposition to India's neoliberal turn; the issue of resistance against neoliberalism in India will be briefly discussed in a separate section later.

It should now be clear that the argument for India's specific dependent capitalist character does not imply complete dependency on metropolitan capital and nor fuller economic independence. India in its own unique way is relatively beholden to TNCs or imperialist demands, whereas its own TNCs are seeking an imperialist stranglehold on some African states—Indian TNCs have a predatory presence to extract iron ore in Liberia or to buy farmland in Ethiopia. The nature of India's dependency and capitalist development—which still relies on support from TNCs for both FDIs and technology transfer and sweetheart deals with imperialist powers (e.g., the agreement with the US for the transfer of civil nuclear technology so that India would distance itself from relying on Iranian natural gas)—is such that India is not the kind of periphery to receive imperialist blessings as did South Korea, Taiwan, Singapore, and Hong Kong (before its reunification). India's experience also differed greatly from Argentina and Brazil's dependent capitalist development: the Brazilian bourgeoisie benefitted significantly by having the state open the country to metropolitan capital, resulting in the most skewed distribution of wealth and privilege among Third World states and horrific living standards among the poor. India's poor fare no better, but the issue of social neglect in India has more to do with how its rural population is treated and how social priorities, rural development, and public outlays, for education as one example, are assigned by the political and bureaucratic elite. However, the nature of Indian dependency is in the realm of technology transfer and FDIs, and in these areas India is vulnerable to the demands of Western and Japanese TNCs. But at the same time, Indian TNCs also have expansionist interests in other parts of the world, which will have to be factored to develop a more accurate analysis of India's capitalist development. .

India's relatively dependent capitalist development will require further research to clarify fully the different types of dependencies and their implications for resistance and being mindful of the predatory urge of Indian TNCs. However, it is clear that analyses of Indian capitalist development needs to move away from the typical characterizations that are popular among Indian scholars, such as identifying state-centered development as "state capitalism"[66] or glorifying the selective and mild resistance of the big Indian bourgeoisie to imperialist domination as the action of a 'national bourgeoisie'. Only by moving away from such lazy characterizations and by avoiding new stereotypes, such as the 'new breed of capitalists' and avoiding binaries between 'traditional' and 'new' capitalists will it be possible to break fresh ground on the subject.

With regard to the 'new breed', there is no doubt that younger, foreign-educated Indian capitalists are more eager for foreign collaboration and differ from their older, more tradition-bound counterparts. These two groups even have a rivalry of sorts, but this does not mean that the former group welcomes foreign capital and TNCs whereas the latter group does not—at least, the evidence does not point in this direction, despite the elaborate arguments constructed by Pedersen and others. Pedersen argued that the Federation of Indian Chambers of Commerce and Industry (FICCI), which was actually formed before decolonization and became an influential body in the post-colonial state's formation, has interests that are diametrically opposed to the new upstarts of Indian capitalism.[67] In other words, the FICCI may be seen as representing the interests of the so-called national bourgeoisie. Pedersen further argued that the 'new upstarts' actually pushed the Indian state to promote the process of economic liberalization. Accordingly, this 'new type of Indian industrialist' is said to have formed links with foreign corporations in India and even to have created joint-venture companies with Western TNCs, the result of which was the 'quiet revolution' that transformed the existing Association of Indian Engineering Industry into the Confederation of Indian Industry, while still coalescing around the industrial body rival to FICCI, The Associated Chamber of Commerce and Industry (Assocham).[68] The presence of rival interests between these two groups does not mean that FICCI can be considered 'nationalist' in some way and that it is therefore unwilling to accept FDIs or collaborate with TNCs. Indeed, the Tata and Birla corporations, two of the strongest and most-established capitalist families in India, have definitely not shied away from forming joint ventures and other collaborative arrangements with Western TNCs. As Baru noted,

> The conventional formulation that the FICCI represents the interests of the 'national bourgeoisie' can no longer remain unchallenged because it has been at least as vocal in its support for an inflow of foreign direct investment into India and import liberalization as the Associated Chambers of Industry and Commerce (Accocham) (traditionally viewed as the representative organization of the 'comprador bourgeoisie').
>
> To suggest that this only proves the comprador nature of all Indian business is begging the question and also goes counter to the actual historical experience of the last forty or fifty years.[69]

The shift towards economic liberalization in India reveals that, whereas imperialist pressure influenced the Indian state with regard to market-based economic reforms, internal demand for this move—both within the public and private sections of state and society—was stronger. Before the introduction of economic liberalization, India's state-centered policies gave its capitalists a protective and nurturing environment in which to consolidate and grow. So, when the shift towards market-orientation was deemed necessary, Indian capitalists eventually came to demand a greater inflow of FDIs and a less active set of *dirigiste* policies, allowing the shift towards economic liberalization to be realized. However, India's pre-liberalization state-directed policy framework was in sharp contrast to the experience of most states in the Third World; in the latter case, most ruling elites and states buckled much earlier than India under the pressure of debt and the demands of the Western imperialist camp to shelve their ISI strategies. When India decided to adopt neoliberalism in the mid-1980s (although the forward and backward movement towards reform began in the late 1970s), many Third World states had already made a number of structural changes towards market-orientation under IMF's structural adjustment program.

Where debt was concerned, however, India's situation was no different from other states in the South: India was heavily in debt and faced considerable pressure from the US, the IMF, and the World Bank to deregulate and otherwise reform its markets. This pressure was significant in terms of the requirements that India follow the regime presented by the IFIs, but the force of this pressure was mitigated by the fact that the Indian state, due to the internal pressure of its bourgeoisie, was developing its own plans to limit state intervention and increase the role of the private sector in India's economy. The timing of the external pressure to liberalize coincided, for instance, with the "changes in policies governing industrial development, trade, foreign investment, the public sector and the financial sector [that were underway from the mid-1980s onwards], and which produced proposals on economic reform from a host of government-appointed committees."[70] The timing was such that India was able to "create a coherent policy package" that was not inimical to its capitalist elite—although the impact of liberalization on the urban and rural poor and the rural landless has since been quite devastating. It was no accident that the steps towards economic liberalization were well-orchestrated by the state in India. In contrast, those other Third World states that were compelled to adopt neoliberal policies have proven to be both ill-equipped and incapable of resisting pressure from the US and IMF to accept market-oriented liberalization and structural adjustments. Consequently, these states have progressively become powerless as they prostrated to imperialist demands, making the post-colonial and Latin American states key instruments in the subordination of the global South.

India's route to economic liberalization has not made the state completely captive to foreign capital and imperialist dictates, and the shift to neoliberalism has benefitted Indian industrialists and professionals, resulting in the expansion of the middle class, which is rushing to embrace conspicuous consumerism. But what about the poor? The social dislocations caused by economic reforms have had an enormous impact for the poor, the landless, the Indigenous, and others that have fallen by the wayside due to abject neglect from the neoliberal state. The poor in India are not a small constituency by any measure, and they appear quite determined not to allow the market to bulldoze their lives.

V RESISTANCE TO NEOLIBERAL REFORMS

Resistance to economic liberalization in India began in the form of protests, boycotts, and occupations by social movement activists and women's groups not long after the Indian state became firmly wedded to the path of neoliberalism. These protests against social and economic dislocations are paralleled by a longer history of resistance against national oppression and the assertion of national identity in Jammu and Kashmir, Assam, and Nagaland. The massive Indian troop presence of almost 700,000 in Kashmir and their violent actions against Kashmiri protestors and activists for national self-determination have been likened to a scorched earth policy of an occupying army.[71] Although space will not permit me to analyze national oppression in India or the violent human rights violations of Kashmiris and other national groups, suffice it to say that the attitude of the Indian state towards the expression of the right to self-determination of Assamese, Kashmiris, and in Nagaland is to address it militarily—an attitude that is common, as the following discussion will show, with the Indian state's response to resistance against economic liberalization and one with many pitfalls.

Until relatively recently, resistance against social and economic displacement has been led largely by well-meaning NGOs and non-violent neo-Gandhian social movements. These forms of resistance have been issues-based and have included actions against the building of dams, loss of biodiversity, poverty, women's oppression, and communalism and linking them to the policies of neoliberalism. This NGO-led resistance (*ngo-ization*)[72] has also been criticized for having displaced mass political mobilization against the state's social neglect, landlessness, corporatization, and class-based policies not just in India but in most post-colonial and Latin American states, with the result that mass movements' resistance has become fragmented and significantly weakened.

With the strong trend of NGO-led movements, resistance against economic liberalization in India remained largely fragmented and did not appear to have mass support until the poor rose up during the 2004 general elections. This poor-led initiative resulted in the Hindu nationalist BJP government being ousted from power, precisely when this fundamentalist/nationalist group appeared unstoppable as a political force. By enabling the Congress to form the government in 2004, the poor in India voted against the BJP's upper caste bias and its over-zealous embrace of neoliberal reforms, articulated in its election slogan, 'India Shining'—which suggested an underlying optimism towards corporatization and market reforms without much recognition of the deplorable social conditions of the poor in urban and rural India. Ironically, the decision of the poor to vote in large numbers against the BJP did not translate into a pro-poor policy shift at the level of the Indian state, as exemplified by the Congress-led government policies over the past six years.

The pathetic conditions of the poor still needed to be addressed; poverty and the forceful takeover of adivasi ('tribals' or Indigenous people's) lands could not be immediately reversed, but an active advocate for poor people's rights has since come forward. This is the hitherto regional grouping of Naxalites or Maoists who began their work of armed resistance initially in West Bengal in the 1960s and 1970s. The Naxalites, since their defeat in the 1970s, have re-emerged in the contemporary period to oppose the takeover of Indigenous people's lands by mining and automotive interests of large Indian corporations and Western TNCs. The Naxalite-led resistance has now spread across various Indian states—from West Bengal, Orissa, Chhattisgarh, and Madhya Pradesh—to about 12 Indian states.[73] As the Congress has gone through the paces of showing it is framing policies to tackle poverty and increase rural development, it has also violently opposed the Maoist/Naxalite movement. There is now a confluence of forces, from the ideological right to the left, that actively opposes the Maoists. In West Bengal, the Left Front led by Communist Party-Marxist, until recently, held power for the last 34 years; it has not only opposed the Naxalite but has also tried to violently crush them. In an ironic political twist, the Left Front was defeated in the May 2011 state elections, which some analysts argue was largely due to the Front's avowed anti-Naxalite policies. The implication of this development is that the Naxalite, rather than being weakened, have gained in strength mainly because of their stand against the neoliberal socio-economic drift and aggressive corporatization from companies like Vedanta, a giant transnational Indian mining corporation, which has made more Indians landless, horribly poor, and very desperate.[74]

The targeting of the Naxalite has accompanied the securitization of the Indian state, which has proceeded alongside the intensification of economic liberalization. The initial push for securitization was partly a response to the movement for self-determination in Kashmir and partly because of the tensions and unease between India and Pakistan. However, the events of 11 September 2001 provided the fillip for securitization and enabled the Indian elite-led state policy of using disproportionate force against demands from oppressed nations and marginalized people as well as protests against neo-liberalism. Whether in the form of peaceful street protests of Kashmiri people for the right to self-determination or the protests of *adivasis* against the forcible corporate takeover of their lands, these actions have been viewed through a security lens and met with brutal force from the Indian state. Some scholars have remarked that this shift towards securitization characterizes the Indian state as a neoliberal security-centric entity.[75] This new character of the capitalist Indian state has also meant that the fragmented and diffused resistance of the NGOs and 'neo-Gandhian' social movements, such as the better known Narmada Bachao Andolan (Save Narmada Movement) led by social activist Medha Patkar, have receded into the background. The more militant armed uprisings led by Maoist/Naxalite for *adivasi* rights are now at the fore: these uprisings have been in support of forest rights and land rights and against corporate mining interests. Even well-known Indian writer and activist Arundhati Roy weighed in to support Maoist resistance against corporate mining interests:

> It's easier on the liberal conscience to believe that the war in the forests is a war between the Government of India and the Maoists, who call elections a sham, Parliament a pigsty and have openly declared their intention to overthrow the Indian State. It's convenient to forget that tribal people in Central India have a history of resistance that predates Mao by centuries . . . The rebellions were cruelly crushed, many thousands killed, but the people were never conquered. Even after Independence, tribal people were at the heart of the first uprising that could be described as Maoist, in Naxalbari village in West Bengal (where the word Naxalite—now used interchangeably with 'Maoist'—originates). Since then, Naxalite politics has been inextricably entwined with tribal uprisings, which says as much about the tribals as it does about the Naxalites.
>
> Over the past five years or so, the governments of Chhattisgarh, Jharkhand, Orissa and West Bengal have signed hundreds of MoUs [memorandum of understandings] with corporate houses, worth several billion dollars, all of them secret, for steel plants, sponge-iron factories, power plants, aluminum refineries, dams and mines. In order

> for the MoUs to translate into real money, tribal people must be moved. Therefore, this war.[76]

In waging this 'war' against the Maoists, the Indian state has implemented a massive security apparatus to defeat them. It has also assembled criminal elements into a militia, the *Salwa Judum*, which as a vigilante group has become a vicious and avowedly anti-*adivasi* and anti-Maoist paramilitary force. The formation of this group and the attack on Indigenous people and the Maoists almost resulted in a civil war in Chhattisgarh and Nandigram.[77] The Chhattisgarh state provided *Salwa Judum* a legal cover, under the colonial-era 1861 Indian Police Act, that made *Salwa Judum* members Special Police Officers (SPOs).[78] In a case that reached the Indian Supreme Court, a group of SPOs in Chhattisgarh attacked and mauled an *adivasi* woman, stripped her, and had her parade naked on the street, all the while beating her in public; the case challenged the state's arming of civilians and the creation of the militia in order to fight the Maoists. In its judgement, the Indian Supreme Court not only declared the appointment of SPOs illegal under Article 14 (equal protection) and Article 21 (right to life) of the Indian Constitution, it asked for the disbanding of the SPOs; remarkably, the judges also criticized the Chhattisgarh state's 'amoral' economic policies and the "culture of unrestrained selfishness and greed spawned by modern neo-liberal economic ideology."[79]

As a consequence of these economic, social, and political developments, the neoliberal 'security-centric' state has made a significant right-ward shift, as have the centrist, Communist, and social-democratic political parties. These parties now openly support the state's right-wing agenda and the ascendency of the repressive, security-obsessed neoliberal policies. In response to state violence, the present conjuncture "opens up the possibility of a response from the masses unimagined by one or the other faction of capital or the state[:] Nandigram showed how this change in the nature and role of social democracy and other left forces opens a possibility for a more radical resistance from the masses."[80]

When the Naxalite movement first emerged in the 1960s in West Bengal, the federal and state-level (provincial) governments were able to 'crush' the Maoist rebellion. In the more recent reincarnation of the Naxalite, the federal government and other states have been unable to stop the movement from spreading across various Indian states. This new-found strength and popularity of the Naxalite has prompted a segment of the Indian left, associated with the IPC, to weigh in on the uprising of the tribals and the peasants. The IPC was once a very influential body tasked with developing India's five-year economic plans and has left a deep imprint on poverty alleviation strategies and socio-economic and development issues with mixed results. Since India's adoption of economic liberalization, the IPC's power base has eroded considerably, and the power centre has moved to the security-obsessed Home (Interior) Ministry. Thus, when the IPC released its recent study, *Development Challenges in Extremist Affected Areas*, it had a two-fold objective.[81] First, it wanted to make the IPC relevant again by challenging the dominance of the Home Ministry and highlighting the value of the state's welfarist role—once prevalent in the Nehruvian developmental state. Second, it wanted to warn security-focused policymakers that a more 'humane' socio-economic approach is needed to contain the Maoist 'problem' before it would affect elite capitalist interests. It noted that "the movement is now active in about 125 districts [and] spread over 12 states."[82]

Saroj Giri provided a perceptive critical analysis of the IPC Report, pointing out that the debate in India on the Maoist uprisings "centres on whether one views this movement as a 'law and order' problem [(security-centric)] or a socio-economic problem."[83] Regardless of how the Maoist movement is perceived, both poles are state-driven imperatives according to Giri, so they tend to privilege either the neoliberal state or the model of the Nehruvian developmental state leading to the monopolization of the political field by different elite interests and end up "blocking off the Maoist alternative from the field of vision."[84] In the absence of a transformative voice in the polarized political environment and the confluence of security/anti-terrorism and democratic forces, the 'war' is not against poverty but rather against the *poor* and the Indigenous and against those asserting their right to national self-determination. India's security state is mobilized against the peoples who are part of the most vulnerable segments of society. Consequently, the lines between democracy and genocide are increasingly blurred. Operation Green Hunt, launched April 2010 by the Indian state, was ostensibly against the Maoist/Naxalite movement, but it ended up targeting *adivasis* who are already facing atrocities from the paramilitary force, *Salwa Judum*. The Naxalite respond to this and other attacks with violence, but because the Operation-like attacks target and terrorize unarmed *adivasis*, these state-sponsored attacks bear the hallmark of a genocide in the making, as evidenced by documentaries and reports of NDTV, the magazines *Frontline* and *Outlook*, and numerous talks by writer and social activist Arundhati Roy.

The security-absorbed segment of the Indian elite is currently buoyed by sustained levels of high growth and capitalist expansion. These movers and shakers have been also embraced by US imperialist interests to nurture India as a foil against China's rising economic, political, and military prowess—not to mention Indian TNCs own predatory impulse in *adivasi* territories and in some African states. India's role in the region as well as the relative weaknesses of its neighbours has further strengthened its aspirations of becoming the regional co-imperialist hegemon. This is apparent from Pakistan's miserable economic and political situation and India's role in neutralizing the political force of the Maoist in Nepal and its tacit approval of the Sri Lankan government's genocide against what it labelled, the 'Tamil terrorism'. These developments and India's international standing will probably make India the next new Permanent Member of the Security Council. However, how the regional capitalism–imperialism nexus will unfold both in the region and in India's internal conflicts and struggles will depend on if or when Pakistan completely implodes and whether the struggle of India's poor will affect the balance of forces within the Indian state. In other words, time will tell whether the polarization between the security-obsessed path and the 'humane' socio-economic approach will end in some kind of a compromise or whether one of the two approaches becomes more pervasive and dominant. The Maoist movement, although currently perceived as a non-urban movement, cannot be written off—not because it has the potential of becoming the dominant narrative but for its potential to influence a wider opposition against neoliberalism. In the face of this opposition, the Indian state, the mainstream Indian media, and the bourgeoisie, in the current period of very high growth, rising consumerism, and an expanding middle class, have also reworked their country's old international image. With slogans like 'India Shining' and 'Incredible India', the country's international image has been transformed from a sleepy, enchanting but a poverty-stricken country "through what the American writer David Rieff calls the most 'successful national re-branding' and 'cleverest PR campaign' by a political and business establishment since 'Cool Britannia' in the 1990s."[85]

India, Argentina, China, Brazil, Malaysia, South Africa, South Korea, Taiwan, Turkey, and possibly Chile and Thailand can all be identified as capitalist Third World states, but these states have achieved this common identity through very different routes and social and economic processes. As a result, their outcomes are socially divergent in terms of the respective underlying political dynamics and economic disparities. In arriving at this common position, these few countries have come to be insulated from the powerlessness experienced by most other post-colonial and Latin American states vis-à-vis the dictates of the US and its Western imperialist allies. The important distinction here is the difference between proto-capitalist and capitalist states. In generalizing about capitalist states, my goal is not to minimize the differences between these few states and their respective abilities to resist imperialist pressure. China and India undoubtedly differ greatly in their ability to withstand imperialist pressure, compared to Taiwan and South Korea, and China and India even differ profoundly. Nevertheless, an emphasis on the shared characteristics of these countries as capitalist states can help distinguish them from most other post-colonial states which, as the discussion of Pakistan in the Chapter 5, this volume, will show, can be identified as proto-capitalist states.

5 Pakistan

The Proto-Capitalist State

The new state of Pakistan was carved out of colonial India and came into existence on 14 August 1947. Whether the Partition of India was the result of religious divisions or deep insecurities related to class and privilege is a question that is tackled in this chapter. In the decade or so before decolonization and the Partition of colonial India, when Hindu-Muslim and/or Sikh-Muslim conflicts were at their peak, religion appears to be the main contradiction affecting these communities and the movement for Pakistan. However, if we focus on the moment of decolonization—the creation of Pakistan supposedly signifying the attainment of the separate homeland for the Muslim *ummah* (nation)—the primacy of religion becomes questionable. This is because the idea of the Muslim *ummah* almost evaporated with the creation of Pakistan, giving way to the assertion of national and ethnic identity of *Baluch*, *Bengali*, *Pushtun*, and *Sindhi*, whereas the bureaucratic elite from the Punjab and its junior partner, the Muslim migrants from North India, became firmly in control of the state apparatus. These Muslim migrants later even claimed their ethnic and national identity of *Mohajir* based on the notion of migrancy.[1] However, ethnic, national, or religious conflicts plaguing Pakistan, India, and other post-colonial societies have a much longer history. This history is rooted in the colonial state's manipulation of colonized people's identity, which created conflicts among the colonized, as I briefly addressed in Chapter 1, this volume. The colonial rulers' level of manipulation was such that even the Muslim League (the political party behind Pakistan's creation) was formed in 1906 at the urging of the then British Viceroy and a British colonial state official, Percival Griffiths. The Indian Congress Party (Congress) is one of the major political parties that monopolized state power in India until the 1980s; it was formed in 1885, and one of its notable founders, A.O. Hume, was also a functionary of the British colonial state.

Ayesha Jalal suggested that Mohamed Ali Jinnah, Pakistan's founder, did not really want the Muslims to separate and divide India. She argued that the main thrust of Jinnah's idea of Muslim separatism was a push for the realization of the shared sovereignty principle between Hindus and Muslims within a united India.[2] However, Jinnah's idea was to treat

Muslims as part of a 'separate electorate', a concept created by the colonial state and which Jinnah had seemingly internalized. Therefore, once Nehru and the Congress effectively closed the door on Jinnah's demand, the only option left for him was to separate and form what he termed the 'moth-eaten' state of Pakistan. So, although Jinnah may not have desired a separate Muslim homeland, his determination to achieve parity between Hindus and Muslims on the basis of separate religious identities (despite a much smaller Muslim population) could have only unfolded along narrow lines of religious or ethnic nationalism. Consequently, the ultimate outcome of a demand for parity on the basis of religious difference—if rejected by the other side, as came to pass with Nehru's rejection—would result in the triumph of ethno-nationalism and the subsequent separation of a significant Muslim population from India. This was how Pakistan's creation unfolded.

Ironically, with Pakistan's inception, the claim of Muslim *ummah's* unity dissolved very quickly and was replaced by different sets of claims based on ethnicity and nationalism. The *raison d'être* of Pakistan's existence, in other words, was in question exactly at the moment of its creation. One plausible explanation for this transient nature of the Pakistan Movement for Muslim unity may be its "shallow roots," which were laid by the Muslim bureaucratic elite in North India.[3] The idea of an independent Muslim homeland originated in North India and was based primarily on fear: privileged Muslims feared being displaced from the bureaucratic positions they held in the colonial state by the surge of Hindu nationalism and the rise of the Hindu bureaucratic elite. The colonial state did nothing to placate these fears; therefore, its role in bringing the Hindu-Muslim antagonism to a head cannot be minimized. But what is confounding in exploring the Pakistan Movement is that the push for the creation of Pakistan overcame "the [. . .] significant and paradoxical fact that the movement was at its weakest in the Muslim majority provinces of [colonial] India which today make up Pakistan."[4] The country's formative years raise two important questions about the role of the post-colonial state in creating identities that may erode and threaten the state itself. The first is related to the manipulative social engineering trope of the colonial state that is structurally embedded in the post-colonial state: is the post-colonial state instrumental in creating certain exclusivist identities based on ethnicity, nation or religion that take on a life of their own and, in the process, threaten to widen conflict in society? As a corollary, if there is strong resistance to such manipulative state practices, will the consequences be devastating for the state itself, in terms of its own breakup or demise? These are not mere rhetorical questions; the following discussion will reveal how they provide clues about the rise of strong national movements in Pakistan and also signal the heavy price the Pakistani bureaucratic and political elite has paid for being inattentive to issues of nationalism and identity and bringing about the country's breakup with the creation of Bangladesh. Similarly, the nurturance of Islamist forces under General Ziaul Haq's military regime has meant that militant Islam has currently emerged as a powerful ideological and military force to create deep insecurities and to perpetuate violence and polarizations in society.

Other issues, such as the military and civil bureaucracy's hold on the state, are related to these questions and go to the heart of this study on state formation in Pakistan. Therefore, the analysis will move from an examination of the social history of the Pakistani state's formative years in the first section to an extended socio-political analysis of Pakistan. My analysis, however, is not limited to the mere unfolding of the social and political situation and the contemporary manifestation reflected in the rise of militant Islam; it also integrates the external dimension, which in Pakistan's case is far more complex than India's socio-political development. In the first section, I critically appraise three significant historical periods in Pakistan's state and societal formation, which roughly coincide with the three periods of Pakistan-US relations. The fourth period, covering the post-Ziaul Haq phase and the contemporary era since General Pervez Musharraf's military coup in 1999, is addressed in its various contexts in the final three sections. Of the three historical periods, two were long periods under military dictatorships, with a brief respite from military rule during Z.A. Bhutto's term in office—although he too did not relax his government's authoritarian grip on society. My analysis of the first period, 1950 to 1970, focuses on General Ayub Khan's martial rule and the efforts of his regime, albeit contrived, to launch capitalist development in the country under the directives of American modernization theorists. My analysis of the second period, from 1971 to 1977, focuses on the state, society, and economy under Z.A. Bhutto, when he was trying to move away from a clientelist relationship with the US. Bhutto undid Ayub Khan's private capitalist-led economic project and tried to introduce an ill-conceived state-led economic development model without a clear strategy for the future direction of Pakistan's economic development. The third period, from 1977 to 1999, marked a most unfortunate phase in Pakistan's history: not only did military rule and clientelism return with a vengeance under Ziaul Haq—with Pakistani military waging US's proxy war in Afghanistan—but Pakistani society also became deeply polarized as Haq began to introduce his version of Islamic revivalism and *jihad*. As the country's rulers moved further to the right and the *jihadist* elements of militant Islam were recruited to fight the Soviet invasion of Afghanistan with US and Saudi Arabian support, Pakistan gradually became more subservient and dependent on the US.

In the second section I focus on Pakistan's rudderless economy and the setbacks it encountered as a result of radical policy shifts of Z.A. Bhutto's government following the end of Ayub Khan's military rule. I also briefly address the contemporary economic lethargy in Pakistan, which is closely linked to the trajectory of clientelism that has intensified since the beginning of the new millennium. In the third section I examine the post-Ziaul Haq era and how his stamp of Islamization has had a very long afterlife in contemporary Pakistan. As a consequence, the state-building project has suffered—being pulled apart by the force of US imperialism on the one hand and on the other by political and militant Islam. None of the expectations people had about the civilian leadership of Benazir Bhutto or Nawaz Sharif, both of whom succeeded Ziaul Haq, materialized, and the economy and society suffered badly in the process. The third section deals with the fourth period and also addresses how Musharraf's military captured state power for the fourth time. Musharraf surrendered Pakistan's sovereignty to the US soon after the 11 September 2001 incident, when Colin Powell, then Secretary of State, threatened to teach him and Pakistan a lesson if he did not accede to US demands of fighting its 'war on terror'.[5] This contemporary period also marked the rise of militant Islam and the Pakistani military's violent confrontation with the Pakistani Taliban.

The Pakistani ruling classes have been unmindful of the consequences of completely aligning with the US almost from the country's inception, although it was obvious that India, Indonesia, China, and other more independent states in the 1950s and 1960s were moving along the path of non-alignment. These other countries formed the important Non-Aligned Movement in Bandung, whereas Pakistan chose to have a close clientelist relationship with the US. This choice has had serious negative outcomes for its people, resulting in dependent and stunted social and economic development, the emergence of *jihadist* culture, and now a full-blown violent militant Islamist move to enforce *sharia* in the country. Thus, in framing its foreign policy, the Pakistani state has taken a contradictory approach: part of the rhetoric is for domestic consumption, whereas much of the policy is aimed to conform to US demands and thereby impress its patron.

In the fourth and fifth sections I focus on the issues of dependency and clientelism, which are two sides of the same coin and have affected Pakistan's state, society, and its economy. The economy, which in any society is the engine of growth and development, is weak in most proto-capitalist post-colonial societies, and it remains seriously neglected in Pakistan. Because the ruling oligarchy of feudal lords and civil and military bureaucracy has become addicted to foreign 'assistance', it has no interest in undertaking the hard work of building a self-reliant economy. In addition, because of political instability and the climate of fear, the Pakistani capitalist class is not investing in the country. But, the capitalists in Pakistan are also very weak and must rely on the state's patronage for access to economic opportunities; they also seek the easy way out by indulging in *rentier* activities instead of undertaking productive steps to build industries and expand the industrial base. The consequence of these policies and actions as well as the burden of subservience and dependency, coupled with long periods of military control of the Pakistani state, has actually retarded industrial development in the country—such that Pakistan's proto-capitalist status has become very prominent. This proto-capitalist status of both state and society along with the burden of clientelism and dependency also signifies Pakistan re-subordination in the new millennium.

I BACKGROUND ON THE MAJOR SOCIO-ECONOMIC AND POLITICAL DEVELOPMENTS IN PAKISTAN

(i) Decolonization and Pakistan's Missed Opportunities

Both Pakistan and India can be portrayed as having relied on the 'strong' state almost from the moment of decolonization. However, this is where the similarity ends when it comes to understanding state formation of these two states. In India, the bureaucratic authoritarian framework played a critical role in constructing the public realm of formal democracy and secularism of a 'strong' nascent capitalist state, whereas the private arena, which was largely left vacant, was taken over by Hindu fundamentalist groups like the Rashtriya Swayamsevak Sangh and Vishwa Hindu Parishad as they promoted Hindu nationalism. In contrast, Pakistan has been marked by brief periods of civilian rule in an otherwise long *duree* of the military's grip on state power. Military rulers have thus shaped the state's perception of India as belligerent and hostile towards Pakistan, which is not without foundation.[6] India had a ready-made colonial state structure that its political and economic elites did not hesitate to re-impose on its polity, in effect removing the possibility of creating an inclusive post-colonial society. Pakistan's emergence from the Partition meant that no remnants of a pre-existing colonial state were available for the new country to salvage or reclaim; Pakistan had to be constructed from scratch. As Jalal pointed out, "[w]hile India inherited the colonial state's unitary central apparatus without seriously rupturing its links with the lower rungs of the administration, Pakistan had to construct an entirely new central government before it could begin coordinating the affairs of the provincial, district and local levels of society."[7] The opportunity to build Pakistan as an inclusive welfare state with an independent foreign policy and a progressive social outlook was completely missed. Pakistani ruling classes chose to emulate India in adopting the colonial state's structures of control and domination. Despite these 'differential inheritances' of India and Pakistan and the unique opportunity for the latter to move away from embedding the structures of the colonial state, Pakistan's ruling classes did not waste time in replicating the structural framework of the colonial state. Remarkably, this replication by the Pakistani ruling classes even involved the adoption of colonial-era penal, criminal, and commercial laws (with minor amendments) as well as other practices of colonial rulers in both state and society: the tendency for Pakistani rulers to be manipulative and callous and to keep themselves separate and apart from ordinary people in order not to address the latter's issues and difficulties. The adoption of the colonial state's structure goes to the heart of the state formation question, and its impact will be explored in the following pages.

Notwithstanding this different history of decolonization in India and Pakistan, the ordinary people of South Asia appear to face a common destiny: they continue to be left out of the calculus of power, and all the while poverty, hunger, misery, and disease has remained rampant in their lives. This entirely avoidable reality is in stark contrast to the lofty principles enshrined in the constitutions of the two states. For instance, the Indian constitution's preamble contains the Enlightenment principles of "liberty, equality and fraternity," whereas the socialist principle of "to each according to his ability and to each according to his [sic] need" is part of the Pakistani constitution's preamble. Despite these lofty ideals in the constitutions of India and Pakistan, the mimetic tendency among the former colonized elites—to embrace colonial-era norms and the structures of the colonial state—has been a source of a serious drag on the populace's social, economic and political development. This tendency which, in its historical context, underlined the collaboration of the colonized elite with colonial rulers, was damaging to the colonized for a host of reasons: the loss of freedom and culture, the emergence of intergroup discord and the treatment of the opposing groups as the 'other', and most important, the fragmentation of resistance to colonial rule. The enduring legacy of this tendency carries over into the post-colonial era and tends not only to reproduce the repressive structure, institutions, and customs of the colonial state but also the presence of a disturbing development among the former colonized to become manipulative in interpersonal dealings and relationships. Colonized elite put up an outward persona of submission, but underlying this facade was an ingrained propensity towards manipulation in order to obtain favours and gain privileged access from colonial rulers. Whether this attitude developed as part of a survival mechanism to retain privilege under colonial rule, its long-term consequences have been devastating for post-colonial societies as ordinary people have emulated the character of the colonized elite in the periods preceding and following decolonization. In essence, they have created a post-colonial state and society that incorporates some of the more troublesome characteristics of the colonial period.

In Pakistan, the post-colonial rulers apparently did not desire a formal separation from their colonial masters because they wasted no time, soon after decolonization in the early 1950s, becoming a junior partner of the new imperialist/capitalist overlord, the US. It is important to note that tendencies towards collaboration with, and submission to, imperialists have not unfolded in a linear manner, and therefore cannot be homogenized for *all* post-colonial societies. The colonized in Asia and Africa had three possibilities for mobilizing resistance: movements of national liberation involving armed struggle against colonial rulers; movements of protest, non-cooperation, non-violent resistance, and strikes; and third, negotiated settlement or acceptance of the colonial ruler's edicts. Given that fewer national liberation struggles ended in victory for the former colonized, a combination of the other two possibilities was largely the norm. The path followed by the leaders of India and Pakistan was a mix of non-cooperation/non-violent resistance and negotiated settlement, and both adopted the colonial state's structures. However, whereas the respective elites of the two states have held somewhat similar attitudes of collaboration and mild resistance towards colonial rulers, the formative development of these two respective states differed. Nehru was a leader of the Non-Aligned Movement; in contrast, Pakistani ruling classes were content with becoming clients of the US.

However, in the Pakistani context, the mimetic tendency among the bureaucratic elite cannot simply be attributed to their collaborative conduct with colonial rulers or the feudal elite's complete dependency on the colonial state. These are partial explanations for the re-incorporation of the colonial state's structures within the post-colonial state, but it is important not to neglect the role of weak social classes in the context of political and economic power. For instance, the capitalists were extremely weak as a class because the privileged among those who migrated from India to Pakistan were generally traders or bureaucrats among the hordes of skilled and unskilled working folks; there were hardly any capitalists to speak of in the region that became Pakistan. Similarly, although the feudal lords may have had their fiefs, they could not negotiate the terrain of political power without the support of the civilian bureaucracy. Neither of these two social classes, therefore, could access political power on their own, which put the colonial-state trained bureaucrats in a commanding position in determining how power would be exercised in the new post-colonial state, reinforcing their experience as colonial state functionaries. As discussed in Chapter 3, this volume, the causality in the ascendancy of weak social classes in proto-capitalist societies is based not on economic power but on accessing political power through the control of the state apparatus. This claim is strengthened by the analysis of how feudal and bureaucratic elites collaborated in sharing state power during the very formative phase of Pakistan's creation and gained significant economic dividend. In privileging causal primacy to the political in proto-capitalist states, the structures of the former colonial state proved to be indispensable to the feudal landlords (in avoiding any tax payments on agricultural income) and the civil and military bureaucratic oligarchy in re-instituting the institutions and processes of control. These processes resulted in the subordination of ordinary Pakistanis, whereas the feudal and bureaucratic oligarchs accrued enormous economic benefits through writing their own rank/position's privileges, land grants, graft, bribery, kickbacks from granting special approvals or sanctions, and so on. In the current conjuncture, these bureaucratic oligarchs have not only entrenched their privileges, they have also become more obliging to their imperialist patrons whose domination is now cleverly camouflaged by clientelist rulers themselves in the guise of extolling the benefits of 'aid', 'assistance', 'democratization', and the 'war on terror'. As a result, resistance to imperialist domination remains a distant mirage at the level of the state in most post-colonial societies—although some Latin American states, in resisting US imperialism, offer a ray of hope.

In the context of resistance against imperialism, it is important to remember that the seeds of resistance can flower any time a populace is determined to resist. Equally, oppressive efforts to crush resistance can nip struggle for change in the bud. The young people's current resistance in Middle East and North Africa (MENA) appears to have gradually overcome the dialectic of collaboration and muted resistance; at least the signs of overcoming oppressive rulers are apparent in Egypt and Tunisia. Whether this resistance will endure and reshape MENA societies will become clearer as the future unfolds. Still, recent events of the Arab uprisings inspire hope, pointing to ways of mobilizing mass/collective resistance by using the very tools of the 'information age' and social media, which were originally introduced to individualize pleasure, pain, and loneliness and divert attention to a host of distractions on the Internet, whereas the social media opened up the possibility for more self-indulgence. The creative inversion of these tools from their intended use has mobilized people on a scale unforeseen in the MENA region to topple authoritarian dictators who have relied on massively violent use of force (even Western societies were inspired to create the 'Occupy Wall Street' and other similar movements).

In Pakistan, the efforts to crush resistance has been in play since the 1960s when protests against the Ayub Khan regime were a regular occurrence and eventually succeeded in toppling him from power. However, the ruling elite have learned their lessons and are now quite adept in overcoming resistance in order to consolidate their power into the present era. They have also continued with the disturbing tropes of manipulation and double-dealing, which the relatively independent Pakistani media now treats as a norm and does not challenge. Consequently, in contemporary Pakistan (and elsewhere), manipulation, corruption, and double-dealing have been normalized and made broadly acceptable. This trend poses problems not just in overcoming the manipulative propensity of those in power; it also makes the elite less introspective about their subjective position as a client of their US patron. The elite in Pakistan have never been self-critical because they have surrounded themselves with toadies who sing their praises. Besides, they are single-mindedly devoted to maintaining their privileged power positions by the only means known to them: subservience to imperialist dictates and manipulative and ruthless use of power against the ruled and the powerless. Therefore, it was an easy choice for Pakistan's ruling classes not just to resurrect the old structures of the colonial state but also to become the subordinate partner of the imperialist overlord to continue the colonial legacy of domination by creating conflicts and divisions in society. In Pakistan, this translates into the rule of civil and military bureaucratic and feudal elites who have denied ethnic and subnational rights to smaller nations and have kept the mass of Pakistanis in a squalid and dreadful existence.

This culture of conflict and authoritarianism can also be examined from the vantage point of the political. As discussed in Chapter 3, this volume, control of political power in proto-capitalist societies through control of the state also enables the acquisition of economic power. The peculiar nature of the Pakistani state, particularly the adoption of the centralized unitary structure of the colonial state, has created more impediments to the resolution of conflicts, specifically those based on religion, ethnicity, language, and region. Instead of playing a pivotal role in resolving these conflicts, the Pakistani state has actually made the situation worse. It first missed the opportunity to build a cohesive society when East Bengal (formerly East Pakistan) was denied its rightful share of state power, which eventually resulted in the formation of Bangladesh. Opportunities continue to be missed as lessons from Bangladesh's separation are ignored: the Pakistani state currently opposes the demands of Baloch, Pushtun, and Sindhi nations for provincial autonomy and for these nations to shape their own destinies. In Balochistan, the anger and resentment against the high handedness of the federal government and military's assault on Baloch nationalists has resulted in a serious conflict that threatens the integrity of the country.

(ii) The Pakistani Ruling Oligarchy and US Imperialist Domination

State power in Pakistan, based on the discussion in the previous section, has effectively been wielded by three sections of the ruling class: the military, the civilian bureaucracy, and the feudal landholders, with a noticeable absence of the capitalist bourgeoisie. This configuration of the exercise of state power can largely be characterized as part of the legacy of colonial rule. All of the three groups that have held power since the Partition of India were close collaborators to the British Raj, although each in different capacities.[8] At the risk of being repetitive, from the very inception of Pakistan (the contemporary situation is different), the Punjabi upper classes from all three sections of the ruling elite have largely controlled state power, although it should be noted that the Muslim migrants from Northern India (who now identify themselves as *Mohajirs*) were junior partners with the Punjabi bureaucratic elite in governing the new state along with a few *Pushtuns* and *Sindhis*. For brief periods, the Sindhi feudal elite has also shared state power. The Bengali population mainly living in the former East Pakistan (now Bangladesh) was effectively excluded (with very few exceptions) from sharing state power, despite having a larger population than West Pakistan. The early exclusion of Bengal really set the tone of domination by the bureaucratic oligarchy. This was soon followed by the establishment of One Unit in 1955, which meant the dissolution of the provinces, the denial of sub-national status, and the domination of the centre, in the name of Muslim *ummah* unity.

This facile agenda was pushed by the tripartite ruling oligarchy through the centralized unitary state, a legacy of the colonial state.

Given the historical links between the South Asian bureaucratic and feudal elite with the English colonial rulers, it was to be expected that the holders of state power in Pakistan (successors of the South Asian oligarchic elite) would collaborate with the new leader of the capitalist world, the US, once the global balance of power began to shift after World War II. When the US decided to expand its sphere of influence, the Americans secured their alliance with a most obliging Pakistani ruling oligarchy in a bid to out-manoeuvre the former Soviet Union. Although to Nehru's credit, India stayed the course of non-alignment, at least until its war with China. The US came looking for anti-communist support from the Pakistani rulers and offered, in return, to strengthen the Pakistani elite through economic and military 'assistance'. In almost blindly pursuing the collaboration with the US, the Pakistani leadership exhibited little concern about how this relationship would affect the sovereignty and independence of the new state.[9] The people of Pakistan were largely unaware that their destinies were being shaped behind their backs by a pernicious ruling class policy that would soon make Pakistan a satellite within the US orbit. To this end, the ruling oligarchs entered into pacts and treaties with the US throughout the decade of the 1950s at an astounding pace.

During a period of five years (1954–1959), Pakistan entered into as many pacts with the US and its allies. One of the first agreements between the US and Pakistan was the Mutual Defence Assistance Agreement (1954), which established a close military, political, and economic alliance with the Americans. This agreement gave the US extra-territorial powers, including the permission to set up military bases in Northern Pakistan, which the Americans used as vantage points from which to spy on the Soviet Union.[10] This agreement was the precursor to Pakistan's inclusion in regional pacts and treaties, such as the Baghdad Pact (1955), later named the Central Treaty Organization (a 1955 pact between England, Turkey, Iraq, and Pakistan), and the South East Asia Treaty Organization (in 1956). All these agreements and pacts were sealed with the overarching US-Pakistan Pact in 1959—once the military dictatorship of Ayub Khan was firmly in place. It goes without saying that the underlying thrust of these agreements was the expectation that Pakistan adopt either a covert or overt anti-communist position.

The US intervention during Pakistan's formative years meant that the Americans played a central role in guiding the country's early quasi-capitalist development.[11] The emerging Pakistani capitalists—a parasitical group of traders that were transformed into industrial capitalists through the patronage of the state—did very well in their embryonic development phase. The power of the feudal elite remained unchecked, especially in Punjab and Sindh. The ruling oligarchs were able to proceed on their chartered course by militarizing society and subduing any opposition through the sheer force of US arms—at least until student demonstrations and public anger against the Ayub Khan regime in the late 1960s finally brought about his downfall.

(iii) Ayub Khan's Martial Rule

Although Pakistan's military was, with prodding from the US, responsible for the installation of former military general Iskander Mirza as the first President of the country, it made its first aggressive political move in 1958. For the next 13 years, the military kept a stranglehold on state power. General Ayub Khan's military dictatorship lasted for 11 years, during which the US intervention in Pakistan's economy and society was greatly intensified. After 1958,

> the dependence on foreign aid increased to enormous proportions, with the process of economic planning becoming completely dominated by foreigners, particularly the large contingent from Harvard University, and Pakistan rapidly moved into the position of a new type of economic colony. The insidious takeover of the Pakistan Planning Commission is described in detail by Albert Waterson, a member of the inner circle of American advisors. The role of foreign advisors and planners was only the beginning: Pakistan became one of the biggest employers of foreign technicians, with no check on their qualifications or on their knowledge of local environmental conditions. In 1967 the number of such technicians in water and electric power departments alone was reported to be more than 1000. At the same time . . . large number of Pakistani technicians and scientists were being forced to leave the country because of a combination of factors: unemployment, misemployment, low salaries [for locals] and arrogant behaviour of Pakistani officialdom.[12]

To finance this pool of largely US technicians and 'experts', and to cover the cost of the US arms it was purchasing, Pakistan had to borrow and incur extensive external debt. This is evident from the fact that the flow of 'aid' to Pakistan, which primarily took the form of interest-bearing loans, increased from $455.8 million from 1950 to 1955 to $3.4 billion from 1960 to 1968.[13] The US placed a great deal of emphasis in configuring Pakistan's economic policy to make it subservient to American economic and global interests. Avowedly anti-communist US economist W.W. Rostow played a pivotal role in the pursuit of this aim, 'helping' Pakistani planners to frame economic policy in line with the tenets of modernization theory, with a particular emphasis on a relationship of dependency on the US.[14]

In following American objectives, the Ayub Khan government protected Pakistani traders-turned-capitalists and gave them lucrative incentives to establish industries, whereas the American transnational corporations were encouraged to set up production facilities in major urban centers to manufacture a wide range of consumer products. Pakistan's support of capitalists differed from India's support of its bourgeoisie during the same period: support for capitalists in Pakistan took the form of the 'bonus voucher' scheme, in which a few traders and industrialists were issued government permits to import goods and machinery at discounted foreign exchange rates and import duties. This offered considerable savings to these chosen few; others wishing to import consumer goods had to pay prohibitive customs duties. Within this protected environment, profits rose dramatically for both Pakistani capitalists and Western transnational companies, whereas working conditions in these very profitable Pakistani factories remained oppressive and miserable. For example, large-scale manufacturing grew at an average annual rate of a phenomenal 22.6% between 1950 and 1956.[15] At the same time, workers' real wages were actually *de*creasing: in 1954, the average wage of industrial workers was estimated at Rupees (Rs.)966.2, but real wages in 1958 were only Rs.936.7 per year.[16] The drop in real wages began around 1955 due to the slump in economic activity because of saturation in the demand for consumer goods, but it started to inch back up around 1957. However, even after economic prosperity had started to become quite visible (at least for the upper classes) and industrial expansion was underway, real wages remained immeasurably low. These conditions contributed to the "large scale immiseration of labour and the population in general."[17]

With regard to women's equality and participation in society, many women who participated in anti-colonial movements hoped that women's rights would be significantly improved once independence was achieved.[18] However, women's equality has remained elusive since the emergence of the post-colonial state—and for most women in the Third World this promise is far from being fulfilled. In the context of Pakistan's creation, the anti-colonial efforts of Muslim women in colonial India were limited to few middle and upper class women who had joined the Muslim League or other movements against British colonial rule, whereas rural women remained outside the active imagining of a 'Muslim nation'. Soon after Pakistan's formation, many women from privileged urban backgrounds decided to form the All Pakistan Women's Association (APWA); it was no coincidence that one of its founding members (and later its president) was the wife of Pakistan's first Prime Minister, Liaquat Ali Khan. APWA did not work with rural women, and it was not keen to see a radical transformation of women's role in society, but it did concern itself with the "general welfare of women, increased educational opportunities and socio-cultural consciousness among them [along with the demand for] better job opportunities."[19] During Ayub Khan's military rule, APWA, as a premier organization of upper class women, launched a campaign against polygamy and to have the state grant Muslim women the right to divorce. The organization also worked to eliminate the traditional prerogative accorded to Muslim men for an instant divorce from their wives simply by uttering *talakh* (divorce) three times. APWA argued that this extremely arbitrary, demeaning, and unilateral patriarchal tradition had to end because it had no consequences for the man, whereas the woman was stigmatized, emotionally scarred, and left with no means of support. They demanded that this measure be replaced by a legal process that protected the rights of women and afforded them the option to seek divorce if they chose. Ironically, it was the military ruler, Ayub Khan, who largely accepted APWA's main demand, and promulgated The Family Laws Ordinance of 1961. This was a move that

> enhanced space—if not actual rights—within the family. A limited number of women gained the right to choose or have a say in whom they would marry. Higher education and remunerative work became acceptable for many, and by 1975, all branches of the civil service had been opened to women. Unfortunately, however, these redefinitions of the parameters of women's personal lives were largely insulated by boundaries of class privilege in metropolitan location [. . . For the less-privileged women], changes were far less dramatic.[20]

The 1961 law was, in effect, a compromise between the state and its somewhat liberal pretensions on one hand and religious parties such as the Jamaat-e-Islami on the other. This compromise essentially "split the legal system in two, with personal status law (marriage, divorce, child custody, inheritance) being articulated in consonance with so-called Islamic principles whereas all other issues were framed in line with secular legal traditions."[21]

As for the aspirations of ethnic and subnational groups for equal treatment and provincial autonomy, the Ayub Khan era was marked by utter failure. By declaring the One Unit, which effectively denied the existence of the five major nations, in effect homogenizing all identities as part of the Muslim *ummah* or nation, Ayub Khan insisted on recreating the unitary state following the pattern of the colonial state. Consequently, his government actively moved to quash demands for provincial autonomy and sharing of power made by *Bengalis* and other national groups. The provincial leaders from Sindh, Baluchistan, and the North West Frontier (now Khyber-Pakhtoonkhwa) were still trying to assess the situation and develop their respective strategies when Maulana Bhashani's group in Bengal called for a broad left-of-centre coalition against the government's intransigence on the issue of provincial autonomy. This call culminated in the formation of the National Awami (People's) Party (NAP). The Pakistani state responded with a myriad of attacks and charges against the Party's leadership. The state was particularly vicious in the former East Pakistan, even going so far as to lay treason charges against Bengali nationalist leaders. The Ayub Khan regime was fixed on the concept of the unitary state and remained steadfast in denying autonomy to the provinces despite rising anger and protests in Bengal and the North West Frontier. These actions on the part of the state (or, more accurately, the elites from the civil and military bureaucracy from the two dominant ethnic/national groups, the Punjabi and the *Mohajir*) with regard to power sharing and national rights eventually led to Pakistan's fragmentation and the creation of Bangladesh in 1971. It is worth noting that the civilian government of Z.A. Bhutto abolished the One Unit with the formation of Bangladesh, by establishing the four provinces (one of which, the Northwest Frontier Province, did not get its national identity of Khyber Pakhtunkhwa until 2010). However, genuine provincial autonomy is still elusive; in the province of Baluchistan, an armed nationalist movement is responding to the military's actions in the province, and confronting the state for real devolution of power to the province.

Despite the widespread perception in Pakistan that the Ayub-era economic policies promoted capitalism, a critical analysis of that period shows the hallmarks of *rentier* capitalism. The state encouraged 'rent-seeking behaviour' through such steps "as protective tariffs, rebates and fiscal subsidies, credit at artificially low rates of financing industrial projects, favourable pricing policies, and protected markets [. . . which thrived as] a kind of mercantilist parody of the market economy."[22] The state also pandered to the feudal elite and supported a class of traders who were willing to submit to every imperialist demand to collaborate with Western transnational corporations, in exchange for opportunities to set up the industry of their choice. The Ayub Khan regime offered a feeble attempt at land reforms, but the problem of landlessness and land concentration remained. As is now a familiar story in the global South, landless peasants in Pakistan were displaced as land concentration and mechanization increased, leaving them no choice other than to flood the urban centres and dramatically expand the ranks of the unemployed. These hardy souls had no choice other than to eke out an existence as the self-employed and self-exploited members of the informal sector. The problem of peasant displacement worsened greatly as Pakistan adopted the American strategy of Green Revolution in the mid-1960s. The situation in West Punjab (Pakistan) was not very different from India's East Punjab, where the most fertile lands had become increasingly concentrated in the hands of fewer and fewer landlords so that peasants either became semi-proletarians or had to scrape an existence while unemployed or under-employed.

The inequities produced by the state under military rule increased social discontent, resulting in a countrywide mass mobilization against Ayub Khan's military regime. He was forced to resign in 1969 and handed over power to another army general, Yahya Khan. Ayub Khan's successor pledged to hold free elections in 1970 and, to his credit, acceded to the popular will of the people. He also presided over the atrocities committed by the military in former East Pakistan, which eventually led to the separation of Bangladesh. The early 1970s were marked by polarization not only of the left and the right but also of religious and secular forces. However, in what was then West Pakistan, the stronger far-left parties, because they did not wish to take the parliamentary road, thus left the terrain open for (and even helped) Zulfikar Ali Bhutto come to power. As a populist, Z.A. Bhutto used the left and leftist rhetoric to promote himself as a 'democrat' and an opponent of military rule. His rhetoric and the developments in West Pakistan were complicated by the fact that a separatist movement in the Eastern half of the country was virtually poised to declare the formation of Bangladesh as a separate and independent state. The military was trying to crush the separatists using brute force and was still committing untold atrocities against the Bengali people. In Bengal, the nationalist movement was being led by another populist, Mujibur Rahman, who was able to garner support from India for his party's cause, which proved to be crucial for the separation of East Bengal from Pakistan. In the 1970 elections, Mujibur Rahman's Awami (People's) League (the largest political party in Bengal) won by a landslide, with its seats concentrated entirely in the former Eastern wing, whereas Zulfikar Ali Bhutto's Pakistan Peoples Party (PPP) won the largest number of seats from West Pakistan. However, the ruling oligarchy in West Pakistan, including the military, were unwilling to hand over power to Awami League, so East Bengal separated to form the new state of Bangladesh, propelling Bhutto to power in what remained of Pakistan in 1971.

(iv) State, Society, and Economy Under Bhutto

Z.A. Bhutto rose to power as a populist, took on the military after its excesses in Bangladesh, and removed certain key offending generals as soon as he took office, thus controlling the military's political ambitions. Bhutto's rule was a bundle of contradictions. He popularized the slogan "*roti, kapra aur makan*" (food, clothes, and shelter) as a populist rhetoric but actually did little to address the immense problem of poverty. Faced with the deep polarization between the Islamists and the left forces during the 1970 elections, Bhutto tried to placate the forces on the right and please his allies on the left through slogans such as "democracy is our politics, Islam is our religion, and socialism is our economy." In reality, he was not committed to any of these three ideologies.

Like most populists (including India's Indira Gandhi), Bhutto quickly turned to authoritarianism. He was fearful of being deposed by the military, so he created the Federal Security Force, which was loyal and answerable to him alone, and used it to intimidate and browbeat his opponents. Bhutto introduced progressive labour legislation, but he also penalized workers and labour groups that were critical of his government. At the level of state functionaries, Bhutto eliminated some of the middle and upper level *Mohajir* bureaucrats who had been entrenched in the bureaucracy, some since 1947. Given his own Sindhi ethnic background, it was not surprising that Bhutto filled these positions with the Sindhi feudal elite and some middle-class bureaucrats, who, along with Baluch and Pushtuns, had been complaining of exclusionary treatment at the hands of the Punjabi elite and the *Mohajirs*.

Bhutto was able to enact the 1973 Constitution with the unanimous consent of all parties in the Parliament. This was the third Constitution of the country, but it was the first of its kind to be voted on and accepted by the first genuinely elected National Assembly, and it came exactly 25 years after the formation of Pakistan. The document enshrined the rights of provinces, at least on paper, giving them a semblance of autonomy; in practice, the situation was very different. For example, Bhutto authorized violent military action against nationalists in the province of Baluchistan. This attack on the Baluch nationalists, whose demands were largely for greater provincial autonomy, demonstrated that neither the military nor Bhutto had learned any lessons from the creation of Bangladesh. The military carried out armed action in Baluchistan for almost three years, and it was evident that even under a supposedly elected civilian political leadership, after the fall of East Pakistan, the civil and military bureaucratic oligarchy were able to recoup their power and begin calling the shots again. The Baluchistan military action ended in a stalemate, but Bhutto and the military claimed victory.

On the economic front, one controversial task undertaken by the state under Bhutto was to nationalize and bring within the public sector certain key industries, including banks and insurance companies, but there was no clear policy outlining how these sectors would contribute to economic development after nationalization. Consequently, the post-nationalization era marked a sharp decline in industrial growth rates: the high gross domestic product (GDP) growth of 9% to 11% in manufacturing, mining, and construction sectors from 1965 to 1969 fell to 4.2% to 5.5% by 1978 to 79, the period marking the overthrow of the Bhutto government.[23] However, real wages of workers actually increased, which was a direct result of the state allowing collective bargaining in public sector corporations and institutions. In 1970 to 1971, before Bhutto took office, the average monthly wage of an industrial worker was Rs.1384 per month; by 1974 to 1975 it had risen to Rs.1730.[24]

In economic terms, Bhutto's era cannot simply be dismissed as a failure. The average annual rate of GDP growth was 5.4%—about the same as it was under Ayub Khan. However, manufacturing and agricultural annual growth rates under Bhutto were down to 2.1% and 5.2%, respectively, in contrast to the growth of 3.9% and 8.9%, respectively, during Ayub Khan's military dictatorship.[25] If Bhutto was trying to set the course in Pakistan towards a state-centered economic development, there was no clear strategy in place. Bhutto's policy (if it could be called that) seemed to be designed to entrench an already over-blown and parasitical bureaucracy in state corporations. In terms of the establishing a stable course of industrial development, Bhutto's era was problematic in a number of ways. If the nationalization scheme was intended to give real public ownership in the operation of these industrial units, this objective was completely missed. Meaningful industrial investment was simply not visible; a number of mega projects were set up with much fanfare, but investment did not follow to build a cohesive industrialization strategy. Eventually, many of these projects had to be closed down or became part of a list of 'sick industries'. Because capitalist development in the private sector was stymied under Bhutto, the Pakistani state became extensively involved in extending the limits of bureaucratic capitalism. The bourgeoisie as a class therefore remained weak whereas the feudal elite as well as the bureaucracy became considerably stronger.

Bhutto's poor economic strategy resulted in a looming economic crisis for a number of years. Fortuitously, he was able to avert a full-blown crisis because he managed to ride the wave of the 1970s economic boom in the Middle East. The economic backsliding in Pakistan can be traced to this period: instead of developing a cohesive economic strategy to create work at home by constructing Pakistan's own industrial infrastructure, Pakistani workers were 'exported' in large numbers at cheap wages to oil-rich sheikhdoms like Saudi Arabia, the Emirates, Iran (under the Shah), and Libya. In one sense, the wages earned by these expatriate workers resolved Pakistan's dollar deficits, but they did so at the cost of neglecting the country's own industrial development. The higher dollar reserves fuelled by high expatriate remittances lulled the government into a false sense of security. In effect, the foreign exchange remittances made by these Pakistani workers in the Middle East from the mid-1970s throughout the 1980s were almost equal to the value of Pakistani exports, which in 1977 to 1978, 1980 to 1981, and 1982 to 1983 were $1.3, $2.8, and $2.4 billion, respectively, whereas workers' remittances in the same period were $1.2, $2.1, and $2.8 respectively.[26] In 1982 to 1983, worker's remittances even exceeded the level of total exports.

If there was any success in the alleviation of poverty in this period, Bhutto's government cannot take any credit. The foreign remittances from expatriate Pakistanis alone played a role in improving the living standards of the families who were left behind as these workers went overseas. Bhutto's government was unimaginative in channelling these significant dollar transfers into the improvement of productive investments and domestic savings. The large amount of disposable cash was mainly spent on consumer durables; individuals with access to speculative capital indulged in land speculation. Of the amounts remitted by expatriate workers back to their families in Pakistan, approximately 63.09% was spent on consumer goods, 22% was spent on real estate, and 12% was saved.[27] Much of the money from overseas Pakistanis was sent to rural areas or smaller towns that depended largely on agriculture, but because most of these rural families either had no land or had land that was not productive, remittances from overseas relatives were spent mainly on survival needs. If land had been made available to the sharecroppers and poor peasants who were receiving this money, it could have been put to productive use. This is not to say that Bhutto did not institute land reforms. In fact, he implemented two sets of land reforms, but neither meaningfully reduced the land holdings of the big landlords, who simply found creative ways to conceal or transfer their landholdings to their relatives and trusted servants.

The imperialist hold on Pakistan, and specifically relations with the US, changed as Bhutto tried to chart a more autonomous course for Pakistan and tried to influence other Muslim-majority states to do the same. Bhutto conceived the idea of making Pakistan a nuclear power through a covert operation of piecing together the technology for this initiative and was eventually successful in bringing this idea to fruition. He was a central figure in politically organizing the Islamic countries and played a major role in strengthening the Organization of Islamic Conference. The Organization of Islamic Conference's objective was to establish a union that would promote interdependency and trade among various Muslim states: facilitating commerce, encouraging the better use of the oil wealth, and establishing an Islamic bank, among other steps. The central leadership of this group was composed of autocrats who were historically allied very closely with the US but also desired to change course and become more independent. The three main figures in this group were Bhutto himself, the Shah of Iran, and King Faisal of Saudi Arabia. Whether by design or coincidence, all three men were either deposed or murdered while in office. Bhutto was deposed from power by General Ziaul Haq and eventually hanged in what many have been called a 'judicial assassination'. The Shah of Iran was confronted with a popular uprising whose leadership was taken over midstream by the religious clergy; when it became clear to the Shah that the US had chosen Ayatollah Khomeini over him, he decided to leave power as well as Iran. King Faisal of Saudi Arabia was murdered by his nephew, who had then recently returned from the US. Bhutto faced clear US ultimatums; one of these was made known to him when he facilitated Henry Kissinger's visit to China, a trip that eventually paved the way for Richard Nixon's famous China visit. During Kissinger's Pakistan visit, Bhutto was threatened with dire consequences for failing to toe the American line.[28] Bhutto tried to publicize these American threats just before the 1977 elections but received little public support because his own credibility had eroded due to his authoritarianism and high-handedness. When Bhutto called a national election in January 1977, a coalition of right-wing groups and religious political parties under the banner of the Pakistan National Alliance was organized relatively swiftly, with the goal of removing Bhutto from power. Bhutto won the election, which was mired in controversy and allegations of vote-rigging.

The vote tampering allegations marred Bhutto's second term in office, and in July 1977 he was forcibly removed in a coup staged by General Ziaul Haq. He was briefly held in military custody before being released. In a major turn of events, his release was marked by huge celebrations, which made the military re-think its strategy of freeing him; he was subsequently re-arrested and eventually hanged by the military ruler.

(v) Haq's Military Rule: Clientelism, Societal Obscurantism, and Islamic Revivalism

Ziaul Haq's rise to power marked Pakistan's return to the status of a US client state. Because the military had been thoroughly discredited in Pakistan after Ayub Khan's 11-year rule and Bhutto's execution, Haq's coup needed a constituency from which to draw its support and rationalize another military general's forcible takeover of state power. Therefore, General Haq sought the support of right-wing groups, especially Islamist political parties, to stay in power. To prove his Islamist credentials, he went through the masquerade of promising to make Pakistan a 'bastion of Islam' and implementing his notion of 'Islamization'. In this Haq was extremely successful and held on to power for another 11 years (1977–1988); he might have kept it longer had he not died in a mysterious plane crash along with the US ambassador to Pakistan. Nevertheless, Haq's reign of fear saw the introduction of public lashings, promotion of obscurantism, restrictions on women to the *chador and char diwari* (a head-to-toe robe and the four walls of the home), diversion of funding from secular public schools to religious *madrassahs*, and the initiation of a US proxy war against the former Soviet Union in Afghanistan, which was fought by the Pakistan army alongside the Afghan Mujahideen (who the Pakistanis also helped train with American arms).

The US President Jimmy Carter (now considered a great champion of human rights and the election monitor for many Third World states) directed his intelligence operatives to actively enlist the support of Islamists for the American Cold War objective of defeating the Soviet Union. The timing of this US initiative could not have been more propitious for Haq and his push towards 'Islamization'. The US support for General Ziaul Haq enabled him to consolidate the military's hold on power, and in return for American favours, he was eager to convert Pakistan into an ever-obliging client state. In propping up the military regime, Haq set dangerous precedents: overriding the Constitution and amending it at will, unleashing a torrent of human rights abuses such as public lashings, restricting women's participation in society, and establishing fear as the overriding deterrent in society—all this as Carter and the US looked the other way. These military actions shook Pakistan's social foundations and sowed the seeds for the emergence of militant Islam that has since devastated and polarized Pakistani society. Furthermore, Haq's military rule and his tight grip on power enabled the Pakistani military, the US, and Saudi Arabia to make Pakistan and Afghanistan serve as grooming environments for *jihadis* from the Middle East, Africa, and Central and West Asia.

To force the former Soviet Union out of Afghanistan (simply a step towards the larger goal of winning the Cold War), the US worked with Saudi Arabia to funnel "billions of dollars worth of secret assistance" through the support of Pakistan's military;[29] the aim here was to set-up *madrassahs* in Pakistan and to build the armies of *jihadis*. The second objective of supporting the Afghan Mujahideen was to help them overthrow the left-leaning Afghan government, a move that would eventually force the former Soviet Union to withdraw from Afghanistan.

Haq's military rule was extremely disabling not just for women, the poor, and religious minorities but also for national struggles towards provincial autonomy, progressive politics, and enlightened intellectual or thoughtful academic activity. His rule was the high point of fundamentalism in Pakistan and represents a confluence of forces representing military rulers and fundamental militant Islamists. Both groups had similar objectives: the former tried to achieve political legitimacy for military rule; the latter attempted to gain state power, which had remained elusive to them through the electoral process. The most venomous attacks of both Haq and the Islamists were directed at women. Although women were made irrelevant to the power contestations taking place in the political arena, gender definition became central to Haq's fundamentalist agenda and "women [as objects] became easy targets."[30] The early compromise reached during the Ayub Khan regime between upper class women, the state, and religious groups in the area of Muslim personal law became the first target of Haq's misogynist enactments. Sections of the colonial-era Evidence Act, specifically those related to the acceptance of evidence during court proceedings, were even amended to inferiorize women, casting their evidence as half as equal to that of men in a court trial.[31] In other words, two women were needed for evidence to be deemed as acceptable as that of one man.

Haq also intervened on the economic front, making changes to the Constitution and banking laws on the pretext of 'Islamizing the economy', while at the same time presiding over the privatization of the public sector. However, enthusiasm for economic liberalization in Pakistan was not strong, so the project advanced in spurts. Haq's experts on 'Islamic economics' claimed that interest charges were 'un-Islamic', so he proceeded to abolish interest and introduced the notion of 'profit and loss' on loans and interest-bearing financial transactions. This measure had very little to do with Islamic concern about usury and everything to do with jugglery because interest has been given another name: profit (or loss, which is hardly ever invoked in practice). The most damaging aspect of Haq's legacy for Pakistan's economy, however, was the military ownership and control of many public corporations, which now rival private investment in the country; this issue will be addressed in the next section.

Islamist forces, even at their peak when they shared power with the military ruler, did not enjoy widespread public support, despite their street power and the capacity to intimidate people. This lack of popular support for religious parties and Islamist groups is exemplified by the results of five elections held between 1970 and 2008. Table 5.1 provides a breakdown of political parties' performance in national elections in the four largely fair and free elections (the 1988 election is generally considered to have been rigged; indicators of 'fair and free' include the absence of intimidation in casting one's vote, the election being generally free of vote-tampering, and the results being considered to be good indicators of public support for a particular party). Table 5.1 demonstrates that religious parties have historically failed to collectively win more than 9% of the seats in any election. The exception was the 2002 election, which was held not long after the October 2001 US and North Atlantic Treaty Organization attack on Afghanistan; the results reflected the general anger against General Musharraf's military government for completely buckling to US pressure in providing military bases and logistical and

Table 5.1 Summary of Pakistan Election Results

	Percentage of Seats Held				
Name of Party	*1970*	*1988*	*1993*	*2002*	*2008*
Awami League (E. Pakistan now Bangladesh)	151	n/a	n/a	n/a	n/a
Pakistan People's Party/Parliamentarians	81	38.8	36.2	23.1	32.5
Pakistan Muslim League–Nawaz	—[b]	—[b]	30.8	6.0	25.0
Pakistan Muslim League (Quaid)	—[b]	—[b]	—[b]	28.4	15.2
Pakistan Muslim League (Qayyum)	9	0	0	0	0
Independents	16	11.4	6.3	8.2	10.4
Islami Jamhoori Ittehad (Islamic Democratic Alliance)	—[b]	23.2	0	0	0
National Awami Party (Wali)	6	0	0	0	0
Awami National Party	—[b]	1.3	1.3	0	3.7
Muhajir Qaumi Mahaz (Migrant National Front)	—[b]	5.5	0	4.8	7.1
Other Parties	10	1.4	6.2	9.7	3.0
[a]Muttahhida Majlis-e-Amal	—[b]	—[b]	—[b]	19.8	2.2
[a]Jamiat-ul-Ulema-e-Islam	7	3.4	4.0	0	0
[a]Jamiat Ahle Sunnat	7	0	0	0	0
[a]Jamaat-i- Islami	4	0	0	0	0
[a]Other Islamic Parties	0	0	3.9	0	0

Note: The 1970 results are taken from—,"Party Positions in N.A. and P.A. at a Glance," Dawn 21 December 1970: 4. November–December 1970: fiche 1, AN D835; the 1988 and 1993 results are from the University of New York, Center on Democratic Performance, "Pakistan: Legislative Elections," 12 July 2004 <http://cdp.binghamton.edu/era/countries/pak.html>. The results of 2002 and 2008 elections were obtained from the Election Commission of Pakistan, "Constituency-Wise Detailed Results: NWFP Province," 20 May 2011 <http://www.ecp.gov.pk/GE/2002/National.pdf> and Election Commission of Pakistan, " General Elections—2008," 20 May 2011 <http://www.ecp.gov.pk/GE2008.aspx>.

[a]Religious party. [b]Party was not yet formed.

material support for the 'war on terror'. In 2002, all major Sunni political parties formed a coalition, the Muttahhida Majlis Amal, which obtained almost 20% of the National Assembly seats and also formed the government in the Northwest province of Khyber Pukhtoonkhwa. The 1988 election saw the revival of the Islami Jamhoori Itehad (IJI), a coalition composed of almost all political parties—both secular and religious—with the goal of defeating Benazir Bhutto and the PPP, but despite its efforts and the efforts of the military to rig the election, IJI failed to win a majority. IJI was created in 1977 with the objective of defeating Z.A. Bhutto, but that too ended in failure. I should also mention that *Mohajir Qaumi Mahaz* (MQM—Migrant National Front) blasted on the city of Karachi's political scene claiming the ethnic and then national identity of a *Mohajir* (migrant) during the Ziaul Haq era. The MQM began by violently confronting the Pushtun settlers in Karachi; later they did the same with the Punjabi settlers and finally confronted the *Sindhis*, the original inhabitants of the Sindh province. I merely mention the MQM, which has now reinvented itself as a mainstream group, the Muttahida Qaumi Movement (United National Movement), as an example of an identity that emerged in conflict (during Partition with Hindu/Sikh–Muslim violence) and how this trajectory of conflict and violence has had an afterlife in the post-colonial era.[32]

What the Pakistani state was unable to do in terms of popularizing conservative Islamists and religious parties, the US has been able to achieve since 11 September 2001 with its reckless saturation bombing of Afghanistan and later with its 'shock and awe' brute display of military force in Iraq. The US attack on the Taliban government of Afghanistan proved to be a bonanza for the wider societal acceptance of religious political parties and militant Islamist groups in Pakistan, as exemplified by the 2002 elections. The popularity of the Islamists, however, was short-lived: as militant Islamists began to promote their obscurantist ideas and started to burn girls' schools and to use extremely violent means to spread their message, their popularity quickly evaporated. This issue will be discussed in more detail in the fourth section of this chapter.

II PAKISTAN'S RUDDERLESS ECONOMY

Pakistan's rulers have claimed their commitment to a path towards capitalist development, but the structure of the Pakistani state has created major impediments to steering the country along this path. In furthering their respective interests, the troika of feudal lords and civil and military bureaucrats has closed off avenues for the capitalist class to become ascendant. Consequently, the lines between feudalism and capitalism are blurred. The feudal elites have remained forceful in oppressing the peasantry while protecting their economic interests and having a share in state power. In contrast, the indigenous bourgeoisie has remained very weak compared with the relative strength of the feudal lords and the bureaucracy, the latter has always acted as an auxiliary class. The power of the feudal elites is illustrated by the fact that the state has not implemented a meaningful taxation regime on agricultural income, whereby even non-agricultural income is declared as agricultural income to evade taxes.[33] A land revenue-based property taxation protocol has been in existence since the British imposed it during the colonial era, but agricultural income taxation revenue earned under this protocol is negligible—given that British colonial rulers were collecting tribute at exorbitant rates. Some form of agricultural income taxation was introduced at International Monetary Fund's (IMF) insistence in the late 1990s and during the new millennium, but these steps were also never seriously implemented. Further, despite the 3 to 4 land reforms introduced by the various governments (another more recently by the present Zardari government), few landless peasants and sharecroppers have benefitted, as very little land has actually been re-distributed.[34] Consequently, feudal lords continue to dominate and oppress peasants, farm workers, and small farmers.

The second impediment to Pakistan's miscued capitalist development trajectory is related to the nature of the over-developed bureaucracy, which has emerged as the classic predator in the post-colonial state and has stifled the bourgeoisie from becoming internally cohesive as a class. The third obstacle involves the inordinate emphasis on the establishment of a consumer goods infrastructure instead of on investment in the enlargement of the capital goods industrial base. Despite Pakistan's urgent need for an industrial infrastructure, 94% of economic 'aid' during the early and mid-1950s was in the form of finished consumer goods, agricultural products, and payment for services to American 'experts', whereas only 6% was spent on capital formation.[35] These patterns of US 'assistance', coupled with the efforts of its economic advisors and modernization theorists, set Pakistan on the course of an industrialization strategy focused on the production of consumer goods. Thus, the main feature that characterized Pakistan's economic development during its first decade of existence (1947–1957) was an emphasis on import substitution of consumer products and a relative absence of capital goods manufacturing.

By 1958 (the year General Ayub Khan captured power), Pakistan's high industrial growth rates had started to level off; manufacturing growth in the private sector stayed within the 4% to 5% range until Z.A. Bhutto began to nationalize industries. The pattern of Pakistan's industrial development was problematic in a number of ways. As mentioned previously, the focus on producing consumer goods during the first three decades took resources away from establishing a production base for capital goods. Bhutto's economic policy of nationalization was an attempt to change this lopsided emphasis on consumer goods production, but it was unsuccessful, largely because of the problems associated with an ill-conceived nationalization and state-led industrialization strategy, as well as corruption, bureaucratic ineptitude, and the dispensation of patronage. The nationalization process itself generated a steep drop in private sector investment, from an annual investment of Rs.1.3 billion in 1970 to 1971 to Rs.500 million in 1973 to 1974.[36] Private sector investment then levelled off to about Rs.600 million a year until 1979 to 1980. Public sector investment compensated for the fall in private investment to a degree, and investment in capital goods started to rise rapidly: from about Rs.100 million in 1971 to 1972, it peaked at about Rs.2.2 billion in 1978 to 1979.[37]

Pakistan's case demonstrates how a highly bureaucratized control of the economy in proto-capitalist societies can have devastating results for economic and social development. Even after following the dictates of US foreign policy and US economic doctrine, not to mention IMF and World Bank dictates for more than five decades and having been identified in the mid-1960s as a country that was at the "take off stage,"[38] Pakistan's economic performance has really deteriorated. The country has experienced significant deindustrialization and has seriously neglected education, health, and programs for social upliftment, all of which have been squeezed out by heavy military spending. Currently, Pakistan faces a ballooning debt burden and has seen an overall increase in poverty since the 1980s. If there was any alleviation in poverty between 1970 (42.5% of the population was classified as poor) and the mid-1980s (31% of the population),[39] it was not really the work of the Bhutto government. Poverty reduction was made possible largely because of the remittances made by overseas Pakistanis to their families as the government's own expenditure on social security and health care remained dismally low. Despite Pakistan's low literacy rate of 56% (2008), the state has done little to increase public expenditure on education, which remains at a low 2.7% (2009) of the GDP—effectively even lower as the figure is based on budgetary commitment that often get reduced as funds are diverted to other heads when it comes to actual spending. Secondary school enrolment has remained stagnant over the past decade at 33% (2009) of all primary school-age children—and yet billons of secret funds from Saudi Arabia have been used to build religious *madrassahs*.[40]

To add to these social woes, the military's intrusion in the economy continues to be a festering problem. This intervention diverts money from ordinary Pakistanis to military officers and their families. The Pakistani military's economic activities are shrouded in secrecy; there is absolutely no accountability to the public about how the defence budget is used—or whether it has even been used for defence purposes instead of being funnelled into the companies run by the four military Foundations (two army, one navy, and one air force).[41] No-one is available to ask these questions of the military, and the defence establishment is not about to volunteer the information. In countries such as Indonesia, where the military held political power longer than in Pakistan, military involvement in business has been used to offset defence budget shortfalls, but "Pakistan's military Foundations (the military's business and welfare arms) continue to be used to divert resources from the annual defence budget for the Foundations' survival."[42] The four Foundations operate a vast number of commercial projects ranging from very large industrial units (fertilizer and cement plants, refineries, and natural gas companies) to financial institutions (banks and insurance companies), a commercial airline, shopping centres, and the largest construction and trucking operations in the country—and these projects complement an enormous military welfare operation used largely for retired military personnel.[43] There is no way of determining the health of these companies or the extent of the Foundations' operations; no way of ascertaining whether they are commercially viable or are simply sucking up public funds:

> Pakistan provides an opportunity to understand the issues that emerge from the financial autonomy of a politically powerful military. Pakistan's military today runs a huge commercial empire. Although it is not possible to give a definitive value of the military's internal economy because of the lack of transparency, the estimated worth runs into billions of dollars. Moreover, the military's two business groups—the Fauji Foundation and the Army Welfare Trust—are the largest business conglomerates in the country.[44]

The military is also the largest owner of real estate—and this is not referring to military bases, barracks, or munitions depots. Through the Defence Officers Housing Authority, military officers have been able to acquire very large tracts of prime real estate in urban centres throughout the country. The Housing Authority allots land (on a 99-year lease) to military officers (but *not* foot soldiers) at very subsidized rates, including some state agricultural land and even prized scenic real estate. These lands are then sold to the general public (largely wealthy, upper class elites) at market rates; this form of legalized corruption enables huge profit for military officers. The transfer of public lands to individual military personnel or military foundations is not a new phenomenon—military intrusion into the economic sphere stretches back to the colonial era, when the military rationalized its limited commercial involvement as a guarantee to the welfare of retired or serving personnel. This idea of the welfare of military personnel was reintroduced during the Ayub Khan regime and greatly expanded by General Ziaul Haq. Since then, the military's predatory impulse to privatize public lands has been completely out of control.

III POST-HAQ PERIOD AND INCOMPLETENESS OF THE STATE-BUILDING PROJECT

Ziaul Haq's death in a mysterious plane crash, which Mohammed Hanif parodied in his *The Case of Exploding Mangoes*,[45] marked a symbolic end to the most troublesome period of Pakistan's history. To the misfortune of most Pakistanis, Haq's policies have had a long and debilitating afterlife: Pakistan has become an obsequious US client and fought its proxy war against the Soviets in Afghanistan and is now deeply enmeshed in the 'war on terror'. His policies have still not been reversed, which promote 'Islamization' as the ideological narrative underlying the exercise of state power and marginalization of women's participation in society. Haq's pernicious legacy also continues: to promote the building of *madrassahs* throughout the country with Saudi funds, to exacerbate sectarianism and target secular and leftwing opposition, and to enable the proliferation of the 'Kalashnikov culture'. The contemporary consequences of Haq's legacy are an unprecedented level of random violence and insecurity stemming from the rise of militant Islam, patriarchal violence against women, sectarianism, and intolerance of dissent and alternative viewpoints—whereas the ideological underpinnings of violent militant Islam have had a deeply polarizing and destabilizing impact on present-day Pakistani society. I will return to the contemporary consequences of Haq's policies in later sections, but first it is important to outline how the Pakistani state-building has remained incomplete in the period following Haq's demise as the state appears incapable of addressing today's social and political realities.

Following Haq's death in 1988, the military reluctantly agreed to Benazir Bhutto becoming Prime Minister as her party had secured most seats in the National Assembly. Still, the spectre of Haq's 11-year rule haunted progressive forces and Bhutto. Before she could complete her term, Benazir Bhutto was unceremoniously removed from power by an appointed President who had acquired extraordinary powers courtesy of Haq's 8th constitutional Amendment. This Amendment was introduced in 1985; it made a draconian addition to section 58 of the 1973 Constitution through clause 58.2(B), providing extraordinary powers to an appointed president to dissolve the National Assembly and remove the Prime Minister at her/his sole discretion. None of the governments that followed Ziaul Haq's regime were able to overturn this unilateral constitutional amendment even when they could muster a two-thirds majority to effect the change; the 8th Amendment was finally expunged in 2010 through the 18th Amendment when the civilian rulers eventually relented due to widespread public anger and protests. After Benazir Bhutto was removed from power in August 1990, a game of musical chairs ensued between her and Nawaz Sharif of the Pakistan Muslim League (Nawaz); they each served two incomplete terms as Prime Ministers. Each was removed twice from office—Bhutto twice and Sharif once by the president.[46] The second time Sharif was removed from office prematurely was the result of a military coup by General Pervez Musharraf—this did not just remove Sharif from power; Sharif was publicly humiliated and exiled to Saudi Arabia.

The two terms of Benazir Bhutto were uneventful in the sense of moving the country towards a path of social and economic development or removing the shackles of clientelism—despite the expectations millions of Pakistanis had of her ascendency to power. On the contrary, her government continued to submit to US demands and did very little towards social upliftment or to alleviate poverty. To make matters worse, Bhutto's husband, Asif Ali Zardari, became involved in corrupt deals and massive kickbacks on government contracts, earning the label of Mr. Ten Per Cent in the process. Because ordinary Pakistanis could not get their political leaders to deliver political and social stability and steer the ship of state from murky waters, they began to grasp at straws and were even willing to install Nawaz Sharif as Prime Minister—despite the fact that he was Ziaul Haq's protégé and had been groomed along authoritarian lines to promote Islamization. Sharif's two terms in office were equally disappointing, and like Benazir Bhutto, he made no effort to reverse the Haq-era policies.

When Musharraf replaced Sharif and gave himself a new title of Chief Executive—instead of the Chief Martial Law Administrator like his three preceding military rulers—he did not fool anyone. Still, Musharraf's martial rule was marginally different in appearance and substance from previous military dictators. During his term the private media became more independent, and he promoted postsecondary education by forming the Higher Education Commission. He desired a secular orientation to his rule and was willing to annul another of Haq's creation, the *Shariah* Law, but backed off when he suspected that the backlash from religious parties and militant Islamist groups could be too much for him to handle. Musharraf did not differ from his predecessors in his cooptation of opportunistic political parties to join the government and give it a degree of legitimacy. This tactic began with Ayub Khan and continued with successive military rulers. Another way the Musharraf's government resembled that of his predecessors was the military's targeting of nationalist groups, especially in Baluchistan, where a targeted military attack killed a long-time Baluch leader, Akbar Bughti, who had been quite acceptable to the bureaucracy and mainstream political parties. Musharraf also stuck to the military doctrine of achieving 'strategic depth' in Afghanistan, a doctrine that developed as a policy during the latter part of Haq's rule. This policy was intended to ensure a Pakistan-friendly government in Afghanistan (or the very least, a neutral one in terms of India and Pakistan's respective interests in the region) so that the Pakistani military would not have to deploy troops and resources on its Western border and could concentrate its attention on its Eastern and Northern borders with India. By fulfilling this military doctrine, the Pakistani military encouraged the Taliban's rise to power and even encouraged the rise of militant Islam within Pakistan. However, the flipside of this doctrine has been that the militant Islamists in Pakistan and Afghanistan are now threatening the Pakistani state itself, with the aim of capturing state power and 'Islamizing' Pakistani state and society. This Islamist threat is substantially the most serious consequence of the rise of militant Islam in Pakistan, but this military doctrine has had an overall corrosive impact on the state and its bureaucratic organs: it is no longer a secret that some civil and military bureaucratic functionaries have divided loyalties with respect to political and militant Islamist groups. Musharraf, given his secular rhetoric, had the opportunity to scrap this military doctrine and build a new non-clientelist relationship with Afghanistan but did not. He actually worsened matters by maintaining this doctrine and submitting completely to US dictates following the 11 September 2001 incident—thereby angering many Pakistanis for failing to implement an independent foreign and domestic policy and simply kowtowing to the US. He buckled under US pressure without much thought about the anti-American 'blowback' that was bound to result. It came in the form of an enormous boost to the recruiting and mobilizing effort of the Tehreek-e-Taliban (TTP—The Movement of Taliban) and other militant groups—as has become apparent given the exponential rise of Taliban-claimed attacks on Sufi shrines, public places, security personnel, and security establishments in Pakistan during Musharraf's rule and since his departure. Near the end of his term, Musharraf made himself President and tried simultaneously to hold the position of Chief of Army Staff. The Supreme Court Chief Justice and other judges opposed this move, resulting in their arrest, but this attack on the judiciary encouraged a valiant protest movement of the lawyers, which greatly weakened Musharraf's position. He was eventually forced to appoint a new military Chief and finally held a national election in 2008. In the aftermath of Benazir Bhutto's assassination, which has been blamed on the Pakistani Taliban (the TTP), the PPP was able to muster the most votes and formed a coalition government with other secular parties. Under the leadership of Benazir Bhutto's widower, Asif Zardari, the PPP succeeded in removing Musharraf as president by threatening him with impeachment.

Curiously, militant Islamist activity has intensified since Musharraf's removal and developed into a full-blown conflict between Pakistani security forces and the TTP and its allies. This development is related to Musharraf's half-hearted effort to go after the Taliban, which allowed them to expand and even to control Swat and other regions. Another contributing factor was the escalation of US intervention in Pakistan, especially the regular aerial drone attacks in Northwest Pakistan.

IV CLIENTELISM AND THE RISE OF MILITANT ISLAM

Although the Pakistani military is currently confronting the TTP and has pushed them back from the Swat region and parts of South Waziristan, the scale of 'blowback' from these military actions in major cities has been phenomenal. However, the state has done very little to limit the expansion of US presence in Pakistan or to stop its aerial drone attacks in Northwest Pakistan. More important, no real effort has been made to challenge political or militant Islam ideologically, a process that will require waging a battle of ideas to expose the narrow, sectarian, anti-women, and intolerant outlooks of both political and militant Islam. The latter part of this section will explore how central ideological challenge will be to defeating militant Islam, but first it is important to distinguish between political and militant Islam and explore how the latter has become a formidable political and military force that can confront the empire as well as the Pakistani state.

The Pakistani state has played a central role in the increasingly right-wing radicalization. At the same time, the post-colonial state worked with right-wing Islamists to target attacks on left-wing groups during much of the Cold War period. Left-wing forces in much of the Third World have largely vanished after more than half a century of attacks by the security organs of the post-colonial and Latin American states and US intelligence and military apparatuses, whereas mainstream Western media's anti-communist hysteria has supported various US imperialist assaults around the world. Within this context, political and militant Islamists have emerged to fill the vacuum left by the progressive left-wing forces. Political Islam has largely retained the constitutional and politico-legal path to assert its influence in Muslim-majority states, whereas militant Islam has now come into its own by taking the extra-constitutional road of military confrontation and violence. Militant Islam was strengthened through various kinds of support, and attacks, from client post-colonial states and now attacks by the imperialist onslaughts of the US and its Western allies. The fact that militant Islamists tend to become stronger when attacked illustrates an important difference between them and the left-wing forces that once had considerable influence, if not the organizational strength, in Pakistan. The Pakistani Taliban is now confronting Pakistani military and paramilitary forces. Many observers see this rise in militant Islam to indicate a strengthening of 'non-state actors' and the weakening of the Pakistani state. I disagree, partly based on my finding that the proto-capitalist post-colonial state tends to be weak in the face of external imperialist impositions but still tend to be internally a 'strong state' that can suppress dissent and oppress its people. In addition, these so-called non-state actors have actually been created by the state itself. Therefore, part of the explanation for the resiliency of militant Islam is that some in the military and bureaucratic apparatus of the client Pakistani state continue to be sympathetic to, and supportive of, this social and political force. Another part is the fact that in the past, ordinary Pakistanis may have been willing to give the militants an opportunity to resist imperialist intervention in Pakistan and the occupation of Afghanistan, based either on the people's genuine anti-imperialist sentiment or simply from being tired of the clientelist sell-out by the indigenous ruling elite (although this attitude has now changed in the face of the scale of TTP's random and targeted violence and sectarianism).

A theoretical exegesis distinguishing political from militant Islam is beyond the scope of this text, and I have already made this distinction in previous work.[47] Here, I will briefly outline how the two overlap and also how they differ. Both constitutional (political) and extra-constitutional (militant) Islam use a narrow interpretation of religious texts as an effective mobilizing tool, with the ultimate aim of capturing state power to enforce the rule of *sharia*. In the contemporary (post-1945) era, followers of political Islam have used limited violence to confront the post-colonial state, whereas militant Islamists have organized mainly as a guerrilla force, first to confront the Soviet Union in Afghanistan, then the US imperialist occupations of Iraq and Afghanistan, and now the post-colonial state has been included along with the attacks on US forces and resources. Militant Islamists have also shown their muscle in a period earlier than the Soviet occupation of Afghanistan: the Indonesian Muslim militia's massacre of Communists with the aid of the Indonesian military and the Central Intelligence Agency,[48] the Moro national struggles against the Philippine state, and the Islamist uprising against the military regime in Algeria. It is important to note that militant Islamists are *not* anti-imperialists. The attempts of militant Islamists to dislodge the US and other allied imperial powers from Afghanistan, Iraq, or Pakistan are *not* meant to end imperialism and move towards a progressive transformation of their respective societies. Rather, the objective is to introduce a narrow, doctrinaire, regressive, and anti-women version of *sharia*. Political and militant Islamists have respectively collaborated with and resisted US imperialism; therefore, they should be viewed within a dialectic of collaboration and resistance. Political Islam, although it has a much longer history, re-emerged during the late-19th century period of colonization and adapted itself to the changed realities of decolonization in Asia and Africa from the 1950s on. During the Cold War, Islamist political parties such as the Jamaat-e-Islami in Pakistan and the Ikhwan al Muslameen (Muslim Brotherhood) in Egypt actively collaborated with the US and its imperialist allies to defeat 'godless Communism'. But with the end of the Cold War and the emergence of the civilizational narrative, courtesy of US's organic intellectuals such as Samuel Huntington and his civilizational clash thesis between Western civilization and Confucianism/Islam (a recreation of the old Occident-Orient civilizational binary),[49] the collaboration with political Islam turned into a confrontation with militant Islamists. Militant Islamists began organizing into groups like the Al Qaeda, the Taliban, and others, so it makes more sense to view the rise of militant Islam and its confrontation with empire within a dialectic of collaboration and resistance instead of seeing it as an anti-imperialist force.

In the Pakistani context, Ziaul Haq's military rule and the early period following Pervaiz Musharraf's military coup captures the interplay of this dialectic. The Islamists had collaborated with the US since the 1950s, but more actively Haq's army was directing the Afghan Mujahideen and their Pakistani and Arab supporters in his patron's proxy war against the Soviet Union. Ziaul Haq, in coming to power, helped to coalesce a fragmented group of Islamist political parties and religious groups, which had been effectively discredited in society,[50] into a reliable constituency for him and the military. General Haq's program of 'Islamization' provided the cover for the inclusion of religious parties in his government. With active military and financial support from the US and Saudi Arabia, religious armies were also assembled in Afghanistan and Pakistan to wage *jihads* in the name of 'saving Islam'.[51] This was unprecedented in a country such as Pakistan with its largely secular public realm. The secular reality, however, began to alter as Ziaul Haq created a framework of *madrassahs* (religious schools) and tried to 'Islamize' criminal and civil laws by introducing an ostensibly *sharia*-based framework under the Hudood Ordinance. Haq's changes intensified the state-driven patronage of the fractured religious parties. As a result, political Islam re-emerged in Pakistan as a very significant social force. Adherents of political Islam have since supported its offshoot, militant Islam, which has become a deadly violent ideological force both within and outside Pakistan. This case demonstrates how the power and patronage of the post-colonial state can effectively resuscitate dying social and political groups, such as Muslim religious parties.[52] In the case of militant Islam, even when state support inverts to confront groups such as the TTP, they can fight back because the latter have core residual support among a small ideological group of state functionaries as well as in pockets of the population. This support for militant Islamists will remain as long as there is continuation of imperialist occupation and intervention. So, the dilemma for Pakistan is how to deal with militant Islam because the US intervention in the region, as the discussion immediately following will show, is not going to end anytime soon.

The consequence of the rise of militant Islam and Pakistan's invidious clientelist relationship with the US has had very costly consequences for the country and its people. "Over the last decade [in Pakistan], 30,000 civilian and around 5,000 security personnel have been victims of extremist violence."[53] The country's economy is in shambles with negligible new industrial investment, and many factories are lying idle. Due to inflation, daily food staples are out of reach for the majority of Pakistanis. The shortfall in power generation is such that electricity is available for only a few hours of the day. After 11 September 2001, and Colin Powell's threat to Musharraf,[54] mentioned earlier, the client state became extremely pliant, providing the US with facilities for its military bases, arresting people involved with planning the 11 September attacks, and fighting the US 'war on terror'. The instability that followed Musharraf's close alliance with the US made Pakistan more dependent on US dictates and its handouts. Since 11 September, the Pakistani political and military elite have effectively mortgaged Pakistan's sovereignty to the US state but pretend to be helpless victims when public anger boils over, for instance, about US aerial drone attacks. Between catering to US demands and addressing their people's anger against US intervention, the manipulative conduct of Pakistan's ruling elite and their divided loyalties only resulted in a half-hearted attempt by the military to confront the TTP. The military is now actively targeting the TTP, but the fact that the Taliban can strike at will, even relatively secure sites, highlights a larger underlying problem related to how the Pakistani state has been forcibly restructured to fight the 'war on terror'. Since 11 September, this restructuring has followed the US concept of the 'security state'. However, what may have worked for the US and other Western states in terms of state securitization is not really applicable in Pakistan. Pakistan's bureaucratic centralized structure, a hold-over from the colonial state, is such that even a police chief in a major city like Karachi cannot be appointed by the municipality or even the province; this is the domain of Islamabad, the federal capital. In other words, the lack of autonomy at the local level inhibits initiative and quick action, which is central in fighting terrorism. So, the Pakistani security state may be complete with anti-terror laws, special anti-terrorism courts—and the police, the Rangers, the Frontier Constabulary, and the military may all try to coordinate their anti-terrorism efforts—but without the resolution of turf issues and immediate decision-making powers at the local level, the exercise will remain futile, as exemplified by the wave of Taliban attacks.

The consequence of the imperialist focus on securitization has not resulted in more protection for the Pakistani state and its populace; rather, it has resuscitated doctrinaire Islam in the form of a strengthened militant Islam. The rise of militant Islam is a direct outcome of attacks on it through military campaigns that were organized within an emulated security state structure, which bears no relationship to indigenous conditions and security needs; rather, it is unified by a joint structure that promotes the participation of Western and key Muslim-majority states in the 'war on terror'—a war that has very little to do with Pakistan's national security interests. This kind of unified structure of the security state forces client states like Pakistan, even under civilian leadership, to claim the 'war on terror' as 'our war'.[55] If there is such a thing as state sovereignty and a country's self-interest, then the US war cannot be Pakistan's war for two good reasons. First, the 'war on terror' is an imperialist war, which the Pentagon has renamed the 'Long War'. This is a perpetual war along the lines of the Cold War for US hegemony and is intended to guard access points of US economic interests, including access to oil in Iraq, energy sources and minerals in Central Asia, and to monitor China and its strategy to access ports off the Baluchistan coast.[56] The Taliban, Al-Qaeda, or 'regime change' in Iraq are really incidental to the larger hegemonic objective of the US. Second, a civilizational narrative is the ideological subtext of this Long War, the push for which comes from US militarism. In turn, US militarism is shaped not just by the US National Security Council and the Pentagon; it is equally formed by the behemoth military-industrial complex and now the accompanying security-industrial complex, and the synergy with Big Oil cannot be ignored.[57] Under the aegis of the Pentagon, these various entities have collectively framed their vision of the Long War, which has the goal of confronting those who oppose their interests and the ideological narrative of Western civilizational dominance and, by implication, those who oppose US hegemony. So, because militant

Islam has an opposing ideology behind the implementation of their version of *sharia* through the capture of state power, they are logically opposed to the civilizational narrative and are therefore a direct target of US militarism. Although these two ideologically motivated foes appear militarily mismatched, militant Islam cannot be written off so easily. Similar to the reasons why the 'war on terror' cannot be Pakistan's war, the interests of the Pakistani state and people cannot be more at odds with the civilizational narrative and Long War objectives. The Pakistani state cannot side with either of the two parties involved in the Long War. But the Pakistani state also cannot remain neutral in this conflict; after all, it nurtured and oversaw the rise of militant Islam. Therefore, it is vital that the Pakistani state confront militant Islam—but this has to be an internal decision with the support of the people and not a result of US prodding. By the same token, Pakistani rulers must muster the courage to resist US pressure and start putting an end to its interference in the country, while taking the difficult steps to become less dependent on the US. None of this will be easy, and one cannot discount the wrath unleashed by an angry imperialist hegemon—but it will be necessary if the client wants to be free of its imperialist patron. Pakistan's survival as a cohesive and viable state depends on whether it can resist the US and take steps to become more autonomous.

Another critical issue related to the confrontation between empire and militant Islam is that a reliance on the old Cold War strategy of perpetual war will not work for a foe that is equally willing to use ideology to meet its larger objective of implementing *sharia*—no matter how much the US tries to demonize militant Islam in Afghanistan, Iraq, Pakistan, and elsewhere or how much force is used against it. The clear conclusion after 10 years of the Long War is that militant Islam *cannot* be defeated militarily. The 'enemy' in this Long War is mobile, faceless, stateless, and geographically untethered. The idea of permanent war may have been integral to the 1947 events that ushered in the Cold War, but militant Islam is a shifting, evolving phenomenon. Followers of political and militant Islam are spread across an enormous geographical terrain, encompassing numerous states as well as having a presence in Western diasporas. The Cold War notion of permanent war was about "peace that was not peace, and war that was not war,"[58] so the Cold War was exhausting on many fronts for the former Soviet Union. For militant Islamists, their sustenance lies in being militarily attacked and confronted—given that ideology is their friend, critical support from ideologically motivated state functionaries is still forthcoming, and callous as it appears, new recruits and suicide bombers are not in short supply. Because militant Islamists are ideologically rooted, and their doctrinaire comrades have a presence both in Muslim-majority states as well as in Western diasporas, the perpetual war will only drain the resources of empire and keep Western states in a state of heightened anxiety and fear.

The Pakistani political leadership also needs to recognize the futility of being a US client for almost 60 years, but this realization will only be driven home to the ruling troika once the people and a set of circumstances force the latter to say *ya basta*! This tipping point may be in sight. To prepare for this eventuality, the leadership needs to consider how it will confront militant Islam as these ideologues are attacking the foundations of the state. So, while the military confronts TTP and other organizations militarily, the Pakistani state needs to have a counter-ideological strategy. This could begin with closing down *madrassahs* and absorbing their students into mainstream educational institutions, whereas also preparing to handle the inevitable backlash. To fill the gap of vanishing *madrassahs*, the state will need to build on an emergency basis quality primary and secondary education institutions and to develop curriculum that directly confronts the narrow ideological and sectarian perspective of militant Islamists, while offering an alternative vision that promotes and realizes shared democratic citizenship, social upliftment, and genuine provincial autonomy along non-denominational lines. The Pakistani media appears to be willing to wage a counter-ideological offensive, and this work will have to be coordinated and encouraged. All of these different ideas will have to be pooled into a well-developed strategy that is comprehensive in scope and implementation. The developers of this strategy will also need to educate policymakers and the public about the patience needed to achieve the long time horizon of this strategy's objectives: the containment and the eventual demise of militant Islam.

V SOCIAL CONTEXT OF ECONOMIC LETHARGY AND PAKISTAN'S RE-SUBORDINATION IN THE 21ST CENTURY

Modernization theorists saw Pakistan's economic development in the 1960s as moving firmly along the axis of the 'take-off stage'. Today, the country's economy is in shambles and dependency on the US has magnified, the society is deeply fragmented and polarized, and the political leaders are not merely asleep at the switch but are busy amassing fortunes in corrupt backroom deals. The country's ill-conceived economic and social development policies have actually led to deindustrialization, rising incidence of poverty, strengthened feudal relations, and the retention of a *rentier* capitalist character of its bourgeoisie. How all this came to pass has already been discussed in the previous sections. This short penultimate section focuses on the consequences of Pakistan's political and military leaders' years of towing a clientelist path, with the exception of Z.A. Bhutto, which has resulted in greater dependency and Pakistan's re-subordination in the 21st century. These ruling oligarchs were not interested in pursuing the difficult task of state-building, nation-building, and guiding the country's socio-economic development trajectory. Instead, they became steadily addicted to the idea of foreign 'assistance'. In addition to US 'aid', Pakistan also became the recipient of long-term, interest-bearing loans from the International

Development Association, a soft-loan window of the World Bank.[59] As Pakistan's dependency on foreign loans increased—an experience echoed in much of the Third World—the rulers made little effort to broaden its industrial base, to encourage the diversification of the country's exports, or even to build an internal market. At the same time, imports rapidly expanded, financed largely through external borrowing. In absolute terms, Pakistan's foreign debt burden is US$53.7 billion (2009 figures) and growing, which amounts to 33% of its GDP of US$162 billion (2009 figures).[60]

The Haq regime started to introduce IMF's Structural Adjustment Programs-induced changes in the 1980s, but the policy lacked the drive to dismantle the feudal and bureaucratic hold on the post-colonial state. Haq's inaction cannot be interpreted as resistance to IMF dictates in the name of protecting state sovereignty; his government was actually trying to preserve civil and military bureaucracy's auxiliary class interests. Generally, the civil and military bureaucracy dragged its feet because Structural Adjustment Programs-induced changes would have undermined the unbridled involvement of the military Foundations in commercial/industrial activities, which have remained secret and unaccountable. Such changes would have also undercut the collective interests of these bureaucratic elites whose members have profited immensely from state-directed activities. Therefore, Pakistan has been a latecomer to the game of economic liberalization: the nudge towards privatization (without a corresponding commitment to market reforms) actually came in 1991. The chief exponent of this privatization move, former finance minister Sartaj Aziz, claimed that Pakistan's experience in the first phase of privatization (1991–1993) was not only 'successful' but was also done quite speedily.[61] For Aziz, the measurement of 'success' was not whether the price obtained from the sale of a state enterprise to the private bidder was comparable to its asset values but simply that these state corporations be privatized—and speedily. Aziz's claim also underplays the real cost of privatization. State-owned enterprises were downsized at public expense before they were handed over to the new owners, a move undertaken through attrition and early retirement by means of a 'Golden Handshake', in which most workers were terminated from their secure jobs with small lump-sum severance payment. The state also failed to reach an agreement with the new owners to minimize any further retrenchment from the remaining employees, which eventually occurred through further attrition but without meaningful compensation. The undervaluing of public assets and providing private capital an opportunity to invest on the cheap was not peculiar to Pakistan; this is how the public sector has been privatized in much of the world in this age of neoliberalism.[62]

The lethargy on the part of the military rulers in Pakistan around the issue of economic liberalization did not translate into a change in Pakistan's client status, and it did not mean that the state would no longer facilitate the external domination of the US and Western transnational corporations. The US was more concerned with the larger objective of ensuring Pakistan's involvement in anti-Soviet actions in Afghanistan, and the Americans were willing to tolerate Haq's feeble attempts at implementing the IMF's dictates for greater market-orientation of Pakistan's economy. The implementation gap of IMF's structural adjustment programs could have had the unintended consequence of weakening the feudal and bureaucratic hold on Pakistani state and society, but this was not to be. Because the US was less willing to enforce IMF dictates, as it needed the services of Haq's Pakistan, it made the ruling troika fairly secure in its ambivalence towards the adoption of neoliberal policies. The avoidance of structural adjustment was also possible because of the weakness of capitalists as a cohesive class in Pakistan.

Capitalists in Pakistan would much rather indulge in backroom deals, pay off bureaucrats, and curry favours from politicians instead of asserting their identity as a class. They would prefer to live off rents or speculative investments or make money by selling their quota of textile exports to Europe and North America instead of actually producing goods for exports. This predatory attitude gives the Pakistani bourgeoisie a *rentier* capitalist character. The subjective position of Pakistani capitalists also contrasts sharply with the comparative strength of the bourgeoisie in India. Whereas the Indian bourgeoisie maintained its hegemony in society, the capitalists in Pakistan have remained dependent on the civil and military bureaucracy. When General Musharraf took power by unseating the elected government of Nawaz Sharif, the military ruler set up the Accountability Bureau on the pretext of rooting out corruption and recovering monies from habitual defaulters of loans from nationalized banks; these happened to be feudal lords, bureaucrats, politicians, and well-connected large commercial and industrial companies. However, what the General failed to tell the public was that this measure represented an IMF-imposed strategy to reduce the high proportion of bad debts on the books of nationalized banks. In reality, the accountability process ended up targeting large and small capitalists and political opponents, but corrupt civil and military bureaucrats were largely spared. Since the Ayub Khan era, capitalists in Pakistan have been particularly vulnerable because of their reliance on state patronage for the success of their respective companies. This relationship with the state affords Pakistani capitalists little bargaining power. The Pakistani state disburses individual favours to groups of capitalists, and in return, state functionaries receive kickbacks, whereas the Pakistani capitalists are simply happy to receive the special favour—in the form of loan approvals, permission to set up operations in a tax-free zone, or some other benefit. Based on these factors and those discussed in the earlier analysis of the weakness of the capitalist class and the relative strength of feudal lords and civil and military bureaucrats, Pakistan remains a *proto-capitalist* state. This means that Pakistan's economy is extremely weak and vulnerable, while the state and its inept political and military leaders—who are dependent on foreign 'assistance'—seem to have no interest in taking advantage of the available talent and resources in Pakistan to grow the economy and give direction to economic and social development. Given this reality, the present Zardari government is quite content in allowing IMF to direct the economy and dictate when to raise electricity rates and gasoline prices and impose value-added tax and higher income taxes on an already overburdened and resource-poor populace.

Within this kind of political, economic, and social environment, an imperial overlord is willing to dole out a few billion in 'aid' and in return receive disproportionate military benefit and advantage. In commercial terms, this has meant a great deal for the US. The US has acquired military bases on Pakistani soil; its intelligence agents are free to roam the country and shoot innocent people at will[63] and violate the country's sovereignty when they please through aerial drone attacks or when capturing bin Laden; it can get physical custody of individuals it wanted to arrest without respecting the writ of habeas corpus; and it has the Pakistani military and security forces attack when and where it wishes, with the quiet assurance that no American lives will be lost. To support my position of the complete dominance of the Pakistani state by the US, the recent Wikileaks's disclosures of memos (compiled by Dawn.com) from the former US ambassador to Pakistan, Anne Patterson, and other consular staff is a treasure trove of incredible revelations about the extremely cozy relationship between different Pakistani political leaders (including the Pakistani President Zardari) and the US Ambassador: these political leaders would much rather consult with, and pour their hearts out to, the American ambassador instead of sharing their respective concerns with other political leaders or even upper level state functionaries, the Pakistani media, or the people of Pakistan.[64] This arrangement and other understandings has been a win-win situation for the US and the Pakistani political and bureaucratic establishment. The latter get to stay in office and amass more wealth because they serve US interests so gallantly—despite the protests and the popular anger against such rulers. Thus, Pakistan's proto-capitalist character (which can be generalized to other proto-capitalist states in Asia and Africa) encompasses a state that is extremely dependent on imperial powers and as such is very weak vis-á-vis external political or economic pressure, whereas internally it remains a 'strong state' that is able to crush popular protests and overcome resistance. In other words, the proto-capitalist post-colonial state in Pakistan is internally 'strong' not only in dominating the bourgeoisie but also oppressing workers and other weaker sections of society. This ruling troika has also become more reliant on the US and international financial institutions whereas greatly compromising Pakistan's sovereignty. As a result, Pakistan has sunk deeper into dependency, and because clientelism is a concomitant offshoot of dependency, Pakistan's subordination to imperial dictates has been re-intensified. In other words, internal conditions have coincided with the externally re-structured imposition of imperialist domination to bring about the re-subordination of the Pakistani state and society since 1990, but more so since 11 September 2001. Pakistan's case is not unique: most other post-colonial states that fit the description of client proto-capitalist states reflect to varying degrees the characteristics of the Pakistani state.

In capitalist post-colonial states such as India, the bourgeoisie was emerging as an ascendant class at the time of decolonization so it could use its strength to consolidate its grip on power—the causal primacy being the economic (i.e. the economic power of Indian capitalists) to further their interests through the political framework of the state. In contrast, proto-capitalist states such as Pakistan have shown that the capture of political (state) power plays a crucial role in enabling access to economic opportunities. In proto-capitalist states, the causal primacy is the political, in direct opposition to capitalist post-colonial states. Further, because the bourgeoisie in proto-capitalist post-colonial states is weak as a class, its economic strength is initially derived from state patronage, a dependency that continues due to the relative strength of the bureaucratic oligarchy and the feudal lords. Accordingly, proto-capitalist states also maintain a higher degree of relative autonomy in relation to capitalist post-colonial states.

Notes

NOTES TO THE INTRODUCTION

1. See Hamza Alavi, "The State in Post-Colonial Societies: Pakistan and Bangladesh," *New Left Review* 74 (July-August 1972): 59–81.
2. This was one of the ways that Benedict Anderson originally identified *nationness* and nationalism; see Benedict Anderson, *Imagined Communities: Reflections on the Origin and the Spread of Nationalism* (London: Verso, 1991) 4.
3. Akhil Gupta and Ardhana Sharma, "Globalization and Postcolonial States," *Current Anthropology* 47.2 (April 2006): 278; Sarah A. Radcliffe, "Imagining the State as a Space: Territoriality and the Formation of the State in Ecuador," *States of Imagination: Ethnographic Explorations of the Postcolonial State,* ed. Thomas B. Hansen and Finn Stepputat (Durham: Duke University Press, 2001) 125; Gilbert Joseph and Daniel Nugent, *Everyday Forms of State Formation: Revolution and the negotiation of rule in modern Mexico* (Durham: Duke University Press, 1994), cited in Radcliffe, "Imagining the State as Space" 123.
4. For a poststructuralist understanding and definition of 'postcolonial', see Ania Loomba, *Colonialism/Postcolonialism* (London: Routledge, 1998).
5. Although Kwame Nkrumah was probably the first one to use the term *neocolonial*, it soon became embroiled in controversy between the 'pro-Chinese' and the 'pro-Soviet' camps in the late 1960s and 1970s. Avoiding the use of the term, therefore, is a way of not wanting to revisit this debate.
6. See Thomas B. Hansen and Finn Stepputat, eds., *States of Imagination: Ethnographic Explorations of the Postcolonial State* (Durham: Duke University Press, 2001) 13.
7. John Dickenson, et al., *Geography of the Third World* (London: Routledge, 1996) 4.
8. See Vijay Prashad, *The Darker Nations: A People's History of the Third World* (New York: New Press, 2007).
9. The work of critical race theorists tends to focus so narrowly on identity, difference, 'whiteness', and representation that the political economy or structural elements of race and racism, which pertain to the theoretical and material significance of race and colonialism, especially in relation to capitalism, remain untheorized. As an example, see the breadth of articles using critical race theory in a special issue of *Critical Sociology*: see Rodney D. Coates, "Introduction to Special Issue of Critical Sociology: Critical Race and Ethnic Theory, Research and Process," *Critical Sociology* 29.1–2 (2002): 7–11.
10. See Ranajit Guha, *Elementary Aspects of Peasant Insurgency in Colonial India* (Delhi: Oxford University Press, 1997); and Edward Said, *Culture and Imperialism* (New York: Knopf, 1993).

11. See Michel-Rolph Trouillot, *Haiti, State Against Nation: The Origins and Legacy of Duvalierism* (New York: Monthly Review Press, 1990).
12. Poulantzas's adherents would probably disagree with such a characterization but that is another discussion.
13. Gupta and Sharma 279.
14. Hansen and Stepputat 14.
15. The interpretation of Foucault is from Timothy Mitchell, "Economy and the State Effect," *State/Culture: State Formation After the Cultural Turn*, ed. George Steinmetz (Ithaca: Cornell University Press) 89, cited in Hansen and Stepputat 4.
16. Mitchell 89, cited in Hansen and Stepputat 17.
17. Nicos Poulantzas, *State, Power and Socialism*, trans. Patrick Camiller (London: New Left Books, 1978) 128.
18. Poulantzas, *State* 129.
19. See Karl Marx and Frredrich Engels, *On the Paris Commune* (Moscow: Progress Publishers, 1971).
20. The quote is from Radcliffe 124.
21. See the edited volumes of Hansen and Stepputat.
22. Hansen and Stepputat claim the opposite, that is, the state is not weak in the 'era of transnationalism' less conclusively—rather than critically assessing whether such an assumption is valid in the first place; Hansen and Stepputat 16.
23. Hansen and Stepputat 2.
24. Hansen and Stepputat 3.
25. Hansen and Stepputat 2.
26. See Antonio Gramsci, *Selections From the Prison Notebooks of Antonio Gramsci*, ed. and trans. Quintin Hoare and Geoffrey Nowell Smith (New York: International Publishers, 1991).
27. Hansen and Stepputat 3.
28. For instance, see the work of the writers on the developmental state, such as Vivek Chibber, Peter Evans, Aseema Sinha, and Jorgen Pedersen; their views are flagged in Chapters 3 and 4.
29. Hansen and Stepputat 9–11.
30. Clyde Barrow tackles the claims of the weakness or the demise of the state in Clyde Barrow, "The Return of the State: Globalization, State Theory and the New Imperialism," *New Political Science* 27.2 (June 2005): 123–145.
31. See William Robinson and Jerry Harris, "Towards a Global Ruling Class: Globalization and the Transnational Capitalist Class," *Science & Society* 64.1 (Spring 2000): 11–54; Robert Burbach and William Robinson, "The Fin de Siecle Debate: Globalization as Epochal Shift," *Science & Society* 63.1 (Spring 1999): 10–39. For a debate on whether the nation-state has weakened, see A. Sivanandan and Ellen Wood, "Globalization and Epochal Shifts: An Exchange," *Monthly Review* 48.9 (February 1997): 19–21.
32. Pheng Cheah, "Given Culture: Rethinking Cosmopolitical Freedom in Transnationalism," *Boundary* 2 24.2 (Summer 1997): 159.
33. For example, Gupta and Sharma identify the Integrated Child Development Services program of the Indian government that was started in 1975 as "part of a *transnational* set of ideas and policies that were global in their reach and effects" contending that it would be hard to argue that before the 1991 market reforms "the Indian state was outside an arena of globalization" (emphasis in original). It is this casual invocation of the transhistorical notion of globalization that is being contested; Gupta and Sharma 278.
34. As an example of this understanding see Amiya Kumar Bagchi, "Parameters of Resistance," *Monthly Review* (July–August 2003): 136.

35. James Petras and Henry Veltmeyer, *Globalization Unmasked: Imperialism in the 21st Century* (Halifax: Fernwood/Zed, 2001).
36. Tariq Amin-Khan, "Is Corporate Globalism an Epochal Shift?" *Gala Conference of Marxism 2000 and the Association of Economic Research,* University of Massachusetts, Amherst, July 2000.
37. On the role of the CIA in eliminating nationalist leaders in the Third World, see William Blum, *Killing Hope: US Military and CIA Interventions Since World War II* (Monroe: Common Courage Press, 2004); on the dismantling of the developmental project in order to implement the globalization project, see Philip McMichael, *Development and Social Change: A Global Perspective* (Thousand Oaks: Pine Forge, 2004) 143–177; and on the "new" international division of labour see F. Fröbel, J. Heinrichs, and O. Kreye, *The International Division of Labour: Structural Unemployment in Industrialised Countries and Industrialisation in Developing Countries*, trans. Pete Burgess (1977; Cambridge: Cambridge University Press, 1980).
38. See Gupta and Sharma.
39. See B. Anderson, *Imagined Communities*.

NOTES TO CHAPTER 1

1. As discussed in the Introduction to this volume, I do not address the different Latin American context as it is outside the purview of this study—although in Chapter 2, I make brief references to Latin American states. However, Eduardo Galeano's work on the impact of European colonialism on Latin America is an excellent source of information on the subject; see Eduardo Galeano, *Open Veins of Latin America* (New York: Monthly Review Press, 1997).
2. See Benedict Anderson, *Imagined Communities: Reflections on the Origin and the Spread of Nationalism* (London: Verso, 1991).
3. For a more detailed analysis, see Earnest Mandel, *Late Capitalism* (London: New Left Books, 1972) 310; for a more involved discussion on "capital as an all-embracing organic system," see Istvan Mézáros, "The Uncontrollability of Globalizing Capital," *Monthly Review* 49.9 (February 1998): 28.
4. See Eric Hobsbawm, *Nations and Nationalism Since 1780, Programme, Myth and Reality* (Cambridge: Cambridge University Press, 1992) and Mandel.
5. Ellen Wood, *Origin of Capitalism: The Longer View* (London: Verso, 2002) 168–169.
6. One of the few theorists to make this link is Mark Burger; see Mark T. Burger, "The Nation-State and the Challenge of Global Capitalism," *Third World Quarterly* 22.6 (2001): 889–907.
7. This universalization of the European experience can be seen in the works on nation and nationalism of Ernest Gellner, *Nations and Nationalism* (Ithaca: Cornell University Press, 1983); Hobsbawm; Elie Kedourie, *Nationalism* (London: Hutchison, 1960); and even B. Anderson, *Imagined Communities.* For a poststructuralist critique of this universalizing trajectory, see Partha Chatterjee, "Transferring a Political Theory: Early Nationalist Thought in India," *Economic and Political Weekly* XXI.3 (18 January 1986): 120. On the support for emulation of the European nation-state model in the Indian context, see Sudipta Kaviraj, "Capitalism and the Cultural Process," *Journal of Arts and Ideas* 19 (May 1990): 61–75.
8. Andreas Wimmer and Nina Glick Schiller, "Methodological Nationalism and Beyond: Nation-State Building, Migration and the Social Sciences," *Global Networks* 2.4 (2002): 301–334.

9. Daniel Chernilo, *A Social Theory of the Nation-State: The Political Forms of Modernity Beyond Methodological Nationalism* (London: Routledge, 2007).
10. See Cornelia Navari, "The Origins of the Nation-State," *The Nation-State: The Formation of Modern Politics*, ed. Leonard Tivey (New York: St. Martin's Press, 1981) 13–38.
11. Quite understandably, this straightforward link between nationalism and territory is bound by complexities, such as nations without states or those occupied and displaced nations that cannot enforce their claim to a territory or even oppressed nations in multinational states. However, what this link tries to establish is the claim that the consciousness of national identity comes with the assertion of political claims to a territory in whatever form.
12. See Gellner, *Nations and Nationalism.*
13. Gellner, *Nations and Nationalism* 20.
14. Navari 34.
15. Navari 35
16. Navari 35–36 (emphasis mine).
17. Navari 26.
18. B. Anderson, *Imagined Communities* 38.
19. B. Anderson, *Imagined Communities* 25
20. B. Anderson, *Imagined Communities* 38–39
21. From the title of her review article, Gail Stokes was expected to shed some light on this linkage but did not do so; see Gail Stokes "How Is Nationalism Related to Capitalism? A Review Article," *Comparative Study of Society and History* 28.3 (July 1986): 591–598. In contrast, Ellen Wood discusses this linkage, but characteristically for her, the link remained "specific to England"; Wood, *Origin of Capitalism* 167.
22. See Tariq Amin Khan, "Colonialism and the Common Origins of Discrete Post-Colonial Identities in India and Pakistan," *Canadian Review of Studies in Nationalism* XXIX.1–2 (2002): 39–52.
23. These developments have been discussed by many theorists, most notably V.I. Lenin, *Imperialism, The Highest Stage of Capitalism* (Peking: Foreign Languages Press, 1973), and in a different light in terms of the "tendency of the surplus to rise" and how the productive absorption of this surplus becomes an issue in the context of the US's monopoly capitalist economy; see Paul Baran and Paul Sweezy, *Monopoly Capital* (New York: Monthly Review Press, 1966).
24. Mandel 311.
25. Franklin W. Knight, "The Disintegration of the Caribbean Slave System," *General History of the Caribbean: The Slave Societies of the Caribbean*, ed. Franklin Knight, vol. III (London: UNESCO/Macmillan, 1997) 332.
26. Eric Williams, *Capitalism and Slavery* (London: Andre Deutsch, 1991) 52.
27. Knight 330, 336.
28. See Ted C. Lewellen, *Dependency and Development: An Introduction to the Third World* (London: Bergin and Garvey, 1995) 42–47; and Walter Rodney, *How Europe Underdeveloped Africa* (Washington, DC: Howard University Press, 1982).
29. For a discussion of the impact of colonial social policy and the social engineering inherent in it, see Amin Khan, "Colonialism and the Common Origins."
30. Hamza Alavi, "Formation of the Social Structure of South Asia Under the Impact of Colonialism," South Asia: *Sociology of "Developing Societies"*, ed. Hamza Alavi and John Harriss (Basingstoke: Macmillan, 1989) 6.
31. See Irfan Habib, "Potentialities of Capitalist Development in Mughal India," *Journal of Economic History* XXIX (March 1969): 32–78; and Bipan

Chandra, *Essays on Colonialism* (New Delhi: Orient Longman, 1999) 259–295.

32. See Irfan Habib, "Processes of Accumulation in Pre-Colonial and Colonial India" and "Colonization of Indian Economy 1757–1900," *Essays in Indian History, Towards a Marxist Perception*, collec. Irfan Habib (Tulika: New Delhi, 1995).
33. See Hamza Alavi's brief account of the benefits that England reaped from the colonization of India: "Formation."
34. See Alavi "Formation;" also see Chapter 3, this volume.
35. Hamza Alavi, "Colonialism and the Rise of Capitalism," *Hamza Alavi Internet Archive*, 18 October 2011 < http://hamzaalavi.com/?p=69> (the figures are from R. Palme Dutt, *India Today* (Delhi: People's Publishing House, 1955) 106).
36. These *zamindari* and *mansabdari* systems were used respectively by the Delhi Sultans and the Mughals to extract surpluses for their monarchies. Although the two systems are representative of the exploitative and expansionist regimes common to most pre-capitalist societies, the *zamindari* system was far more exploitative; see Abdul Aziz, *The Mansabdari System and the Mughal Army* (New Delhi: Idarah-i-Adabiyat-I-Delhi, 1972) 79–83. The *zamindar* under the Delhi Sultans was more like a warlord with a substantial military force, who claimed the hereditary right to collect a share of the harvest; see John Richards, *The New Cambridge History of India—The Mughal Empire* (New Delhi: Foundation Books, 1993) 80.

    Because *zamindari* was a much more extractive system, it suited the needs of colonial rulers; therefore, the British re-adopted this system and replaced the *mansabdari* system (A. Aziz 80). For information on the oppressive means of control employed by the English through the re-introduction of the *zamindari* system, see Habib, "Colonization".
37. See Ellen Wood, *The Pristine Culture of Capitalism, A Historical Essay on Old Regimes and Modern States* (London: Verso, 1991). See also Robert Brenner, "The Agricultural Roots of European Capitalism," *The Brenner Debate: Agrarian Class Structure and Economic Development in Pre-Industrial Europe*, ed. T.H. Ashton and C.H.E. Philpin (Cambridge: Cambridge University Press, 1985) 10–63.
38. See Chris Fuller, "British India or Traditional India?: Land, Caste and Power," *Sociology of "Developing Societies": South Asia*, ed. Hamza Alavi and John Harriss (Basingstoke: Macmillan, 1989) 28–40.
39. Habib, "Colonization," 305–306.
40. See Habib, "Processes."
41. Alavi, "Formation" 11.
42. Landes points out that "the 'threshold' of the industrial revolution in England was first crossed in cotton manufacture"; David Landes, *The Unbound Prometheus: Technological Change and Industrial Development in Western Europe From 1750 to the Present* (Cambridge: Cambridge University Press, 1969) 82.
43. Alavi, "Colonialism."
44. Alavi, "Formation" 15.
45. Alavi, "Formation" 15 (emphasis mine).
46. Amiya Kumar Bagchi, *The Political Economy of Underdevelopment* (Cambridge: Cambridge University Press, 1982).
47. Pererea discusses the "logic of apartness and separation" in the context of "official policy-making" from "colonial Ceylon to republican Sri Lanka;" see Suvendrini Pererea, "Unmaking the Present, Remaking Memory: Sri Lankan Stories and a Politics of Coexistence," *Race and Class* 40.4 (July–December 1999): 189–195.

48. The case of Latin American states as settler colonies is very different from the Northern European settler colonies, but these differences cannot be addressed here.
49. The terms 'ethnic' and 'sub-national' as they are used throughout this book refer to ethnic groups within multiethnic/multinational post-colonial states who assert their identities to gain recognition of their cultural distinctiveness or to seek redress of real or perceived wrongs. Sub-national groups are smaller or weaker nations in multinational states who have become conscious of their national identity within the larger multinational state.
50. For an account of how these nationalist leaders were eliminated, see William Blum, *Killing Hope: US Military and CIA Interventions Since World War II* (Monroe: Common Courage Press, 2004).
51. The reference is to B. Anderson, *Imagined Communities*. B. Anderson's universalization of the European experience becomes more apparent in his later text; Benedict Anderson, *Spectres of Comparisons: Nationalism, Southeast Asia and the World* (London: Verso, 1998).
52. B. Anderson, *Imagined Communities* 26.
53. See Partha Chatterjee, "Transferring a Political Theory" 120–128; Partha Chatterjee, "Whose Imagined Communities," *Mapping the Nation*, ed. Gopal Balakrishnan (London: Verso, 1996) 214–225; and Partha Chatterjee, "Anderson's Utopia," *Ground of Comparison: Around the Work of Benedict Anderson*, spec. issue of *Diacritics* 29.4 (Winter 1999): 128–134.
54. Chatterjee, "Anderson's Utopia" 130.
55. Chatterjee, "Transferring a Political Theory" 121.
56. Chatterjee, "Transferring a Political Theory" 121.
57. Partha Chatterjee, *The Nation and Its Fragments: Colonial and Postcolonial Histories* (Princeton: Princeton University Press, 1993).
58. Chatterjee has relied upon Bengali-language school history texts and *Puranic* history to construct the "historical claims of *hindutva*" in Partha Chatterjee, "History and Nationalization of Hinduism," *Social Research* 59.1 (Spring 1992): 111–149.
59. Chatterjee, "History and Nationalization of Hinduism" 112 (emphasis in original).
60. For instance, Chatterjee cites Tarinicharan Chattophaday's 1878 text, *History of India* in the Bengali language in which Tarinicharan glorifies the sacrifices of Hindu men and women in fighting off the invasion of the Arabs led by Muhammed bin Kasim: Chatterjee, "History and Nationalization of Hinduism" 141–142
61. See the brief explanation about Haiti in this volume's Introduction.
62. Frantz Fanon expresses poignantly the impact of the process of inferiorization and cultural devaluation in Frantz Fanon, "Racism and Colonialism," *Toward the African Revolution: Political Essays*, collec. Frantz Fanon (New York: Monthly Review Press, 1967) 29–44.
63. As an example, following the 1857 Rebellion (see note 82), the Muslims were identified as the instigators of the rebellion (although Hindus and Muslims fought together against the British), prompting the colonial state to promote Hindu elite interests over the Muslims. Later, as Hindu nationalism began to assert itself in the late 1800s, the British partitioned Bengal into Hindu and Muslim Bengal, and this time supported the Muslim elite.
64. Most theorists of nation and nationalism have largely ignored the role of women in the construction of national identities, and B. Anderson is no exception. Despite a general interest among many scholars on the differential participation of various other groups, women are largely overlooked in the literature on nation and nationalism. I also recognize the omission of gender

in the present section of this volume, however, I have addressed the role of women in national struggles separately in another paper; see Tariq Amin-Khan, "Nation, Gender and Development: The Differential Experience of Women in the South," *2002 Canadian Sociology and Anthropology Association Conference at the Congress of the Humanities and Social Sciences*, University of Toronto, 29 May–1 June 2002.

65. B. Anderson, *Imagined Communities* 4.
66. B. Anderson, *Imagined Communities* 47–70.
67. B. Anderson, *Imagined Communities* 86 and 159 (emphasis in original).
68. B. Anderson, *Imagined Communities* 87–99.
69. B. Anderson, *Imagined Communities* 109–110.
70. B. Anderson, *Imagined Communities* 99.
71. B. Anderson, *Imagined Communities* 4.
72. See B. Anderson, *Imagined Communities.*
73. B. Anderson, *Spectres* 173.
74. B. Anderson, *Spectres* 40.
75. B. Anderson. *Spectres* 43.
76. Because patriarchal values influenced both the census takers and those being enumerated, the identity of women from any group remained invisible in this enumeration.
77. Sugata Bose and Ayesha Jalal, *Modern South Asia: History, Culture, Political Economy* (London: Routledge, 1998) 107–108.
78. Bose and Jalal 108.
79. It is generally accepted that the rise of nationalism in Europe started around the late eighteenth century; see E.J. Hobsbawm.
80. J.G. Fichte dealt in a novel way with the French occupation of Germany. He not only propounded a narrow concept of the German nation, but also addressed the Germans on the question of resistance without alarming the French; see J.G. Fichte, *Addresses to the German Nation*, trans. R.F. Jones and G.H. Turnbull (Chicago: Open Court Publishing, 1922).
81. Many accounts support this position. For instance, see D. Maclean, *Religion and Society in Arab Sindh* (Montreal: McGill University Press, 1989)—Maclean points out that the conversions to Islam during the Arab conquest of Sindh were mainly of persons from the Buddhist community who were trying to escape the oppression of the dominant Hindu majority; and Asghar Ali Engineer, "Hindu—Muslim Relations Before and After 1947," *Anatomy of Confrontation: The Babri Masjid—Ramjamnabhumi Issue*, ed. Sarvepalli Gopal (New Delhi: Viking, 1991).
82. The May 1857 Rebellion was a revolt of the cavalry serving the Company's army in Meerut, which was put down with the help of the colonized recruits in the colonial army. The revolt spread to the North and West of Delhi. It had popular support from various sections of both Hindus and Muslims. The British believed and popularized the idea that the Rebellion was led by Muslims because its symbolic head was the aging last Mughal emperor, Bhadur Shah Zafar, who was too frail to wage any kind of resistance.
83. There are a number of examples of religious, ethnic, and national conflicts in post-colonial Africa and Asia, including Rwanda, Nigeria, and India, taking on a genocidal dimension.
84. Ayesha Jalal suggests that the goal of Mohammed Ali Jinnah, Pakistan's founder, was not separation; this issue is discussed in Chapter 5, this volume. See Ayesha Jalal, *The Sole Spokesman: Jinnah, the Muslim League and the Demand for Pakistan* (Cambridge: Cambridge University Press, 1990) and Ayesha Jalal, *The State of Martial Rule: The Origins of Pakistan's Political*

Economy of Defence (1990; Cambridge: Cambridge University Press; Lahore: Vanguard Press, 1991).

85. See Tapan Basu et al., *Khaki Shorts Saffron Flags: A Critique of Hindu Right* (Bombay: Orient Longman, 1993).
86. Tanika Sarkar, "Semiotics of Terror: Muslim Children and Women in Hindu Rashtra," *Economic and Political Weekly* 37.28 (13 July 2002): 2874.
87. See Fanon, "Racism and Culture" and Frantz Fanon, *The Wretched of the Earth*, trans. Constance Farrington (New York: Grove Weidenfeld, 1963).
88. Fanon, "Racism and Culture" 36.
89. See Bipan Chandra, "Colonialism, Stages of Colonialism and Colonial State," *Journal of Contemporary Asia* 10.3 (1980): 272–285.
90. For a fuller discussion on tribute extraction, see Habib, "Colonization."
91. See Habib, "Colonization" and Alavi, "Formation."
92. Satyananda Gabriel and Evgenia Todorova, "Racism and Capitalist Exploitation: An Overdetermined Nexus," *Critical Sociology* 29.1(2003): 29; also see Williams.
93. Gabriel and Todrova 31–32.
94. See Fanon, *The Wretched.*
95. See Blum.

NOTES TO CHAPTER 2

1. The field of state theory is largely silent on the theorization of the post-colonial state. Even the ethnographical studies of the post-colonial state, mentioned in the Introduction of this volume, do not analyze the impact of imperialism or the capitalism–imperialism nexus and the enormous burden it places on post-colonial and Latin American states.
2. See Thomas B. Hansen and Finn Stepputat, eds., *States of Imagination: Ethnographic Explorations of the Postcolonial State* (Durham: Duke University Press, 2001).
3. Cardoso's articulation of the developmental state, offered in the early 1970s, has been incorporated as a contemporary understanding of the post-colonial state by a number of scholars; see F.H. Cardoso and E. Faletto, *Dependency and Development in Latin America*, trans. M.M. Urquidi (Berkeley: University of California Press, 1971).
4. Vivek Chibber, "Reviving the Developmental State? The Myth of the 'National Bourgeoisie'," *Socialist Register 2005: The Empire Reloaded,* ed. Leo Panitch and Colin Leys (London: Merlin, 2004) 144–165.
5. See Loïc Wacquant, *Punishing the Poor: The Neoliberal Government of Social Insecurity* (Durham: Duke University Press, 2009); Holger Henke, "Jamaica's Decision to Pursue a Neoliberal Development Strategy: Realignments in State-Business-Class Triangle," *Latin American Perspectives* 26.5 (September 1999): 7–33; Werner Bonefeld, "Free Economy and the Strong State: Some Notes on the State," *Capital & Class* 34.1 (2010): 15–24.
6. See Douglas T. Stuart, *Creating the National Security State: A History of the Law That Transformed America* (Princeton: Princeton University Press, 2008).
7. See Bill Moyers, "The Secret Government," *What I've Learned From US Foreign Policy: The War Against the Third World*, dir. Frank Dorrell, DVD (Culver City, 2002).
8. The Green Revolution emphasized the deployment of high-yield hybrid seed technology, farm mechanization, and an exaggerated use of irrigation, fertilizers, and pesticides, which led to the catastrophic displacement of the

peasantry and small-scale farmers in the South. The resulting displacement compelled the rural migrants to move into urban centres in search of work—a process that continues to this day: see J. Abraham, "The Green Revolution Revisited," *Food and Development*, ed. J. Abraham (London: Worldwide Fund for Nature, 1991).

9. The Dollar-Gold Convertibility Accord was reached during the 1944 Bretton Woods Conference that made the US dollar the supreme international currency, and other currencies of the world were pegged to it in the sense that central banks of different countries could convert US dollars into gold at fixed rates. This allowed a reasonably stable international currency exchange rate, especially for the global South, until the US's Vietnam War-induced high deficit triggered the unilateral abrogation of the agreement in 1971.
10. For instance, Martijn Konings argues for the utility of Marxist state theory's insights to account for the complexities of the present conjuncture; see Martijn Konings "Renewing State Theory," *Politics* 30.3 (2010): 174–182.
11. For a distinction in the two trajectories of modernity, see Tariq Amin-Khan, "Issues of Power and Modernity in Understanding Political and Militant Islam," *Comparative Studies of South Asia, Africa and the Middle East* 29.3 (2009): 544–555.
12. P.K. Lawrence, "Enlightenment, Modernity and War," *History of the Human Sciences* 12.1 (1999): 3–4.
13. Lawrence 4.
14. Lawrence 4.
15. The internalization of the "normal" nation-state by the former colonized elite in post-colonial societies tries to mimic state formation on the model of European nation-states; see Hansen and Stepputat 8–27.
16. Hamza Alavi developed the notion of the *salariat* to specify an auxiliary class to the bureaucracy; see Hamza Alavi "Formation of the Social Structure of South Asia Under the Impact of Colonialism," South Asia: *Sociology of "Developing Societies"*, ed. Hamza Alavi and John Harriss (Basingstoke: Macmillan, 1989) 5–19; and Hamza Alavi "Nationhood and Communal Violence in Pakistan," *Journal of Contemporary Asia* 21.2 (1991): 152–178.
17. John D. Kelly and Martha Kaplan, "Nation and Decolonization: Toward a New Anthropology of Nationalism," *Anthropology Theory* 1.4 (2001): 419.
18. See Tariq Amin-Khan, "The Rise of Militant Islam and the Security State in the Era of the 'Long War'," *Third World Quarterly* 30.4 (2009): 813–828.
19. See William Blum, *Killing Hope: US Military and CIA Interventions Since World War II (*Monroe: Common Courage Press, 2004); John Stockwell, *In Search of Enemies: A CIA Story* (New York: Norton, 1978).
20. Immanuel Wallerstein, "The Rise and the Future Demise of the World Capitalist System: Concepts for Comparative Analysis," *The Capitalist World Economy* (Cambridge: Cambridge University Press, 1979).
21. Blum contains well-documented cases of CIA's and US military's covert and counter-insurgency operations throughout the world; other older sources are A. Sampson, *The Sovereign State of ITT* (New York: Stein and Day, 1973); and Thomas Ross, *The Invisible Government* (New York: Random House, 1964).
22. See Alvin So, *Social Change and Development: Modernization, Dependency and World System Theories* (Newbury Park: Sage, 1990).
23. Talcott Parsons, "Evolutionary Universals in Society," reprinted in J. Timmons Roberts and Amy Hite, *From Modernization to Globalization: Perspectives on Development and Social Change* (Oxford: Blackwell, 2000) 85.
24. Parsons, reprinted in Roberts and Hite 85.
25. Parsons, reprinted in Roberts and Hite 85.
26. Parsons, reprinted in Roberts and Hite 85–86.

27. Parsons, reprinted in Roberts and Hite 85.
28. Parsons, reprinted in Roberts and Hite 87.
29. Parsons, reprinted in Roberts and Hite 86–94.
30. Parsons, reprinted in Roberts and Hite 86.
31. Samuel Huntington, "The Change to Change: Modernization, Development, and Politics" *Comparative Politics*, 3.3 (April 1971): 286.
32. Huntington, "Change to Change" 288.290.
33. Samuel Huntington, *Political Order in Changing Societies* (New Haven: Yale University Press 1968) 2.
34. Huntington, *Political Order* 2.
35. For an explanation of 'blowback', see Chalmers Johnson, *Blowback: The Costs and Consequences of American Empire* (New York: Henry Holt, 2004); for other interpretations of blowback, see Mahmud Mamdani, *Good Muslim, Bad Muslim: America, The Cold War and Roots of Terror* (New York: Three Leaves Press, 2004); and Gabriel Kolko, *Another Century of War* (New York: New Press, 2002).
36. See Samuel Huntington, *The Clash of Civilizations and the Remaking of the World Order* (New York: Simon Schuster, 1996); for a critical perspective on Huntington, see Ervand Abrahamian, "The US media, Huntington and September 11," *Third World Quarterly* 24.3 (2003): 529–544.
37. See Tariq Amin-Khan, "New Orientalism, Western Media's Incendiary Racism and the 'Long War'," *Journal of Postcolonial Writing* 48.3 (July 2012) forthcoming.
38. A. Escobar, *Encountering Development: The Making and Unmaking of the Third World* (Princeton: Princeton University Press, 1995).
39. US President, Harry S. Truman, proposed the idea of developmentalism in his speech in January 1949; see Philip McMichael, *Development and Social Change: A Global Perspective* (Thousand Oaks: Pine Forge, 2004) 22.
40. See Rex A. Hudson, ed., *Brazil: A Country Study* (Washington, DC: GPO for the Library of Congress, 1997), 5 February 2011<http://countrystudies.us/brazil/62.htm>. In the section "Import-Substitution Industrialization: 1945–64," the author argues that the commitment to ISI policies in Brazil was at its peak between 1950 and 1961, but by 1963 when growth began to slip, Brazil opted for economic liberalization, and ISI began to be dismantled.
41. Research and Information System for the Non-Aligned and Other Developing Countries, *Raul Prebisch and Development Strategy* (New Delhi: Research and Information System for the Non-Aligned and Other Developing Countries, 1987).
42. Werner Baer, "Import Substitution and Industrialization in Latin America: Experiences and Interpretations," *Latin American Research Review* 7.1 (Spring 1972): 95–96.
43. See Eul-Soo Pang, "The Financial Crisis of 1997–98 and the End of the Asian Developmental State," *Contemporary Southeast Asia* 22.3 (2000): 570–593; S.J. Maswood, "Developmental States in Crisis," *Reconfiguring East Asia: Regional Institutions and Organisations After the Crisis*, ed. M. Beeson (London: Routledge, 2002).
44. See Stockwell.
45. See Huntington, *Political Order.*
46. See Peter Evans, "The State as Problem and Solution: Predation, Embedded Autonomy and Structural Change," *The Politics of Economic Adjustment*, ed. S. Haggard and R.R. Kaufman (Princeton: Princeton University Press, 1992) 139–181.
47. Aseema Sinha, "Rethinking the Developmental State Model: Divided Leviathan and Subnational Comparisons in India," *Comparative Politics* 35.4 (July 2003): 460.

48. See Shigeko Hayashi, "The Developmental State in the Era of Globalization: Beyond the Northeast Asian Model of Political Economy," *The Pacific Review* 23.1 (March 2010): 45–69.
49. See N. Hamilton, "State Autonomy and Dependent Capitalism in Latin America," *British Journal of Sociology* 32.3 (1981): 305–329.
50. Cardoso and Faletto 145–148.
51. The influence was on many political leaders in the former colonies, based on the experience of the Soviet Union's very rapid transformation from a feudal to an industrialized society, largely during the early years of the Russian Revolution.
52. Export orientation was the hallmark of colonial division of labour, and although the early period of decolonization was a move towards becoming self-reliant, post-colonial economies reverted to export-reliance as the new IDL was introduced in the late 1970s.
53. Cited in F. Fröbel, J. Heinrichs, and O. Kreye, *The New International Division of Labour: Structural Unemployment in Industrialised Countries and Industrialisation in Developing Countries*, trans. Pete Burgess (1977; Cambridge: Cambridge University Press, 1980) 1, cited in Business International Corporation, *Business International Weekly Report to Mangers and World-wide Operators* (7 January 1977) 1.
54. The larger discussion on the ballooning debt of Third World states cannot be undertaken here. Rising and unstable exchange rates are one part of the puzzle, but the dismantling of the Bretton Woods Dollar-Gold Convertibility Accord meant that countries that were repaying the loan in US dollars had to pay higher rates to convert their currencies as these had lost in value; see M. Mason, *Development and Disorder: A History of the Third World Since 1945* (Toronto: Between the Lines, 1997) 410–419; also see D. Green, *Silent Revolution: The Rise and Crisis of Market Economics in Latin America* (New York: Monthly Review Press, 1995) 32–59.
55. Baer 108.
56. See Blum.
57. The G-7 is the meeting of the finance ministers in France, Germany, Italy, Japan, UK, US, and Canada.
58. The South Commission, *The Challenge to the South: The Report of the South Commission* (London: Oxford University Press, 1990) 216.
59. Julius Ihonvbere, "The Third World and the New World Order in the 1990s," *Futures* (December 1992), reprinted in *Annual Editions, Developing World 99/00* (Guildford: Dushkin/McGraw Hill, 1999) 10.
60. Ihonvbere, reprinted in *Annual Editions* 11.
61. McMichael, *Development and Social Change.*
62. Carlos Vilas, "Neoliberal Social Policy Managing Poverty (Somehow)," *NACLA Report on the Americas* XXIX.6 (May-June 1996): 19.
63. Vilas 18, 19.
64. The G-8 is a forum of eight major economies including France, Germany, Italy, Japan, the UK, the US, Canada, and Russia.
65. Vilas 16.
66. Vilas 18.
67. See Helen Caldicott, *The New Nuclear Danger: George W. Bush's Military-Industrial Complex* (New York: The New Press, 2002).
68. For a searing indictment of free trade and economic liberalism from a historical perspective, see F. Clairmont, *The Rise and Fall of Economic Liberalism: The Making of the Economic Gulag* (Kuala Lumpur: Southbound and Third World Press, 1996).
69. I. Bensidoun and A. Chevallier, "Indicators of Regionalization in North America, Asia, Central and Eastern Europe and the Mediterranean Basin,"

OECD Proceedings: Globalisation, Migration and Development (Paris: OECD, 2000) 15–16 ; the quote of Oman is from C. Oman, "The Policy Challenges of Globalisation and Regionalisation," *Migration, Free Trade and Regional Integration in Central and Eastern Europe* (Paris: OECD, 1997) (emphasis mine).

70. Bensidoun and Chevallier 16.
71. See Anna Tsing, "Supply Chains and the Human Condition," *Rethinking Marxism* 21.2 (April 2009): 148–176.
72. Cited in Tsing 148.
73. Most publications of the OECD that I have examined reflect this imperialist arrogance. Even the use of language such as "human capital," "social capital," or the "cost advantage of low wages" is made so mechanistically that there is no allowance for even mild introspection of such usage and its implications.
74. The ILO maintains large databases of key indicators of the labour market. However, although they do not have hourly wage statistics of some of the poorest countries in Southern Africa and South Asia, even a comparison of the "hourly compensation costs of employees" in Mexico and Philippines, not by far the poorest countries in the world, with European states such as Norway and Belgium or the US and Canada, shows the astounding gulf in hourly wages (in US dollars) between the North and the South based on 2008 figures:
    Belgium: $33.07
    Canada: 21.50
    UK: 28.29
    US: 24.77
    Mexico: 1.06
    Philippines: 1.54

    See International Labour Office, "Key Indicators of the Labour Market," 12 February 2011 <http://kilm.ilo.org/KILMnetBeta/default2.asp>.
75. The ILO introduced the concept of the informal sector in early 1970s and defines it currently as "consist[ing] of small-scale, self-employed activities (with or without hired workers), typically at a low level of organization and technology, with the primary objective of generating employment and incomes. The activities are usually conducted without proper recognition from the authorities, and escape the attention of the administrative machinery responsible for enforcing laws and regulations." See International Labour Office, "The Informal Sector," 9 February 2011 <http://www.ilo.org/public/english/region/asro/bangkok/feature/inf_sect.htm>.
76. See International Labour Office, "Social Security Department: The Informal Sector," 9 February 2011 <http://www.ilo.org/public/english/protection/secsoc/areas/policy/informal.htm>.
77. Chavanov developed the concept of self-exploitation when examining the Russian peasant economy, although D. Thorner interpreted Chavanov's notion of self-exploitation more broadly for the work done by peasant families; see A.V. Chavanov, *On the Theory of the Peasant Economy*, ed. Daniel Thorner, Basile Kerblay, R.E.F. Smith (Homewood: Irwin, 1966). Also see the application of the concept in the work of tenant farmers in post-colonial India, S.N. Sanyal, "Land Holdings in Punjab: An Analysis," *Economic and Political Weekly* 5.34 (22 August 1970): 1425–1428.
78. Biel hints in passing at the concept's application in the period of capitalist globalism and imperialism, Robert Biel, *The New Imperialism: Crisis and Contradictions in North/South Relations* (London: Zed Books, 2000) 5–6.
79. The nature of proto-capitalism is discussed in Chapter 3 of this volume.

80. For a discussion of home-based and subcontracted work, and the push-pull factors that facilitate outsourcing, see Radhika Balakrishnan and Asad Sayeed, "Subcontracting: The Push-Pull Factors," *The Hidden Assembly Line: Gender Dynamics of Subcontracted Work in a Global Economy*, ed. R. Balakrishnan (Bloomfield: Kumarian, 2002) 15–34.
81. See Anjan Chakrabarti and Anup Dar, *Dislocation and Resettlement in Development: From Third World to the World of the Third* (New York: Routledge, 2010).
82. See Chavanov.
83. Biel 5.
84. R. Balakrishnan 7.
85. R. Balakrishnan and M. Huang, "Flexible Workers-Hidden Employers: Gender and Subcontracting in the Global Economy," *Draft Report of the Women's Economic and Legal Rights Program* (Washington, DC: 2000), cited in R. Balakrishnan 7.
86. Biel 146; also see Samir Amin, "For a Progressive and Democratic New World Order," *Globalization and the New Dilemmas of the State in South*, ed. Francis Adams, Satya Das Gupta, and K. Megisteab (New York: St. Martin's Press, 1999) 17–32.
87. Henry Veltmeyer, "The World Economy and Labour," *Canadian Journal of Development Studies, Special Issue on Labour and Employment Under Globalization* XX (1999): 689–690.
88. Henk Overbeek, "Globalization, Sovereignty and Transnational Regulation: Reshaping the Governance of International Migration," *Managing Migration: Time for a New International Regime?* ed. Bimal Gosh (Oxford: Oxford University Press, 2000) 51. Overbeek's citation of Fröbel relies on the same edition as used in this volume.
89. Fröbel et al. 46
90. See Tsing.
91. Bensidoun and Chevallier 16.
92. Fröbel et al. 46.
93. Fröbel et al. 2.
94. Fröbel et al. 3.
95. The fear among capitalists about the possible demise of the capitalist epoch, as Mies seems to suggest, may be exaggerated. However, given the economic crises, the fear of social upheaval has been a real threat for most capitalist states; see Maria Mies, *Patriarchy and the Accumulation on a World Scale: Women in the International Division of Labour* (London: Zed Books, 1986) 113.
96. It should be noted that Germany and Japan were less vulnerable to this phenomenon because they had built or were in the process of rebuilding their industrial infrastructure along technologically advanced and less labour intensive lines, following the end of World War II.
97. Fröbel et al. 3.
98. Abraham 61, 70; Fröbel et al. 6.
99. The theme of the peasantry's displacement and their migration to urban areas has been the subject of many feature films produced in India and in other parts of the South. The films depict quite graphically the socially ravaged lives of these new proletarians.
100. See H. Bernstein, T. Hewitt, and A. Thomas, "Capitalism and the Expansion of Europe," *Poverty and Development Into the 21st Century*, ed. T. Allen and A. Thomas (Oxford: Open University in association with Oxford University Press, 2000) 181.
101. Since the signing of the North American Free Trade Agreement, capital investments in Mexico's *maquiladora* have jumped from about $3 billion

FDIs in 1993 to $7.6 billion in 1996 to $24.3 billion in 2006. World Bank, "Foreign Direct Investment, Net Inflows (Mexico)" 25 October 2011 2011 <http://data.worldbank.org/indicator/BX.KLT.DINV.CD.WD/countries/MX?display=graph>

102. See International Labour Office, "Key Indicators."
103. Makdisi has used the concept of "duality of labour" in his paper on the rebuilding of Lebanon; see Saree Makdisi, "Laying Claim to Beirut: Urban Narrative and Spatial Identity in the Age of Solidere," *Critical Inquiry* 23.3 (Spring 1997): 661–705.
104. This wage gap, which is as much as 30% between White workers and new non-White immigrants or between new White and new non-White immigrants in Canada, has been documented by Galabuzi's research; see: Grace-Edward Galabuzi, *Canada's Economic Apartheid: The Social Exclusion of Racialized Groups in the New Century* (Toronto: Canadian Scholars' Press, 2006).
105. See Ghazi Hidouci, "The Geopolitical Dimension of Regional Integration," *OECD Proceedings: Globalisation, Migration and Development* (Paris: OECD, 2000): 183–186.
106. Sarah Anderson, ed., *Views From the South: The Effect of Globalization and WTO in Third World Countries* (Oakland: Food First Books, 2000) 8.
107. S. Anderson 9.
108. William K. Tabb, "The World Trade Organization? Stop World Take Over," *Monthly Review* 51.8 (January 2000): 6.
109. Tabb 44.
110. Harry Shutt, *The Decline of Capitalism: Can a Self-Regulated Profits System Survive?* (New York: Zed Books, 2005) 2–3.

NOTES TO CHAPTER 3

1. See Hamza Alavi, "The State in Post-Colonial Societies: Pakistan and Bangladesh," *New Left Review* 74 (1972): 59–81; for Miliband-Poulantzas debates, see Nicos Poulantzas, "The Problem of the Capitalist State," *New Left Review* 58 (November–December 1969): 67–78; Nicos Poulantzas, "The Capitalist State: A Reply to Miliband and Laclau," *New Left Review* 95 (January–February 1976): 63–83; Ralph Miliband, "The Capitalist State: Reply to N. Poulantzas," *New Left Review* 59 (January–February 1970): 53–60; Ralph Miliband, "Poulantzas and the Capitalist State," *New Left Review* 82 (November–December 1973): 83–92.
2. See Issa Shivji, *Class Struggles in Tanzania* (New York: Monthly Review Press, 1976); and John Saul, "The State in Post-Colonial Societies: Tanzania," *Socialist Register* (London: Merlin, 1974) 349–372.
3. The exception being the bureaucratic authoritarian state form, which is applicable in the Latin American context; see Guillermo O'Donnell, *Modernization and Bureaucratic Authoritarianism: Studies in South American Politics* (Berkeley: Institute of International Studies, University of California, 1973).
4. See Hamza Alavi, "The Structure of Peripheral Capitalism," *Introduction to the Sociology of "Developing Societies,"* ed. Hamza Alavi and Teodor Shanin (New York: Monthly Review Press, 1982) 172–194.
5. See Alavi, "The Structure."
6. Karl Marx, *On Colonialism*, collec. Karl Marx and F. Engels (Moscow: Progress Publishers, c. 1970) 83. The article in which this quote appears, "The Future Results of the British Rule in India," was first published in *New York Daily Tribune* (22 July 1853) (emphasis mine).

7. Alavi, "The Structure" 172; Alavi's reference in the quote is to Bill Warren, *Imperialism: Pioneer of Capitalism* (London: New Left Books, 1980).
8. Alavi, "The Structure" 174 (emphasis in original).
9. Alavi, "The Structure" 173.
10. Alavi, "The Structure" 174 (emphasis mine).
11. Irfan Habib, "Processes of Accumulation in Pre-Colonial and Colonial India," *Essays in Indian History: Towards a Marxist Perception*, collec. Irfan Habib (New Delhi: Tulika, 1995) 273.
12. Habib, "Processes" 289.
13. See Alavi, "The State in Post-Colonial Societies."
14. See Alavi, "The State in Post-Colonial Societies."
15. Hamza Alavi, "State and Class Under Peripheral Capitalism," *Introduction to the Sociology of "Developing Societies,"* ed. Hamza Alavi and Teodor Shanin (New York: Monthly Review Press, 1982) 298.
16. Alavi has identified the same three classes as being also pivotal in the post-colonial state: Alavi, "The State in Post-Colonial Societies" 59.
17. Alavi, "State and Class" 298.
18. Alavi, "State and Class" 298–299.
19. Alavi, "The Structure" 181.
20. It should be said that although surplus value remained largely unrealized in the colonial Indian context, in some cases, such as mining in South Africa, where wage-labour was introduced, surplus value was extracted from the labour of indigenous South Africans.
21. See the explanation provided earlier on the role of primary accumulation in capitalist expansion; Luxemburg, however, essentializes the role of non-capitalist social relations or primary accumulation for capitalist development—seeing this relationship continuing in perpetuity. A modified view acknowledges Luxemburg's contribution of non-capitalist social relations or primary accumulation but (i) does not see non-capitalist relations as unchanging and (ii) attributes a limit to how much benefit capitalists can derive from primary accumulation; see Rosa Luxemburg, *The Accumulation of Capital—An Anti-Critique*, ed. and intro. Kenneth J. Tarbuck (New York: Monthly Review Press, 1972).
22. See Chris Fuller, "British India or Traditional India?: Land, Caste and Power," *South Asia: Sociology of "Developing Societies,"* ed. Hamza Alavi and John Harriss (Basingstoke: Macmillan, 1989) 34–35; and Irfan Habib, *The Agrarian System of Mughal India (1505–1707)* (Bombay: Asia Publishing, 1963).
23. Alavi, "State and Class" 297.
24. See Hamza Alavi, "Formation of the Social Structure of South Asia Under the Impact of Colonialism," *South Asia: Sociology of "Developing Societies,"* ed. Hamza Alavi and John Harriss (London: Macmillan, 1989) 5–19.
25. Alavi, "Formation" 6.
26. Alavi, "Formation" 10.
27. R. Palme Dutt, *India Today and Tomorrow* (Delhi: People's Publishing House, 1955) 73.
28. Dutt 72.
29. Dutt 72 (emphasis mine—"modern" for Dutt implies the contemporary period).
30. Dutt 74.
31. Dutt 75.
32. See Irfan Habib, "Processes" 273–274. Also see Dutt 81–84.
33. Habib, "Colonization of the Indian Economy 1757–1900," *Essays in Indian History: Towards a Marxist Perception*, collec. Irfan Habib (New Delhi: Tulika, 1995) 332.

34. Dutt 84.
35. Habib, "Processes" 289 (emphasis added).
36. The concept of 'outside labour' can arise from various social sanctions or circumstances. It can be due to the non-economic demand created by the particular social conditions of the *Jajmani* system, a hierarchical system where strict followers of Hindu caste system, as upper caste members, are prohibited from performing manual labour. Another reason for use of 'outside labour' is based on short-term seasonal needs of the small family farm that cannot cope with the harvesting or planting work. Therefore, demand for outside labour becomes necessary. Rastayannikov, cites India's Eighth Round of the National Sample Survey which has a section on "farming conditions and practices" that shows "11% of the cultivators' households were 'wholly or mainly' based on 'hired labor'; Victor G. Rastayannikov, "The Social Types of Rural Hired Workers in Independent India," *Soviet Scholars View of South Asia*, ed. Yuri V. Gankovsky (Lahore: People's Publishing House, 1975).
37. Rastayannikov 60.
38. See K.N. Raj, "Land Reforms in India and Pakistan: A Comparative Review," *The Post-Colonial State and Social Transformation in India and Pakistan*, ed. S.M. Naseem and Khalid Nadvi (Karachi: Oxford University Press, 2002) 131–141.
39. Luxemburg's view of non-capitalist markets is more clearly expressed in the editor's introduction of her and Nikolai Bukharin's work, which is published as one volume; see Luxemburg*;* also, see Habib's comment in the Habib, "Processes" 282–283.
40. Organic composition of capital is a technical or physical relationship between the mass of machinery, raw materials, and labour necessary to produce commodities at a given level of productivity, and the value relationship between constant capital (factory, machinery) and variable capital (wages) determined by these physical properties.
41. Alavi, "The Structure" 181 (emphasis mine).
42. Nicos Poulantzas, *State, Power and Socialism*, trans. Patrick Camiller (London: New Left Books, 1978).
43. Saying that Euro-American societies do not have 'remnants' of pre-capitalist social forms, such as the presence of slavery (which survived for a long time under capitalism in the US), is merely to acknowledge this fact in a formal sense—as the present-day consequences of race and racism continue to adversely impact racialized peoples in these societies.
44. See Pranab Bardhan, *The Political Economy of Development in India* (Oxford: Basil Blackwell, 1984).
45. See Noman Omar, *The Political Economy of Pakistan, 1947–85* (London: KPI, 1988); Tariq Ali, "Revolutionary Perspectives for Pakistan," *New Left Review* 63 (September–October 1970): 43–55; Hamza Alavi, "Social Forces and Ideology in the Making of Pakistan," *Economic and Political Weekly* 37.51 (21 December 2002): 5119–5124
46. See Tariq Amin Khan, "Economy, Society and the State in Pakistan," *Contemporary South Asia* 9.2 (2000): 181–195.
47. See Mick Moore, "Economic Liberalization Versus Political Pluralism in Sri Lanka," *Modern Asian Studies* 24.2 (1990): 341–383.
48. I have avoided giving these indigenous capitalists a 'nationalist' tinge as suggested in the much overused term 'national bourgeoisie', which assumes an anti-imperialist character to this class that does not square with the conduct of most indigenous capitalists in post-colonial societies.
49. Japan, in colonizing South Korea, was probably the only colonizing power to have introduced meaningful land reforms in the colony which, in Korea's case,

had a transformative effect as the country gained independence from Japan; see Parvez Hasan, *Korea: Problems and Issues in a Rapidly Growing Economy* (Baltimore: John Hopkins Press (published for the World Bank), 1976).

50. See, for example, the reports of United Nations Development Programme spanning a number of years, which have repeatedly raised the issue of land reforms.
51. For example M.L. Sharma discusses how land reforms in the Indian state of Rajasthan did not take into account the land tenure system or even the caste system; see M.L. Sharma "Altering Agrarian Structure: Rajasthan Land Reforms," *Green Revolution and Social Change*, ed. M.L. Sharma and T.M. Dak (Delhi: Ajanta Publications, 1989) 171–109.
52. P.S. Appu, *Land Reforms in India—A Survey of Policy, Legislation and Implementation* (mimeograph). Mussorie: Land Reforms Unit, Shastri National Academy of Administration. 1995, cited in Raj 138–139.
53. See Raj; for the discussion on three separate land reforms in Pakistan, see Omar.
54. See Saturnino Borras Jr., "Questioning Market-Led Agrarian Reform: Experiences of Brazil, Colombia, and South Africa," *Journal of Agrarian Change* 3.3 (July 2003): 367–394.
55. Thomas B. Hansen and Finn Stepputat , eds., *States of Imagination: Ethnographic Explorations of the Postcolonial State* (Durham: Duke University Press, 2001) 10.
56. Benedict Anderson, *Imagined Communities: Reflections on the Origin and Spread of Nationalism* (London: Verso, 1991) 9–46.
57. Abbas Rashid and Farida Shaheed, *Pakistan: Ethno Politics and Contending Elites* (New York: UN Research Institute for Social Development, June 1993).
58. Hansen and Stepputat 10–11.
59. See Vivek Chibber, "Bureaucratic Rationality and the Developmental State." *American Journal of Sociology* 107.4 (January 2002): 951–989.
60. Ayesha Jalal, *The State of Martial Rule: The Origins of Pakistan's Political Economy of Defence* (1990; Cambridge: Cambridge University Press; Lahore: Vanguard Press, 1991).
61. B.B. Misra, *The Bureaucracy in India* (Delhi: Oxford University Press, 1977, cited in Hamza Alavi, "Formation" 17.
62. Alavi, "Formation" 17.
63. For instance, many writers have argued that as a result of British colonial rulers' manipulative social policy in India, such as the Separate Electorate Act of 1906, and other measures, glimpses of ethno-nationalism were visible in Muslim League's demand for separatism; see Hafeez Malik, "Sir Sayyid Ahmed Khan's Contribution to the Development of Muslim Nationalism in India," *Modern Asian Studies* 4.2 (1970); Hamza Alavi, "Social Forces."
64. For an example of the former, see Alavi, "Formation," for the use of the term *salariat*; and Hamza Alavi, "Politics of Ethnicity in India and Pakistan," *Sociology of "Developing Societies": South Asia*, ed. Hamza Alavi and John Harriss (London: Macmillan, 1989) 225–228.
65. See Peter Evans, *Embedded Autonomy: States and Industrial Transformation* (Princeton: Princeton University Press, 1995).
66. Notice my class categories are different than Alavi's three propertied classes (the indigenous bourgeoisie, the metropolitan bourgeoisie, and capitalist landowners).
67. Alavi, "The State in Post-Colonial Societies" 61 (emphasis mine).
68. Frantz Fanon, *The Wretched of the Earth*, trans. Constance Farrington (New York: Grove Weidenfeld, 1963) 150, 159, 165.

69. Hassan Nawaz Gardezi, *A Re-Examination of the Socio-Political History of Pakistan, Reproductions of Class Relations and Ideology* (Lewiston: The Edwin Mellon Press, 1991) 30.
70. See Samir Amin, *Unequal Development: An Essay on the Social Formations of Peripheral Capitalism* (New York: Monthly Review Press, 1976); Emmanuel Arghiri, *Unequal Exchange: A Study of the Imperialism of Trade* (New York: Monthly Review Press, 1972).
71. Alavi, "The State in Post-Colonial Societies" 61.
72. The idea of the 'weakness of the nation-state' has been argued in a number of articles; two examples are Roger Burbach and William Robinson, "The Fin De Siecle Debate: Globalization as Epochal Shift," *Science and Society* 63.1 (Spring 1999) 10–39; William Robinson and J. Harris, "Towards a Global Ruling Class: Globalization and the Transnational Capitalist Class," *Science & Society* 64.1 (Spring 2000) 11–54.
73. Jean-Francois Medard, "The Underdeveloped State in Tropical Africa: Political Clientilism or Neo-Patrimonialism," *Private Patronage and Public Power*, ed. Christopher Clapham (London: Pinter, 1982), cited in Adrain Leftwich, "States of Underdevelopment: The Third World State in Theoretical Perspective," *Journal of Theoretical Politics* 6.1 (1993): 67.
74. See Shivji.
75. See Nicos Poulantzas, *Political Power and Social Classes*, trans. Timothy O'Hagan (London: New Left Books, 1975); and Bob Jessop, *State Theory: Putting the Capitalist State in Its Place* (University Park: Penn State University Press, 1990).

NOTES TO CHAPTER 4

1. The Rashtriya Swayamsevak Sangh (Hindu national volunteer organization) was founded in 1925, Vishwa Hindu Parishad (World Hindu Council) was founded in 1964, and the Bharatiya Janata Party (Indian People's Party) was established in 1980.
2. K.N. Raj, "Land Reforms in India and Pakistan: A Comparative Review," *The Post-Colonial State and Social Transformation in India and Pakistan*, ed. S.M. Naseem and Khalid Nadvi (Karachi: Oxford University Press, 2002) 133.
3. Raj 36; Raj cited the figure from the work of P.S. Appu, *Land Reforms in India: A Survey of Policy, Legislation and Implementation*, mimeograph (Mussorie: Land Reforms Unit, Shastri National Academy of Administration, 1995).
4. Stuart Corbridge and John Harriss, *Reinventing India: Liberalization, Hindu Nationalism and Popular Democracy* (Cambridge: Polity, 2000) 21–22.
5. Corbridge and Harriss 22.
6. See the works of Ashis Nandy, Ronald Inden, and T.N. Madan; these writers contrasted the Nehruvian project with the Gandhian view of India, that is, as a collection of decentralized village communities, with an emphasis on the rural rather than on the urban. In making this comparison, these writers contend that Nehru's vision of India is symptomatic broadly of an Orientalist view of development and change, especially on India's experiments with modernism. Also see Corbridge and Harriss 31.
7. Ayesha Jalal, *Democracy and Authoritarianism in South Asia: Comparative and Historical Perspectives* (Cambridge: Cambridge University Press, 1995) 25.
8. Jalal, *Democracy* 25; also see Arundhati Roy, "Instant-Mix Imperial Democracy, Buy One Get One Free—An Hour With Arundhati Roy," speech

at the Riverside Church, *Democracy Now! The War and Peace Report,* 23 October 2003. 7 May 2011 <http://www.democracynow.org/2003/10/24/instant_mix_imperial_democracy_buy_one>.

9. See P.K. Tripathi, "Secularism: Constitutional Provisions and Judicial Review," *Secularism: Its Implications for Law and Life in India*, ed. G.S. Sharma (Bombay: Tripathi, 1966) 193. The 12 articles of the Indian Constitution are mentioned by Tripathi as having relevance to the concept of secularism; these same articles have been also cited in Thomas Pantham, "Indian Secularism and Its Critics: Some Reflections," *The Review of Politics* 59.3 (Summer 1997): 526–527.
10. Pantham 525.
11. See T.N. Madan, "Secularism in Its Place," *Journal of Asian Studies* (November 1987): 747–759; Ashis Nandy, "The Politics of Secularism and the Recovery of Religious Tolerance," *Mirrors of Violence*, ed. V. Das (Delhi: Oxford University Press, 1990).
12. The reference to the phrase "night-bitten dawn" is from Faiz Ahmad Faiz's well-known poem, "Morning of Freedom" (*Subha-e-Azadi*) on what was not to be at the dawn of Pakistan's inception and India's 'independence'. In his poem, Faiz takes aim at the "reactionary views of the ruling elite and obscurantist mullahs" in the partitioning of India; the quote is from S.M. Mehdi, "Faiz—The Voice of Asia's Revolt," *Business Recorder* (27 December 1984)—cited in Estelle Dryland, *Faiz Ahmad Faiz: Urdu Poet of Social Realism* (Lahore: Vanguard Books, 1993) 58.
13. Kalpana Wilson, "Class Alliances and the Nature of Hegemony: The Post-Independence Indian State in Marxist Writing," *State and Nation in the Context of Social Change,* vol. 1 of *Social Change and Political Discourse in India: Structures of Power, Movements of Resistance*, ed. T.V. Sathyamurthy (Delhi: Oxford University Press, 1994) 249–250 (emphasis added).
14. Corbridge and Harriss 11.
15. D. Thorner and A. Thorner, *Land and Labour in India* (Bombay: Asia Publishing House, 1965).
16. Amiya Kumar Bagchi, "Dialectics of Indian Planning: From Compromise to Democratic Decentralization and Threat of Disarray," *Industry and Agriculture in India Since Independence*, vol. 2 of *Social Change and Political Discourse in India: Structures of Power, Movements of Resistance*, ed. T.V. Sathyamurthy (Delhi: Oxford University Press, 1995) 57 (emphasis added).
17. Bagchi 57, 59.
18. See Bagchi, "Dialectics"; see Corbridge and Harriss.
19. Bagchi, "Dialectics" 49.
20. Bagchi, "Dialectics" 49.
21. See Raj.
22. Pramit Chaudhuri, "Economic Planning in India," *Industry and Agriculture in India Since Independence,* vol. 2 of *Social Change and Political Discourse in India: Structures of Power, Movements of Resistance*, ed. T.V. Sathyamurthy (Delhi: Oxford University Press, 1995) 97.
23. See Purshotamdas Thakurdas, *A Brief Memorandum Outlining a Plan of Economic Development for India*, 2 vols. (Harmondsworth: Penguin, 1945). Note that Sir Purshotamdas Thakurdas and his fellow contributors in these two volumes — J.R.D. Tata, Sir Ardeshir Dalal, Sir Shai Ram, Kasturbahai Lalbhai, A.D. Shroff, and John Matthai—as knighted big bourgeoisie have proudly addressed themselves with their titles and abandoned any concern with anti-imperialism; this is the paradox of the "national bourgeoisie," a term whose application I have contested in this and earlier chapters.
24. See Thakurdas.

25. Jawaharlal Nehru, *Nehru Papers (G5A–1936)* (New Delhi: Nehru Museum and Memorial Library, 1936), cited in Chaudhuri 96
26. Bagchi 48.
27. Chaudhuri 97.
28. Chaudhuri 97.
29. Bagchi, "Dialectics" 48.
30. See the report of the IPC's press conference; Indian Planning Commission, "India's Poverty Declined to 32% in 2009–10," press conference, 20 April 2011 <http://www.moneycontrol.com/news/current-affairs/indias-poverty-declined-to-322009–10-plan-panel-est_537354.html>.
31. For a somewhat different take on Nehru's social democratic outlook that sees him reluctantly accepting India becoming part of the WCS, see Corbridge and Harriss.
32. Chaudhuri 98.
33. See Aseema Sinha, "Rethinking the Developmental State Model: Divided Leviathan and Subnational Comparisons in India," *Comparative Politics* 35.4 (July 2003): 459–472; and JØrgen Dige Pedersen, "Explaining Economic Liberalization in India: State and Society Perspectives," *World Development* 28.2 (2000): 265–282.
34. See Sinha.
35. See note 13.
36. Jalal, *Democracy* 71.
37. Jalal, *Democracy* 71
38. Jalal, *Democracy* 71.
39. Jalal, *Democracy* 72.
40. Jalal, *Democracy* 73.
41. Narendra Panjwani, "Some Hazards of Universalism in the Indian Polity," *Class Formation and Political Transformation in Post-Colonial India,* vol. 4 of *Social Change and Political Discourse in India: Structures of Power, Movements of Resistance*, ed. T.V. Sathyamurthy (Oxford: Oxford University Press, 1996) 345.
42. There are many excellent and easily accessible books and articles written on the RSS, BJP, and the rise of the *hindutva* phenomenon; some examples are Tapan Basu et al., *Khaki Shorts and Saffron Flags: A Critique of the Hindu Right* (Bombay: Orient Longman, 1993); Achin Vaniak, "Situating Threat of Hindu Nationalism. Problems With Fascist Paradigm," *Economic and Political Weekly* 29.28 (9 July 1994): 1729–1748; Aijaz Ahmad, "Fascism and National Culture: Reading Gramsci in the Days of Hindutva," *Lineages of the Present: Political Essays, collec.* Aijaz Ahmad (New Delhi: Tulika, 1996) 221–266.
43. It should be emphasized that these neo-Malthusian ideas were encouraged by only a section of the Indian ruling elite as there were many instances when Indian political leaders and even capitalists themselves came out strongly against these Orwellian moves of the state. As for the inspiration of neo-Malthusians, Malthus himself and his anti-poor perspective is critically assessed in an excellent piece; see John Bellamy Foster, "Malthus' Essay on Population at Age 200: A Marxian View," *Monthly Review* 50.7 (December 1998): 1–18.
44. Debabar Banerji, "Violation of Human Rights in India's Birth Control Initiatives," *Class Formation and Political Transformation in Post-Colonial India,* vol. 4 of *Social Change and Political Discourse in India: Structures of Power, Movements of Resistance*, ed. T.V. Sathyamurthy (Delhi: Oxford University Press, 1996) 379.
45. Sumit Roy, "Liberalization and the Indian Economy: Myth and Reality," *Industry and Agriculture in India Since Independence,* vol. 2 of *Social Change and*

Political Discourse in India: Structures of Power, Movements of Resistance, ed. T.V. Sathyamurthy (Delhi: Oxford University Press, 1994) 141.

46. World Bank, "GDP Growth (Annual %)," 24 April 2011 <http://data.world-bank.org/indicator/NY.GDP.MKTP.KD.ZG>.
47. See Rajni Kothari, *State Against Democracy: In Search of Human Governance* (New Delhi: Ajanta, 1988).
48. Kothari 138.
49. Saroj Giri, "The Maoist 'Problem' and the Democratic Left in India," *Journal of Contemporary Asia* 39.3 (August 2009): 463–474.
50. See Prabhat Patnaik, "On the Political Economy of Economic Liberalisation," *Social Scientist* 13.146–147 (July–August 1985): 3–17.
51. Sanjaya Baru, "Continuity and Change in Indian Industrial Policy," *Industry and Agriculture in India Since Independence,* vol. 2 of *Social Change and Political Discourse in India: Structures of Power, Movements of Resistance*, ed. T.V. Sathyamurthy (Delhi: Oxford University Press, 1994) 130.
52. See S. Mundle, "Growth, Disparity and Capital Reorganization in Indian Economy: Some Speculations," *Economic and Political Weekly* 16.10/12 (March 1981): 393–408.
53. For instance, Baru cites Ahluwalia on this view; I. J. Ahluwalia, *Industrial Growth in India, Stagnation Since the Mid-Sixties* (New Delhi: Oxford University Press, 1985).
54. Baru attributes this view to "neo-Marxists" in India; see Baru 127.
55. See Michael Hudson, *Super Imperialism: The Origin and Fundamentals of US World Dominance* (London: Sterling; Virginia: Pluto Press, 2003).
56. See Pranab Bardhan, *The Political Economy of Development in India* (Oxford: Basil and Blackwell, 1984); and Pedersen 275.
57. S. Roy 139.
58. S. Roy 139.
59. Baru129.
60. Baru129.
61. Baru 129.
62. Government of India, "Agriculture and Food Management," *Economic Survey 2010–11,* 30 April 2011 <http://indiabudget.nic.in>, Table 8.1: GDP for Agriculture and Allied Sectors.
63. Utsa Patnaik, "Poverty and Neo-Liberalism in India," *Rao Bahdur Kale Memorial Lecture,* delivered at Gokhale Institute of Politics and Economics, Pune, 3 February 2006, Table 2: Reduction in Rural Development Expenditures Under Economic Reforms, Selected Years 1985–90 to 2000–01."
64. Baru 129.
65. Baru 130.
66. See Baru.
67. See Pedersen.
68. Pedersen 268–270.
69. Baru 130.
70. Pedersen 277.
71. See Victoria Schofield, *Kashmir in Conflict: India, Pakistan and the Unfinished War* (London: Tauris, 2003).
72. For a critique of *ngo-ization*, see James Petras and Henry Veltmeyer, *Globalization Unmasked: Imperialism in the 21st Century* (Halifax: Fernwood/ Zed, 2001).
73. Indian Planning Commission, *Development Challenges in Extremist Affected Areas: Report of an Expert Group to the Planning Commission* (New Delhi: Government of India, April 2008), 7 May 2011<http://planningcommission.nic.in/reports/publications/rep_dce.pdf>, 3.

74. See Arundhati Roy, "Walking With the Comrades," *OutlookIndia.com* (29 March 2010), 7 May 2011<http://www.outlookindia.com/article.aspx?264738–0>.
75. See Giri.
76. A. Roy, "Walking With the Comrades."
77. See the television documentary by mainstream Indian news channel, NDTV, "Operation Green Hunt: War Without End" (2 April 2010), 8 May 2011 <http://www.ndtv.com/video/player/ndtv-special-ndtv-24x7/operation-green-hunt-war-without-end/135562>.
78. Madhav Khosla, "Salwa Judum and the Supreme Court," *The Hindu* (13 July 2011), 14 July 2011 <http://www.thehindu.com/opinion/lead/article2221935.ece?homepage=true>.
79. Cited in Khosla.
80. Giri 472.
81. Indian Planning Commission, *Development* 3.
82. Indian Planning Commission, Development 3.
83. Giri 464.
84. Giri 464.
85. Pankaj Mishra, "Pakistan: A Hard Country by Anatol Lieven—Review," *The Guardian on the Web (30 April 2011),* 28 May 2011 <http://www.guardian.co.uk/books/2011/may/01/pakistan-hard-country-anatol-lieven-review>.

NOTES TO CHAPTER 5

1. For a discussion of the *Mohajir* identity and the violence surrounding its assertion, see Tariq Amin Khan, "Colonialism and the Common Origins of Discrete Post-colonial Identities in India and Pakistan," *Canadian Review of Studies in Nationalism* XXIX.1–2 (2002): 39–52.
2. Ayesha Jalal, *The State of Martial Rule: The Origins of Pakistan's Political Economy of Defence* (1990; Cambridge: Cambridge University Press; Lahore: Vanguard Press, 1991).
3. Hamza Alavi has suggested the idea of Pakistan's "shallow roots" ; see Hamza Alavi, "Nationhood and Communal Violence in Pakistan," *Journal of Contemporary Asia* 21.2 (1991): 152–178. In contrast, Imran Anwar Ali questions quite unconvincingly whether the Pakistan Movement has a far longer history, one going back to Mahmud Ghaznawi (11th century) or even Muhammed bin Qasim (8th century); see Imran Anwar Ali, "Past and Present: The Making of the State in Pakistan," *Pakistan: The Contours of State and Society*, ed. Soofia Mumtaz, Jean-Luc Racine, and Imran Anwar Ali (Karachi: Oxford University Press, 2002) 24–42.
4. Alavi, "Nationhood" 153.
5. Pervez Musharraf, *In the Line of Fire: A Memoir* (New York: Free Press, 2006).
6. This apprehension of Pakistan's military and the Indian ruling classes' hostility towards Pakistan is also acknowledged by Imran Anwar Ali and Soofia Mumtaz, "Preface: Understanding Pakistan—The Impact of Global, Regional, National and Local Interactions," *Pakistan: The Contours of State and Society*, ed. Soofia Mumtaz, Jean-Luc Racine, and Imran Anwar Ali (Karachi: Oxford University Press, 2002) xi.
7. Jalal, "The State of Martial Rule" 18.
8. Members of these different ruling groups either held lower administrative positions in the colonial state or, like the feudal land holders, had collaborated

with colonial rulers in the extraction of tribute from the peasantry; see Irfan Habib, "Colonization of the Indian Economy 1757–1900," *Essays in Indian History, Towards a Marxist Perception*, collec. Irfan Habib (New Delhi: Tulika, 1995).

For another view of how the Punjabi landed elite—whether Hindu, Muslim, or Sikh—were the beneficiary of land grants from English colonial rulers in the newly created canal colonies of Punjab that were given to the former as reward for assisting the colonial regime, such as in putting down the 1857 Rebellion, see Hamza Alavi, "Nationhood" 158–159.

9. For some revealing behind-the-scenes pro-American moves of Pakistani bureaucrats in the early and mid-1950s, see "Darkness at High Noon: The Anglo-US Bloc and Middle East Policy" in Mazhar Ali Khan, *Pakistan: The First Twelve Years: The Pakistan Times Editorials of Mazhar Ali Khan* (Karachi: Oxford University Press, 1996) 441–481.
10. Surveillance flights of the high-flying U2 spy plane were regularly undertaken from the airbase near Peshawar, Pakistan; however, this covert operation was exposed when the Soviet Union downed a US spy plane in 1964.
11. For a critical view of American-inspired economic policies that were implemented in the early 1950s, see M.A. Khan 439–578.
12. H.N. Gardezi, *A Re-Examination of the Socio-Political History of Pakistan, Reproductions of Class Relations and Ideology* (Lewiston: The Edwin Mellon Press, 1991) 30. Also see Albert Waterson, *Planning in Pakistan* (Baltimore: Johns Hopkins University Press, 1963), cited in Gardezi. For W.W. Rostow's outlook on dependant economic development for emerging decolonized states, see W.W. Rostow, *The Stages of Economic Growth: A Non-Communist Manifesto* (Cambridge: Cambridge University Press, 1971).
13. Figures are cited from Government of Pakistan, *Interim Report of Pakistan's Third Five Year Plan 1965–1970* (Islamabad: Government Printing Press, 1970), cited in Gardezi 31.
14. For another critical view of the US's deep involvement in Pakistan's political and economic development, see Gardezi 92–94.
15. This average figure has been culled from the Government of Pakistan's statistics, cited in Noman Omar, *The Political Economy of Pakistan 1947–85* (London: KPI, 1988) Table 2, 17.
16. From A.R. Khan, "What is Happening to Real Wages in Pakistan?" *Pakistan Development Review* (Autumn, 1967), cited in Gardezi 20.
17. Gardezi 62.
18. See Kumari Jayawardena, *Feminism and Nationalism in the Third World* (London: Zed Books, 1986) 86.
19. Iftikhar H. Malik, *State and Civil Society in Pakistan: Politics of Authority, Ideology and Ethnicity* (Basingstoke: Macmillan, 1997) 145.
20. Farida Shaheed, "The Other Side of the Discourse: Women's Experience of Identity, Religion and Activism in Pakistan," *Appropriating Gender: Women's Activism and Politicized Religion in South Asia*, ed. Patricia Jeffery and Amrita Basu (London: Routledge, 1998) 155–156.
21. Shahnaz Rouse, "Liberation From Above or Within: Nationalism, Gender and Space in Pakistan," *Against the Current* 97 (March–April 2002): 14.
22. I.A. Ali and Mumtaz, "Preface: Understanding Pakistan" xxii–xxiii.
23. Omar, Table 6, 164; also, see Government of Pakistan, Finance Division, *Pakistan Economic Survey 1978–79* (Islamabad: Government Printing Press, 1980).
24. Omar, Table 8, 96.
25. Shahid J. Burki, *Pakistan: Fifty Years of Nationhood* (Boulder: Westview, 1999) Table 3.4, 103.

26. Burki, Table 3.6, 118.
27. Burki 165.
28. See Z.A. Bhutto, *If I Am Assassinated* (New Delhi: Vikas, 1979).
29. Support for the statement on funding by the US and Saudi Arabia is from The 9/11 Commission, "The 9/11 Commission Report," 23 July 2004 <http://news.bbc.co.uk/nol/shared/bsp/hi/pdfs/22_07_04911Report.pdf>; also see Tariq Ali, *Clash of Fundamentalisms* (London: Verso, 2003).
30. Rouse 14.
31. Based on Ziaul Haq's amendment to the Evidence Act, whereas a lone male can provide evidence in a court case, two women are needed for their evidence to be of equal weight to the single male's evidence in Pakistani courts. Haq even renamed the Act to Qanoon-e-Shaadat (law of evidence) where he retained all of the clauses of the colonial-era Evidence Act, and added the new clauses related to women's evidence.
32. See Amin Khan, "Colonialism and the Common Origins."
33. See World Bank, *Report No. 18395–PAK: Agricultural Taxation in Pakistan* (Washington: World Bank, 1999).
34. See K.N. Raj, "Land Reforms in India and Pakistan: A Comparative Review," *The Post-Colonial State and Social Transformation in India and Pakistan*, ed. S.M. Naseem and Khalid Nadvi (Karachi: Oxford University Press, 2002) 131–141.
35. M.A. Khan 463.
36. Omar, Figure 1, 85.
37. Omar 85.
38. Based on Rostow's five stages of economic growth.
39. World Bank, "Social Indicators of Development 1995," 23 July 2004 <http://www.worldbank.org/cgi-bin/sendoff.cgi?page=%2Fdata%2Fcountrydata%2Faag%2Fpak_aag.pdf>.
40. Figures are from World Bank, "Country Data 2010," 24 June 2011<http://data.worldbank.org/country/pakistan>.
41. The two army Foundations are Fauji Foundation and Army Welfare Trust, whereas others are Bharia Foundation (Navy) and Shaheen Foundation (Air Force). Besides, there is the Frontier Works Organization involved in a range of high-value construction projects, from building dams to highways; alongside, the National Logistics Cell has the largest fleet of commercial trucks in the country.
42. Ayesha Siddiqa Agha, "Power, Perks, Prestige and Privileges: Military's Economic Activity in Pakistan," *International Conference on Soldiers in Business: Military as an Economic Actor*, Jakarta, 17–19 October 2000.
43. See Ayesha Siddiqa, *Military Inc.: Inside Pakistan's Military Economy* (Karachi: Oxford University Press, 2007).
44. Siddiqa 2.
45. Mohammed Hanif, *The Case of Exploding Mangoes* (New York: Vintage Books, 2009).
46. See John Bray, "Pakistan at 50: A State in Decline," *International Affairs* 73.2 (1997): 315–331.
47. Tariq Amin-Khan, "The Rise of Militant Islam and the Security State in the Era of the 'Long War'," *Third World Quarterly* 30.4 (2009) 813–828.
48. William Blum, *Killing Hope: US Military and CIA Interventions Since World War II* (Monroe: Common Courage Press, 2004).
49. See Samuel Huntington, *The Clash of Civilizations and the Remaking of the World Order* (New York: Simon and Schuster, 1996).
50. The religious parties in Pakistan had been discredited because they were seen by a large cross-section of people as being too close to the US and also for

having allied with the men in uniform, triggering the military coup against the government of Zulfikar Ali Bhutto.

51. Reference here is to the *jihad* against the Soviet Union's occupation of Afghanistan—seen by many as a proxy war of the US—and the other *jihad* for the 'liberation' of Kashmir.
52. The reference here is to *Jamaat-e-Islami*, *Jamiat-e-Ulema Islam*, and other smaller religious parties that had effectively lost political and social support in Pakistan until Ziaul Haq's Islamization agenda resuscitated them.
53. Irfan Husain, "OBL: A Martyr of Islam?" 21 May 2011–31 May 2011 <http://www.dawn.com/2011/05/21/obl-a-martyr-of-islam.html>.
54. See Musharraf.
55. The current Pakistani government headed by the Peoples Party claims quite openly that the 'war on terror' is 'our' war: both President Zardari and Prime Minister Gilani are on record making this claim; see Amir Waseem, "Zardari Has Become Army's Spokesman, Says PML-N," 23 June 2011. 4 July 2011 <http://www.dawn.com/2011/06/23/zardari-has-become-armys-spokesman-says-pml-n.html>.
56. See Amin-Khan, "The Rise of Militant Islam" 824–825.
57. See Jim Holt, "It's the Oil," *London Review of Books* 29.20 (2007), 18 October 2007 <http://www.lrb.co.uk/v29/n20.holt01html>.
58. Bill Moyers, "The Secret Government," *What I've Learned from US Foreign Policy: The War Against the Third World*, dir. Frank Dorrell, DVD (Culver City, 2002).
59. Burki 114.
60. World Bank, "Country Data 2010."
61. Sartaj Aziz, *Privatization in Pakistan* (Paris: Development Centre, OECD, 1996) 10.
62. Harry Shutt, *The Decline of Capitalism: Can a Self-regulated Profits System Survive?* (New York: Zed Books, 2005) 45–48.
63. While there are a number of instances involving the murder of Iraqi civilians at the hands of the US military and US security contractors in Iraq, reference here is to the well-known Raymond Davis incident in Pakistan involving an alleged US security contractor with supposed links to the Central Intelligence Agency who killed two young men riding a motorcycle on a busy Lahore thoroughfare whom he deemed as a threat to him. This act, according to news reports, was apparently without provocation. Davis was initially arrested and then freed by Pakistani authorities when blood money was paid as compensation to the victims' families. See Dawn.com, "Davis Leaves Pakistan," 16 March 2011. 31 May 2011 <http://www.dawn.com/2011/03/16/court-frees-cia-contractor-accused-of-murder-rana-sanaullah.html>.
64. See Dawn.com, "Dawn Presents Wikileaks' Pakistan Papers," 20 June 2011 <http://www.dawn.com/pakistan-papers>.

Bibliography

Abraham, J. "The Green Revolution Revisited." *Food and Development*. Ed. J. Abraham. London: Worldwide Fund for Nature, 1991.

Abrahamian, Ervand. "The US Media, Huntington and September 11." *Third World Quarterly* 24.3 (2003): 529–544.

Adams, Francis, Satya Dev Gupta, and Kidane Mengisteab, eds. *Globalization and the Dilemmas of the State in the South*. New York: St. Martin's Press, 1999.

Agha, Ayesha Siddiqa. "Power, Perks, Prestige and Privileges: Military's Economic Activity in Pakistan." *International Conference on Soldiers in Business: Military as an Economic Actor*. Jakarta, 17–19 October 2000.

Ahluwalia, I.J. *Industrial Growth in India, Stagnation Since the Mid-Sixties*. New Delhi: Oxford University Press, 1985.

Ahmad, Aijaz. "Fascism and National Culture: Reading Gramsci in the Days of Hindutva." *Lineages of the Present: Political Essays*. Collec. Aijaz Ahmed. New Delhi: Tulika, 1996. 221–266.

———. "Postcolonialism: What's in a Name?" *Late Imperial Culture*. Ed. Roman De La Campa, Ann Kaplan, and M. Sprinker. London: Verso, 1995.11–32.

Alavi, Hamza. "Colonialism and the Rise of Capitalism." *Hamza Alavi Internet Archive*, 18 October 2011 < http://hamzaalavi.com/?p=69> .

———. "Formation of the Social Structure of South Asia Under the Impact of Colonialism." South Asia: *Sociology of "Developing Societies."* Ed. Hamza Alavi and John Harriss. Basingstoke: Macmillan, 1989. 5–19.

———. "Nationhood and Communal Violence in Pakistan." *Journal of Contemporary Asia* 21.2 (1991): 152–178.

———. "Politics of Ethnicity in India and Pakistan." *Sociology of "Developing Societies": South Asia*. Ed. Hamza Alavi and John Harriss. London: Macmillan, 1989. 222–246.

———. "Social Forces and Ideology in the Making of Pakistan." *Economic and Political Weekly* 37.51 (21 December 2002): 5119–5124.

———. "The Social Origins of Pakistan and Islamic Ideology." *South Asia in Transition*. Ed. Kalim Bahadur. New Delhi: Patriot Publishers, 1986. 95–132.

———. "State and Class Under Peripheral Capitalism." *Introduction to the Sociology of "Developing Societies."* Ed. Hamza Alavi and Teodor Shanin. New York: Monthly Review Press, 1982. 289–307.

———. "The State in Post-Colonial Societies: Pakistan and Bangladesh." *New Left Review* 74 (1972): 59–81.

———. "The Structure of Peripheral Capitalism." *Introduction to the Sociology of "Developing Societies."* Ed. Hamza Alavi and Teodor Shanin. New York: Monthly Review Press, 1982. 172–194.

Ali, Imran Anwar. "Past and Present: The Making of the State in Pakistan." *Pakistan: The Contours of State and Society*. Ed. Soofia Mumtaz,

Jean-Luc Racine, and Imran Anwar Ali. Karachi: Oxford University Press, 2002. 24–42.

Ali, Imran Anwar, and Soofia Mumtaz. "Preface: Understanding Pakistan—The Impact of Global, Regional, National and Local Interactions." *Pakistan: The Contours of State and Society*, Ed. Soofia Mumtaz, Jean-Luc Racine, and Imran Anwar Ali. Karachi: Oxford University Press, 2002. ix–xxxvi.

Ali, Tariq. *Clash of Fundamentalisms*. London: Verso, 2003.

———. "Revolutionary Perspectives for Pakistan." *New Left Review* 63 (September–October 1970): 43–55.

Althusser, Louis, and Étienne Balibar. *Reading Capital*. Trans. Ben Brewster. London: Verso, 1997.

Amin, Samir. *Delinking: Towards a Polycentric World*. Trans. Michael Wolfers. London: Zed Books, 1990.

———. *Eurocentrism*. New York: Monthly Review Press, 1989.

———. "For a Progressive and Democratic New World Order." *Globalization and the New Dilemmas of the State in South*. Ed. Francis Adams, Satya Das Gupta, and K. Megisteab. New York: St. Martin's Press, 1999.17–32.

———. *Unequal Development: An Essay on the Social Formations of Peripheral Capitalism*. New York: Monthly Review Press, 1976.

Amin-Khan, Tariq. "Colonialism and the Common Origins of Discrete Post-Colonial Identities in India and Pakistan." *Canadian Review for Studies in Nationalism* XXIX.1–2 (2002): 39–52.

———. "Economy, Society and the State in Pakistan." *Contemporary South Asia* 9.2 (2000): 181–195.

———. "Is Corporate Globalism an Epochal Shift?" *Gala Conference of Marxism 2000 and the Association of Economic Research*. University of Massachusetts, Amherst, July 2000.

———. "Issues of Power and Modernity in Understanding Political and Militant Islam." *Comparative Studies of South Asia, Africa and the Middle East* 29.3 (2009): 544–555.

———. "Nation, Gender and Development: The Differential Experience of Women in the South." *2002 Canadian Sociology and Anthropology Association Conference at the Congress of Social Sciences and Humanities*. University of Toronto, 29 May–1 June 2002.

———. "New Orientalism, Western Media's Incendiary Racism and the 'Long War'." *Journal of Postcolonial Writing* 48.3 (July 2012) forthcoming.

———. "The Rise of Militant Islam and the Security State in the Era of the 'Long War'." *Third World Quarterly* 30.4 (2009): 813–828.

Anderson, Benedict. *Imagined Communities: Reflections on the Origin and the Spread of Nationalism*. London: Verso, 1991.

———. *Spectres of Comparisons: Nationalism, Southeast Asia and the World*. London: Verso, 1998.

Anderson, Perry. *Lineages of the Absolutist State*. London: Verso, 1993.

Anderson, Sarah, ed. *Views From the South: The Effect of Globalization and WTO on Third World Countries*. Oakland: Food First Books, 2000.

Arghiri, Emmanuel. *Unequal Exchange: A Study of the Imperialism of Trade*. New York: Monthly Review Press, 1972.

Aston, T.H., and C.H.E. Philpin, eds. *The Brenner Debate: Agrarian Class Structure and Economic Development in Pre-Industrial Europe*. Cambridge: Cambridge University Press, 1993.

Aziz, Abdul. *The Mansabdari System and the Mughal Army*. New Delhi: Idarah-i-Adabiyat-I-Delli, 1972.

Aziz, Sartaj. *Privatization in Pakistan*. Paris: Development Centre Studies, Organization for Economic Cooperation and Development, 1996.

Baden-Powell, B.H. *The Land Systems of British India: Being a Manual of the Land Tenures and the Systems of Land-Revenue Administration Prevalent in the Several Provinces.* 1892. New York: Johnson Reprint, 1972.

Baer, Werner. "Import Substitution and Industrialization in Latin America: Experiences and Interpretations." *Latin American Research Review* 7.1 (Spring 1972): 95–122.

Bagchi, Amiya Kumar. "Dialectics of Indian Planning: From Compromise to Democratic Decentralization and Threat of Disarray." *Industry and Agriculture in India Since Independence.* Vol. 2 of *Social Change and Political Discourse in India: Structures of Power, Movements of Resistance.* Ed. T.V. Sathyamurthy. Delhi: Oxford University Press, 1995. 46–93.

———."Parameters of Resistance." *Monthly Review* (July–August 2003): 136–143.

———. *The Political Economy of Underdevelopment.* Cambridge: Cambridge University Press, 1982.

Balakrishnan, Radhika, and Asad Sayeed. "Subcontracting: The Push-Pull Factors." *The Hidden Assembly Line: Gender Dynamics of Subcontracted Work in a Global Economy.* Ed. R. Balakrishnan. Bloomfield: Kumarian, 2002. 15–34.

Banerji, Debabar. "Violation of Human Rights in India's Birth Control Initiatives." *Class Formation and Political Transformation in Post-Colonial India.* Vol. 4 of *Social Change and Political Discourse in India: Structures of Power, Movements of Resistance.* Ed. T.V. Sathyamurthy. Delhi: Oxford University Press, 1996. 360–387.

Banks, M. *Ethnicity and Anthropological Constructions.* London: Routledge, 1996.

Baran, Paul, and Paul Sweezy. *Monopoly Capital.* New York: Monthly Review Press, 1966.

Bardhan, Pranab. *The Political Economy of Development in India.* Oxford: Basil and Blackwell, 1984.

Barrett, Michèle. *Women's Oppression Today: Problems in Marxist Feminist Analysis.* London: Verso, 1980.

Barrow, Clyde. *Critical Theories of the State: Marxist, Neo-Marxist and Post-Marxist.* Madison: University of Wisconsin Press, 1993.

———. "The Return of the State: Globalization, State Theory and the New Imperialism," *New Political Science* 27.2 (June 2005): 123–145.

Barsamian, David, ed. *Eqbal Ahmad, Confronting Empire: Interviews With David Barsamian.* Cambridge: South End Press, 2000.

Baru, Sanjaya. "Continuity and Change in Indian Industrial Policy." *Industry and Agriculture in India Since Independence.* Vol. 2 of *Social Change and Political Discourse in India: Structures of Power, Movements of Resistance.* Ed. T.V. Sathyamurthy. Delhi: Oxford University Press, 1994. 115–134.

Basu, Tapan, et al. *Khaki Shorts and Saffron Flags: A Critique of Hindu Right.* Bombay: Orient Longman, 1993.

Beck, Ulrich. *What Is Globalization.* Cambridge: Polity, 2000.

Bensidoun, I., and A. Chevallier. "Indicators of Regionalization in North America, Asia, Central and Eastern Europe and the Mediterranean Basin." *OECD Proceedings: Globalisation, Migration and Development.* Paris: OECD, 2000. 15–33.

Bernal, Martin. Black Athena: The Afro-Asiatic Roots of Classical Civilization. London: Free Association Books, 1987.

Bernier, Francois. *Travels in the Mughal Empire, AD 1656–1668.* Trans. Archibald Constable. 1710. Oxford: Oxford University Press, 1934.

Bernstein, H., T. Hewitt, and A. Thomas. "Capitalism and the Expansion of Europe." *Poverty and Development In the 1990s.* Ed. T. Allen and A. Thomas.

Oxford: Open University in association with Oxford University Press, 1992. 168–184.

Bhutto, Z.A. *If I Am Assassinated*. New Delhi: Vikas, 1979.

Biel, Robert. *The New Imperialism: Crisis and Contradictions in North/South Relations*. London: Zed Books, 2000.

Blaney, David, and Mustapha Kamal Pasha. "Civil Society and Democracy in the Third World: Ambiguities and Historical Possibilities." *Studies in Comparative International Development* 28.1 (Spring 1993): 3–24.

Blum, William. *Killing Hope: US Military and CIA Interventions Since World War II*. Monroe: Common Courage Press, 2004.

Bonefeld, Werner. "Free Economy and the Strong State: Some Notes on the State." *Capital & Class* 34.1 (2010): 15–24.

Borras, Saturnino, Jr. "Questioning Market-Led Agrarian Reform: Experiences of Brazil, Colombia, and South Africa." *Journal of Agrarian Change* 3.3 (July 2003): 367–394.

Bose, Sugata, and Ayesha Jalal. *Modern South Asia: History, Culture, Political Economy*. London: Routledge, 1998.

Bray, John. "Pakistan at 50: A State in Decline." *International Affairs* 73.2 (1997): 315–331.

Brenner, Robert. "The Agricultural Roots of European Capitalism." *The Brenner Debate: Agrarian Class Structure and Economic Development in Pre-Industrial Europe*. Ed. T.H. Ashton and C.H.E. Philpin. Cambridge: Cambridge University Press, 1985. 10–63.

Burbach, Roger, and William Robinson. "The Fin de Siecle Debate: Globalization as Epochal Shift." *Science & Society* 63.1 (Spring 1999): 10–39.

Burger, Mark T. "The Nation-State and the Challenge of Global Capitalism." *Third World Quarterly* 22.6 (2001): 889–907.

Burki, Shahid J. *Pakistan: Fifty Years of Nationhood*. Boulder: Westview, 1999.

Burstyn, Varda, and Dorothy Smith. *Women, Class, Family and the State*. Toronto: Garamond, 1985.

Business International Corporation. *Business International Weekly Report to Mangers and Worldwide Operators* 7 January 1977: 1.

Caldicott, Helen. *The New Nuclear Danger: George W. Bush's Military-Industrial Complex*. New York: The New Press, 2002.

Carby, Hazel. "White Woman Listen! Feminism and the Boundaries of Sisterhood." *The Empire Strikes Back*. Ed. Centre for Contemporary Cultural Studies. London: University of Birmingham Press, 1982. 211–234.

Cardoso, F.H., and E. Faletto. *Dependency and Development in Latin America*. Trans. M.M. Urquidi. Berkeley: University of California Press, 1971.

Chakrabarti, Anjan, and Anup Dar. *Dislocation and Resettlement in Development: From Third World to the World of the Third*. New York: Routledge, 2010.

Chandra, Bipan. "Colonialism, Stages of Colonialism and Colonial State." *Journal of Contemporary Asia* 10.3 (1980): 272–285.

Chandra, Bipan, et al. *Indian Economy in the 19th Century: A Symposium*. Delhi: Indian Economic and Social History Association, 1969.

Chatterjee, Partha. "Anderson's Utopia." *Ground of Comparison: Around the Work of Benedict Anderson*. Spec. issue of *Diacritics* 29.4 (Winter 1999): 128–134.

———. "History and Nationalization of Hinduism." *Social Research* 59.1 (Spring 1992): 111–149.

———. *The Nation and Its Fragments: Colonial and Postcolonial Histories*. Princeton: Princeton University Press, 1993.

———. "Transferring a Political Theory: Early Nationalist Thought in India." *Economic and Political Weekly* XXI.3 (18 January 1986): 120.

———. "Whose Imagined Communities," *Mapping the Nation*, ed. Gopal Balakrishnan (London: Verso, 1996)

Chaudhuri, Pramit. "Economic Planning in India." *Industry and Agriculture in India Since Independence*. Vol. 2 of *Social Change and Political Discourse in India: Structures of Power, Movements of Resistance*. Ed. T.V. Sathyamurthy. Delhi: Oxford University Press, 1995. 94–114.

Chavanov, A.V. *On the Theory of the Peasant Economy*. Ed. Daniel Thorner, Basile Kerblay, and R.E.F. Smith. Homewood: Irwin, 1966.

Cheah, Pheng. "Given Culture: Rethinking Cosmopolitical Freedom in Transnationalism." *Boundary 2* 24.2 (Summer 1997): 157–197.

Chernilo, Daniel. *A Social Theory of the Nation-State: The Political Forms of Modernity Beyond Methodological Nationalism*. London: Routledge, 2007.

Chibber, Vivek. "Bureaucratic Rationality and the Developmental State." *American Journal of Sociology* 107.4 (January 2002): 951–989.

———. "Reviving the Developmental State? The Myth of the 'National Bourgeoisie'." *Socialist Register 2005: The Empire Reloaded*. Ed. Leo Panitch and Colin Leys. London: Merlin, 2004. 144–165.

Clairmont, F. *The Rise and Fall of Economic Liberalism: The Making of the Economic Gulag*. Kuala Lumpur: Southbound and Third World Press, 1996.

Coates, Rodney D. "Introduction to Special Issue of Critical Sociology: Critical Race and Ethnic Theory, Research and Process." *Critical Sociology* 29.1–2 (2002): 7–11.

Colletti, Lucio. "Introduction." *Karl Marx: Early Writings*. Ed. and Trans. Rodney Livingstone and G. Benton. Middlesex: Penguin, 1977. 7–56.

Corbridge, Stuart, and John Harriss. *Reinventing India: Liberalization, Hindu Nationalism and Popular Democracy*. Cambridge: Polity, 2000.

Davis, Mike. *Late Victorian Holocausts, El Niño Famines and the Making of the Third World*. London: Verso, 2001.

Dawn.com, "Dawn Presents Wikileaks' Pakistan Papers." 20 June 2011 <http://www.dawn.com/pakistan-papers>.

Dawn.com. "Davis Leaves Pakistan." 16 March 2011. 31 May 2011 <http://www.dawn.com/2011/03/16/court-frees-cia-contractor-accused-of-murder-rana-sanaullah.html>.

Dickenson, J., et al. *Geography of the Third World*. London: Routledge, 1996.

Donnell, Guillermo, O. *Modernization and Bureaucratic Authoritarianism: Studies in South American Politics*. Berkeley: Institute of International Studies, University of California, 1979.

Dryland, Estelle. *Faiz Ahmad Faiz: Urdu Poet of Social Realism*. Lahore: Vanguard Books, 1993.

Durkheim, Emile. *The Division of Labour in Society*. Basingstoke: Macmillan, 1984.

Dutt, R. Palme. *India Today and Tomorrow*. Delhi: People's Publishing House, 1955.

Election Commission of Pakistan. "Constituency-Wise Detailed Results: NWFP Province." 20 May 2011 <http://www.ecp.gov.pk/GE/2002/National.pdf>.

Election Commission of Pakistan. "General Elections—2008." 20 May 2011 <http://www.ecp.gov.pk/GE2008.aspx>.

Elster, Jon. *Making Sense of Marx*. Cambridge: Cambridge University Press, 1985.

Emmer, Pieter C., and Geman Demas, eds. *General History of the Caribbean, New Societies: The Caribbean in the Long Sixteenth Century*. Vol. 2. London: UNESCO Publishing/Macmillan, 1999.

Engineer, Asghar Ali. "Hindu—Muslim Relations Before and After 1947." *Anatomy of Confrontation: The Babri Masjid—Ramjamnabhumi Issue*. Ed. Sarvepalli Gopal. New Delhi: Viking, 1991. 179–182.

Escobar, A. *Encountering Development: The Making and Unmaking of the Third World*. Princeton: Princeton University Press, 1995.

Evans, Peter. *Embedded Autonomy: States and Industrial Transformation*. Princeton: Princeton University Press, 1995.

———."The State as Problem and Solution: Predation, Embedded Autonomy and Structural Change." *The Politics of Economic Adjustment*. Ed. S. Haggard and R.R. Kaufman. Princeton: Princeton University Press, 1992. 139–181.

Evans, Peter, Dietrich Rueschemeyer, and Theda Skocpol, eds. *Bringing the State Back in*. Cambridge: Cambridge University Press, 1985.

Fanon, Frantz. *A Dying Colonialism*. Trans. Haakon Chevalier. New York: Grove, 1965.

———. "Racism and Culture." *Toward the African Revolution: Political Essays*. Collec. Frantz Fanon. New York: Monthly Review Press, 1967. 29–44.

———. *The Wretched of the Earth*. Trans. Constance Farrington. New York: Grove Weidenfeld, 1963.

Fichte, J.G. *Addresses to the German Nation*. Trans. R.F. Jones and G.H. Turnbull. Chicago: Open Court Publishing, 1922.

Foster, John Bellamy. "Malthus' Essay on Population at Age 200: A Marxian View." *Monthly Review* 50.7 (December 1998): 1–18.

Foucault, Michel. *Power/Knowledge: Selected Interviews and Other Writings, 1972–1977*. Ed. and Trans. Colin Gordon, et al. Brighton: Harvester, 1980.

———. "Power and Sex: An Interview with Bernard-Henri Lévy." *Michael Foucault: Politics, Philosophy, Culture: Interviews and Other Writings 1977–1984*. Ed. Lawrence Kritzman. New York: Routledge, 1988. 110–124.

Frank, Andre Gunder. *Dependent Accumulation and Underdevelopment*. New York: Monthly Review Press, 1979.

Frankel, B. *Beyond the State? Dominant Theories and Socialist Strategies*. London: Macmillan, 1983.

Fröbel, F., J. Heinrichs, and O. Kreye. *The New International Division of Labor: Structural Unemployment in Industrialised Countries and Industrialisation in Developing Countries*. Trans. Pete Burgess. 1977. Cambridge: Cambridge University Press, 1980.

Fuller, Chris. "British India or Traditional India?: Land, Caste and Power." *South Asia: Sociology of "Developing Societies"*. Ed. Hamza Alavi and John Harriss. Basingstoke: Macmillan, 1989. 28–40.

Gabriel, Satyananda, and Evgenia Todorova. "Racism and Capitalist Exploitation: An Overdetermined Nexus." *Critical Sociology* 29.1 (2003): 29–46.

Galabuzi, Grace-Edward. *Canada's Economic Apartheid: The Social Exclusion of Racialized Groups in the New Century*. Toronto: Canadian Scholars' Press, 2006.

Galeano, Eduardo. *Open Veins of Latin America*. New York: Monthly Review Press, 1997.

Gardezi, Hassan Nawaz. *A Re-Examination of the Socio-Political History of Pakistan, Reproductions of Class Relations and Ideology*. Lewiston: The Edwin Mellon Press, 1991.

Gellner, Ernest. *Encounters With Nationalism*. Oxford: Blackwell, 1994.

———. *Nations and Nationalism*. Ithaca: Cornell University Press, 1983.

Gilbert, Paul. *The Philosophy of Nationalism*. Boulder: Westview, 1998.

Gimenez, Martha. "The Oppression of Women: A Structuralist Marxist View." 1978. *Materialist Feminism: A Reader in Class, Difference, and Women's Lives*. Ed. Rosemary Hennessy and Chrys Ingraham. New York: Routledge, 1997. 71–82.

Giri, Saroj. "The Maoist 'Problem' and the Democratic Left in India." *Journal of Contemporary Asia* 39.3 (August 2009): 463–474.

Government of India. "Agriculture and Food Management." *Economic Survey 2010–11*. 30 April 2011 <http://indiabudget.nic.in>.

Government of Pakistan. *Interim Report of Pakistan's Third Five Year Plan (1965–1970)*. Islamabad: Government Printing Press, 1970.
Government of Pakistan, Finance Division. *Pakistan Economic Survey 1978–79*. Islamabad: Government Printing Press, 1980.
Gramsci, Antonio, *Selections From the Prison Notebooks of Antonio Gramsci*. Ed. and trans. Quintin Hoare and Geoffrey Nowell Smith. New York: International Publishers, 1991.
Green, D. *Silent Revolution: The Rise and Crisis of Market Economics in Latin America*. New York: Monthly Review Press, 1995.
Guha, Ranajit. *Elementary Aspects of Peasant Insurgency in Colonial India*. Delhi: Oxford University Press, 1997.
Gupta, Akhil. "Narratives of Corruption: Anthropological and Fictional Accounts of the Indian State." *Ethnography* 6.1 (2005): 5–34.
Gupta, Akhil, and Ardhana Sharma."Globalization and Postcolonial States." *Current Anthropology* 47.2 (April 2006): 277–307.
Habib, Irfan. *The Agrarian System of Mughal India (1505–1707)*. Bombay: Asia Publishing, 1963.
———. "Colonization of the Indian Economy 1757–1900." *Essays in Indian History, Towards a Marxist Perception*. Collec. Irfan Habib. New Delhi: Tulika, 1995. 296–335.
———."Potentialities of Capitalist Development in Mughal India." *Journal of Economic History* XXIX.1 (1969).
———. "Processes of Accumulation in Pre-Colonial and Colonial India." *Essays in Indian History, Towards a Marxist Perception*. Collec. Irfan Habib. New Delhi: Tulika, 1995. 259–295.
Hamilton, N. "State Autonomy and Dependent Capitalism in Latin America." *British Journal of Sociology* 32 (1981): 305–329.
Hanif, Mohammed. *The Case of Exploding Mangoes*. New York: Vintage Books, 2009.
Hansen, Thomas B., and Finn Stepputat, eds. *States of Imagination: Ethnographic Explorations of the Postcolonial State*. Durham: Duke University Press, 2001.
Harvey, David. "Capitalism: The Factory of Fragmentation." *From Modernization to Globalization: Perspectives on Development and Social Change*. Ed. J. Timmons Roberts and Amy Hite. Oxford: Blackwell, 2000.
———. *The New Imperialism*. New York: Oxford University Press, 2005.
Hasan, Parvez. *Korea: Problems and Issues in a Rapidly Growing Economy*. Baltimore: John Hopkins Press (published for the World Bank), 1976.
Hayashi, Shigeko. "The Developmental State in the Era of Globalization: Beyond the Northeast Asian Model of Political Economy." *The Pacific Review* 23.1 (March 2010): 45–69.
Henke, Holger. "Jamaica's Decision to Pursue a Neoliberal Development Strategy: Realignments in State-Business-Class Triangle." *Latin American Perspectives* 26.5 (September 1999): 7–33.
Hidouci, Ghazi, "The Geopolitical Dimension of Regional Integration," *OECD Proceedings: Globalisation, Migration and Development* (Paris: OECD, 2000): 183–186.
Hilton, R.H, ed. *The Transition From Feudalism to Capitalism*. London: Verso, 1976. Hobsbawm, Eric. *Nations and Nationalism Since 1780, Programme, Myth and Reality*. Cambridge: Cambridge University Press, 1992.
Holt, Jim. "It's the Oil." *London Review of Books* 29.20 (2007). 18 October 2007 <http://www.lrb.co.uk/v29/n20.holt01html>.
Hudson, Rex A., ed. *Brazil: A Country Study*. Washington, DC: GPO for the Library of Congress, 1997. 5 February 2011 <http://countrystudies.us/brazil/62.htm>.

Hudson, Michael. *Super Imperialism: The Origin and Fundamentals of US World Dominance*. London: Sterling; Virginia: Pluto, 2003.

Huntington, Samuel. "America in the World." *Hedgehog Review* 5.1 (Spring 2003): 7–18.

———. "The Change to Change: Modernization, Development, and Politics." *Comparative Politics* 3.3 (April 1971): 283–322.

———. *The Clash of Civilizations and the Remaking of the World Order*. New York: Simon Schuster, 1996.

———. "Dead Souls: The Denationalization of the American Elite." *National Interest* 75 (Spring 2004): 5–14.

———. *Political Order in Changing Societies*. New Haven: Yale University Press, 1968.

Huntington, Samuel, and M. Weiner, eds. *Understanding Political Development: An Analytic Study*. Boston: Little Brown, 1987.

Husain, Irfan. "OBL: A Martyr of Islam?" 5 May 2011–31 May 2011 <http://www.dawn.com/2011/05/21/obl-a-martyr-of-islam.html>.

Ihonvbere, Julius. "The Third World and the New World Order in the 1990s." *Futures* December 1992. Rpt. in *Annual Editions: Developing World 99/00*. Ed. Robert J. Griffiths. Guilford: Dushkin/McGraw Hill, 1999. 10.

Inden, Ronald. *Imagining India*. Oxford: Blackwell, 1990.

Indian Planning Commission. *Development Challenges in Extremist Affected Areas: Report of an Expert Group to the Planning Commission*. New Delhi: Government of India, April 2008. 7 May 2011<http://planningcommission.nic.in/reports/publications/rep_dce.pdf>

———. "India's Poverty Declined to 32% in 2009–10." Press Conference. 20 April 2011 <http://www.moneycontrol.com/news/current-affairs/indias-poverty-declined-to-322009–10-plan-panel-est_537354.html>.

International Labour Office. "The Informal Sector." 9 February 2011 <http://www.ilo.org/public/english/region/asro/bangkok/feature/inf_sect.htm>.

———. "Key Indicators of the Labour Market." 12 February 2011 <http://kilm.ilo.org/KILMnetBeta/default2.asp>.

———. "Social Security Department: The Informal Sector." 9 February 2011 <http://www.ilo.org/public/english/protection/secsoc/areas/policy/informal.htm>.

Jalal, Ayesha. *Democracy and Authoritarianism in South Asia: A Comparative and Historical Perspective*. Cambridge: Cambridge University Press, 1995.

———. *The Sole Spokesman: Jinnah, the Muslim League and the Demand for Pakistan*. Cambridge: Cambridge University Press, 1990.

———. *The State of Martial Rule: The Origins of Pakistan's Political Economy of Defence*. 1990. Cambridge: Cambridge University Press; Lahore: Vanguard, 1991.

Jani, Pranav. "Karl Marx, Eurocentrism, and the 1857 Revolt in British India." *Marxism, Modernity and Postcolonial Studies*. Ed. Crystal Bartolovich and Neil Lazarus. Cambridge: Cambridge University Press, 2002. 81–100.

Jayawardena, Kumari. *Feminism and Nationalism in the Third World*. London: Zed Books, 1986.

Jeffery, Patricia, and Amrita Basu, eds. *Appropriating Gender, Women's Activism and Politicized Religion in South Asia*. New York: Routledge, 1998.

Jessop, Bob. *The Capitalist State*. Oxford: Blackwell, 1982.

———. *State Theory: Putting the Capitalist State in Its Place*. University Park: Penn State University Press, 1990.

Johnson, Chalmers. *Blowback: The Costs and Consequences of American Empire*. New York: Henry Holt, 2004.

Joseph, R.A. "Class, State and Prebendal Politics in Nigeria." *Journal of Commonwealth and Comparative Politics* XXI.3 (1983): 21–38.
Kaviraj, Sudipta. "Capitalism and the Cultural Process." *Journal of Arts and Ideas* 19 (May 1990): 61–75.
Kazancigill, Ali, ed. *The State in Global Perspective*. Aldershot: Gower/UNESCO, 1986.
Kedourie, Elie. *Nationalism*. London: Hutchison, 1960.
Kelly, John D., and Martha Kaplan. "Nation and Decolonization: Toward a New Anthropology of Nationalism." *Anthropology Theory* 1.4 (2001): 419.
Khan, A.R. "What Is Happening to Real Wages in Pakistan?" *Pakistan Development Review* (Autumn, 1967).
Khan, M. Ayub. *Friends Not Masters: A Political Autobiography*. New York: Oxford University Press, 1967.
Khan, Mazhar Ali. *Pakistan: The First Twelve Years: The Pakistan Times Editorials of Mazhar Ali Khan*. Karachi: Oxford University Press, 1996.
Khilnani, Sunil. *The Idea of India*. London: Penguin, 1997.
Khosla, Madhav. "Salwa Judum and the Supreme Court." *The Hindu* (13 July 2011). 14 July 2011 <http://www.thehindu.com/opinion/lead/article2221935.ece?homepage=true>.
Knight, Franklin W. "The Disintegration of the Caribbean Slave System." *General History of the Caribbean: The Slave Societies of the Caribbean*. Ed. Franklin Knight. Vol. III. London: UNESCO/Macmillan, 1997.
Kolko, Gabriel. *Another Century of War*. New York: New Press, 2002.
Konings, Martijn. "Renewing State Theory." *Politics* 30.3 (2010): 174–182.
Kothari, Rajni. *State Against Democracy: In Search of Human Governance*. New Delhi: Ajanta, 1988.
Krueger, Anne O. "The Political Economy of the Rent-Seeking Society." *The American Economic Review* 64.3 (June 1974): 291–292.
Landes, David. *The Unbound Prometheus: Technological Change and Industrial Development in Western Europe From 1750 to the Present*. Cambridge: Cambridge University Press, 1969.
Lawrence, P.K. "Enlightenment, Modernity and War." *History of the Human Sciences* 12.1 (1999): 3–25.
Leftwich, Adrian. "Governance, Democracy and Development in the Third World." *Third World Quarterly* 14.3 (1993): 605–624.
———. "States of Underdevelopment: The Third World State in Theoretical Perspective." *Journal of Theoretical Politics* 6.1 (1993): 55–74.
Lenin, V.I. *Imperialism, The Highest Stage of Capitalism*. Peking: Foreign Languages Press, 1973.
Lewellen, Ted C., *Dependency and Development: An Introduction to the Third World*. London: Bergin and Garvey, 1995.
Leys, Colin. "The 'Overdeveloped' Post Colonial State: A Re-Evaluation." *Review of African Political Economy* 5 (1976): 39–48.
Lipsett, Seymour M. *Political Man*. London: Heinemann, 1960.
Loomba, Ania. *Colonialism/Postcolonialism*. London: Routledge, 1998.
Luxemburg, Rosa. *The Accumulation of Capital—An Anti-Critique*. Ed. and Intro. Kenneth J. Tarbuck. New York: Monthly Review Press, 1972.
Maclean, D. *Religion and Society in Arab Sindh*. Montreal: McGill University Press, 1989.
Madan, T.N. "Secularism in Its Place." *Journal of Asian Studies* 46.4 (November 1987): 747–759.
Makdisi, Saree. "Laying Claim to Beirut: Urban Narrative and Spatial Identity in the Age of Solidere." *Critical Inquiry* 23.3 (Spring 1997): 661–705.

Malik, Hafeez. "Sir Sayyid Ahmed Khan's Contribution to the Development of Muslim Nationalism in India." *Modern Asian Studies* 4.2 (1970).
Malik, Iftikhar H. *State and Civil Society in Pakistan: Politics of Authority, Ideology and Ethnicity*. Basingstoke: Macmillan, 1997.
Mamdani, Mahmud. *Good Muslim, Bad Muslim: America, The Cold War and Roots of Terror*. New York: Three Leaves Press, 2004.
Mandel, Earnest. *Late Capitalism*. London: New Left Books, 1972.
Marx, Karl. *The 18th Brumaire of Louis Bonaparte (1852/1988)*. Moscow: Progress Publishers, 1986.
———. *On Colonialism*. Collec. Karl Marx and F. Engels. Moscow: Progress Publishers, c. 1970.
———. *Economic and Philosophical Manuscripts of 1844*. Moscow: Progress Publishers, 1977.
Marx, Karl, and Fredrick Engels. *The Holy Family: Or, Critique of Critical Critique*. Moscow: Foreign Languages Press, 1956.
———. "Manifesto of the Communist Party." *Marx and Engels Selected Works*. Moscow: Progress Publishers, 1986. 31–62.
Mason, M. *Development and Disorder: A History of the Third World Since 1945*. Toronto: Between the Lines, 1997.
Maswood, S.J. "Developmental States in Crisis." *Reconfiguring East Asia: Regional Institutions and Organisations After the Crisis*. Ed. M. Beeson. London: Routledge, 2002.
McMichael, Philip, *Development and Social Change: A Global Perspective*. Thousand Oaks: Pine Forge, 2004.
———. "State Formation and the Construction of the World Market." *Political Power and Social Theory*. Vol. 6. Ed. Maurice Zeitlin. Greenwich: JAI, 1987. 187–237.
McNally, David. *Bodies of Meaning: Studies on Language, Labour and Liberation*. New York: SUNY Press, 2001.
Medard, Jean-Francois. "The Underdeveloped State in Tropical Africa: Political Clientilism or Neo-Patrimonialism." *Private Patronage and Public Power*. Ed. Christopher Clapham. London: Pinter, 1982.
Mehdi, S.M. "Faiz—The Voice of Asia's Revolt." *Business Recorder* 27 December 1984.
Mézáros, Istvan. "The Uncontrollability of Globalizing Capital." *Monthly Review* 49.9 (February 1998): 27–37.
Mies, Maria. *Patriarchy and the Accumulation on a World Scale: Women in the International Division of Labour*. London: Zed Books, 1986.
Miliband, Ralph. "The Capitalist State: Reply to N. Poulantzas." *New Left Review* 59 (January–February 1970): 53–60.
———. "Poulantzas and the Capitalist State." *New Left Review* 82 (November–December 1973): 83–92.
———. *The State in Capitalist Society: The Analysis of the Western System of Power*. London: Quartet Books, 1973.
Mill, James. *The History of British India*. Vol. 1 and 2. New York: Chelsea House, 1968.
Miller, L. "Foucault, Nietzsche, Enlightenment: Some Historical Considerations." *Postmodernism and the Enlightenment: New Perspectives in Eighteenth-Century French Intellectual History*. Ed. D. Gordon. New York: Routledge, 2001. 179–200.
Mishra, Pankaj. "Pakistan: A Hard Country by Anatol Lieven—Review." *The Guardian on the Web* 30 April 2011. 28 May 2011 <http://www.guardian.co.uk/books/2011/may/01/pakistan-hard-country-anatol-lieven-review>.
Misra, B.B. *The Bureaucracy in India*. Delhi: Oxford University Press, 1977.

Moore, Mick. "Economic Liberalization Versus Political Pluralism in Sri Lanka." *Modern Asian Studies* 24.2 (1990): 341–383.

Moyers, Bill. "The Secret Government." *What I've Learned From US Foreign Policy: The War Against the Third World.* Dir. Frank Dorrell. DVD. Culver City, 2002.

Mukherjee, Aditya and Mridula Mukerjee. "Imperialism and Growth of Indian Capitalism in Twentieth Century" *Economic and Political Weekly* 23.11 (12 March 1988) 531–546.

Mumtaz, Soofia, Jean-Luc Racine, and Imran Anwar Ali, eds. *Pakistan: The Contours of State and Society.* Karachi: Oxford University Press, 2002.

Mundle, Sudipto. "Growth, Disparity and Capital Reorganization in Indian Economy: Some Speculations." *Economic and Political Weekly* 16.10/12 (March 1981): 393–408.

Musharraf, Pervez. *In the Line of Fire: A Memoir.* New York: Free Press, 2006.

Nandy, Ashis. "The Politics of Secularism and the Recovery of Religious Tolerance." *Mirrors of Violence.* Ed. V. Das. Delhi: Oxford University Press, 1990.

Navari, Cornelia. "The Origins of the Nation-State." *The Nation-State: The Formation of Modern Politics.* Ed. Leonard Tivey. New York: St. Martin's Press, 1981. 13–38.

NDTV. "Operation Green Hunt: War Without End." 2 April 2010. 8 May, 2011 <http://www.ndtv.com/video/player/ndtv-special-ndtv-24x7/operation-green-hunt-war-without-end/135562>.

O'Donnell, Guillermo. *Modernization and Bureaucratic Authoritarianism: Studies in South American Politics.* Berkeley: Institute of International Studies, University of California, 1973.

Oman, C. "The Policy Challenges of Globalisation and Regionalisation." *Migration, Free Trade and Regional Integration in Central and Eastern Europe.* Paris: OECD, 1997. 29–44.

Omar, Noman. *The Political Economy of Pakistan 1947–85.* London: KPI, 1988.

Opello, Walter, Jr., and S. Rosow. *The Nation-State and the Global Order: A Historical Introduction to Contemporary Politics.* Boulder: Lynne Rienner, 1999.

Overbeek, Henk. "Globalization, Sovereignty and Transnational Regulation: Reshaping the Governance of International Migration." *Managing Migration: Time for a New International Regime?* Ed. Bimal Gosh. Oxford: Oxford University Press, 2000, 51.

Pang, Eul-Soo. "The Financial Crisis of 1997–98 and the End of the Asian Developmental State," *Contemporary Southeast Asia* 22.3 (2000): 570–593

Panitch, Leo. "The New Imperial State." *New Left Review* 2 (March–April 2000): 5–20.

Panitch, Leo, and Colin Leys, eds. *The Empire Reloaded: Socialist Register 2005.* London: Merlin, 2004.

———, eds. *The New Imperial Challenge: Socialist Register 2004.* London: Merlin, 2003.

Panjwani, Naren. "Some Hazards of Universalism in the Indian Polity." *Class Formation and Political Transformation in Post-Colonial India.* Vol. 4 of *Social Change and Political Discourse in India: Structures of Power, Movements of Resistance.* Ed. T.V. Sathyamurthy. Oxford: Oxford University Press, 1996. 342–359.

Pantham, Thomas. "Indian Secularism and Its Critics: Some Reflections." *The Review of Politics* 59.3 (Summer 1997): 523–541.

Parsons, Talcott. *Structure and Process in Modern Societies.* Glencoe: Free Press, 1960.

Patnaik, Prabhat. "On the Political Economy of Economic Liberalisation." *Social Scientist* 13.146–147 (July–August 1985): 3–17.

———. *Whatever Happened to Imperialism and Other Essays.* New Delhi: Tulika, 1995.

Patnaik, Utsa. "Poverty and Neo-Liberalism in India." *Rao Bahdur Kale Memorial Lecture*. Delivered at Gokhale Institute of Politics and Economics, Pune, 3 February 2006.

Pavier, B. *The Telengana Movement*. New Delhi: Vikas, 1981.

Pedersen, JØrgen Dige."Explaining Economic Liberalization in India: State and Society Perspectives." *World Development* 28.2 (2000): 265–282.

Pererea, Suvendrini. "Unmaking the Present, Remaking Memory: Sri Lankan Stories and a Politics of Coexistence." *Race and Class* 40.4 (July–December 1999): 189–195.

Petras, James, and Henry Veltmeyer. *Globalization Unmasked: Imperialism in the 21st Century*. Halifax: Fernwood/Zed, 2001.

Poulantzas, Nicos. "The Capitalist State: A Reply to Miliband and Laclau." *New Left Review* 95 (January–February 1976): 63–83.

———. *Classes in Contemporary Capitalism*. Trans. David Fernbach. London: New Left Books, 1974.

———. *Political Power and Social Classes*. Trans. Timothy O'Hagan. London: New Left Books, 1975.

———. "The Problem of the Capitalist State." *New Left Review* 58 (November–December 1969): 67–78.

———. *State, Power and Socialism*. Trans. Patrick Camiller. London: New Left Books, 1978.

Prashad, Vijay. *The Darker Nations: A People's History of the Third World*. New York: New Press, 2007.

Prazniak, Roxann, and Arif Dirlik. *Places and Politics in an Age of Globalization*. Lanham: Rowman and Littlefield, 2001.

Radcliffe, Sarah A. "Imagining the State as a Space: Territoriality and the Formation of the State in Ecuador." *States of Imagination: Ethnographic Explorations of the Postcolonial State*. Ed. Thomas B. Hansen and Finn Stepputat. Durham: Duke University Press, 2001.

Raj, K.N. "Land Reforms in India and Pakistan: A Comparative Review." *The Post-Colonial State and Social Transformation in India and Pakistan*. Ed. S.M. Naseem and Khalid Nadvi. Karachi: Oxford University Press, 2002. 131–141.

Rashid, Abbas, and Farida Shaheed. *Pakistan: Ethno Politics and Contending Elites*. New York: UN Research Institute for Social Development, June 1993.

Rastayannikov, Victor G. "The Social Types of Rural Hired Workers in Independent India." *Soviet Scholars View of South Asia*. Ed. Yuri V. Gankovsky. Lahore: People's Publishing House, 1975.

Research and Information System for the Non-Aligned and Other Developing Countries. *Raul Prebisch and Development Strategy*. New Delhi: Research and Information System for the Non-Aligned and Other Developing Countries, 1987.

Richards, John. *The New Cambridge History of India—The Mughal Empire*. New Delhi: Foundation Books, 1993.

Roberts, J. Timmons, and Amy Hite. *From Modernization to Globalization: Perspectives on Development and Social Change*. Oxford: Blackwell, 2000.

Robinson, William, and Jerry Harris. "Towards a Global Ruling Class: Globalization and the Transnational Capitalist Class." *Science & Society* 64.1 (Spring 2000): 11–54.

Rodney, Walter. *How Europe Underdeveloped Africa*. Washington, DC: Howard University Press, 1982.

Ross, Thomas. *The Invisible Government*. New York: Random House, 1964

Rostow, W.W. *The Stages of Economic Growth: A Non-Communist Manifesto*. Cambridge: Cambridge University Press, 1971.

Roth, G. "Personal Rulership, Patrimonialism and Empire-building in the New States." *World Politics* 20.2 (1968): 195–206.

Rouse, Shahnaz. "Liberation From Above or Within: Nationalism, Gender and Space in Pakistan." *Against the Current* 97 (March–April 2002): 14–16.

Roy, Arundhati. "Instant-Mix Imperial Democracy, Buy One Get One Free—An Hour With Arundhati Roy." Speech at the Riverside Church. *Democracy Now! The War and Peace Report*. 23 October 2003. 7 May 2011 <http://www.democracynow.org/2003/10/24/instant_mix_imperial_democracy_buy_one>.

———. "Walking With the Comrades." *OutlookIndia.com*. 29March 2010. 7 May 2011 <http://www.outlookindia.com/article.aspx?264738-0>.

Roy, Sumit. "'Liberalization' and the Indian Economy: Myth and Reality." *Industry and Agriculture in India Since Independence*. Vol. 2 of *Social Change and Political Discourse in India: Structures of Power, Movements of Resistance*. Ed. T.V. Sathyamurthy. Delhi: Oxford University Press, 1994. 135–194.

Said, Edward. *Culture and Imperialism*. New York: Vintage Books, 1993.

Sampson, A. *The Sovereign State of ITT*. New York: Stein and Day, 1973.

Sanyal, S.N. "Land Holdings in Punjab: An Analysis." *Economic and Political Weekly* 5.34 (22 August 1970): 1425–1428.

Sarkar, Tanika. "Semiotics of Terror: Muslim Children and Women in Hindu Rashtra." *Economic and Political Weekly* 13 July 2002: 2872–2876.

———. "Women, Community and Nation: A Historical Trajectory of Hindu Identity Politics." *Appropriating Gender: Women's Activism and Politicized Religion in South Asia*. Ed. Patricia Jeffery and Amrita Basu. New York: Routledge, 1998. 89–105.

Saul, John. "The State in Post-Colonial Societies: Tanzania." *Socialist Register*. London: Merlin, 1974. 349–372

Shaheed, Farida. "The Other Side of the Discourse: Women's Experience of Identity, Religion and Activism in Pakistan." *Appropriating Gender: Women's Activism and Politicized Religion in South Asia*. Ed. Patricia Jeffery and Amrita Basu. London: Routledge, 1998. 143–166.

Shanin, Teodor , ed. *Late Marx and the Russian Road: The Peripheries of Capitalism*. New York: Monthly Review Press, 1983.

Sharma, Ardhana, and Akhil Gupta. *The Anthropology of the State: A Reader*. Oxford: Blackwell, 2006.

Sharma, M.L. "Altering Agrarian Structure: Rajasthan Land Reforms." *Green Revolution and Social Change*. Ed. M.L. Sharma and T.M. Dak. Delhi: Ajanta Publications, 1989. 171–109.

Shivji, Issa. *Class Struggles in Tanzania*. New York: Monthly Review Press, 1976.

Schofield, Victoria. *Kashmir in Conflict: India, Pakistan and the Unfinished War*. London: Tauris, 2003.

Shutt, Harry. *Beyond the Profits System: Possibilities for a Post-Capitalist Era*. New York: Zed Books, 2010.

———. *The Decline of Capitalism: Can a Self-Regulated Profits System Survive?* New York: Zed Books, 2005.

Siddiqa, Ayesha. *Military Inc.: Inside Pakistan's Military Economy*. Karachi: Oxford University Press, 2007.

Sinha, Aseema. "Rethinking the Developmental State Model: Divided Leviathan and Subnational Comparisons in India." *Comparative Politics* 35.4 (July 2003): 459–472.

Sivanandan, A., and Ellen Wood. "Globalization and Epochal Shifts: An Exchange." *Monthly Review* 48.9 (February 1997): 19–21.

Skocpol, Theda, and Dietrich Rueschemeyer, eds. *States, Social Knowledge, and the Origins of Modern Social Policies*. New York: Russell Sage Foundation, 1996.

Smith, Adam. *An Inquiry Into the Nature and Causes of the Wealth of Nations*. Vol. 1. Ed. R.H Campbell and A.S. Skinner. Liberty Classics: Indianapolis, 1981.

So, Alvin. *Social Change and Development: Modernization, Dependency and World System Theories*. Newbury Park: Sage, 1990.

The South Commission. *The Challenge to the South: The Report of the South Commission* London: Oxford University Press, 1990.

Stockwell, John. *In Search of Enemies: A CIA Story*. New York: Norton, 1978.

Stokes, Gail. "How Is Nationalism Related to Capitalism? A Review Article." *Comparative Study of Society and History* 28.3 (July 1986): 591–598.

Stuart, Douglas T. *Creating the National Security State: A History of the Law That Transformed America*. Princeton: Princeton University Press, 2008.

Tabb, William K. "The World Trade Organization? Stop World Take Over" *Monthly Review* 51.8 (January 2000): 1–12.

Thakurdas, Purshotamdas, ed. *A Brief Memorandum Outlining a Plan of Economic Development for India*. 2 vols. Harmondsworth: Penguin, 1945.

Thapar, Romila. *History and Beyond*. New Delhi: Oxford University Press, 2000.

———. "State Formation in Early India." *The State in Global Perspective*. Ed. Ali Kazancigill. Aldershot: Gower UNESCO, 1986. 55–71.

Thorner, D., and A. Thorner. *Land and Labour in India*. Bombay: Asia Publishing House, 1965.

Tonkin, E., M. Chapman, and M. McDonald. *History and Ethnicity*. London: Routledge, 1988.

Toutain, F. "Trade Liberalisation, Foreign Direct Investment and Growth in Semi Industrialized Countries: Overview and Empirical Analysis." *OECD Proceedings: Globalisation, Migration and Development*. Paris: OECD, 2000. 128–147.

Trimburger, E.K. *Revolution From Above: Military Bureaucrats in Japan, Turkey, Egypt and Peru*. New Brunswick: Transaction Books, 1978.

Tripathi, P.K. "Secularism: Constitutional Provisions and Judicial Review." *Secularism: Its Implications for Law and Life in India*. Ed. G.S. Sharma. Bombay: Tripathi, 1966. 165–194.

Trouillot, Michel-Rolph. *Haiti, State Against Nation: The Origins and Legacy of Duvalierism*. New York: Monthly Review Press, 1990.

Tsing, Anna. "Supply Chains and the Human Condition." *Rethinking Marxism* 21.2 (April 2009): 148–176.

Tucker, Vincent, "The Myth of Development: A Critique of Eurocentric Discourse." *Critical Development Theory: Contributions to a New Paradigm*. Ed. Ronaldo Munck and Denis O'Hearn. London: Zed Books, 1997. 1–26.

University of New York, Center on Democratic Performance. "Pakistan: Legislative Elections." 12 July 2004 <http://cdp.binghamton.edu/era/countries/pak.html>.

Vaniak, Achin. "Situating Threat of Hindu Nationalism. Problems With Fascist Paradigm." *Economic and Political Weekly* 29.28 (9 July 1994): 1729–1748.

Veltmeyer, Henry. "The World Economy and Labour." *Canadian Journal of Development Studies, Special Issue on Labour and Employment Under Globalization* XX (1999): 689–716.

Verkaaik, Oskar. *A People as Migrants: Ethnicity, State and Religion in Karachi*. Amsterdam: Vanderbilt University Press, 1994.

Vilas, Carlos. "Neoliberal Social Policy Managing Poverty (Somehow)." *NACLA Report on the Americas* XXIX.6 (May-June 1996): 16–19.

Vishvanathan, Nalini, et al. *The Women, Gender and Development Reader*. London: Zed Books, 1997.

Wacquant, Loïc. *Punishing the Poor: The Neoliberal Government of Social Insecurity*. Durham: Duke University Press, 2009.

Walby, Sylvia. "Woman and Nation." *Mapping the Nation*. Ed. Gopal Balakrishnan. London: Verso, 1996. 235–254.

Wallerstein, Immanuel. "The Rise and the Future Demise of the World Capitalist System: Concepts for Comparative Analysis." *The Capitalist World Economy.* Cambridge: Cambridge University Press, 1979.

Warren, Bill. *Imperialism: Pioneer of Capitalism.* London: New Left Books, 1980.

Waseem, Amir. "Zardari Has Become Army's Spokesman, Says PML-N." 23 June 2011. 4 July 2011 <http://www.dawn.com/2011/06/23/zardari-has-become-armys-spokesman-says-pml-n.html>.

Waterson, Albert. *Planning in Pakistan.* Baltimore: Johns Hopkins University Press, 1963.

Weber, Max. *The Protestant Ethic and the Spirit of Capitalism.* Trans. Talcott Parsons. London: Routledge, 2001.

White, G., and R. Wade, eds. *Developmental States in East Asia.* Brighton: Institute of Development Studies, 1985.

Williams, Eric. *Capitalism and Slavery.* London: Andre Deutsch, 1991.

Wilson, Kalpana. "Class Alliances and the Nature of Hegemony: The Post-Independence Indian State in Marxist Writing." *State and Nation in the Context of Social Change.* Vol. I of *Social Change and Political Discourse in India: Structures of Power, Movements of Resistance.* Ed., T.V. Sathyamurthy. Delhi: Oxford University Press, 1994. 246–273.

Wimmer, Andreas, and Nina Glick Schiller, "Methodological Nationalism and Beyond: Nation-State Building, Migration and the Social Sciences," *Global Networks* 2.4 (2002): 301–334.

Wood, Ellen. *Origin of Capitalism: The Longer View.* London: Verso, 2002.

———. *The Pristine Culture of Capitalism, A Historical Essay on Old Regimes and Modern States.* London: Verso, 1991.

World Bank. "The 9/11 Commission Report." *BBC.* 23 July 2004 <http://news.bbc.co.uk/nol/shared/bsp/hi/pdfs/22_07_04911Report.pdf>.

———. "Country Data 2010." 24 June 2011<http://data.worldbank.org/country/pakistan>.

———. "Country Data and Statistics." *World Bank.* 23 July 2004 <http://www.worldbank.org/cgi-bin/sendoff.cgi?page=%2Fdata%2Fcountrydata%2Faag%2Fpak_aag.pdf>.

———."Foreign Direct Investment, Net Inflows (Mexico)" 25 October 2011 <http://data.worldbank.org/indicator/BX.KLT.DINV.CD.WD/countries/MX?display=graph>

———. "GDP Growth (Annual %)." 24 April 2011 <http://data.worldbank.org/indicator/NY.GDP.MKTP.KD.ZG>.

———. "India at a Glance." *World Bank.* 23 July 2004 <http://search.worldbank.org/data?qterm=India%20ata%20a%20glance&language=EN> >.

———. "Industry, Value Added (Annual Percentage Growth)," 24 April 2011 <http://databank.worldbank.org/ddp/html-jsp/QuickViewReport.jsp?RowAxis=WDI_Series~&ColAxis=WDI_Time~&PageAxis=WDI_Ctry~&PageAxisCaption=Country~&RowAxisCaption=Series~&ColAxisCaption=Time~&NEW_REPORT_SCALE=1&NEW_REPORT_PRECISION=0&newReport=yes&ROW_COUNT=1&COLUMN_COUNT=51&PAGE_COUNT=1&COMMA_SEP=true>.

———. *Report No. 18395–PAK: Agricultural Taxation in Pakistan.* Washington: World Bank, 1999.

———. "Social Indicators of Development—Pakistan 1991–2010" 27 October 2011 <http://search.worldbank.org/data?qterm=pakistan+1994+to+2010&language=-EN&format=>

Index

For Product Safety Concerns and Information please contact our EU
representative GPSR@taylorandfrancis.com
Taylor & Francis Verlag GmbH, Kaufingerstraße 24, 80331 München, Germany

www.ingramcontent.com/pod-product-compliance
Ingram Content Group UK Ltd.
Pitfield, Milton Keynes, MK11 3LW, UK
UKHW022001180926
475701UK00003B/136

* 9 7 8 0 4 1 5 7 1 9 7 6 6 *